THE
POSTWAR TRANSFORMATION
OF
ALBUQUERQUE, NEW MEXICO
1945–1972

To Jimmy and Hayden Pickel
in appreciation of their
friendship and for all they
have done for the MBA class
of 1960.

April 24, 2015

Bobby Wood

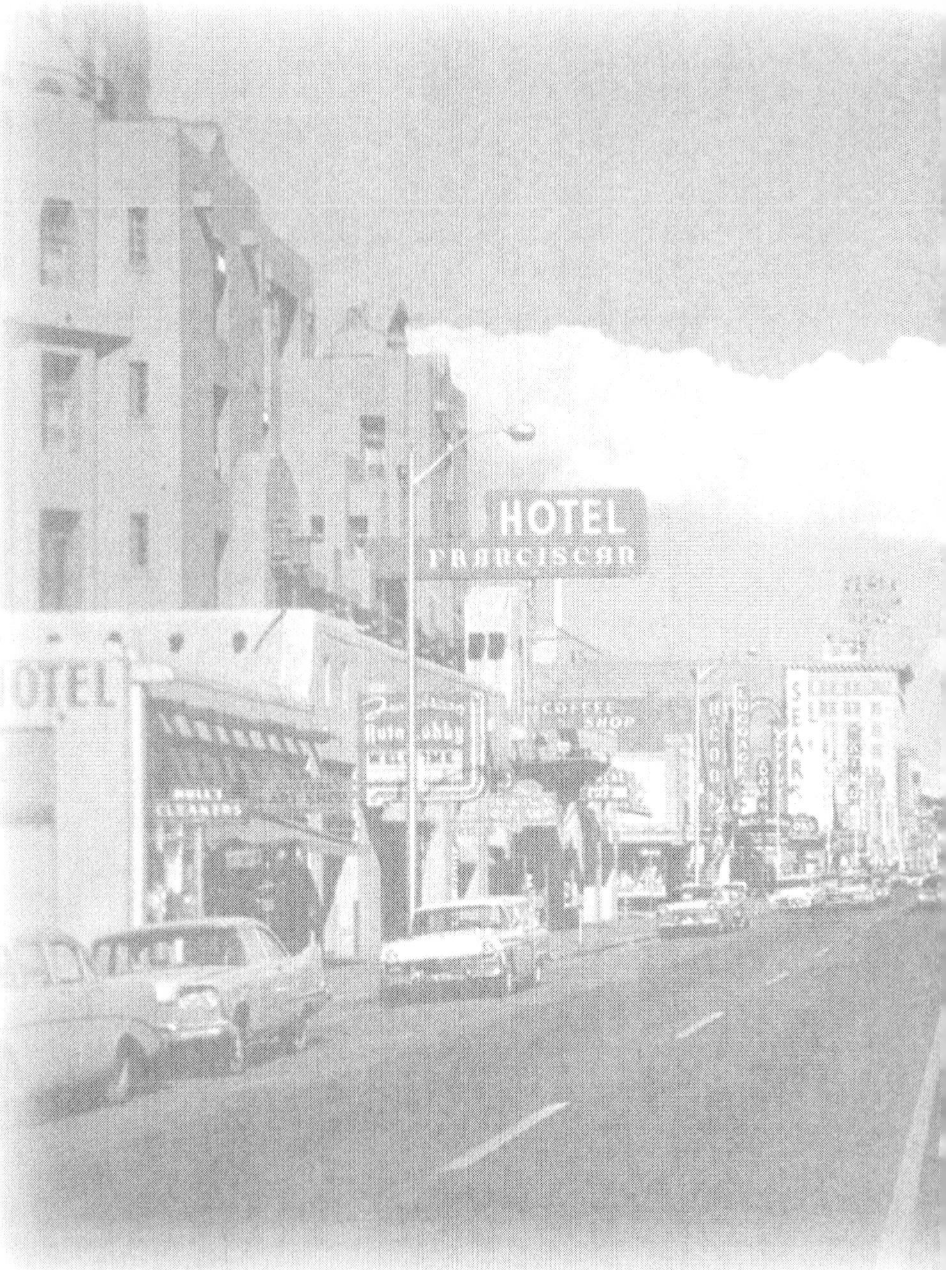
HOTEL
FRANCISCAN
COFFEE SHOP
CLEANERS
SEARS

The
Postwar Transformation
of
Albuquerque, New Mexico
1945–1972

Robert Turner Wood, PhD

Sunstone
Press

SANTA FE

Sunstone books may be purchased for educational, business, or sales promotional use.
For information please write: Special Markets Department, Sunstone Press,
P.O. Box 2321, Santa Fe, New Mexico 87504-2321.

Book and cover design › Vicki Ahl
Body typeface › Minion Pro
Printed on acid-free paper
∞
eBook 978-1-61139-310-1

Library of Congress Cataloging-in-Publication Data

Wood, Robert Turner, 1942-
  The postwar transformation of Albuquerque, New Mexico, 1945-1972 / by Robert
Turner Wood.
      pages cm
  Includes bibliographical references and index.
  ISBN 978-1-63293-019-4 (softcover : alk. paper)
  1. Albuquerque (N.M.)--History--20th century. 2. Albuquerque (N.M.)--Politics
and government--20th century. 3. Albuquerque (N.M.)--Social conditions--20th
century. 4. Social change--New Mexico--Albuquerque--20th century. 5. Albuquerque
(N.M.)--Biography. I. Title.
  F804.A3W66 2014
  978.9'61053--dc23
                         2014026031

WWW.SUNSTONEPRESS.COM
SUNSTONE PRESS / POST OFFICE BOX 2321 / SANTA FE, NM 87504-2321 /USA
(505) 988-4418 / ORDERS ONLY (800) 243-5644 / FAX (505) 988-1025

CONTENTS

1

THE NATURE OF THE TRANSFORMATION

Like many other Americans, most Albuquerque residents have become accustomed to living in a time of rapid change. In fact, for more than a century our technologies, our standards of living, and the physical and cultural world around us have all undergone a profound transformation. Preoccupied with the present day, we marvel at the changes brought about by the Internet, cell phones, robotization and other technological innovations, paying little attention to the profound cultural shifts which have taken place and are still under way. To better understand the nature of what has been going on, it can be helpful to look closely at a particular place and time. From 1945—the end of World War II—to 1972—when the intensity of the decade of the 1960s began to subside—Albuquerque, New Mexico, went through more pronounced and more dramatic changes than most of the rest of the country. Its transformation helps illuminate what was taking place more gradually elsewhere.

The general shape of what was going on across the country is easy to discern. From approximately the late 1940s to the early 1970s the manmade landscape shifted and took on new forms as millions of citizens abandoned their small towns and surged into the metropolises and their suburbs, as gigantic transportation systems and networks streamed with traffic, and as huge and opulent structures spread out over city blocks and soared toward the skies. The growth of the cities and the buildings within them was paralleled by a spectacular increase in disposable income. Goods and services that were lavish by former standards abounded, making possible more comfortable and more secure lives for many. Yet instead of basking in contentment, large groups of people, including both have nots and haves, asserted themselves against the established social order, shaking it until it trembled and bent. Equally disconcerting to those who were comfortable with the ways things had been was a wave of new mores which seemed to countenance sexual permissiveness, sloppiness in manner and dress, and rampant disrespect for authority. The persons in the vanguard of the changes, on the other hand, waxed enthusiastic over the apparent new openness all around them. But what was actually taking place—whether society was becoming more or less restrictive, whether the individual was counting for more or less than in the past, whether people were treating one another much differently than before—was difficult to untangle amid the claims and counterclaims.

During these years Albuquerque, located at an important transportation intersection in the growing sunbelt of the United States, gained population at a faster rate than most other American cities, and the attitudes and behaviors of the people that made up the character of the society changed at a similar pace. As was the case with all cities, many of the problems and opportunities which the residents of Albuquerque wrestled with during this time appeared in forms which were peculiar to the unique circumstances of their time and place, but the deep patterns of the ways the people coped with them and of what emerged were representative and significant.

A brief look at Albuquerque's recent history can cast light on these patterns. At the end of World War II the reins of city government were concentrated in the forceful hands of a small band of leaders, foremost of whom was the boisterous and colorful Clyde Tingley. The assertiveness of the political leaders was matched by the lively, aggressive and competitive spirit of most of the other members of the community, including businessmen, professionals, laborers and charity workers. Their money and ambitions for self-improvement, pent up during the war years, were just beginning to be unleashed. During the course of the ensuing boom the residents' wealth and material possessions increased at a prodigious rate; their appetites for more and better city services grew just as rapidly. At the same time large numbers of educated middle-class professionals were pouring in from out of state to work at Sandia Corporation and other defense-related industries. Their incomes further fueled the economic expansion, and their desires for orderly, efficient and relatively elaborate services put added pressure on city government. The old political order was swept out of office, to be replaced eventually by the somewhat technocratically oriented functionaries of the Albuquerque Citizens' Committee. Making greater use than their predecessors had of such impersonal management techniques as pyramidal organization and the merit system, these officials and their employees were able to expand the reach of local government while making it operate smoothly and efficiently. Meanwhile, other institutions, especially businesses, were also expanding, becoming more bureaucratic, and delivering goods and services more effectively. In order to keep these institutions humming like well-oiled machines, the workers in them had to submit to demanding discipline; but away from their jobs, enjoying their newly gained affluence, they came to assume a more relaxed and less formal style of life. For most of the 1950s the city seemed fairly happy and harmonious. The most spectacular occurrence was a weeklong festival in the summer of 1956 during which residents from every level of society came together to celebrate the 250th anniversary of the founding of Albuquerque.

With the advent of the sixties a more restless, adventurous and outgoing spirit entered city life. Not so preoccupied with their jobs and families as before, many people began to assert themselves vigorously into the world outside. The smoothly running machinery of city government and other institutions developed friction as persons at every level of the power structures demanded more voice in the decisions that affected them. Many members of identifiable groups which had previously had little power—young people, ethnic minorities, women, the poor—banded together in drives for more influence, rights and privileges. The assertiveness of the masses of the people also manifested itself in aggressively informal behavior—on the job, at school, in the political arena. Yielding to the mounting pressures, institutional authority became more dispersed and permissive. Yet the overall influence of the institutions did not recede: governments, businesses and other types of organizations continued to grow larger and more inclusive to meet the continuously rising demand for their goods and services. People wanted better health care, more social programs and more elaborate education, and only large organizations could satisfy these wants. Loosely hierarchical organizational structures emerged in which the persons at the top had more power than those below, yet virtually everyone at each of the levels had some measure of influence. The evolution of such structures—and the changes in attitude and behavior that made them possible—was not easy and smooth, however. From the latter part of the sixties on into the early seventies Albuquerque was wracked by rising crime, bitter political struggles and conflicts among ethnic groups, sexes and generations. The single most newsworthy event of the period was the eruption in June 1971 of two days of rioting, looting and destruction starting in Roosevelt Park and spreading into the downtown.

As this sketch of the post-World War II history of Albuquerque has indicated, the complexion of the city underwent dramatic fluctuations between 1945 and 1972. And as will be apparent, the facets of urban life and its transformation during this period were much more varied and complex than can be shown in a page or two of summary. But amid all the drama and confusion can be discerned two highly significant and constant trends. In the first place, organizations of all kinds grew larger and more dominant in the lives of the people. Second, authority and control became looser. Much about the nature of these two trends and about their possible interrelationship can be learned from a close examination of their unfolding. Their manifestation and development in the dense texture of twenty-eight years of Albuquerque's history is the primary focus of this book. Yet they did not originate during this time or a few years earlier; their seeds had been germinating and sprouting for a long time before they began to affect people's behavior and perceptions very radically. In order to glimpse their beginnings, one has to step back further into the past.

Much of the forcefulness, competitiveness, acquisitiveness and spirit of restless striving that were characteristic of the residents of the city in the 1940s had been present for as long as there had been an Albuquerque. Acting on orders from the Spanish governor, in 1706 twelve families moved from nearby Bernalillo to a portion of vacant high ground near a section of the Rio Grande that could easily be forded. The tiny settlement was named after the Duke of Alburquerque (note the additional "r" in the Spanish title); soon it had a central plaza, a cluster of adobe buildings including a church with a bell tower, and outlying irrigated farmland. Withstanding the ravages of the periodic droughts, floods and attacks by bands of marauders, the community prospered modestly and continued to grow. In the nineteenth century came more tumultuous upheavals. The Spanish flag was replaced by the Mexican, then by the American, then briefly by that of the Confederacy, and finally again by the American. Already accustomed to a rugged and tenuous existence, the people accepted these changes of government with resilience, if not quite equanimity. In 1880, however, came a bigger shock. The Santa Fe Railroad had been making plans to build tracks through the area, but the community balked at donating land for the right-of-way. Instead, Franz Huning, a prosperous merchant of German extraction who resided just outside of town, deeded the company land about a mile to the east. The railroad came through, and with it came swarms of energetic and competitive Americans from the East, eager to seek their fortune and build a new community. So New Albuquerque was born around the Santa Fe shops. To the west, extending toward Old Albuquerque, sprang up a bustling American-style business district; to the east were built ornate wooden residences. In the twentieth century the easterners continued to stream in, many of them convalescing from tuberculosis and attracted by the warm, dry climate. The violence of the Old West was channeled more and more into aggressive business enterprise; persons arriving in town with almost nothing of their own accumulated fortunes and political power. The new city came to dwarf Old Albuquerque, yet the Spanish language, the customs, the foods and the attitudes of the original community continued to exert a stubborn and pervasive influence. Although in many ways the two cultures provided a startling contrast, their common ruggedness and political acumen provided much of the basis for the different people's working together with a substantial degree of harmony.

The general tendency of the people to expose themselves to risks and to strive vigorously for the sake of material betterment, then, had a long tradition. The Spanish explorers, the early settlers in the New World, the Mexican farmers and the American railroad workers—most of these could have opted for a more secure existence, but they chose instead to brave the uncertainties attendant upon building a prosperous life in New Mexico. The energetic competition and risk taking by the Albuquerque businessmen around the end of the Second World War had ample precedent.

This restless striving had been an important feature of Western civilization since the time of the Renaissance, when the medieval world order, with its complex of political and religious hierarchies, began to break down and people turned more of their attention to the quest for material betterment. As society and culture became more fragmented, the individual person became more on his own, not having the involved network of medieval systems and hierarchies to buttress him, and self-reliance was especially necessary for those who dared to venture into new areas of endeavor or to compete vigorously with other people. Nerve, ingenuity, stubbornness, self-discipline, inner-directedness and a thick skin became much-valued traits. The condition of hardy individuals competing energetically for what the world and society had to offer extended into politics and other fields as well.

Yet in spite of the widespread social fragmentation and the attendant attacks on traditional authority, in spite of the strife which frequently grew out of the rampant competition, society continued to function, for the most part, in a disciplined and orderly manner. Most people were seeking after the same end, the economic betterment which they believed would bring them the "good life," and most were in agreement that hard work and earnestness were necessary for accomplishing their goal. The system of social stratification was no longer so imposing or highly involved as before, but it continued to be an important source of authority. The persons at the top, their positions usually ratified by their accumulations of worldly goods, had a substantial stake in the maintenance of order, and they felt a responsibility to see that the new social and economic system operated smoothly. People at every level of society came to perceive the world around them as acting according to orderly, clear-cut and impersonal rules. The universe, they came to believe, operated according to the laws of nature like a gigantic and perfectly constructed clock; the marketplace enforced an equilibrium between supply and demand; the ideal of justice was fair and equal treatment of all before the law; in sports and other competition fair play was honored nearly as much as winning.

In such a fragmented and impersonal world the people became highly dependent on a limited number of close personal relationships for emotional support. Protestant religions might lack the color and the network of saints found in Catholicism, but the personal relationship with God was all the more intense. Friendship among people might be transient, but while it lasted high demands were placed on personal loyalty. As the extended family was displaced by the smaller nuclear family, sexual love was elevated to an almost sacrosanct level. The gradual supplanting of the sprawling and intricate medieval system of social relationships by the less extensive yet more intense bonds of persons struggling to succeed in an impersonal world by no means heralded unbridled permissiveness. In this dynamic system more freedom of movement was permitted and encouraged than formerly, but greater burdens and responsibilities were placed on the individual. The Puritan conscience, self-discipline, and self-restraint in matters of sex and other types of expression all rose to the fore along with the work ethic. The people no longer had to be so obedient to imposed authority as before, but the internalized disciplines that went hand in hand with their new way of life were rigorously demanding.

The intense focus on the individual also extended to the world of the mind. Works of art became more individualized and more self contained.

Most people were too preoccupied with getting ahead to pay much attention to art, but everyone had access to language, and verbal ability, especially the power to influence and persuade others, was highly valued.

Such a world of strong individuals competing for wealth and political power while forming intense alliances and undergoing heated conflicts with one another can be found in Albuquerque around the end of World War II. It had actually been present, in one form or another, for as long as the community had existed. And the temperament and social interactions of the people were reflected in their culture—their favorite books and movies, their conversations and celebrations, and even the urban landscape of their streets and buildings.

In time, though, the system of individuals competing among themselves underwent fundamental change. Their competition changed the nature of the world in which they functioned to such an extent that individuals came to have more difficulty accomplishing their objectives and making a difference.

The first way in which the competition among individuals for the rewards of society changed their world was that it eventually led to the growth of large organizations. In the contest for goods and glory, people began to band together to pool their resources, and a large group could often compete more effectively in the marketplace than a small one or an individual. It had the advantages of less duplication of effort, more specialized expertise and greater accumulation of working capital. As time went on and more industries became dominated by large firms, the economic ideal of perfect competition receded further into the mythology of the past. The competitive advantage of large organizations became pronounced also in the realm of politics. Within a single government the influence of pressure groups began to dwarf that of isolated individuals, and among nations the old balance-of-power approach was undermined as large nations dominated or swallowed up smaller ones and the centers of significant power grew fewer. The people's styles of living shifted in this direction for similar reasons. More moved to large cities, where they could find a larger variety of job opportunities and a greater abundance of consumer goods and public services. The tendency of large industries to locate in population centers accelerated this trend. A growing number of persons who could afford to do otherwise chose to reside in apartment houses, for such a living arrangement could provide conveniences and luxuries which they would otherwise have to forego. Even scholarship and the arts, where individualism was still fairly firmly entrenched, were affected. Large universities could pay higher salaries and provide more elaborate facilities than small ones; thus they tended to win out in the competition for more illustrious faculty and more and better students. Certain types of research, especially large, prestigious and well-funded projects, could be performed better by teams of scholars or scientists than by individuals working alone. Many solitary thinkers and artists continued to ply their trade in the time-honored manner, nursing their unique flashes of insight and inspiration, but large group projects became prominent in the cultural realm. Expensive and impressive building complexes were more likely to be entrusted to a sizable architectural firm than to a talented individual, and movies produced on a lavish scale and aimed at a mass audience could only be made through the combined efforts of many.

As Albuquerque grew, the typical business enterprises also got bigger. Franchises and branch offices, almost unheard in earlier years, became more common. New projects involved greater numbers and more kinds of workers. Politics, once mainly the province of powerful and colorful leaders, became spread out into committees, interest groups and public relations campaigns.

A second factor in the new transformation of society was the limits of available natural and social resources on which the old system could build. The world, after all, contained a finite amount of natural resources and space, and a limited number of possible new markets. The individualistic and competitive spirit of the culture could best thrive and justify itself when there was an abundance of new territory to discover, new natural resources to develop and exploit, new groups of people to bargain with—in other words, when there was plenty of room to move. When shortages of raw materials arose, the advantage shifted from those who were the most energetic and enterprising to those who were already sitting on top of the desired substances. When people became more concerned with the shrinking availability of land for such activities as farming and recreation, and when they began to worry more about the despoliation of natural beauty, entrepreneurs had less freedom to locate new industries where they chose. Noneconomic considerations grew more significant. As the limits to growth pressed more forcefully against the old dynamic system, much of its attractiveness waned.

As parcels of vacant land with clear titles were absorbed in the Albuquerque metropolitan area, the builders had to struggle more with the complexities of multiple ownership of land grants and with growing demands from environmentalists. Local manufacturers also had to be concerned with the fluctuations of national and international markets, as well as with pollution controls. Albuquerque no longer felt located in the old wild west.

And in the third place, the very success of the old system in supplying the people with what they wanted in the way of material goods, services and glory tended to change their motivations. Some continued to strive for more and more in the style of their forebears, but a growing number felt like relaxing their efforts. They had attained a substantial measure of success—why not devote more of their time and attention to enjoying what they had? The shift to a more relaxed spirit often occurred from one generation to the next: the parents, thoroughly imbued with the work ethic, would strive vigorously to make their way in the world and arrive at a relatively high standard of living, and their children, reared in a more comfortable and less strenuous environment, would feel less impetus to strain so hard. And as the people relaxed their drive for worldly success, their goals tended to broaden and become less tightly focused. They grew more interested in such areas as recreation and art—fields of endeavor which were more ends in themselves and not so much vehicles for pushing on ahead. People began to pay more attention to present enjoyment and fulfillment and less to long-range schemes for success. As a result of their changed orientation, they fit less into the old system of dynamic individualism.

On the Albuquerque scene, young people began to develop their own culture, partially insulated from the stresses of their parents. Their music and their language helped set them off. Not being so preoccupied with making a living and getting ahead, they could investigate alternative life styles, such as the beatniks of the late 1950s or the counterculture of the following decade. Meanwhile, many of their elders also felt freer to turn away from long accepted patterns in their work and their politics.

These three factors—the increasing importance of large organizations, the limitations of resources and room for growth, and the growing tendency of the people to relax their efforts—are conceptually distinct, but in practice they were interrelated to a high degree. Membership in a large organization encouraged a person to become less competitive and more cooperative than if he were on his own, for the organization as a whole stood a better chance of succeeding and thus bringing success to its members if everyone got along well together. Furthermore, the organization provided some shelter for its members, and they therefore felt less need to depend so much on their individual resources for survival and success. So the sheer fact of belonging to an organization, whether that organization reaped large benefits for its members or not, tended to make the people relax. And so did the limits to growth. If one's exertions were less likely to bring increased success than in the past, or if the success was likely to come in smaller increments, then the rewards for striving were diminished, and people grew less likely to strive so hard. The limits to growth also tended to further encourage the development of large organizations. A large group had the resources to make a large investment or expend much time and energy for only a small unit gain for each product manufactured, say, or each person affected; a single individual did not. And there were smaller and less obvious ways in which the three overall causes operated together and reinforced each other's effects to produce pressure for a new social transformation. Their combined force was overwhelming.

As these causal factors converged across twentieth-century America, the two broad trends which we earlier glimpsed in the recent history of Albuquerque began to develop. People came to interact with one another not so much as independent and competing individuals but as members of groups, and a loose structure of interrelated hierarchies gradually emerged. And self-discipline and many other forms of control significantly relaxed. The strenuous and dynamic system which had dominated for centuries was undergoing fundamental changes.

Of these two trends or broad dimensions of the social and cultural transformation now underway, the easier to recognize is the general loosening of control and authority. Fundamentally it came about because the conditions of society had changed, or were perceived to have changed, in such a way that the people felt less need to exert control over themselves and their surroundings than before, and they felt ready to relax. Through the use of their technology they had attained a high degree of control over their natural environment; the beast of nature, somewhat tamed, seemed less dangerous than in earlier times. By means of this technology, their powerful organizations and the cumulative effect of their strivings over the years, they had been able to garner a substantial portion of the worldly goods and comforts which they had sought; having arrived nearer to their goal, they could relax. The old system of competitive striving seemed to work less well than previously, yet there seemed to be enough of what the world and society had to offer to satisfy most people's needs and appetites: this perception also influenced the people to slow down. Furthermore, some of the greatest dangers to society that the people recognized—global nuclear war and poisoning of the environment by industrial pollution, for example—seemed to be aggravated by too much competitive striving and excessive consumption. So they relaxed, and this relaxation spread, like ripples after a splash, further and further until it permeated almost every aspect of their lives.

In thousands of ways across the Albuquerque metropolitan area, the society was becoming less authoritarian and controlling. In the 1960s groups like the Grass Roots Committee challenged the established political leaders and structures. Liberal judges threw out city ordinances which they felt had been used to harass people the police did not like. Schools embraced more active participation by students in the learning process, and they began to allow girls to wear pants.

Regardless of the times, competitive striving has always been a demanding activity; it requires toughness, the ability to direct one's energies toward a distant goal, and self-discipline. In order to compete successfully, the individual must control and channel his impulses. The conscious part of his mind must forcefully assert its dominance over the rest of his personality. If the motivation for competitive striving is diminished and if nothing else in the person's environment demands such tight control, then his consciousness has a tendency to become more relaxed and permissive. This type of relaxation is characteristic of people affected by the contemporary social and cultural transformation.

Less stringent control of people's whole personalities by their conscious minds—or, more simply, less rigorous self-discipline—has led to a general lessening of control in other levels of activity. Individuals have felt less impetus to control, dominate or manipulate all things outside themselves. No longer viewing the natural world so much as a source of raw material to be shaped to satisfy man's needs, they have grown more sensitive to the requirements and limitations of nature. In a sense, they have paid more attention to feedback from nature and tried harder to fit themselves into the natural system. They have come to regard themselves more as occupying a crucial but not unexpendable position in that system rather than being apart from it and above it. This change in attitude, stemming largely from a diminution in the human desire to dominate, has been an important impetus for the growing interest in ecology and the environment. It had much to do with such local movements as Save the Volcanoes in the early 1970s.

Individuals have also relaxed their drive to control other people. In most human relationships, particularly in large modern organizations, the dominance of the strongest person or persons has grown less pronounced. More heed has been paid to feedback from those not in the focus of power, and a more cooperative spirit has been stressed. Less common than in the past are the political boss who runs his government with an iron hand, the entrepreneur who treats his business as his personal domain, the pastor who talks down to his congregation, the teacher who has all the answers, the husband whose word is law in his own family.

The decreasing interest on the part of the controlling individual in exerting dominance, however, is only half of the reason for this loosening of authority; the other half is the decline in the appetite and tolerance for domination on the part of that which was being controlled. People were growing less eager to follow their leader's demands. Along with the slackening self-discipline came a lessening tolerance for discipline imposed from above, particularly if that discipline seemed to interfere unduly or unnecessarily with the people's more relaxed posture toward life. Many persons, their energies less tightly focused on getting ahead by competing according to the old rules, wanted more satisfaction and self-fulfillment, and they wanted them now. They were growing more assertive; their demands had to be taken into consideration. The leader or boss who tried to impose his will on his underlings in the traditional manner was likely to meet with frustration.

The loosening of the structure of authority among people also influenced the way they perceived and related to the spiritual realm. If man towered above nature less grandly than before, God Himself seemed to become less remote and imposing. Many Christian denominations made their services less formal, and the language of the church services became more vernacular. In many instances the altar, previously at the extreme end of the room in which the people worshipped and as far from the congregation as possible, was moved to a position between the priest and the people. God seemed to be made more accessible, and He mingled more intimately with the devout. Church architecture changed: the typical tall spire of the steeple, commonly the dominant feature of the building, came to receive less emphasis, and structures which seemed to emphasize the continuity of the highest point with the ground, such as A-frames, hyperbolic paraboloids and other sweeping, graceful and expressive shapes, grew in popularity. The swooping roof lines of St. Paul Lutheran Church on Indian School Rd. in northeast Albuquerque are particularly dramatic. Theologians wrote of the need to "demythologize" religion and described God as the "ground of all being." Christian teaching became less a source of absolute answers and more a guide to be adapted to particular situations.

The relaxation of authority and control had a wide impact on everyday human behavior as well. Interactions between people became less formal, conventionalized and studied; spontaneity seeped in more. Speeches and greetings grew less elaborate and dress less formal. Traditional rules about appearance and decorum were enforced less rigorously as more and more persons went their own way, doing what struck their fancy and that of their comrades. Sexual expression and behavior, restricted fairly tightly during the preceding centuries, were given freer rein, and the people felt less inclined to suppress their desires. Around the University of New Mexico in the late 1960s, the fight to overturn pornography laws became a cause célèbre. The growing permissiveness was being felt in every aspect of social existence.

While this general loosening of control and relaxation of authority was taking place, the second broad shift, the emergence of a loose hierarchical structuring of society and culture, was becoming more pronounced. This development grew out of the dynamic and competitive struggle of the people to better themselves, yet in important respects it conflicted with the basic attitudes and values of the old system. Bit by bit, however, the persons involved, or most of them at any rate, made adjustments to the new way of life it ushered in.

It is true that large organizations had already become common before the ongoing transformation of society and culture really got underway. The competition among individuals led to the formation of larger groups, more potent than isolated individuals and thus better able to compete. However, as long as the people who comprised these organizations retained such traditional values as stubbornness, forcefulness and individual competitiveness, the effectiveness of group action was seriously limited. A small organization could be run smoothly by a single person who was determined to make all the important decisions and to impose his will on the group; a large organization could not be steered so easily. Subordinates would have a tendency to tell their boss what he wanted to hear rather than what he needed to know, and even with the best possible communication he would not be able to assimilate and assess all the incoming information. Furthermore, if the people in the lower ranks shared his traditional values, they would chafe under the rigidly imposed authority and want to strike out on their own, becoming their own bosses.

In time, though, the attractiveness of large-scale organization and what it could deliver rendered changes in the psychologies of the people. Leaders and underlings alike grew to be a little more cooperative and flexible, a little less competitive and forceful. And at the same time that organizational pressures were leading to more cooperativeness, the overall relaxation of control and authority was making all the people less insistent on imposing their will and getting their way. It was also making them more resistant to authority and discipline imposed from above. So little by little, the leaders loosened their grip on the powers of decision making, delegating their authority and allowing more other people a voice. At the same time that organizations were growing larger, influence was being dispersed among the ranks. Local examples of this trend include the evolution of the Albuquerque Public Schools system and of the University of New Mexico. The growing tendency toward group decision-making further contributed to the emphasis on cooperation throughout the society. In the political forums, in the factories, in the schools, in the families, more and more was being said about cooperation, less about competition. And as cooperation came more to displace competition as a basic cultural value, the people sought out the company of one another all the more avidly. In addition to the material benefits that such large groupings as cities and big companies had to offer, the opportunities for socializing were making them increasingly appealing.

Although most of the resistance to the newly emerging organizational structures came from the old guard of rugged individualists, many persons who prided themselves on being forward looking, including much of the younger generation, also had trouble making adjustments. The rising wave of permissiveness often clashed with the institutional requirements for structure and order. As bureaucracies grew larger and less susceptible to influence by isolated individuals, they had a tendency to become more impersonal. As they became more intricately developed, more rules and regulations were promulgated to ensure that disorderly or uncooperative persons did not disrupt the complex structures. So at the same time that the rising level of material living was tending to make society more permissive and indulgent, the rise of complex organizations was bringing new pressures toward order and conformity. Large numbers of people rebelled against such institutional pressures. Sometimes they failed and were pushed into roles which they resented; at other times they met with some measures of success as they forced the large organizations to be more open and flexible. They were most often successful when they banded together in organized groups to oppose the power of the organized groups which they considered repressive. As a result of the long and often heated struggles between the assertive subordinates and those higher up in the administrations of the organizational structures, new adjustments were made on all sides. Standardization of procedures increased, but so did opportunities for self-expression, and the pressure on the individual to produce tended to abate. The large organizations became less like smoothly running machines, more like complex living organisms.

The looseness of organizational structures sometimes obscured the pervasive tendency of the people to relate to hierarchical structures. Formal organizations, which are relatively easy to recognize, were growing rapidly, including governments, financial institutions, major universities, big businesses, apartment complexes and many other varieties of organizational structures. Furthermore, they were growing more interdependent. Government regulations and regulatory agencies were extending their influence and control deeper into areas that had traditionally been outside their province, and nongovernmental organizations found themselves having to comply with an increasing number of government rules and policies, as well as having to alter their approaches and programs in order to obtain government assistance. A decision made by a bureaucracy in Washington, for example, might affect an academic program under consideration at a religious college in Arkansas or a building project being pondered in Albuquerque. On the other hand, big government was growing more susceptible to the demands made by outside pressure groups, whether these were industries, consumer groups, ethnic groups or whatever. So the influence worked in both directions. Looking at the interdependence of the organizations rather than at their formal designations and structures, one could say that they were all functioning together as a single, although quite loosely structured, organization.

Even nominally unassociated individuals were affected by the giant organization. Everyone had to respect the growing body of laws or pay the consequences. Everyone qualified for some form of assistance by government or other large institutions if he happened to find himself in dire need. A single nonaligned individual could exert some influence on government and public opinion, although not so much as if he belonged to a large, cohesive and well-known group. Society as a whole was evolving into a large, loosely structured organization composed of thousands of smaller organizations and individuals who were not aware of joining anything. The various component organizations and individuals were jostling for power and influence, seeking out their respective positions in the vast emerging hierarchy. People were coming to relate to one another not so much as individuals competing for the prize but as members of a single loosely cohesive group.

Just as the organizational tendency transcended formal organizations with their precisely defined lists of members, it also leaped across national boundaries and was manifested wherever other people with this same tendency came in contact with one another. Associations with persons with whom one was in closest contact or felt most in common were, of course, the strongest. Friends would gather and speak mistrustfully of big government or big business or the establishment or other countries, even though these very persons depended on the distant structures being denigrated for the way of life they were leading. But they felt ties to larger groups than their immediate circles as well. The strength of their feelings of loyalty and identification was generally weakest for the largest and most distant of the organizational structures; nevertheless, even remote structures were growing more important. As the economies of the various countries became more interrelated, as the disadvantages of warfare between countries became more apparent, and as the citizens of each nation became more aware of what was going on elsewhere, the entire world moved slowly toward becoming a single, unified organization.

Each person related to this emerging hierarchical structure in a slightly different fashion, yet there tended to be similar techniques and mechanisms. A hypothetical example may illustrate a typical pattern. A poor person on welfare might feel that his benefits were being unfairly restricted, and he might resolve to do something about the situation. He might complain to the other members of his community association, to his welfare caseworker, to a broadly based state or national welfare rights organization, and to anyone else who would listen. Each of his listeners or each group of listeners might decide that the person had a legitimate grievance, that he did not, or somewhere in between. The community association might air the matter before the local Model Cities Citizens Board and/or the directors of the Economic Opportunity Board. The issue might come before the City Commission; it might be deliberated at any number of levels of local, state or national bureaucracies concerned with welfare; it might be debated in the State Legislature or in the halls of Congress; it might be submitted directly to public opinion through the communications media. Although there were generally established channels for the matter to pass through—for example, it was not likely to be heard by the City Commission unless it had the backing of a substantial number of influential citizens, and the national news media would be more inclined to take it up if it had first made an impact locally—it might bypass some of the foci of decision making on its way up. The City Commission might rule against the person, but a concerned official in Washington or the groundswell of public opinion stirred up by an investigative reporter might ultimately decide the case in his favor. So there were many points and places at which the matter could be fully or partially resolved. If it became important enough to preempt the attention of a wide audience, the decisions of millions of people might be brought to bear on it. Sooner or later, it would probably be taken care of at the level or levels that seemed appropriate to most of the people that came to be involved. And such a process was also available to a small businessman, a college student, a government administrator and just about anyone else, although the formal and informal channels could be different.

As the hierarchy of organizations became more firmly established and deeply entrenched, less importance was attached to individual effort. Each person came to gain a measure of identity and personal security just from belonging to a group, and as long as he did what was expected of him he did not need to depend so much on his own talents and energies to survive. The organizational structures took on more of the responsibility for their members' welfare, and a formidable complex of insurance and pension plans, health care programs, welfare agencies and other institutional activities directed toward succor arose. The traditional emphasis in American society on equality of opportunity began to give way to a stress on equality, or at least diminished inequality, of material welfare, whether obtained through individual striving or not. Society was coming more and more to look after all its members.

As a result of the overall relaxation of authority and of the diminishing emphasis on individual striving, ethnic groups became more assertive, demanding and getting more influence and more of the other rewards society had to bestow. Black Americans, Spanish-Americans, American Indians and members of other conspicuously identifiable ethnic minorities could contend that their heritage and ways were just as acceptable as those of white, mainstream America, and white Americans, their own social conventions looser and more open than earlier, were more ready to accept them. With more influence to be gained through association with groups and less through individual striving, the ethnic minorities could make headway in American society even if many of the individual members did not plunge vigorously into the traditional competitive swirl; this was an important new advantage since their cultures did not generally emphasize individual competition to the extent that that of mainstream America had. As the ethnic groups became more self-conscious and demanding, various institutions of society were forced to recognize the need to keep open the channels of communication, so there developed the practice of installing representatives of the more important of these groups in decision-making bodies such as subcommittees and boards of directors, even though these representatives had not risen to their new positions of prominence and power through the time-honored channels. With their increased status and influence, members of minority groups were becoming more assimilated to American society in significant ways than ever before, but their ethnic identifications and organizational structures remained important avenues to public influence. Like other groups in the overall hierarchical structure, they served as functioning levels of decision making, as loose organizations with a measure of authority and influence.

Another group that began to gain new power and prestige in somewhat the same fashion as the ethnic minorities was women. Women were by no means a minority in America, but for the most part they had traditionally occupied positions of less influence than men. In a restlessly striving and fairly power-conscious society, women had generally filled subordinate and supportive roles. The question of inherent differences between men and women is a controversial one, but a few generalizations can be made which may illuminate the shifting roles of the sexes. Men are usually larger and stronger than women, and many psychologists argue that male hormones tend to lead to more aggressive personalities than are characteristic of females. Furthermore, the fact that only women can bear children pushes many of them to divert much of their attention to the young. Men may work hard at caring for children, but their biological makeup does not direct them so much in this way. For these reasons and perhaps others, men have tended to be more adept at exerting their control over their surroundings. They have been more inclined to focus their attention and to take risks, since they have not been so tied down to children who made demands on their time and energy or who depended upon them for their continued existence and well-being. As a result of these tendencies and capabilities, men usually occupied the positions of greatest influence during the years from the Renaissance well into the twentieth century, while most women devoted themselves largely to less prestigious but no less necessary tasks centered around their families. But with the advent of the contemporary social and cultural transformation, the inherent differences between the sexes became less important. The male physical, psychological and cultural advantages that fitted him for individual striving became less significant. Authority and power continued to be necessary, but on a more relaxed scale than formerly. As society became more concerned with welfare and succor, and as cooperation became more important and competition less so, women found their abilities more in demand. As society beyond the immediate family took on more of the responsibilities traditionally left up to the family members, the nuclear family became looser and the wife and mother was freed for more outside activity. As traditional social conventions relaxed their grip, more freedom of movement became possible for the hitherto restricted and protected women. So like the members of the ethnic minorities, women demanded and got more influence and prestige. The ascent of woman to greater parity with man was made possible by the social and cultural transformation taking place, and her improved position contributed to the transformation as well.

The changes sweeping through human behavior were also making a dramatic impact on culture and thought patterns. These shifts are treated in more detail in the last chapter, but in general they occurred in the same direction as the other changes. No longer focusing their attention so intently on individual striving, the people at large slowly became more interested in artistic expression. Music and visual arts, particularly on the popular level, began to flourish, for these made an immediate appeal to the senses. On the other hand, literature and other verbal expression underwent a decline: their appeal was less direct and depended more on the highly conventionalized medium of language. The general loosening of authority found throughout society was also felt in culture. What had traditionally been considered high culture, such as orchestral music, carefully wrought theater, and paintings by the old masters, lost some of its prestige; the influence of illustrious critics and other arbiters of taste waned; persons enamored of traditional art bewailed what they regarded as the declining standards. Indeed, many of the younger artists seemed to go out of their way to flout authority, often mixing their media and producing works that appeared vulgar. But much of the new art had an exuberance and a spontaneous popular appeal. Students thronged to rock concerts; housewives flocked to art classes; arts and crafts fairs grew more common and more heavily attended; advertising displays became more elaborate and sophisticated; cities built impressive and attractive malls to draw people in. In one form or another culture became accessible to everyone, not just the members of the educated elite. It became something to be savored for its own sake and for the enrichment it could bring to life in the freer, more open and more relaxed atmosphere.

The broad picture of the social and cultural transformation presented here can help illuminate what happened in postwar Albuquerque and much of the rest of the country. Years after the time period covered, the changes are still unfolding. Although everyone has been affected by the growth of large, hierarchically structured organizations and by the general relaxation of control, different individuals, groups and subcultures react in different ways. The following pages trace many of these ways in the course of the development of the city of Albuquerque from 1945 through 1972. The drama of the growing metropolis contains millions of shifts and individual stories, of which this book can only offer some of the most representative. Yet every person in the area came to be influenced by the ongoing transformation.

2

ALBUQUERQUE IN 1945

Around the end of World War II Albuquerque was a bustling small city of about fifty thousand persons. Outlying beginnings of suburbs, neighboring Southwestern villages and small farms scattered along the Rio Grande brought the total population in Bernalillo County close to ninety thousand. The majority of the people in the area were Anglo—the Spanish-American name for non-Spanish whites—and except for their openness, boisterousness and other remnants of the frontier spirit, they were much like the residents of similar-sized cities of the time elsewhere in the country. The Spanish-Americans constituted an important minority, about 35 percent; although proportionately they had less power than the Anglos, their presence was responsible for much of the area's cultural distinctness. Indians (about 2 percent) and Blacks (around 1 percent) also contributed to the ethnic mix, as did a sprinkling of Orientals and recent immigrants from Europe.[1] But for all the diversity of the people's backgrounds and in spite of the sturdy individualism which most of them shared, they had little trouble functioning together as a coherent community. Almost everyone believed in traditional American values, in fair play and in fighting the good fight and getting ahead, and they were proud of their city, old in years but brimming with youthful possibility.

The story of Albuquerque during the years after the war is the story of these people, them and the newcomers who moved in to join them. In later years the immense population growth and the rise of large organizations tended to mute the impact of individual personalities; in 1945, however, the individual was very much in the limelight. Most people felt that through hard work and self-discipline they could shape their destinies. That they were responsible for what they were, not some impersonal and amorphous forces. And to a large degree, their experiences seemed to bear out their beliefs. As a consequence, one can peer deeply into the nature of their society by starting with their composite portraits.

To a much greater extent than in later years, the community leaders and other prominent citizens set the tone for Albuquerque of 1945. The people looked to them for direction, inspiration and models for behavior. Their words and actions as revealed on public occasions, as filtered through newspaper editions and radio broadcasts, and as passed on by word of mouth constituted high drama, drama in which everybody who lived in Albuquerque had at least a small part to play. So the prominent citizens tended to be strong, colorful figures. Some had come from other parts of the country to make their fortune and spread their influence, such as Congressman Clinton P. Anderson; the wealthy Simms brothers; Ex-Governor A. T. Hannett and his brother Dr. James G. Hannett; the funeral director Chester T. French; Clyde Oden, president of the Chamber of Commerce; Dr. W. R. Lovelace, who gave his name to Lovelace Clinic; and Kathryn Kennedy O'Connor, founder of the Albuquerque Little Theatre. Several of these transplants had contracted tuberculosis in their youth, come to Albuquerque because of its reputation for having a healthful climate with its abundance of clean dry air, and stayed on to thrive. Some of the prominent figures were local products—U.S. Senator Dennis Chavez; the writer Erna Fergusson; State Representative Joe A. Montoya; Philip and Harold Hubbell, long active in Republican politics; Manuel Sanchez, chairman of the county Democrats; and the Keleher family. Most of these leading citizens knew each other, planned strategies with each other in mind, and enjoyed good fights that frequently resulted in shifting alliances and vehement declarations. And at the center of the stage was the chairman of the City Commission, the most flamboyant figure in New Mexico politics, Ex-Governor Clyde Tingley.

Tingley had enormous vitality, and he stamped his imprint on city political life for many years. He was born on a farm in Madison County, Ohio, in 1881, and grew up in that part of the country. While working for the Graham Motor Company in Bowling Green, Ohio, he met the well-to-do Carrie Wooster. She moved to Albuquerque for her health in 1910; he followed and they were married the next year. His chosen career was machinery work, but he also spent time as a farmhand, a railroad fireman and a chauffeur. His easy familiarity with working men and their life became one of his chief assets after he entered politics. After his marriage Tingley, now independently wealthy, plunged headlong into the political arena. He served two terms as alderman of Albuquerque, and when the city shifted to the city manager-commission form of government in 1922, he was elected to the City Commission, where he served until 1934, and again from 1940 to 1955. Twelve of those years he was chairman, and when he was chairman he was, one could say with little exaggeration, the City Commission. He was also district supervisor of the State Highway Department from 1921 to 1924, and governor of New Mexico for two terms in the 1930s. In every capacity, from every position he held, he exerted his influence as a builder. Senator Chavez said that more schools were built throughout the state during his governorship than in all other administrations, and Tingley was also credited with establishing the state fair at Albuquerque, the Carrie Tingley Hospital for Crippled Children at Truth or Consequences, and the tuberculosis hospital at Socorro. He directed the building of the Albuquerque airport and other local projects.[2] Years after his death monuments to his name remained, including Tingley Coliseum, Tingley Field, Tingley Drive and Tingley Park.

He was not an educated man—the lawyer-writer Will Keleher doubted that he had ever read an entire book in his life[3]—but he had a colorful tongue. Once, when he was giving a luncheon at the governor's mansion, a guest commented on how well one of the maids was serving the meal. "Where did you get her?" he asked Governor Tingley.

"Out of the penitentiary."

"What was she in for?" the guest asked.

"For life—she murdered her husband by feeding him ground glass."

"Aren't you afraid she'll serve you ground glass?"

"Hell no!" Tingley answered. "Her brother is over in the prison and she wants a pardon for him."[4]

As the story illustrates, he demanded loyalty and favorable treatment from those around him. Such behavior was not always forthcoming. During his second term as governor he decided he wanted to run again, but the state constitution prohibited his serving for three consecutive terms. Acting on the advice of Will Keleher, he called a meeting with three of the chief Democratic leaders in the state—former governor A.T. Hannett, Senator Dennis Chavez and John Miles—and asked their support in amending the constitution.[5] The three were noncommittal—Senator Chavez declared, "I will have to go home and consult my God, my wife and my conscience."

"By—" Tingley exploded. "If I had consulted my God, my wife and my conscience, I never would have appointed you to the U.S. Senate!"[6] . . . The three leaders united behind Miles, who was elected the next governor as Tingley lost his bid.

In 1945 Clyde Tingley, as chairman of the City Commission and a striking figure in his own right, was the leading personality in Albuquerque. The city's largest newspaper, the *Albuquerque Journal*, gave him prominent coverage, as his activities made good copy and the paper sided with him politically. (In contrast, the *Albuquerque Tribune* opposed him and mentioned him less often and less vividly.) His gestures and his tactical maneuvers, his charities and his fights were all in the limelight. Albuquerque followed avidly his efforts to disperse Chinese elm trees all over town to make the city a more pleasant place to live in, his complicated and bitter fights with Governor Dempsey, and his spontaneous clowning.

Tingley loved shady trees, parks, the Rio Grande Zoo, things that had the vitality that could make Albuquerque a satisfying home for its residents, and many of the other townspeople felt the same way. (Perhaps he, like many others, wanted to transplant memories of his native state to the arid land of New Mexico.) Chinese elms grew fast, and he undertook to spread them with evangelical zeal. A typical news item of 1945: "Five hundred Chinese elms as big around as Clyde Tingley's wrist will be given to Albuquerque residents willing to dig them up, Tingley said Sunday." These were available at the city nursery in Rio Grande Park the following weekend.[7]

His conflict with Governor Dempsey was longstanding. The incidents and episodes which it comprised were as involved and dramatic as those of a daytime radio or television serial. Unlike a fictional soap opera, however, the prolonged fight between these two powers and their cohorts was very real, and the destinies of living people hung in the balance. What follows are some of the highlights of this struggle during the year of 1945.

January 4—Tingley attempts to revoke the liquor licenses of two retail stores for selling liquor to Indians. (Such sales were illegal in New Mexico.) An episode in his continuing battle with the State Liquor Commission.[8]

January 9—He announces he will send letters to heads of counties and municipalities in New Mexico recommending the revival of the Municipal League. He favors the League acting to transfer the power to issue liquor licenses from the State Liquor Tax Division to local governments. He indicates annoyance that Governor Dempsey has not replied to his demand that illegal liquor sales be stopped. The old liquor dealers resent the large number of new applications for licenses.[9]

January 27—A reorganizational meeting of the Municipal League is held, and interest is shown in restoring liquor-licensing powers to cities and counties. Annual dues are set at one dollar for each hundred dollars of a city's general fund budget, with a minimum of twenty-five dollars.[10]

January 29—Tingley announces his resignation as chairman of the board at Carrie Tingley Hospital for reasons of the current and anticipated press of city business and poor health.[11]

February 5—A legislative report on Carrie Tingley Hospital is made public. Governor Dempsey says he would have felt compelled to ask for Tingley's resignation "for cause" if it had not already been submitted.[12]

Two men, Manuel Sanchez, supported by Tingley, and Ralph Keleher, backed by Dempsey, claim to be chairman of the Democratic Party in Bernalillo County. The County Commission recognizes Sanchez as the legitimate chairman.[13]

March 13—Assistant Attorney General Harry L. Bigbee rules that the state constitution forbids the Municipal League to use public funds.[14]

October 24—Tingley accuses Dempsey of "continually stealing and trying to steal" Albuquerque policemen for the state police force. He charges the governor with playing politics.[15]

November 5—Dempsey denies Tingley's charges.[16]

And so on, with more in the same vein. Nor were the public attacks and rivalries aired in the Albuquerque papers limited to conflicts on the scale of the one with Governor Dempsey. Alliances were forged and broken, and restless maneuvering and infighting were constants in Albuquerque politics. And almost always, Clyde Tingley had an interest in the outcome and played a part in the struggle.

One sometime ally, sometime opponent was State Representative Joe A. Montoya. Born in the Old Town section of Albuquerque, the son of a former Bernalillo County probate judge, Montoya had been a water meter reader, an insurance agent, a conductor for a travel agency and a business agent for a labor union, and he had been continuously involved in state and local politics.[17] When Tingley promoted the reorganization of the Municipal League in January of 1945, Montoya supported the commissioner's stand.[18] But just two months later, Montoya sponsored a bill designed to place employees of the City of Albuquerque under civil service. It sailed through the House of Representatives.[19] Since it made a special case of Albuquerque, naturally it upset Tingley and his cohorts.[20]

But whatever his political troubles, Clyde Tingley remained irrepressible. A few days before the fourth of July, he came across a 1906 ordinance prohibiting throwing snowballs, and he publicly announced that anyone celebrating Independence Day in such fashion would be prosecuted. And as an afterthought, he said shooting fire-crackers was against the law too.[21] A few weeks later, when he was walking through Conservancy Beach, he noticed dead leaves on the Chinese elm trees planted twelve years earlier by city employees. Consulting with his advisers, he learned that the culprits were probably Thomomys Talpoides (pocket gophers), which had been chewing bark off the trees. "They moved here last winter because of the warm climate, but they can't come in here and kill our trees," he declared. "We'll run 'em out of town." He deputized three men to lay traps.[22]

Tingley was by no means the only strong and colorful leader in Albuquerque of 1945, although none of the others basked in such publicity. On the national scale U.S. Senator Dennis Chavez was more powerful, and the senator exerted his considerable influence in local politics from time to time. Like Tingley and others, Chavez thrived in the rough and tumble atmosphere of hard fights and shifting alliances characteristic of New Mexico at this time. When he died in 1962, his obituary writer characterized him as a fighter:

> He was a fighter, the lad who was born 74 years ago in a poor adobe home in Los Chavez [a small community a few miles south of Albuquerque] and was baptized Dennis Chavez. He fought his way out of the poverty of his early days, battled his way to one of the most powerful posts in the U.S. Senate, kept on fighting to better the conditions of those who had not been able to work their own way above poverty.
>
> He was uncompromising in his beliefs—even to the point of giving up a needed job rather than deliver groceries to strikebreakers. He early broke from his father's political party [the Republican Party] because he didn't think it had the interests of the common man at heart—but was not adverse [sic] in later years to withholding support from the nominee of his own party. He was beloved by thousands of his fellow New Mexicans—and hated by almost as many.[23]

34

Before becoming a U.S. Senator, he had been a deputy game warden, a newspaper editor, an engineer, a lawyer (he had put himself through law school at Georgetown University) and a member of the State Legislature. In 1930 he defeated the incumbent Albert G. Simms in a contest for a seat in the U.S. Congress. In 1934 he ran against Bronson Cutting, then the greatest power in New Mexico politics, for the U.S. Senate. Cutting was declared the winner, Chavez contested the election, Cutting was killed in an airplane accident, and Governor Tingley appointed Chavez to fill the vacancy. From the Senate, Chavez used his influence, especially after becoming chairman of the Committee on Public Works and the Subcommittee on Defense Appropriations, to direct federal projects into New Mexico. He feuded openly and vigorously with such prominent state figures as Governor John J. Dempsey and Governor John Miles (despite their alliance at the time when Tingley wanted a third term as governor), but his battles seemed mainly to increase his power in the state, especially among the Spanish-Americans. Toward the end of his career, he looked back over his life and wrote:

> It was the early years, the hard years of growing up in a poor country, that made the difference. They were years rich in human warmth, They taught me a knowledge of New Mexico, her people and problems, that has enabled me to serve effectively through more than 30 years in high office.[24]

Not all of the influential people in Albuquerque of 1945 were so flamboyant and public. Two whose quiet manner belied their broad impact were Albert G. and John Simms, born in the 1880s in Washington, Arkansas, the sons of a former Confederate soldier. Albert attended the University of Arkansas, contracted tuberculosis, and in 1907 travelled for his health to Monterrey, Mexico, where he worked as an accountant. John, meanwhile, earned a law degree at Vanderbilt University, moved to Texarkana to practice law, and served a term in the Arkansas Legislature. Tuberculosis, however, brought the brothers together again. In 1912 Albert moved to Silver City, New Mexico, seeking a more salubrious climate, and John, now sick himself, came the following year. Albert studied in the office of a prominent lawyer there, and then the brothers moved to Albuquerque and set up their own firm, Simms and Simms.

Albert was especially active during his early years in Albuquerque. Like his brother, he had been a staunch Southern Democrat, but he became a Republican in New Mexico, then a Republican state. He left the law firm in 1919 and plunged into banking, ranching and politics. In the next ten years he founded and served as president of the Citizens National Bank (it went under during the Great Depression); was a co-founder of the Albuquerque National Bank (by 1972 the largest bank in the state) and served as chairman of its board of directors; established a real estate company; was elected to the chairmanship of the Bernalillo County Commission, to the State Legislature and to the U.S. House of Representatives; and bought a six-hundred-acre ranch in northwest Albuquerque. In 1930, when the Democratic tide swept the state, he was defeated in his bid for reelection to Congress by Dennis Chavez, and he never ran for another elective office. He continued to prosper, however. He bought one-half of the Elena Gallegos Grant, a sixteen-thousand-acre strip of land running three miles wide from North Edith Street to the top of Sandia Crest. In the years after World War II this became one of the most valuable tracts in the rapidly expanding northeast heights of Albuquerque.

His first wife, whom he had met at Silver City when they were both tubercular, never recovered from her illness and died in 1921. While serving in Congress from 1929 to 1931, he met and fell in love with one of the few congresswomen of the day, Representative Ruth Hanna McCormick, Republican from Illinois, daughter of Senator Marcus Hanna of Ohio and widow of Senator Medill McCormick of the Chicago McCormicks. They were married, and her enormous fortune added to his made the Albert G. Simms family one of the richest in New Mexico.[25] Together they founded the Manzano Day School for Girls and Sandia School and gave substantial support to the Albuquerque Little Theatre. On the last day of 1944, the second Mrs. Albert Simms died. Residents honored her memory as they would for few other citizens: on the day of her funeral the City and County Commissions closed down for an hour, and the Albuquerque National Bank and Manzano Day School closed for half a day.[26]

Albert's younger brother John remained a Democrat and a lawyer, and partly as a result his political fortunes did well. He served for many years on the State Supreme Court. His law firm became one of the biggest in New Mexico, and his business interests prospered as well, although not so spectacularly as Albert's. Not least of his contributions was the fathering of two sons, John, who later was to become governor of New Mexico, and Albert, who grew up to be a prominent doctor.[27]

The most literary of the Albuquerque political leaders at this time was William A. Keleher, a member of an illustrious local family which included his brother, Ralph, one of the rival claimants to the chairmanship of the Democratic Party in the county, and his sister, Julia, an English teacher at the University of New Mexico. His father had come to Albuquerque in 1881, just after the Santa Fe Railroad had been built through the area causing the boom of New Albuquerque. Then the Kelehers moved briefly to Lawrence, Kansas, where Will was born, so he was not a native, strictly speaking. Then back to Albuquerque, and school and a variety of jobs, including work at the Western Union, reporting for the *Albuquerque Journal*, then city editor for that newspaper and later for the now-defunct *Albuquerque Herald*. In 1913 he went east for a year of law school and another of studying American and English history and poetry. Returning, Will practiced law and served as city attorney from 1916 to 1922. From this point onward, he held a number of important offices, including Democratic state chairman in 1928, member of the State Finance Board under six Democratic governors, and member of the Board of Regents of New Mexico A & M from 1940 to 1942.

From the early 1940s, Will became increasingly occupied with his law practice and writing about New Mexico history. In 1942 he wrote *Maxwell Land Grant*, treating the history and problems of land grants in the state; *The Fabulous Frontier*, about southeastern New Mexico during the territorial period, came out in 1945. His keen interest in life in the early days shone through the pages.[28] His friends and associates appreciated his skill with words, and they called on him frequently to speak. In 1945 he was the toastmaster at the Democrats' annual Jefferson Day dinner. John Simms was the principal speaker; Tingley, among others, also spoke a few words.[29]

The Albuquerque political leader destined to make the greatest impact nationwide over the ensuing years was U.S. Congressman Clinton P. Anderson. His father had migrated from Sweden to South Dakota, where young Anderson was born. After college he moved to Albuquerque for his health (he had tuberculosis) and worked as a newspaperman. For a while he was editor of the *Albuquerque Journal*. When the paper was sold, he went into the insurance business, bought out the company, and eventually made the Clinton P. Anderson Agency one of the largest in the state. He also became increasingly active in politics. After a succession of state offices, in 1940 he was elected to the U.S. House of Representatives. In May of 1945, President Truman appointed him Secretary of Agriculture. Anderson was kept busy directing the dispersal of food to overseas countries, but he still managed to exercise his considerable influence on politics back home.

In his memoirs he gave his version of his active career. Certain motifs stand out, and these mark him as sharing similar experiences and attitudes with many of his contemporaries. They include a strenuous youth, love of action and being productive, enjoying a good fight (but observing the rules), a sense of being right, respect for good leaders, especially Roosevelt, obligation to the public, and enduring ties with the Democrats and antagonism toward the Republicans and their causes.[30]

The cast of characters who performed on the political scene of Albuquerque 1945 was very large. The preceding brief sketches have presented a few representative personalities and incidents; they have by no means delineated the limits of the political behavior of the time. To do so fully would be impossible even if this chapter were stretched out into many volumes, for the varieties of political behavior, all the declarations, struggles and intrigues, were as great as the size of the population and the time span the people had in which to act. A fuller, but still miserably finite, study would expand the treatment of the leading personalities touched upon here, and it would provide biographies of other influential personages. It would discuss Clyde Oden—member of the City Commission; president of the Albuquerque Chamber of Commerce; founder and president of Oden Motor Company, the largest Buick dealership in the area; the man who, born in Corsicana, Texas, moved to Oklahoma and worked for an express company with only a sawed-off shotgun to fight off robbery attempts and, afterwards, came to Albuquerque and became active in Democratic politics.[31] It would treat Art Westerfeld, a small, wiry man, the son of a former Albuquerque mayor, the fire chief who presided over the expansion of the City Fire Department and who was proud of never losing a man to death by fire and of getting to fires as fast as possible.[32] It would deal with Philip Hubbell, the realtor who in the 1920s led the fight to move the county courthouse from Old Town to New Town.[33] Also his brother Harold, the sheriff. But however the numbers might expand, any more complete presentation of the city's politics in those days would have to treat the controlled turbulence, the struggle within mutually acceptable limits that has been indicated here.

The business community of Albuquerque 1945 was more fragmented than the political one. True, there were several towering figures whose deals had widespread repercussions, people such as Albert Simms and Fred Luthy, president of the Albuquerque National Bank, and it is also true that business was not completely separate from politics. Such political decisions as where a new government building would be erected and who would win a government contract naturally interested businessmen, and a substantial amount of hidden bargaining could be expected. Nevertheless, the Albuquerque economy was much closer to a state of perfect competition, with businesses competing vigorously among themselves for trade and few monopolies or oligopolies, than it was to become in later years. A few statistics, culled from the classified section of the May 1945 telephone book, may illustrate this point. In the city there were 28 drug stores, and only 3 were operated by the same chain or under the same franchise. There were 151 grocery stores, of which 5 were operated by the same firm (several months later, the respective numbers were 154 and 0). Of the 15 department stores, the only examples of multiple ownership were 2 Montgomery Wards and 2 Sears Roebucks. There were also 27 hotels, 56 tourist courts, 79 restaurants and 3 banks in Albuquerque, and apparently no company or individual owned or operated more than a single place of business in any of these fields. Contrast that state of affairs with the situation in any city in America of today, with chains and conglomerates on nearly every thoroughfare and in nearly every shopping center. The composition of Albuquerque business changed too, as a later chapter will discuss. The business competition in Albuquerque at this time was not perfect, of course—it never has been anywhere—but these numbers and the widespread single ownership which they indicate support the conclusion that competition was as important in the economic sphere, perhaps more so, as it was in politics.

The largest employer was the Santa Fe Railroad, with twenty-five hundred workers and over half a million in monthly paychecks.[34] As the railroad was not locally owned, it afforded little opportunity for Albuquerque people to make fortunes. Fortunes were being made, though, and mainly by hard-driving Anglos. (Spanish-Americans had a number of small businesses, but on the whole they were not so successful in business as in politics.) Many of the people who did the best came from far-off places.

Fred Luthy, president of the Albuquerque National Bank, was born in Albuquerque in 1894, the son of a Swiss immigrant who was at that time mayor of the city. He attended the University of New Mexico and Yale, studying geology and economics. Graduating Phi Beta Kappa in 1917, he entered the army but saw no overseas action. He then went to work in the Texas oil fields as a scout and a roustabout for two years until malaria forced him to return to Albuquerque. In 1921 he joined the Citizens National Bank as a bookkeeper, and advanced to the position of vice president before it closed in 1924. Then he became vice president and executive officer of the newly opened Albuquerque National Bank.

On June 23, 1938, he and George Kaseman, president of the bank, were visiting an oil field in Hobbs, New Mexico, to watch an oil well "shot" to increase its flow. Workmen had just unloaded nitroglycerin from a truck and were getting ready to lower it into the well. "All of a sudden there was a flash," Luthy recalled. "I first thought of my wife and my boy. I tried to get to Mr. Kaseman to see if I could help him." His next memory was waking up in a Hobbs hospital, the course of his life changed. Kaseman was dead, and Luthy was elected the next president of the bank as soon as he was well enough to be released from the hospital. He never did fully recover from the explosion, however; over the next few years he gradually lost his eyesight. Every morning secretaries would read him the news and the mail, and they would also make recordings of published articles of special interest to him for him to listen to at nights and on weekends. Under his leadership, the Albuquerque National Bank grew to become the largest bank in the state.[35]

One of the most energetic of the city's businessmen in 1945 was Chester T. French, senior partner of the French-Fitzgerald Mortuary. Born on a farm in East Tennessee, he moved to Albuquerque with his brother, who was sick with tuberculosis, in 1904, and three years later became owner of a mortuary. In 1914 he conducted the first motorized funeral in the state. From time to time he held various elective offices; the one he was the proudest of was the post of county commissioner from 1926 to 1930, which he won by beating Clinton P. Anderson in the last race Anderson lost. Long interested in young people, he taught Sunday school at a Methodist church for many years, and he founded the Chester T. French Boys' Choir in 1936 and funded it until 1941, when it became the Albuquerque Boys' Choir. He had the first large flower garden in Albuquerque. Upon request, he mailed thousands of packages of blue morning glory seeds all over the United States, and he sponsored many flower growing contests for young people. Meanwhile, his mortuary service flourished, moving from location to location as he felt the need to expand his facilities.[36]

Throughout his long life he emphasized clean living and self-discipline. In his biography, which he commissioned, is presented the Chester T. French Creed, summing up much of his attitude toward life:

> Four major thoughts I would leave with you, to help you build a rich, full and rewarding life. Four sides you should have in your building to make it stand firm and four square.
> First—The Physical
> Do not neglect to take this daily round of exercise, if only for one minute each day. It will bring you clear eyes to see the truth, pure blood and bubbling energy that you must have to carry on your work.
> Second—The Mental
> Spend at least an hour each day in reading good literature, written by dedicated and educated men, remembering always to find guidance in the pages of the greatest book ever written—The Holy Bible!
> Third—The Social
> Rub elbows with your fellow man! Share pleasant hours of association with those whose hearts are light, whose thoughts are pure, and whose lives are filled with acts of kindness.
> Fourth—The Spiritual
> Never forget that your church is the bulwark of your life! That around you is a world created by the Master's Hand! That more than two thousand years ago the Son of God came into the world, lived as a man for a brief time, and died on the cross FOR YOU!
> These four major building planks would I leave with you. If you use them wisely and well, when the sun of your life nears the horizon, you can look back with few regrets.[37]

The discipline and industry which French manifested were characteristic of many businessmen whose backgrounds were very unlike his. One ethnic group that thrived in the Albuquerque business world, partly as a result of these traits, was the Italians, who migrated to the city in large numbers during the early part of this century. One of the most striking of their success stories was that of Pompilio Matteucci, founder and owner of Paris Shoe Store.

In 1904 Matteucci left Lucca, Italy, and his wife and son, and followed his two older brothers to Albuquerque. (The older brothers Alesandro and Amadeo soon became successful retail grocers.) On his way he passed through Paris, France; the city impressed him so much that he subsequently named his business after it. Pompilio arrived in town with about a hundred dollars in his pocket and went to work at a sawmill, and by the end of the year the rest of his family joined him. In 1905 he set up a small shop for making and repairing shoes. At this time Albuquerque was still a town of the old west, with lively cowboy bars and gunfights in the streets, but he stayed away from the wild side. "I had a family to take care of," Matteucci said. "I stayed home nights." He worked steadily. In 1924 he moved his operation to a bigger location; by now he was employing an extra cobbler as well as his five sons. In 1932, in the depths of the Depression, he moved to a still larger downtown location, and again Paris Shoe Store thrived. By the end of the Second World War, it was one of the biggest retail businesses in the city.[38]

As different as Matteucci, French and Luthy were, they shared a common orientation among themselves and with many others who were doing well in the Albuquerque business community at this time. By and large, they were not so outgoing as the politicians (although, as with French, there was a certain amount of overlap), but they tended to have a high degree of self-discipline and perseverance. They worked hard, they believed in themselves and in the growth of Albuquerque, and events generally vindicated their faith.

In the areas of education, culture and civic affairs, the leadership also tended to be varied and diffuse, ranging from the autocrats of educational administration John Milne and Dr. John Wernette to more gently persuasive yet highly influential individuals such as the writer Erna Fergusson and the actor-director Kathryn Kennedy O'Connor. These people were impelled by a sense of duty to lift the cultural level of the people of Albuquerque. And they were generally acquainted with and often a part of the leadership in local business and politics.

John Milne, superintendent of Albuquerque Public Schools, knew how to spot business trends and influence politicians, and during his long tenure in office he utilized both abilities to his own advantage and to that of the school system. Born in Scotland in 1880, he came to Albuquerque and started teaching in 1907. He served as principal of Albuquerque High School from 1908 to 1911, when he became superintendent of schools. Over the following decades, the canny administrator was always able, through judicious buying of valuable land, to keep school building abreast of the growing population. Around the time of World War I, for instance, he bought a piece of property for three thousand dollars that much later became the site of the Public School Stadium.[39]

But it was as a ruler of the school system itself that Milne exerted the most influence. He ran the system almost singlehandedly, sharing little of his authority with committees, subordinates or even the elected school board. His concentration of power sometimes reassured and comforted the other people working in the school system, sometimes it frustrated and antagonized them, but always it was effective. One school principal commented: "I enjoyed being a principal under John Milne. He made the rules and we enforced them. Furthermore, we knew he would back us up, right or wrong. When a question came up, we could call him and receive an immediate answer. We all knew where we stood." Another administrator, however, gave a less favorable viewpoint. "John Milne was a complete tyrant, He allowed no freedom of action for anyone in the system; teachers, administrators, or even board members. He made all the important educational decisions and insisted on absolute submission on the part of school personnel and patrons alike."[40]

Much of Milne's authority came from his long stay in office and from his intimate knowledge of the city. Dr. John P. Wernette, appointed by the regents in 1945 to be the new president of the University of New Mexico, was just as assertive as Milne but lacked such a firm power base. Born in Michigan, Wernette attended the University of Southern California at Los Angeles and then Harvard, where he got a master's and a doctorate. He taught at Harvard for eighteen years, rising to prominence as a professor of economics.[41] When he arrived in Albuquerque in August, a man of a medium build bedecked with a Tom Dewey moustache,[42] the university community had little idea what to expect. He lost little time making his presence felt. Later that month he spoke before the Kiwanis Club and startled his audience by announcing that the university would play a large part in the creation of a new American culture. In the next twenty years, he said, the university would more than double its enrollment [it was only 1009 at the beginning of the year[43]] and quadruple the value of its physical plant. More important, he prophesied, with the national goal pointed toward full employment and with more time for recreation, American thought would turn away from the New England culture, which frowned on pleasure, and toward the Spanish-American culture, which stressed happiness.[44] But if Wernette saw himself as playing a leading role in this transformation of values, he did not peer deeply enough into his crystal ball.

The realm of cultural affairs in Albuquerque 1945 was open to women, and some of them made a greater ultimate impact in this area than Wernette and Milne. The most illustrious was Erna Fergusson, the most prominent daughter of one of the oldest and most prominent families in the city. Her grandfather Franz Huning had come over from Germany in 1851, become an enormously successful merchant, and erected a massive, Bavarian-style structure on the edge of Old Town that was still known in 1945 as Huning Castle. His daughter Clara, the first Anglo born in Albuquerque, married Harvey Fergusson, a young lawyer from Alabama who became very active in territorial and then state politics, serving two terms in Congress.[45] The Fergussons had four children, three of whom became nationally recognized writers. Besides Erna, there was Harvey, who moved to California, and Francis, who taught at Rutgers and became a drama critic. Erna, who stayed in Albuquerque most of her life, outshone her brothers in the hearts of the townspeople.

She was born in 1888 and grew up, not in Huning Castle, but in an old adobe house, which later became the Manzano Day School. She earned degrees from the University of New Mexico and Columbia University, and taught in the Albuquerque Public Schools for several years. Among her more notable activities were stints as a reporter for the *Albuquerque Herald*, as state supervisor for the Red Cross during World War I, as partner in a tour business, as a lecturer in seminars on Latin America, and as program officer for the Inter-American Educational Foundation's division of science and education. She gained her greatest fame from her books; among them are *Dancing Gods*, on Southwestern Indian ceremonies; *New Mexico, A Pageant of Three Peoples*; and *Mexican Cookbook*. Much of her influence around Albuquerque stemmed from her lectures and her talks on topics of civic interest. She inaugurated and was a frequent speaker in the annual "Under the Stars" lecture series at the University of New Mexico.[46] In May 1945 she was moved to speak out on suffering in the United States: all illiteracy, disease, poverty or social injustice discovered abroad can be matched in this country, she told a group of local educators.[47]

Another of the first ladies of Albuquerque cultural activities was Kathryn Kennedy O'Connor, who directed all the plays of the Albuquerque Little Theatre since its founding and acted in many of them. She was born in Cortland, New York, studied at the Syracuse University College of Oratory, and went on to become a professional actress. While playing a minor role and understudying the star in a Broadway production of *Rain*, she was struck down by tuberculosis. So like many others from various parts of the country, in 1927 she came to Albuquerque to recuperate.

Kathryn Kennedy was a patient at St. Joseph Sanatorium when she met James O'Connor, a ward visitor. O'Connor, a native of Ireland, had come to Albuquerque after being gassed as a British soldier in World War I. At this time he worked in a storeroom for the Santa Fe Railroad, but before immigrating he had acted in England and at the Abbey Theater in Dublin, Ireland. Their common interest in the theater blossomed into friendship and then marriage in 1928. Two years later they founded the Albuquerque Little Theatre, with Mrs. O'Connor as founding director and Mr. O'Connor as business manager and director of publicity and advertising. Their first play was *This Thing Called Love*. From the start the Albuquerque Little Theatre had substantial support from the leading citizens. Clinton P. Anderson was its first president; Ruth Hanna McCormick Simms was its second. In 1936 a new building was erected for the Theatre as a result of a WPA project on land donated by W.A. Keleher and A.R. Hebenstreit.[48] Under the direction of the O'Connors, especially Kathryn Kennedy, it continued to flourish. The newspapers in 1945 gave it prominent coverage.

Another field in which women were quite active was civic and charitable work. Good deeds and helping those less fortunate than oneself were considered duties in Albuquerque of 1945. Of course some people heeded the call of this sort of duty more than others, but association with and leadership in worthy causes could bring eminence and respect in the community. A number of local personages, notably the Tingleys, especially Carrie Tingley, and Chester T. French, worked energetically for numerous charitable causes. Most of the aid to the sick and the poor was given on a volunteer basis rather than through governmental agencies. Most of it was in the form of educational opportunities or youth organizations or, occasionally, medical treatment and food; outright transfers of money were rare. The society's unfortunate, it was generally felt, should not remain in a state of dependency but should work to better themselves. What they needed, so went the belief, was opportunity, help in times of dire emergency, and moral support.

A representative instance of citizens providing help for other citizens occurred in March of 1945. Mrs. Maria Vergara, chairman of the Committee on Survey of the Nutrition Problem in the City for the Bernalillo County Nutrition Council, made a report that sixty children were "starving to death." The Hugh A. Carlisle Post of the American Legion decided to contribute fifty dollars a month toward whatever program was found necessary and practical to combat malnutrition. The Nutrition Council voted to adopt one family and see that its nutritional needs were being met, and to guide two other families in food purchasing over a period of several weeks. The department adjutant for the American Legion expressed the opinion that the problem could be solved by a long-time educational campaign on nutrition.[49]

Charity work sometimes took on ceremonial overtones. In the annual March of Dimes campaign for funds to combat infantile paralysis, two of the most important channels for donations were the movie theaters, where collections were taken up, and ticket sales for the Infantile Paralysis Dance. Most of the movie theaters participated in collecting for the drive. Afternoon collections were made by high school girls, who did their work as part of the Junior Red Cross extension program, and evening collections by student nurses from the Regina School of Nursing. At the same time, a number of organizations busily sold tickets to the ball. The group selling the most tickets was honored by having the pleasure of eating Tojo, a blue-ribbon Japanese black-tail bantam rooster, a la king. The dance was held simultaneously at the four largest downtown hotels—the Hilton, the Alvarado, the Franciscan and the Fidel. During the festivities home-baked cakes were auctioned off.[50]

Some of the charitable and civic work was centralized under the auspices of the Community Chest, a loosely knit group of organizations banded together for the purpose of raising funds. Typically a prominent man in the community would lead a drive, and the newspapers would give the drive and its beneficiaries wide coverage. Two of the institutions which at this time received most of their financial support through the Community Chest were the Barelas Community Center and St. Anthony's Boys' Home.

The Barelas Center, established in 1942, was run by the Barelas Community Council since 1944. Members of the council and other volunteers conducted most of the regularly scheduled activities, including classes in crafts and first aid, Girl Scouts meetings, physical education for boys, fraternal club and church group gatherings, educational movies, and lecture and discussion groups. A paid instructor taught music four days a week, and once a month maternal and health clinics were conducted by the district health department. Council members were also involved in remodeling the center. Most of the labor they provided with their own hands; costs were covered by benefit functions held at the center.[51]

St. Anthony's Boys' Home was established on fifty acres of swampy land by two nuns who arrived from Indiana in 1913. More nuns came to help within the next few months, and by the second year they had sixty boys to look after and an elementary school as well. As the years passed by, the facilities, the staff and the enrollment grew. In the depths of the Great Depression, when many Albuquerque families were unable to support their children, the number of boys at St. Anthony's peaked at 250 or more. Until the time when the institution became a beneficiary of the Community Chest, the sisters had to garner financial support by travelling through the state and collecting contributions.

In 1945 the home was an almost self-contained community of the staff and over a hundred boys. Most of the boys were Spanish-American, but other ethnic groups were represented as well. Much of their food, including livestock for meat and milk, was grown on the premises. In addition to the regular school work, each boy was given two hours of study period daily. Every boy old enough to work was also assigned a specific job, such as work in the dining hall, the bakery, the laundry, the barn and the chapel, and the assignments were shifted every month to vary the routine. The boys had athletic activities as well, and their football, basketball and baseball teams competed with those of other schools in the city. After graduating from the eighth grade, they would leave the home and move in with relatives, strike out on their own and go to work full time, or go on to high school.[52]

By and large, the Anglos and the Spanish-Americans worked together in the civic and governmental organizations in 1945, and their attitudes and their goals were similar. The Anglos did, however, put greater emphasis on individual initiative and self-help, whereas the Spanish-Americans, perhaps because of their political and social traditions and perhaps because of their poverty, tended to stress people helping each other and getting help from the government. One of the more influential of the Spanish-American organizations was the League of United Latin-American Citizens (LULAC), a largely middle-class group concerned with improving the standard of living of their ethnic group.

Early in 1946 Ernest Salazar, president of LULAC Council No. 34, announced a program to be taken up by the League. The overall goal, he said, was to raise the social and economic standards of the lower classes of Spanish-speaking people and to aid in veteran rehabilitation. The specific points of the program included industrial development in the state, a city-county general hospital, higher wages for university professors and school teachers, support of federally controlled credit unions and of consumer cooperatives, creation of community centers throughout the Southwest patterned after the Barelas Community Center, and efforts to see that all Spanish-speaking veterans take advantage of the G.I. Bill of Rights and that all civic organizations give more responsibility to Spanish-speaking communities in all civic matters, such as drives for the Red Cross, infantile paralysis and the Community Chest.[53] Although these points were designed to help the poorer Spanish-Americans in particular, they were also directed toward bringing them more into the larger community.

The attitudes, values and structures embodied in the patterns of leadership and the institutions in Albuquerque were manifested in the day-to-day lives of the thousands of ordinary citizens as well. Such motifs as the importance of strong leaders, formal celebrations, love of competition and combat, fascination with the spoken and written word, and self-discipline were recurrent in hundreds of news accounts of 1945 and for a while thereafter.

Large, formal parties were in the social spotlight. Even the students at the University of New Mexico, that hotbed of informality and general raucousness of later years, loved them. Early in the year they held their annual Mirage Beauty Ball, featuring the beauty queen for their yearbook. As customary, chaperones were present.[54] Many of their festivities and those of other groups were held at the large downtown hotels, for the central location and the stately mien of these edifices seemed to enhance the celebrations. Spanish-American organizations often added a distinctive accent to this pattern. Lodge 178 of Alianza Hispano-Americans held its annual costume ball at the Hilton and modeled the event after the fiestas of Latin-American countries.[55]

If people took their festivities seriously, they were even more serious about their vocations. A local dentist, Dr. Howard R. Raper, published a book in 1945 entitled *Man Against Pain: The Epic of Anesthesia*, and the Scientific

Book Club selected it for promotion.[56] Imagine, if you can, how a book with such a grandiose title on such a mundane subject would have been received some twenty-five years later.

Women, including housewives, took their tasks and duties no more lightly. One of their models for inspiration was Eleanor Roosevelt, whose syndicated column "My Day" appeared in the *Albuquerque Tribune*. The same paper also carried a daily advice column, "As One Woman Looks at Life" written by Mrs. Walter Ferguson. Some of the topics she dealt with were "Wastrels," "Happy Homes" and "Delinquent Parents." At the beginning of the year, when people were making their New Year's resolutions, several women expressed noble, dutiful sentiments. Mrs. L.A. Wilkins: "I hope the war will end in 1945, and I have resolved to be the best wife possible and devote all my time and attention to my two children and my husband!" Mrs. J.D. Simpson: " I want to live a more useful life and do my best to make others happy." Mrs. Allen Bemis: "I resolve to do all I can to bring victory sooner."[57]

The written and spoken word loomed large in the lives of the people of Albuquerque. There was radio, which broadcast among other things political speeches and highly charged dramas, but no television. The newspapers were thin, but they were filled with articles and advertisements written in a more dramatic and colorful style than was likely to be found in papers of later years. Few photographs. The public library received a lot of attention; the *Tribune* published a weekly list of its new books. Among the most popular were *Forever Amber* by Kathleen Winsor, *The Robe* by Lloyd Douglas, *A Tree Grows in Brooklyn* by Betty Smith, and *Immortal Wife* by Irving Stone. War books were also in demand, especially *A Bell for Adano* by John Hersey and *Here Is Your War* and *Brave Men* by Ernie Pyle, whose home was then in Albuquerque. Readers devoured crime stories as well. The *Tribune* had a column of mystery reviews, "Report Card of Crime," and the Sunday *Journal* always carried four or five one-page stories of romance, adventure or crime. Typical of these was "The Case of the Miner's Daughter" by Terry McShane, about a rich, popular young man who got a miner's daughter pregnant, killed her to prevent his misdeed from becoming known, and then was apprehended.[58]

Going to the movies was a favorite activity. Albuquerque had nine movie theaters, and usually the feature attraction changed twice a week. Every day a different advertisement would run in the newspapers, employing slightly different captions or pictures to draw in more patrons. The variety of movies was wide, including war dramas such as *Thirty Seconds over Tokyo* starring Spencer Tracy; Bob Hope comedies; suspense thrillers like *The Woman in the Window* with Edward G. Robinson and Joan Bennett; high romances like *A Song to Remember* with Paul Muni and Merle Oberon ("Blazing with human conflict . . .it sweeps into your heart with all the emotional impact that only a really great picture can convey!"); heartstring twangers such as *National Velvet* with Elizabeth Taylor and Mickey Rooney; John Wayne westerns; boys-meet-girls musicals like *Anchors Aweigh* with Frank Sinatra, Gene Kelly and Kathryn Grayson; and many other sorts as well. A number were based on novels, including Betty Smith's *A Tree Grows in Brooklyn* and A.J. Cronin's *Keys to the Kingdom*. Hemingway was a favorite; two much-ballyhooed movies that came into town that year were *For Whom the Bell Tolls* with Gary Cooper and Ingrid Bergman and *To Have and Have Not* starring Humphrey Bogart and Lauren Bacall. There were no adults-only movies and no rating system, so local viewers had God's plenty to choose among. Some, like Carrie Wooster Tingley, chose nearly all of them.[59]

Varied as the fare was, certain similarities can be discerned from the perspective of a few decades later. The action and the emotion were intense, fast-paced and easy to follow. The leading actors were stars and stood out dramatically. The men were generally strong, brave and, except for the villains, honorable; the women dramatic and beautiful. In comparison with the techniques of later movie actors, their gestures were pronounced and forceful, and their poses were studied. All in all, the movies provided a heightened and more dramatic reality for the moviegoers in somewhat the same fashion that novels did for readers of fiction and politics did for active participants in the political process. It would be misleading to call what they had to offer escapism, for although they provided emotional fulfillment that was sometimes in short supply in the ordinary lives of the viewers, they also presented models of behavior. The brave man who fought against the odds, the patient and loyal and courageous woman, the adorable young children, the funny man who quipped at adversity but never gave up, the gangster who paid for his transgressions, and the weak person who gave into temptation and met his destruction—all these types had tremendous relevance to the way society functioned around 1945. If courage, loyalty, strength of character, perseverance, kindness and so forth were not often so exciting in everyday life, they were still valued, and they did lead to success, so people believed.[60]

Overshadowing all other events and developments in the lives of the people of Albuquerque 1945 was the Second World War. The war touched everybody: it was daily in the news, shortages and rationing crimped people's spending, and most of the residents had friends and relatives fighting overseas. Albuquerque was probably affected more by the war than most other cities of its size. Ernie Pyle, the most famous war correspondent of the time, had moved to Albuquerque, and his daily column was featured in the *Tribune*. Early in the war, a company of New Mexico boys, many from Albuquerque, had been captured by the Japanese in the Philippines and forced to go on the notorious Bataan Death March. The city reeled from the shock. And Kirtland Air Force Base, located just east of the city limits, assumed wartime importance and brought young men from all over the country to Albuquerque.

In early February came the news that a Japanese prisoner-of-war camp had fallen and that many of the soldiers from New Mexico's 200th were among the captives freed.[61] The next month five came home to a heroes' welcome in Albuquerque. When three of them flew in on the same plane and landed at Albuquerque Municipal Airport, they were met by a cheering throng of over five hundred. The papers carried full accounts of the exuberant celebrating, the joyous reactions of the soldiers, their friends and their relatives, and the food they were offered.[62] Thanks were given at church services, and at a ceremony at the Alianza Club, willow trees were planted for the two returning Anglos and Chinese elms for the three Spanish-Americans who had come home safely.[63] The memory of Bataan did not die away. In December a parade was held honoring the men of Bataan and other veterans of the war.[64] Later that month fifteen hundred people attended a memorial service to the fallen soldiers of the 200th. Drums rolled and commanding officers spoke. Colonel Memory Cain: "At Clark Field and Bataan Peninsula and in the prison camp there were no Anglos, natives, Protestants, Catholics, or Jews. They were all welded into an American organization that did their duty and fought the enemy as a team." Colonel Harry M. Peck: "They were so intent on winning that orders weren't necessary." City Commission Chairman Clyde Tingley added, "Anything we can say or do can only be inadequate . . . mere words can never fill the void. . . . May God forever keep them . . . may we forever cherish their memory."[65] In the ensuing years a hospital and a city park came to bear the name of Bataan.

Another war loss that struck hard at Albuquerque was the death in April of Ernie Pyle, killed by Japanese machine gun fire on an island near Okinawa.

His widow was notified at their little white house on the eastern edge of town, and prominent citizens praised his bravery and patriotism.[66] Three months later a movie depicting his exploits, *The Story of G.I. Joe*, premiered at the biggest downtown theaters, the Kimo and the Sunshine. Its director and several of the stars were on hand for the ceremony, which was broadcast by Radio Station KOB. Lines more than a block long formed at each theater.[67]

Just as much as the American soldiers were honored, the enemy was hated. And to a large extent, the enemy was hated for not fighting fairly. While speaking of the Germans, Pfc. Eloy Tafoya said, "They're cowards. They'll sneak up on you, shoot a few rounds and then run like everything. That's no way to fight."[68]

Then at last, on August 14, came the word that the war was over. The years of sacrifice and intense struggle had paid off, and the people tasted the exultation of victory. The restraint of wartime relaxed, and the time of wild celebration was at hand. The following are excerpts from an account of the occasion in the *Journal*:

> With the official announcement of Japan's surrender, Albuquerque went into its victory celebration late Tuesday afternoon.
>
> The news, which came at 5 o'clock, was greeted with silence by persons in cafes and other downtown establishments with radios. For about five minutes it was as if the announcement had concerned a baseball score or some other everyday occurrence.
>
> Then a single auto horn sounded on Central Avenue swelling quickly into a roar from hundreds of cars as pent up emotions, whetted by the many days of suspense while awaiting Japan's official capitulation, were loosened in a noisy demonstration that lasted far into the night.
>
> Confetti began drifting into the streets tossed out from upper story office windows but appearing to come out of thin air.
>
> Excited persons smiled at one another, stranger to stranger. Sometimes there was a brief comment: "Wonderful, isn't it?" or "I'm still numb."
>
> The crowds of homeward bound office workers slowed their usual hurried pace and groups of friends or strangers stood on the corners and even in the street. Slow moving automobiles wended their way along the streets, every car with its horn blasting full, Santa Fe Railway Shop whistles, locomotive whistles, sirens and church bells added to the din.

A shower which fell in the downtown area at the height of the early celebration failed to dampen it in the slightest. A clap of thunder added to the noises.

In residential districts, housewives opened their doors to call to passers-by with joyful remarks. . . .

After a brief lull around evening meal time, the celebration whooped into tremendous proportions, with downtown streets filled with cars fender-to-fender and bumper-to-bumper. The sidewalks were jammed to overflowing, and at Fourth and Central it was impossible to cross the street on frequent occasions.

The noisiest thing on wheels was a car with four pipes attached to its exhaust, which sounded off like Gabriel's trumpet. The driver made the circuit of the crowded streets dozens of times with his noise maker going full blast.

Some of the downtown cafes and soda fountains, swamped by the crowds, closed up, and their proprietors and employes joined in the merrymaking.

Gasoline rationing was forgotten for the night, and the largest number of automobiles was seen on Albuquerque streets since the war began. They paraded up and down Central, with horns going full blast, until late at night. . . .

Patrolman Dan Martinez had difficulty at Fourth and Central when a conga-line of about forty high school youths danced in the path of traffic.

Theaters and restaurants were jammed, but with bars and night clubs closed, much of the late celebrating was done at private parties at home.

One unknown person or group of persons had a unique method of celebrating. It was the blinking of the "V for Victory" signal from the top of the Sandias.

Retail stores, the university, and federal, city and county offices were closed on Wednesday, and federal employees had a holiday Thursday as well. Almost every church in Albuquerque had special services Wednesday. In addition, the Ministerial Alliance sponsored services at the Kimo and Sunshine Theatres.[69]

The war was over, the victory celebration subsided, but some of the wartime habits and attitudes lingered on. The emphasis on combat, courage and heroism continued, and it was manifested in hundreds of incidents and statements over the following months and years. Two examples of this emphasis were a football game and a domestic tragedy.

In the fall of 1945 the University of New Mexico had a championship football team, and it went to the Sun Bowl in early January to play against the team from Denver University. New Mexico won in an exciting game; an editorial in the Journal telling about the game follows:

> The Lobo accomplishment took a lot of courage. Twice the Denver Pioneers were ahead—at one time 10 points ahead in the first quarter. Denver University again was ahead as the fourth quarter opened.
>
> Then that great Lobo combination of skill and courage went to work. Three blazing touchdowns in that final quarter brought the magnificent win.
>
> Our sincere congratulations go to a fine squad and its coaches. Every Lobo player participating was a football hero on the auspicious occasion. But there's one name we must specifically mention. The name is Fred Doar, the Lobo center. On the first play of the game he sustained a broken jaw. He didn't tell anyone or else the coaches would certainly have removed him from the game. Doar played almost the entire contest and his play had much to do with the result.
>
> It was that sort of fortitude and courage spread throughout the entire team that brought victory.[70]

One month later, in the mountain village of Escabosa, not far from Albuquerque, a woman was accidentally burned to death, leaving a nine-year-old boy an orphan. The boy, Alonzo Lopez, told the story to Assistant District Attorney Harry D. Robins. On a Sunday evening Mrs. Hernandez, his foster mother, threw some coal oil on the wood in her stove and stooped down to light it. It flared up and she was badly burned. Alonzo led her outside, took off his pants, and wrapped them around her to put out the flames. Mrs. Hernandez lay down on the ground. The boy dragged her inside and put her to bed, but it took him four hours to do so. He stayed in the house and watched over her. There was nothing to eat, for the past summer's drought had killed their crops and they had been subsisting on a little food supplied by a neighbor who was slightly better off then they. Around noon the next day Mrs. Hernandez died, and Alonzo went for help. Asked why he had not gone sooner, he said, "I was afraid to leave her alone." In front of Robins, a few officers, some neighbors and some relatives, he tried to keep from crying but could not. A deputy sheriff gave him money for a haircut, and some policemen dug into their pockets for change to buy him half a dozen hamburgers and a sack of doughnuts. Tentative plans were made for the neighbor who had been helping out with food to adopt him. All present admired his heroism.[71]

The distinctive flavor of attitudes and actions in Albuquerque 1945 pervaded all aspects of the society—even crime and law enforcement. Albuquerque's problems and concerns in the realm of crime and social disorder were different from what they were to become in later years. The crime rate in the city was fairly low, lower than for most urban areas of its size.[72] One of the main functions of the law enforcement agencies was to protect public morality against the so-called victimless crimes and to make sure that the citizens adhered to certain high standards of conduct. Albuquerque had little tolerance for licentious behavior, in public at any rate. At the swearing-in ceremony at the end of 1944 for elected county officials, Sheriff Harold Hubbell made his pledge: "Gambling all has to quit. Bootlegging on Sunday has to stop. Joints staying open after hours and selling liquor on Sunday have to stop. We'll raid every one of them and enforce the law as it is." He also included prostitution and selling liquor to minors among the major vices in the county, and promised to put an end to them.[73]

Crimes against property seldom attracted very much attention, but violent crimes, especially gang fights among young men, were regarded as more of a problem. Early in 1944 strife among "zoot-suiters"—groups of young men flamboyantly dressed, frequently Spanish-American—gained public attention. Their activities continued, although their attire became more subdued. William Apodaca, investigator for the district attorney's office, described a typical incident. "A bunch from Barelas will be at a dance and they'll see a gang from Armijo they don't like, and a fight will start. It's gotten so bad that at many dance halls, where your wife and mine used to be able to go and have a good time, you wouldn't dare take your wife now." The gangs sometimes attacked solitary individuals, beating and robbing their victims. Former Sheriff Ed Donohue spoke of loosely organized gangs roaming the suburban sections of town fighting each other or, if an opposing gang was not handy when a group felt the urge to fight, attacking whatever persons happened to be near.[74] As was the case all over America, fights and violent crimes became more numerous after the war's end.

Lawless combat was not peculiar to the poorer young men of Albuquerque, it could be found at the university as well. Early in 1946 a long-standing feud between engineering students and arts and science students flared up. Four girls who were contestants for the position of Engineer Queen were "kidnapped" by a group of arts and sciences students. The coeds were picked up on the pretext that they were going to have their pictures taken, and three of them were taken to a hideout in the Sandia Mountains. (The fourth was able to talk her way out of her captivity.) Meanwhile, another A. and S. student climbed a tree on campus in an effort to take the engineers' flag, but a branch broke and he fell twenty feet, eventually landing in the infirmary. Then a group of engineers learned of the hideout location and fought the A. and S. students off to rescue the girls. That evening students tried to wreck the dance decorations, but they were chased away. The honor of arts and sciences was salvaged, however, when a few managed to let the air out of the tires of the car selected to carry the queen to the dance.[75]

A year later three young men were suspended from the university for setting fire to a building owned by a rival fraternity. The fraternity rivalry was particularly heated at that time, and outlaw groups with mysterious initials were often involved in criminal and destructive activity.[76]

The physical layout of Albuquerque in 1945—the distribution of buildings, the architecture and the street pattern—was also distinctive and significant. For the streets and buildings of a city are like footprints—their distribution and design show how the people moved about over a long period of time. The placement of an office or a road is a very deliberate act, and it is as revealing of the nature of the people as a spontaneous outcry or a deed of the moment.

The *Albuquerque City Directory, 1945-46* (Hudspeth Directory Company: El Paso, Texas, 1946) shows an enormous concentration of business and governmental activity in the heart of the Albuquerque downtown area, and a smaller, more diffuse one about two miles east, around the intersection of Richmond and Central. The strong central focus of the city consisted of a twenty-block area bounded by the Santa Fe Railroad on the east, Tijeras Avenue on the north, Sixth Street on the west, and Silver Avenue on the south. Through the middle of it ran Central Avenue, the most important street in town. This area contained 24 of the 25 office buildings in the city, 8 of the 9 movie theaters, 23 of the 27 loan companies, 84 of the 103 insurance agencies, 2 of the 3 banks, 19 of the 25 hotels, 11 of the 13 department stores, 7 of the 9 other dry goods stores, 9 of the 15 furniture stores, and 12 of the 20 jewelry stores. Sixty-two of the 64 lawyers had their offices in this area, as did 28 of the 32 dentists and 48 of the 62 physicians. In addition, there were numerous other offices and stores dispersed throughout the section, and quite a few just outside the twenty-block area. Not all businesses clustered there; automobile dealers were mostly outside, with a number on North Fourth Street, and a slight majority of the real estate agencies were in other parts of the city. Churches, schools, grocery stores, restaurants and bars were scattered out wherever people lived. In general, one could say that the downtown area was the focus of recurrent important business (shopping for items more permanent than food, consulting a doctor or a lawyer, attending a political event) and important entertainment (seeing a movie, going to a big party). Less portentous activities (buying groceries, having a car repaired, downing a few beers) could be undertaken elsewhere. Almost everyone had occasion to go downtown and fairly frequently. The effort involved bothered few—it was like dressing up for a party. Downtown, things were more important, more formal, more ceremonial. The strong downtown focus of Albuquerque was analogous to the strongly focused leadership in political, business and civic organizations in the community.

Much smaller but a sign of things to come was the emerging cluster in the neighborhood of Richmond and Central, just east of the university. Here were located the only bank and movie theater outside of the downtown area, as well as a few offices for doctors and dentists, some insurance and real estate agencies, and several shops. This area catered to the interests of some of the university people and some of the new residents who had moved into the heights on the eastern side of town.

Photographs of the Albuquerque downtown in the 1940s show a variety of massive structures. A motorist driving west on Central would go through the underpass for the railroad and then be in the midst of the bustling activity of the city's core. On the right would be the First National Bank Building, nine stories high and the tallest on the street, and on the left the Sunshine Building, a little shorter. Most of the buildings were older than these two and about as wide as they were tall. Hulking rectangular solids with much external ornamentation. On Central there were the Alvarado Hotel in the Spanish mission style; the Albuquerque National Bank, with arches and an ornamental rail along the top; the Armijo Building, a stone structure with Romanesque arches; and the Franciscan Hotel, a striking edifice that has been variously labeled pueblo and expressionist. A block south, on Gold Avenue, were the Occidental Life Building, with pointed arches all in a row, a row of quatrefoils above them, and an elaborate cornice on top; the Commercial Club, featuring a Norman-style pointed tower; and the brick, colonial-style Post Office and Federal Building, topped off with an octagonal cupola. And there were other structures in the area that were equally impressive. With all the diversity of architectural styles, the group of buildings had a fundamental unity. They were big, solid, square-cornered for the most part, ornate, self-confident to the point of brashness, full of vitality. Like a gathering of frontiersmen in an old painting or old movie. One is reminded of the preamble to Chester T. French's creed: "Four major thoughts I would leave with you, to help you build a rich, full and rewarding life. Four sides you should have in your building to make it stand firm and four square."

Looking at a map of the city in 1945, one is struck by the predominant grid pattern of the streets. In the downtown and much of the surrounding area, most streets run either parallel with or perpendicular to the railroad tracks. A couple of miles to the east there is a slight shift; right angles are still dominant, but the streets are aligned with the old section boundaries, which are not quite lined up with the railroad. Here and there, however, are found a few curved and diagonal streets, mostly in the newer residential areas.

For all its shortcomings, the grid pattern has a number of features which could have been expected to appeal to the people of Albuquerque 1945. In the first place, it is orderly, disciplined and rational. Provided that the streets are named or numbered according to some overall pattern and a person has a basic familiarity with the city, he can find his way quite easily. Second, it is flexible. Although some streets are bigger than others and can accommodate more traffic, they all have somewhat the same shape and the same number of intersections in a given distance. So an established part of town does not have a great advantage over a newly developed area in regard to accessibility. The focus of Albuquerque had shifted from Old Town to the area just east of the Santa Fe Railroad in the 1880s; it might move again. The streets, then, existed in a rough kind of democracy of equal opportunity, just as did the people who used them. And finally, there is the psychological symbolism of the right angles. Remember the shape of the buildings, remember French's words, think of the orderliness and discipline of the grid pattern—do they suggest a kind of mental set, a habit of perception that the people of this time had to a strong degree? It seems very likely; a later chapter focusing on changing modes of perception and thought will explore the matter further.

Looking back over the physical appearance of the city, the typical activities and attitudes of the residents, the pivotal events, and the sketches of the prominent people, one is struck by the extent to which the different pieces of the picture fit to form an integrated whole. From the perspective of a later and more permissive society, Albuquerque around the close of World War II appears almost as tightly unified as a movie of the time. For all their vitality and color, the people operated, for the most part, according to regular rules and within the broad confines of recognizable roles.

A generalized biography of a representative prominent male figure of Albuquerque 1945 would include a strenuous childhood and youth, enthusiasm for work and competitive activity from an early age, and work experience in a wide variety of jobs. This rough and tumble background would forge the young man into a sturdy character, sure of himself and directed from within to make a mark on the world. He would have a substantial amount of self-discipline as well as respect for discipline in society, manifested by his interest in duty and his admiration for strong, honorable leaders. His concern for charity would be genuine but different from later conceptions of social welfare: through providing basic opportunities for survival and advancement and through exhortation, he would try to help others to rise as he has done. And having risen to a position of prominence himself, he would be decisive, direct his affairs with a strong hand, have a flair for the colorful gesture, and bestow his name on whatever landmarks and institutions he could.

About the typical prominent female of the time we know less, for women were less in the news. Her background was less strenuous and less competitive, for presumably she was more protected by her family and not encouraged so much to be assertive. Her sense of duty was, if anything, stronger than the man's; she could be very forceful in the pursuit of what she believed was right. More concerned with making society stable and homelike, less interested in getting ahead, she did much to help the unfortunate, elevate the cultural and educational tone of the community, and work for social cohesion in general.

The less prominent members of the society imitated and complemented their leaders. Their orientations and goals were not so much different, but they tended to be less ambitious, less assertive, less outgoing. Most acted their parts with enthusiasm and the awareness that they, also, were vital components of Albuquerque. The men, by and large, did what were considered manly things; the women acted in their womanly fashion. People did not question their roles to any great extent—they were quite sure who they were.

Most of the experiences and attitudes which they shared were not unique to the men and women of Albuquerque; similar phenomena could be found in much of the rest of America. Yet one does not have to go beyond Albuquerque to look for causes; the most fundamental cause lay in the character of the citizens. Even important external influences, such as books, movies and the war itself, resulted to a large degree from the tastes, habits and actions of millions of people substantially like those living in this city. The books and movies that came to town from outside did not significantly change the people; rather they were written and produced to appeal to such people as lived in Albuquerque. This is why they found such an eager audience here.

Even World War II, bearing down on the lives of everyone in town, did not fundamentally alter people's directions. Competitiveness and combativeness had been ingrained in their character for a long time past; the war provided a huge focus for much of their aggressiveness. I am not arguing that the people of Albuquerque wanted the war, or that it was a necessary result of orientations such as theirs; still, it was competition and combat on a titanic scale, and the people were ready to throw themselves into it with gusto. The young men of Albuquerque who, in the early months of 1945, were fighting fiercely on the German and Japanese fronts, those who survived the war and were toughened by it, these were well trained to come home (as well as veterans who grew up elsewhere and elected to make Albuquerque their new home) and compete in the business and political fronts of the explosive postwar boom.

Just as the people of Albuquerque 1945 had characteristic habits and motivations, so did they also have characteristic patterns of thought. Their emphasis on language, their preference for massive structures and right angles— these have all been indicated, but they can best be treated in a later chapter. One outstanding feature, though, which calls for immediate comment was their tendency to formalize. All societies tend to formalize and ritualize certain activities which possess for them heightened significance, for traditional forms and social conventions provide the structure necessary to ensure that people act in socially acceptable ways. Formality is an important means of and an outward and visible sign of social control and cohesion. Some societies, however, are more formal than others; Albuquerque in 1945 was considerably more formal than it was to become later. People dressed formally; men commonly wore coats and ties, and women dresses. They dressed up more for special occasions, like attending church, meetings and parties. Political gatherings were more structured, such as the annual Jackson Day dinner for the Democrats with elaborate speeches. Parties and other celebrations were elaborate. Even going to the movies usually involved taking a trip to the downtown area, the most formal part of the city. And abiding by such forms as these gave the participants a heightened sense of doing something important and special; their lives were temporarily elevated above their routine existences and intensified.

The dynamics of the society included both a substantial degree of social control and of flux. Rules of behavior were binding and leaders were strong. The agencies of law enforcement were as concerned with protecting the morals of the community—remember Sheriff Hubbell's stand against prostitution, gambling and Sunday liquor sales—as with protecting people and property from criminal marauders. Community leaders made a show of being strong, and frequently they were. Autocracies such as John Milne's in the public school system were common in business. People expected their leaders to be decisive, not to consult with their subordinates every step of the way.

On the other hand, there was also much freedom of movement in Albuquerque society. The self-made man was widely respected. One of the chief functions of education was seen to be to provide opportunities for advancement for as many people as possible. The political and business worlds may not have been as wide open as many wished and believed, yet they were fairly open. The humble beginnings of Tingley and Chavez won many votes. Business was highly competitive, and many of the successful businessmen started, like French and Matteucci, on not much more than a shoestring.

The city of Albuquerque in 1945 functioned as a vital and cohesive society. The population was diverse, but most of the citizens adhered to a common set of rules in their pursuit of a common goal. That goal was the good life—more wealth and greater happiness. As long as that goal could be seen in the not-too-distant future and the way there seemed to be individual striving within the rules of the game, the people were eager to discipline themselves and strive. But if at some future time playing by the traditional rules did not seem to bring about the desired result—if the goal were reached and turned out not to be worth the trouble, or if, upon reaching the goal, the people decided in large numbers to relax their efforts, or if conditions changed in such a way that individual striving seemed to get one nowhere—then the structure of society would be ripe for a breakdown or a transformation. That, however, would come later. At the close of the war Albuquerque was poised, brimming with energy, eager to venture into the promised land of economic expansion.

3

YEARS OF STEADY EVOLUTION, 1945–1959

Measures of the Transformation

Over the ensuing years of headlong economic and population growth, Albuquerque society changed so dramatically that many of its salient features in 1972 would have been almost unrecognizable to a local citizen of 1945. Most of the aspects of the transformation which affected the people most directly and personally are not easily measurable—new styles of dress and of architecture, more government involvement in the lives of ordinary persons, greater tendency to identify with groups, more spontaneity and expressiveness, and so forth. As we trace the emergence of the newer Albuquerque, we can perceive their development, but seldom do we have the opportunity to quantify them. The most fundamental of the trends, however, cut paths so deep and broad that they are as obvious in historical statistics as in evidence more subject to impressionistic interpretation.

The first dimension which we noted of the profound social and cultural transformation was the tendency of the people to interact in larger and larger groups. One of the most primary levels of this group interaction was population growth. In 1940, according to the U.S. Census, there were 69,391 persons living in Bernalillo County; the number catapulted to 145,673 in 1950, 262,199 in 1960, and 315,774 in 1970 for an increase of 355.1 percent over the thirty-year span.[77] During this period the population of New Mexico grew at a far smaller rate, 91.1 percent;[78] consequently, one cannot attribute the growth of the Albuquerque metropolitan area simply to the increase which most of the southern regions of the country were undergoing. As a matter of fact, thirteen of the thirty-two counties in the state, comprising 42.7 percent of the land area, were actually losing population.[79] Another way of looking at the same general phenomenon in New Mexico is through measures of urbanization: the number of people living in municipalities of 2,500 or larger grew by 301.8 percent, while those living in smaller towns or off by themselves declined by

13.6 percent.[80] Clearly people across the state were shifting their residential patterns and relocating in larger groups, and the trend was particularly pronounced in the largest city.

The jobs the people held also reflected this shift to interaction in larger groups. The percentage of the working population in Bernalillo County employed by some branch of government rose from 17.2 in 1950 to 19.3 in 1960 to 23.9 in 1970. In contrast, the percentage that was self-employed declined over these years from 13.9 to 8.7 to 6.0.[81] Most of the workers continued to be associated with private firms, and the average size of such establishments grew from 8.58 employees in 1908 to 13.14 in 1959 to 15.98 in 1972.[82]

In considering such statistics as these last, one does well to investigate the possibility that the increased size of the private firms located in Albuquerque could be accounted for simply by the population growth of the city. Inspection of county business patterns across the country does indeed reveal the fact that counties with 20,000 to 25,000 workers—Bernalillo County had 21,676 in 1948—generally have smaller business establishments than those with 90,000 to 100,000 workers—and there were 94,482 in Bernalillo County in 1972. Further examination of the available data, however, indicates that population growth was not the sole cause of the shift during the period, in Albuquerque or elsewhere. The average size of business firms of counties with 20,000 to 25,000 workers in 1948 was 13.32 employees; the average size for counties with the same number of workers in 1972 was 16.63. For counties with 90,000 to 100,000 workers, the comparable figures are 15.01 in 1948 and 17.22 in 1972.[83] So throughout the country, the growth of businesses took place even when population increase was not a factor. It is reasonable to assume, then, that although private firms and municipalities both grew during these years, and both growth trends interacted with and augmented one another, neither was the fundamental cause for the other. Rather, both were manifestations of the same overall shift toward large groups which was acting on the whole social fabric.

Statistical data on the second primary dimension of the transformation—the overall relaxation of authority and self-control—are harder to come up with. Certain aspects of this deep trend, however, were highly publicized, among them the so-called "sexual revolution." Although complete and reliable figures on the rise of sexual activity and expressiveness in Albuquerque are not available, it is safe to assume that people in the city changed in substantially the same manner as Americans did in general. Since in most areas of inquiry that can be documented, Albuquerque altered more radically than the country as a whole, this assumption is probably conservative.

In 1948 Dr. Alfred C. Kinsey, a biologist working at Indiana University's Institute of Sex Research, and his colleagues published *Sexual Behavior in the Human Male*, and they followed this up in 1953 with *Sexual Behavior in the Human Female*. Twenty-two years later the women's magazine *Redbook* ran a series of two articles by a team of social scientists which presented the results of a recent survey of the sexual attitudes and practices of its readers. The methods of the 1953 Kinsey report and the 1975 *Redbook* articles were not the same—the earlier study was based on extensive interviews of fewer than 8,000 women scientifically selected from a larger population, whereas the later one depended on the responses of more than 100,000 women who answered a questionnaire they had received in the mail—but both studies focused most heavily on the same group—women who were under 50 years of age, had completed high school, were white, had an above-average income, and felt open enough about their sex lives to communicate with the researchers.[84] The studies are sufficiently comparable to demonstrate broad changes in the behavior of mainstream American women. No similar survey of American men has been made since Dr. Kinsey's 1948 report; impressionistic evidence, however, strongly suggests that male sexual attitudes and practices have loosened in much the same way but that the traditional gap between male and female sexual activity, the "double standard," has significantly narrowed.

Taken together, the two studies indicate a dramatic relaxation of traditional restraints and an upsurge of sexual activity, both inside and outside of marriage. Of the married women interviewed for the 1953 work, 54 percent acknowledged they had experienced cunnilingus and 49 percent fellatio;[85] the comparable figure in the later report is 91 percent, with no significant difference between the two kinds of oral-genital sex.[86] Premarital sex became much more common: 33 percent of the women under 25 interviewed by the Kinsey researchers said they had had premarital intercourse as contrasted with 90 percent of the same category who answered the *Redbook* questionnaire. According to the 1975 articles, the likelihood of premarital coitus rose steadily through the years. Of all the women married before 1964, 69 percent had experienced intercourse before their marriage; the proportion grows to 81 percent for women married between 1964 and 1969, 89 percent for those married between 1970 and 1973, and 93 percent for the women whose marriage took place after 1973. Furthermore, the typical age at which the women's initial sexual intercourse took place dropped. Regardless of educational level, women under 25 reported that their first such encounter was, on the average, a full year earlier than had been the case for those over 25.[87] And after marriage, women became more likely to enter into affairs with other men. Kinsey found that 9 percent of the 25-year-old married women had experienced extramarital sex; the 1975 study showed that 25 percent of the wives surveyed from 20 to 24 years of age had done so. By age 40, Kinsey reported, 26 percent of the married sample had been unfaithful; the most comparable figure in the later study, that for the 35-to-39-year-old age group, is 38 percent.[88] These dry and impersonal numbers indicate a momentous change in deeply personal attitudes and behaviors on a scale seldom to be encountered.

If national or local figures had been collected on such matters as provocativeness of clothing, suggestiveness of advertisements, sexual content of language and abundance of topless bars, the data would undoubtedly point in the same direction. In the 1972 Albuquerque telephone directory were listed four bookstores and six movie theaters devoted exclusively to erotic material; twenty-seven years earlier there had been none. And substantial as the shift in sexual mores clearly was across the society, it was just one aspect, one manifestation of the general loosening of traditional control suffusing the culture.

Population Growth and Political Change

During the decade and a half following the Second World War, Albuquerque boomed spectacularly, and the growth in population and average income was instrumental in bringing about gradual yet profound changes in the makeup of the city. The population increase was particularly apparent to the city fathers as hordes of new voters with new attitudes streamed in. The number of people residing within the city limits rose from about 50,000 in 1945 to 96,815 in 1950 to 201,189 in 1960; in Bernalillo County as a whole it went up over those same years from approximately 90,000 to 145,673 to 262,199.[89] Broken down by ethnic groups, 0.9 percent of the net increase in the entire metropolitan area between 1950 and 1960 were Indians, 2.6 percent Blacks, 20.9 percent Spanish-surnamed (not an ethnic group, strictly speaking, but the figure corresponds closely to the number of people who considered themselves Spanish-Americans since the number of Spanish-Americans with Anglo surnames would be more or less offset by the number of Indians with Spanish last names), and 75.6 percent other. For practical purposes, "other" can be considered Anglos, since only a scant smattering of foreign-born and persons of Oriental extraction were included. During the 1950s this group increased its dominance from 67.3 percent of the population in the metropolitan area to 71.0 percent,[90] and most of the newcomers were better educated, more affluent and readier to follow an independent course than the long-time residents.

Among the early contributors to the influx were veterans who had been stationed in Albuquerque during the war. As a result of the clear New Mexico weather, the excellent conditions of the terrain, and the central location of the city in the southwestern United States, Albuquerque had become a vital link in military communications and air transport network. Shortly after the bombing of Pearl Harbor, the U.S. government had taken over the municipal airport just southeast of the city and made it Kirtland Air Force Base; a little later the army established Sandia Base further to the east. The military activities fueled the local wartime economy, and they also strained the capacity of the city to accommodate the new people. Rental housing was tight; hotels were jammed; even cemeteries were overcrowded.[91] But with the cessation of hostilities came the eventual lifting of building restrictions, and many of the soldiers and airmen who had come to know the city decided to remain in its moderate climate and informal atmosphere. In 1946 more than fifteen hundred veterans from elsewhere were living in the city,[92] and more would soon be arriving. With their youthful energy, their accumulated savings and their veterans benefits, they were in good position to take advantage of and contribute to the postwar boom.

At the war's end most people did not foresee this boom and feared a recession or depression instead. One of the reasons for the economic upturn was the continuation of defense spending. When the city got back its airport, Kirtland continued on adjoining land, and the military installations kept up their eastward spread. Meanwhile, civilian scientists were flocking into the area to work on projects related to weapons development. In 1946 a group from Los Alamos, New Mexico, where much of the basic research for the development of the atomic bomb had been conducted, set up a branch laboratory at Sandia Base, and thus was born Sandia Corporation, soon to become the largest private employer in the state. At this time Sandia Corporation was run by the University of California, which also operated the Los Alamos Scientific Laboratory, both under contract with the Atomic Energy Commission.[93] When the operation of the corporation was transferred to Western Electric in 1949, its size expanded substantially.[94] Little affected, however, was the nature of the work conducted there—ordnance engineering and weapons development.[95] As the Cold War with Russia and the Korean War fed the demand for this type of defense work, other organizations, including ACF Industries and the Atomic Energy Commission, set up operations in the same part of the metropolitan area and expanded.[96]

By the late 1950s this complex of private industries and military bases had attained enormous size and influence. In 1957 approximately 30 percent of the city's labor force worked at Kirtland Air Force Base or Sandia Base, including Sandia Corporation.[97] The elite of these were probably the employees at Sandia Corporation, who together with their families constituted about one-ninth of the Albuquerque population. Their average age was thirty-five, most were married and had two or three children, and 70 percent owned their homes. Having come from about everywhere in the country, they were willing, for the time being at any rate, to call Albuquerque their home,[98] but Albuquerque had better move toward compliance with their well-scrubbed, efficient and altogether exacting standards.

The newcomers' impact on the city grew steadily throughout the late forties and the fifties, but even in early 1946 Albuquerque was changing faster than City Commission Chairman Clyde Tingley and his cohorts realized. City elections were to be held in April, and most observers took it for granted that the Tingley-dominated machine would retain the grip it had held on city hall for years. In March Antonio Morelli, a retired Santa Fe Railroad worker and an old friend of Tingley's, announced his bid for a City Commission post. He did not have Tingley's support, and he offered a ten-point program which included putting city employees on a merit system,[99] a change which the machine in power had long resisted.

A week later Tingley, whose own four-year term was not yet up, announced his slate of candidates. A writer for the *Albuquerque Journal* described the drama of this point in the campaign:

It has been a practice in the past for "Greater Albuquerque" tickets to let the rumors steam until just before the deadline for filing. Then the bombshell drops, the political banners come out in the open, and the brief campaign is a whirlwind.

"A 'Greater Albuquerque ticket' has never been defeated," said Tingley with Churchillian determination. "It will not be defeated at this time."

Tingley's Greater Albuquerque slate consisted of the incumbents from the old commission whose terms had expired—Pete A. Mosier, William M. Wylie and Clyde Oden, who was also considering running for governor.[100]

The deadline for filing, however, was still two days away. On March 18, the last possible day, Owen B. Marron, a prominent attorney and son of a former mayor, and Al E. Buck, a steel manufacturing plant proprietor, announced, and the race was on. In the following days these two combined with Morelli to form the Better Government ticket. On April 2, in the midst of a heavy dust storm, Albuquerque voters went to the polls and elected the Better Government candidates by a substantial margin. It was the people from the heights, the rapidly growing east side of town, who made the difference, piling up majorities in their precincts of as much as four to one for the victors, while the lowlands near the Rio Grande, the older part of town and traditionally the mainstay of the Tingley machine, did not support the Greater Albuquerque candidates as heavily as in the past. The only post retained by the Tingley people was police judge, won narrowly by the incumbent E.C. Gober. State Representative Joe A. Montoya finished a poor third in that contest and immediately announced he would start circulating petitions for the recall of City Commissioner Clyde Tingley.[101]

So new hands held the reins of political power. Al Buck was elected chairman, and Tingley had to content himself for a while with being a loud voice in the minority. In the meeting during which the new members were sworn in, the old commission, as its last act, reduced the water rate from $1.50 per household per month to $1.00, and the new commission promptly rescinded the change.[102] A few days later heads began to roll. The city manager Charles Wells managed to stay in office, but some others were not so lucky. He fired Wallace N. Davidson, city garbage inspector, apparently on orders from Buck. Several days earlier Marron had said publicly that he had heard Davidson ordering a clerk at a polling place not to allow anyone to vote whose name did not appear on a type-written list, and the suspicion of dirty politics was immediate. Other "deadwood and excess baggage on the city payrolls" were also slated for dismissal.[103]

Out of power, Tingley could only mourn stridently when his favorite projects went neglected. In late May fifty Chinese elms in North End Park were dead and falling down; he claimed the trees had not been watered. He pointed out that he had called the attention of the commission to the matter two weeks earlier.[104] A more severe blow fell the following month when the city sanitarian announced the closing of the fifteen-year-old municipal beach because samples of the water revealed the presence of coliform bacteria.[105] But the foremost concerns of the new commissioners and their supporters were not those of Tingley and his camp; instead they pushed relentlessly such issues as business growth and municipal expansion.

Expansion and Political Stalemate

Throughout the next several terms of the City Commission Clyde Tingley continued to be an important factor in Albuquerque politics, often a dominant one. But neither he nor his followers could check the tide of growth that was steadily eroding his support. As a result of the increasing population and the growing appetite for more public services, the municipal expenditures skyrocketed. In the fiscal year beginning in 1945, the budget for the general fund was $409,963, and the total city government budget was $1,230,231. One year later the respective figures jumped to $589,555 and $1,528,082; by fiscal year 1951 they were $1,541,192 and $4,384,423.[106] In just six years the general fund had risen 275.9 percent and the total budget 256.4 percent. To pay for these escalating expenses a broader tax base was needed, and annexations proceeded at a similar pace. The area encompassed by the city boundaries grew from eleven square miles in 1945 to forty-nine in 1950.[107] Soon thereafter, however, the adding of new land slowed—only seven more square miles were annexed during the next nine years[108]—as new sets of concerns came to preoccupy the leaders in city government.

The city commissioners who had defeated Tingley's slate in 1946 moved to increase the city's size dramatically, but public resistance eventually forced them to moderate their ambitions. In late 1946, acting upon the behest of the Chamber of Commerce, the commission submitted a petition to district court to annex all the densely populated areas contiguous to Albuquerque, thereby doubling the city's population and increasing its area to approximately one hundred square miles at a single stroke. Clyde Tingley cast the only dissenting vote, claiming that it would cost at least $12 million just to provide sewer service for the new areas.[109] Many of the residents of the affected areas also opposed the measure, and amid the ensuing storm of protest it died. Not without some retribution, however—in February 1947 the City Commission, with Tingley voting by himself in the minority, doubled the water rates for the residents outside the city limits.[110]

The following month the New Mexico legislature gave final passage to an annexation bill which was regarded as a compromise between the wishes of cities wanting to annex and residents outside those cities. According to this statute, a city would designate an area to be taken in and would appoint three members to a seven-member arbitration board with the responsibility of deciding the issue. Then the residents of the designated area would elect three other members to the board. (If they did not, three representatives of the area would be appointed by district court.) The seventh member, who could generally be expected to cast the deciding vote, would be elected by the other six or, if that proved impossible, appointed by district court. The arbitration board would be charged to base its decision solely on whether municipal services could be extended to the area in question within a reasonable length of time. This 1947 law, which was destined to be applied on numerous occasions to resolve the annexation disputes, had been very nearly aborted when State Representative Joe A. Montoya, head of the Taxation and Revenue Committee and a reputed opponent of the measure, had gone to El Paso with the official copy of the bill a few days before the deadline for the close of the legislative session, allegedly under doctor's orders for asthma treatment, but a certified copy had been borrowed from the Senate, voted through, and signed by the governor.[111]

Meanwhile, Clyde Tingley was maneuvering energetically, attempting to regain control of the City Commission. Antonio Morelli, like Tingley a union man, felt uncomfortable with Al Buck and Owen Marron, and under Tingley's influence he broke with them. The most dramatic early manifestation of the rift came in June 1947 over a fairly trivial issue, allocation of office space. At a commission meeting Morelli pointed at Buck and Marron and recalled that the three of them had campaigned together on a platform "pledged against one-man rule." "But now instead of one-man rule," he declared, "we have two-man rule, which I think is a hell of a lot worse."[112] For the remainder of his term Morelli was a Tingley alley. This shift was not enough to give the former chairman back his power, however, for Frank Darrow, the other holdover commissioner, generally voted with Buck and Marron. Two months after this Morelli outburst, Buck withdrew from his position as chairman in a surprise move, and Darrow was elected to replace him.[113]

By this time the officeholders and the people were beginning to look ahead to the next city election, and Tingley saw the opportunity to improve his position. He charged the commission majority with wasting several thousand dollars of public money on a storm sewer project, which had been planned for a year and a half but had been "saved up for just before the city election." Over that period, he averred, "Construction costs have gone up; the cost of pipe, by the city manager's own word, has increased 12 or 15 percent since the first of the year."[114] In September Tingley formally announced his bid for reelection and said he was running with Colonel Ernest N. Everly, a veteran of both world wars. Among the planks of their platform were pledges to work for a substantial reduction of water rates, rehabilitation of the city zoo, and reopening the municipal beach.[115] Outshone in the vigorous campaign were their chief opponents, Louis A. McRae and Edmund Ross, who had ties with Buck and Marron. On election day, October 7, 1947, Tingley led everyone, and Everly had about seven hundred more votes than the third-place finisher.[116]

At the first meeting of the new commission Clyde Tingley, with the support of Morelli and Everly, regained his chairmanship. He immediately moved to consolidate his hold on city government. Right after the election he had asked Charles Wells to resign his position as city manager; at this meeting the resignation was offered and accepted. Building Supervisor Herbert W. Rankin was appointed acting city manager,[117] and the following month he, in turn, appointed Waldo Rogers and Gino Matteucci, who had been campaign managers for Tingley and Everly, to be the new city attorneys.[118]

Commissioner Tingley's success, however, was as fleeting as it was sweet. In early December he had Charles Wells appointed manager and chief engineer of the City Water Department at an annual salary of $6,000 (his salary as city manager had been $6,600).[119] Later that month William B. Catchings of Baton Rouge, Louisiana, was chosen the new city manager by a vote of four to one, with Tingley opposing apparently because he did not like the designated salary of $12,000.[120] A few days afterwards Catchings turned down the job, referring to a telephone conversation with Tingley and Morelli during which the two commissioners had suggested he might settle for less money. Commissioner Ernest Everly, who had assumed the task of searching for a suitable man to fill the post, was livid; he told the press, "I think it is a cheap political trick perpetrated by two members of the commission, and I think that their action has brought embarrassment upon the applicant himself, upon the entire commission and on the city of Albuquerque itself."[121] Several days later, when the second leading candidate for the position withdrew because of discord in the City Commission, Everly announced he would have nothing further to do with the search.[122] Nevertheless, another candidate was found, and on January 27, 1948, Lyle Rosenberg from Berkeley, California, was installed as city manager. At this same commission meeting Everly, thoroughly disenchanted with Tingley by this time, was elected chairman.[123] But the rambunctious former chairman continued to try to get his way, and a little over a week later Rosenberg quit, blaming harassment and interference.[124] One of Tingley's ploys had been to ask Ms. Irene Teakell, whom Rosenberg had appointed director of recreation facilities, including the zoo, if she was ready to give the elephants an enema. He had then asked her not to take the job. Upon hearing of the incident, the incensed commission majority voted over Tingley's opposition to issue Mrs. Teakell an apology. Determined to fill the still-vacant manager's position, the majority then voted to make Charles Wells acting city manager; he accepted on the conditions that he receive the same $12,000 salary the others had been offered and that he retain his post as head of the water department.[125] The following September he was reinstalled as permanent city manager.[126] So less than a year after Clyde Tingley's latest triumph at the polls, he had lost his control of the commission and Wells had had his salary almost doubled.

Despite the turbulence in the commission, the reach of city government continued to extend. During this term it took over the operation of the local garbage collecting firm, United Service Corporation, owned by Abe Sour, had had the garbage contract with the city for years, but in 1946 it began to have financial problems. In December the City Commission voted to raise residential rates from forty cents a month to a dollar, but heated opposition from the citizens of Albuquerque led them to the rescind the hike. In February of the next year the rates were raised to seventy cents, and the city began negotiating with Sour to buy the company. Sour wanted $65,000 for the firm; Morelli said the firm's assets were worth only $25,000 according to the company's own books.[127] The bargaining dragged on until May 1948, when the company notified the city it would stop garbage collections because of inability to meet payrolls. Under the press of this emergency a compromise was reached: the commission voted to buy United Service Corporation for $43,772.37, the appraised value of its equipment. Tingley opposed the deal, arguing that they should wait until the day the garbage collections stopped and "collect $10,000 on the company's bond," but the majority was firmly convinced that the city should not miss a day of garbage service.[128]

In the following months the City Commission again turned its attention to forceful expansion of the municipal boundaries. A number of parcels of land with more or less cooperative residents had been annexed on the east, but heavily populated areas on the other side of town had remained sturdily resistant. In June the commission availed itself of the procedure set forth in the recently enacted annexation law and designated a substantial portion of the north valley along the Rio Grande as territory to be brought in.[129] The following month, while the arbitration board was still in session, it applied the so-called Roswell law, "which authorizes municipalities to annex, by simple resolution, areas contiguous to two or more sides of the city limits, provided that such areas have been platted into tracts of five acres or less, are built up, have two or more business establishments, and the city can provide municipal services to such area," to much of Old Albuquerque, whose history stretched back for more than a century and a half beyond the founding of the incorporated city.[130] In August the arbitration board trimmed off the northernmost mile of the north valley tract, which was mostly farmland, from the original proposal and annexed the rest.[131] The residents of these two absorbed areas, however, expressed vehement dissatisfaction, and it was apparent the disputes were not settled.

The contentiousness of the citizens of the greater Albuquerque area on this issue was paralleled by more strife within the City Commission. In September 1948 the commission passed on the first of its three readings a proposed revenue bond issue of $2,910,000 for a program of water and sewer line expansion. (According to state law, revenue bonds must be approved by a four-fifths majority of the commission and are retired from department earnings, whereas general obligation bonds must be approved by the voters and are retired with tax money.) Tingley voted against the issue, but Morelli, while making unenthusiastic noises, went along.[132] Three days later, however, after two hours of asking questions and commenting, Morelli balked and withheld the required fourth vote. The commission majority exploded. Everly: "The rankest piece of obstructionism I've ever seen in thirty years of attending meetings all over the world. . . ." Marron: "This is the most evil thing, the most wicked thing you have ever done . . . why don't you resign and let a man sit there?" Buck: " I condemn you for your stand . . . I thought there was some semblance of man, of the humanitarian in you, but it's all gone." Tingley was conspicuously absent from this meeting, but it was clear that he was directing the opposition because of its costliness and because of reluctance to finance expansion of utilities into such areas as North End and Old Albuquerque that were contesting their annexation in court.[133] Months of infighting ensued, but the matter was finally resolved in a secret deal the following January when the commission voted unanimously to give final passage to the entire amount originally proposed.[134]

In the meantime, litigation on the North End and Old Albuquerque annexations was progressing. Because the annexation of much of Old Albuquerque by means of the Roswell law had met such vigorous opposition, the city was attempting to bring in the area by still another legal approach: landowners requested the city to annex their property, and contiguous lands not exceeding 49 percent of the land owned by petitioning landowners could be taken in at the same time. The validity of some of the signatures was called into question, and some of the property owners asked that their names be withdrawn, so after some fruitless legal maneuvering the City Commission resorted to the 1947 annexation law, which had been used for the North End territory. The commission appointed its three members to the seven-member arbitration board, and Old Albuquerque, by a margin of more than two to one, elected three representatives opposed to the annexation. Following the election an impromptu celebration was held in the Old Albuquerque plaza with speeches and torchlights.[135] But the jubilation of the foes of annexation was short-lived. On June 29, 1949, came a State Supreme Court decision declaring the North End annexation and the 1947 law under which it had been conducted valid;[136] the next day the recently set-up arbitration board voted to annex Old Albuquerque, which later became known as Old Town.[137]

Other pieces of land were absorbed into the city during this commission term, but in most instances the residents either put up little resistance or were eager to be taken in. Most of the old communities of North Barelas and San Jose were added on to the south side of Albuquerque.[138] The largest annexations were in the east; most of these consisted of undeveloped mesa land brought in on the request of the property owners.[139] As a consequence of these piecemeal additions, the eastern border of the city took on a jagged, irregular pattern, and land developers there acquired easy access to municipal services.

Although the commission majority was almost always on the side of expanding the powers of city government during these years, on one occasion it pushed to shrink its sphere of control. Such expensive undertakings as the recent acquisition of the garbage collecting operation were causing financial strain, and someone hit upon the idea that the city could save money if it did not have to pay for maintaining the municipal airport. The airport included twenty-three hundred acres of land just to the west of and adjoining Kirtland Air Force Base, and the U.S. Air Force could use more space and facilities than it presently had. In late 1949 over the vociferous opposition of Tingley and Morelli, the majority—Everly, Buck and Marron—negotiated and voted through a contract with the air force that gave title to all but fifty-three acres of the airport to the government under the condition that fifty nonmilitary flights a day could use the facilities, Trans World Airlines flights were exempted from this restriction, and when the number of other non-military flights per day reached forty, the limit would be renegotiated. To prevent the federal government from attempting to condemn the remaining fifty-three acres at some future time, a clause was inserted stating that if the government did so, title to the entire airport would revert to the city. So the government would have to condemn and pay for the whole 2300 acres. The commission majority pointed out that the air force could spend no money on improvements for the area unless it held title. Tingley, however, perhaps imagining future possible complications, protested that the deal was "giving away a multi-million dollar airfield to the government for nothing."[140]

The next City Commission election was held on April 4, 1950. The campaign had been heated; in all, thirty candidates had announced for the race, the most that had ever run at one time for the City Commission.[141] Tingley had backed the Independent Progressive ticket, and the commission majority had thrown their support to the People's ticket. When the votes were counted, Don Wilson, an attorney, emerged as the leader, followed by Tony Gilbert, operator of a laundry, and Paul Batsel, a real estate broker.[142] Wilson was a member of the slate supported by Tingley, and Gilbert and Batsel were People's candidates. Since the commission members to be replaced were Buck, Marron and Morelli, the election left the three-two division unchanged.[143] The voters' lack of clear alignment with either side had left the City Commission to continue in its old ways—more headlong annexation, more heated wrangling.

The election in October of 1951 pitted Clyde Tingley and Dan O'Bannon, on the Good Government ticket, against Hugh Graham and O.C. McCallister, on the Community slate, which was supported by the same people who had backed Tingley's Albuquerque opposition since 1946. O'Bannon, a native Albuquerquean, had worked as a cigar maker and a machinist in his early days, and since 1930 had been in the county assessor's office as assessor or deputy.[144] Graham was president of Albuquerque Federal Savings and Loan Association, and McCallister headed McCallister Auto Company.[145] Tingley and O'Bannon won by respective majorities over Graham, who came in third, of about thirteen hundred votes and seven hundred votes. As usual, the Tingley team did best in the lowlands and lower highlands, whereas his opposition carried the heights on the east.[146] On October 9 Tingley, with the support of O'Bannon's and Wilson's votes, took over the chairman's seat.[147]

In apparent control for the first time since his brief stint following the 1947 city election, Commission Chairman Tingley immediately began flexing his political muscle. The City Garbage Department was now a $340,000-per-year item in the municipal budget;[148] it was his first target. He had the head of that department, among others, suspended on the charge of conducting political activity during working hours,[149] and he announced that the department was $307,377.77 "in the red" and was sinking further into debt by the month. "I think," he commented, "the city manager should put a businessman in charge of the department, someone who can keep expenses down." The money was owed to three other city sources: $68,128.32 to the water fund, $194,667.40 to the general fund, and $44,572.05 to the retirement fund. Upon prodding from the chairman, the city attorney ruled that the garbage department had violated New Mexico statutes in borrowing from the water department, for which bonds had been issued.[150] Operating expenses throughout city government were cut in order to pay off the illegal debt.[151] In December 1951 a new business manager was named for the garbage department, Richard C. Schoor, a recent county manager.[152]

Clyde Tingley widened his fire and found other financial mismanagement in city government. Tallying up additional deficits to bring the total shortage to "over half a million dollars," he declared, "I say the City of Albuquerque is broke and we have to do something at once." City Manager Charles Wells and the minority commissioners denied that the situation was so bad, but publicity, the ledger sheets and Tingley's declamations had a telling effect.[153] On the last day of 1951 Wells announced he had asked for retirement and this time would accept no other position in city government.[154] Four days later Edmund Engel, head of the City Planning Department, was hired as his replacement at a starting salary of $8,000.[155]

Throughout 1952 and 1953 the chairman continued to assert his power, but increasingly the other commissioners and the growing city bureaucracy resisted his moves. Don Wilson, always a more independent voice than O'Bannon, often voted with the opposition. In the aftermath of a flood in the summer of 1952, Tingley attacked the competency of the engineering department, headed by E.O. Betts, who had been temporarily suspended following the previous city election. Betts, however, weathered this and subsequent storms and remained in office.[156] The following March Tingley, now disenchanted with Richard Schoor, whom he had had installed as manager of the garbage department, made a bid to take over direct control of the operation of that department. Gilbert and Batsel, however, took a strong opposing stand, and the attempt ground to a halt.[157] In spite of his intelligence and the force of his personality, Clyde Tingley was having growing difficulty coping with the pervasive forces that were opposing his will. The last month of 1953 found him prodding City Manager Engel to investigate the city zoo as a result of a report of the death of an emu.[158]

Citizen Activism in the Tingley Years

The spirit of assertiveness and contentiousness that marked the Albuquerque City Commission during the late forties and early fifties was paralleled by a rise in citizen activism. Particularly in the university community, large groups of people were forming strong opinions about what they wanted done in local government, and they were ready to do battle with established powers in their efforts to get their way. Although their protests were mild mannered by later standards—they generally stayed within legally sanctioned channels—their influence was often decisive.

One of the issues which came to generate strong public feeling was the passage of a new bus franchise.[159] All the local bus companies were privately owned, and the largest by far was the Albuquerque Bus Company, which ever since 1928, when street cars had been discontinued, had operated under a twenty-five-year franchise with the city. According to the terms of the agreement, the firm paid 2 percent of its net earnings to the city in addition to an occupation tax limited to $200 a year.[160] In 1945 the company was bought by a group of five men headed by Joseph Land, who already owed the smaller Armijo and Isleta bus lines.[161] As a result of the change in ownership and management, of the short time remaining on the original franchise, and of the growing numbers of riders, a new arrangement would soon have to be negotiated. And the riders, who constituted a much larger proportion of the local population than in later, more affluent days, were determined to have a say in the financial details.

After several proposals and counterproposals and much pressure exerted on both sides, the city and the Albuquerque Bus Company reached tentative agreement in early 1948. The company would pay a premium of $12,000 plus 1% percent of its gross profits until January 1, 1953, and 2 percent thereafter. Regular adult fares were set at ten cents, but the firm was not prohibited from applying to the State Corporation Commission for higher rates, thus bypassing the City Commission and local voters. Such matters as discontinuing old routes and adding on new ones would be left to the discretion of the company. At public hearings on the proposed franchise many citizens expressed vehement opposition, for they felt it slighted their interests and was too favorable to the company. Nevertheless, on May 29, 1949, at a City Commission meeting for which it was not even on the agenda, the new twenty-five-year franchise was voted through with only Tingley dissenting.[162]

The next day a group of angry citizens began making plans to force a referendum on the issue. They came to call themselves the Citizens Committee for a Fair Bus Franchise; chairing the organization was Joel V. Barrett, a graduate assistant in government at the University of New Mexico, and Dorothy I. Cline, a professor in the same department, was active on the steering committee.[163] According to New Mexico Statutes, Chapter 14-3501, 1941, a referendum election was required if petitions were signed by "bona fide adult residents of such municipality to a number equivalent to ten per cent of the population of such municipality as shown by the most recent federal census";

in this case 3545 valid signatures of such residents were needed. Less than a month later the committee turned in petitions bearing 5264 names to the city clerk.[164] The signatures were validated, an election was ordered, and the campaign became more earnest. City Commissioners Buck, Marron and Everly and two local unions of the Brotherhood of Railroad Trainmen, one of them composed of Albuquerque Bus Company drivers, supported the franchise; Tingley, local unions affiliated with the American Federation of Labor, and the Citizens Committee for a Fair Bus Franchise fought against it. On December 20, 1949, a snowy and rainy day, the franchise went down to defeat 3477 to 2749.[165]

Over the following years came more developments which put pressure on the Albuquerque Bus Company to be sensitive to the public's wishes. In early 1950 a new bus line, Duke City Transportation Company, began operating two routes in the metropolitan area, one of which serviced Bel-Air, a community that the Albuquerque Bus Company had refused to enter. Then the larger firm began to send buses to Bel-Air, and the City Commission vacillated on giving the new company permission to make stops inside the city limits.[166] Duke City Transportation Company collapsed in the face of these difficulties, convincing more people of the need for municipal control of bus routes. In April three new city commissioners were elected, two of whom, Tony Gilbert and Paul Batsel, had campaigned for a 3 percent tax on the company's gross profits. More months of negotiation ensued.[167] In March of 1951 the bus drivers went on strike and won from the company standby pay and also contributions to the union health and welfare program and to the pension plan.[168] Now feeling the pinch of increased expenses, the bus firm asked in October for a fare increase, but Clyde Tingley, who had just won in a city election and regained his position as chairman of the commission, insisted it would not be granted until a new franchise had been passed. More deliberations.[169] Finally, on March 18, 1952, about a year before the original franchise was to run out, the City Commission voted in a new franchise which gave the city increased regulatory powers over the bus company effective immediately and 2 percent of its gross profits as soon as a new fare ordinance was passed.[170] It was estimated that the new agreement would bring the city $15,000 to $20,000 annually as compared to about $1,700, which had been its take in recent years.[171]

Controversy flared up again when the City Commission voted in early June to raise bus fares from ten cents for adults and five cents for school children to fifteen cents and seven cents respectively, subject to an ordinance amendment. This time Tingley and his two allies on the commission were on the side of the Albuquerque Bus Company, and Batsel and Gilbert were opposed. Tingley pointed out that the city was losing money by not taking advantage of the revenue provisions of the new franchise. Joel Barrett hinted that there might be another referendum to counter the increase.[172]

At the end of the month a new organization was formed to combat the raise, Fighters for Fair Fares. Many of the members of the old Citizens Committee for a Fair Bus Franchise joined the new group, but the leadership was different.[173] The organization immediately set out collecting names for a petition to force a referendum. Their task was more difficult than had faced the earlier group, for the 1950 census had been published showing a large increase in the population of Albuquerque, and thus many more signatures of registered adult voters living inside the city were required. Nevertheless, on July 23 the petition was turned in to the city clerk's office bearing 17,293 names.[174]

Soon, however, signs began to crop up that this second petition might meet a different fate from the one the first one had. Rumors spread, which Tingley neither confirmed nor denied, that he had said that a check of the petition would find only about seven thousand signatures of qualified voters, not enough to force an election. Charles Albaugh, acting chairman of the Fighters for Fair Fares, issued a statement which read in part as follows:

> Tingley is running the show his own way. He doesn't care who, or how many, people sign the petitions so long as he can throw out enough so that he doesn't have to call an election, which he knows will surely and soundly defeat the ordinance providing for the rate increase.
>
> He has hired workers at bus company expense to check and count the names. He allowed the bus company representatives and workers to count the names and look the petitions over before the City Commission had seen them or taken any action on them.[175]

A little over a week later, Tingley reported to the Commission that all but 5843 names of the 17,293 submitted had been disallowed. His report did not indicate who was in direct charge of the count or what the precise criteria for disqualifying signatures were.[176] The Fighters for Fair Fares sought legal recourse, District Judge Edwin L. Swope deliberated about a month and declared that determining the sufficiency of the petition was the commission's job, and the commission then threw it out. On September 28, 1952, just in time to catch thousands of people flocking to the state fair, the Albuquerque Bus Company raised its rates.[177]

Having been thwarted by Tingley's strong-armed tactics, all the frustrated petitioners could do was await the next city election. They had, however, attained some of their goals: the enacted franchise was clearly more favorable to the public than the one the Citizens Committee for a Fair Bus Franchise had fought against. And around the same time some of these same people were pushing to a successful conclusion another grass-roots issue—the passage of an anti-discrimination ordinance.

By the standards of the day Albuquerque was one of the most liberal cities in the country in regard to racial distinctions. Anglos and Spanish-Americans had a long tradition of sharing political power, newcomers tended to be judged by what they could do rather than the way they looked, and Blacks constituted less than 2 percent of the population.[178]

In 1951 the University of New Mexico was proud to proclaim it was one of thirty-seven institutions of higher learning in the country that omitted all "discriminatory" questions on its applications for admission.[179] Nevertheless, many persons were coming to feel that present community practice did not go far enough, that all forms of public racial discrimination should be outlawed. In 1951 students at the university conducted boycotts of business establishments that refused service to Blacks, and various social groups throughout the community rallied to the cause. Finally, on February 12, 1952, the city passed an ordinance prohibiting discrimination in public places because of race, creed, ancestry or color, becoming one of the first American cities to do so. A minimum fine of $100 was the penalty for breaking the law. Bill Upchurch, son of a restaurant owner, protested. He identified himself as "a good Christian" and criticized the measure as "more of this old socialistic stuff being forced on us by Truman and his gang." He went on, "It's a question of whether or not we'll have private ownership." Hobart La Grone, president of the local chapter of the National Association for the Advancement of Colored People, supported it: "It is fitting that this should come up for its final reading on the birthday of the Great Emancipator. . . ."[180] Upchurch led a group which attempted to get enough petition signers to force a referendum on the ordinance, but when the deadline came the petition bore only about 1,840 names instead of the required approximately 8,000.[181] The flurry of excitement subsided, and the law eventually became established, unquestioned custom. Although the drive for its passage had been briefer and had met with less resistance than the citizen efforts regarding the Albuquerque Bus Company, it probably had greater significance for the future.

Efficiency and Rationality in City Government

In the late 1940s and early 1950s citizen activism was sometimes a problem for Clyde Tingley and others who were accustomed to governing with a strong hand, but the veteran commissioner generally managed to ride out the storms. A greater source of difficulty was the growth of population and of city government, yet the people always reelected him to the City Commission, and he regained his chairman's post in 1951. A still more serious threat to his leadership, however, had been apparent for some time—the growing emphasis on standardized, rational and efficient procedures. Big government required a certain systematic delegation of decision making; the educated and affluent defense industry workers who were moving into the eastern heights demanded order and reason in public life; the whole country seemed to be seeking a return to quietness and sanity. Tingley, on the other hand, remained as rambunctious as ever. His arbitrary maneuvers regarding the city manager's position and the Albuquerque Bus Company cost him some support, but he felt he knew what he was doing. On other important issues of the day—the merit system for city employees, the construction of a civic auditorium, the expansion of the water system and the handling of traffic control—he antagonized more people by opposing the rising tide of disciplined reasonableness.

Much of Tingley's power was based on a foundation of personal loyalties and favors, and he had long opposed applying something as impersonal as a merit system to employment by the city. The loss by his slate of candidates in the 1946 election, however, foreshadowed his defeat on this issue. The next year the City Commission put most municipal workers on a merit system.[182] Early in 1948, at the same meeting at which Tingley lost his newly regained chairman's post to Everly, a resolution was passed making it grounds for dismissal for any department head or employee to obey orders from any commissioner and instructing the city manager to employ personnel "without regard to partisan or factional alignments."[183] A merit approach was followed rigorously during the search for a new police chief the following fall; Paul Shaver won the job partly because he made the highest score on a special examination administered to all applicants for the position.[184] To a much greater extent than before, hirings and promotions were being handled on a scientific basis.

When Tingley again became chairman, he could not turn back the clock, but he was able to help install a counterweight to the merit system. Many city workers did not feel that the system sufficiently looked after their interests, and in 1952 they joined forces with the Albuquerque Central Labor Union in a successful drive for unionization. Tingley, who held a union card and enjoyed widespread labor support, favored recognizing the union, as did O'Bannon, also a union member, and Wilson, who had frequently served as legal representative for labor groups. Gilbert and Batsel were more noncommittal.[185] In February the entire commission approved the AFL as bargaining agent for the city workers,[186] thus giving them the protection of their own organization in addition to that provided by the impersonal regulations of the merit system.

Although Clyde Tingley was adroit at political wrangling, often casting himself in the role of the people's champion, he was frequently more successful at blocking the opposition than at working with them to resolve problems. One apparently simple issue that lingered on for years was the location and construction of a proposed civic auditorium. The idea of a civic auditorium had been introduced back in the 1930s, most people seemed to favor it, but it was delayed by an almost incredible sequence of difficulties and disagreements. One general obligation bond issue for construction funds was defeated; another was declared invalid. In 1946 a bond issue of $500,000 was approved by the voters, but increasing building costs made the amount insufficient. Four years later another bond issue and an auction of city land boosted the fund to $894,000;[187] there remained, however, the sticky question of what kind of auditorium to build. Tingley insisted on a structure which could accommodate athletic events as well as cultural ones, whereas his opposition on the commission wanted some kind of auditorium and soon, even if the available money would cover the cost of only a small building. The commission majority overrode Tingley's opposition and approved a contract with the University of New Mexico for an auditorium on university land,[188] but rising costs and legal complications stymied the work.[189] By now the public was getting amused and impatient. At the convention of the New Mexico Education Association in October 1953, Superintendent of Albuquerque Public Schools John Milne invited the teachers to return to Albuquerque. "We hope to have a city auditorium for you next year," he said. "Of course, there are some technical things yet to be ironed out, but I can be sure of this . . . ." Milne paused. "Completion of the auditorium is twenty years closer today than the first time I mentioned it." The audience whooped.[190] The following month the City Commission voted approval for a contract for the building to be erected on a different parcel of university land,[191] but Tingley, who was the chairman, refused to sign unless the other commissioners took legal action to force him to do so.[192] In January 1954 university officials, discouraged by all the difficulties, asked that the contract be canceled, and the city was back where it had started.[193] The weary public was growing less amused and more resentful of the way the affair was being handled.

Commissioner Tingley and his allies had even more trouble dealing with issues which were complicated and technical, such as expansion of the water system. As more suburbs sprang up on the outskirts of town and as per capita consumption of water increased, the city expanded its network of wells, pumping stations and water mains, but seldom fast enough to meet the demand. Shortages necessitating emergency rationing measures arose in 1946, 1948, 1951, 1952, and 1953. Under constant public pressure to alleviate the problem, the City Commission took a number of halting steps toward improving the operation of the water department. In late 1947 a ten-year master plan for water and sewer lines was voted through,[194] and it was around the same time that Charles Wells, who had temporarily been bumped from his position as city manager, was installed in the newly created post of head of the water department. In October 1951 Albuquerque voters overwhelmingly approved a $3,458,000 general obligation bond issue for water system improvements, but the City Commission did not convert it all into cash until about midway into 1953. Before that time, however, much more money was needed. The 1947 master plan, which had been rendered obsolete by the population growth, was replaced by a new one in 1952 calling for an ambitious program of new construction.[195]

In July 1953 the matter came once more to a head. A Water Board was created and appointments were made to it.[196] On the twenty-ninth of the month a revenue bond of $3,000,000 for water and sewer improvements was put to a vote at the City Commission meeting, but Tingley and O'Bannon, one of whose votes was needed to give it the legally required four-fifths majority, opposed it. O'Bannon declared, "This is too complicated for me," and Tingley asserted, "That's too much money."[197] Upon hearing of the commission action, Don Johnstone, Chairman of the Water Board, tendered his letter of resignation:

Dear Mr. Tingley:

I have just read of the action of the City Commission in connection with water bonds at this afternoon's meeting. If I may be permitted to borrow a phrase, this is so rotten it stinks.

It has taken me just two weeks on the newly appointed Water Conservation Board to satisfy myself that Albuquerque's water problems are not the fault of the master plan, or of the men who are operating the system, but of the short-sighted, penny-pinching, obstructionist tactics in regard to financing in which you are indulging. It seems you are unable or unwilling to grow with the City. What you did today, if not reversed immediately, guarantees that next year we will look back on 1953 as a year of water plenty.

I had looked forward to being of service to the community on the Water Conservation Board (created by Commission in your absence), but the opportunity for useful public service as a citizen must apparently await a time when the Commission is composed entirely of men who do not find the City's problems "too complicated to understand."

This is my resignation.

Very truly yours,
DON JOHNSTONE[198]

The next day Commissioner Don Wilson proposed as a compromise measure a bond issue of $2,400,000 and it passed unanimously,[199] bringing to a close yet another cliff-hanging episode in municipal politics.

The issue unfolding over these years which best illustrates the clash between the old ways and the new stress on rationality and expertise was traffic control. The rapid growth of population and average income was flooding the city with automobiles, and many once-adequate streets were being jammed. From 1946 to 1947, for example, automobile registrations in Bernalillo County jumped from about fifteen thousand to around twenty thousand.[200] Numerous persons were becoming convinced that systematic and well-thought-out measures would have to be taken to cope with the matter.

The first steps were tentative, slow and resisted by some of the entrenched leadership. In mid-1946 a no-parking zone was established on Fourth Street, the main north-south road of the city, in the vicinity of its intersection with Central in an effort to expedite the flow of traffic,[201] and soon other sections of downtown streets were closed to parking. Clyde Tingley opposed these measures, contending that more traffic would be created by cars circling blocks in search of parking space. The commission began negotiating with the Federal Bureau of Public Roads for funding for a proposed traffic survey. Tingley blasted this idea as well, branding it a "waste of the taxpayer's money" and declaring it would accomplish "nothing that we couldn't do by hiring three taxicabs and an engineer."[202] The months and years dragged on with little being done to ameliorate the traffic situation.

Finally, in 1949, the traffic survey was begun, and on May 22, 1950, exactly one year later, the results were announced at a public meeting at the University of New Mexico. The survey had been conducted by the Automotive Safety Foundation out of Washington, D.C., and had cost $60,000, $8,000 of which was paid by the city and the remainder by the state and federal governments. The report noted that Albuquerque had no centralized agency for dealing with traffic problems, and it recommended the establishment of a department of traffic engineering, headed by a trained and experienced traffic engineer, and a traffic board, composed of certain designated city officials. In order to improve downtown traffic flow, it urged that a number of streets be made one-way and that parking be prohibited on more blocks. Since downtown land was expensive, open deck parking buildings not taller than four stories should be constructed. More and better trained police should be hired to help reduce Albuquerque's high accident rate. A model traffic ordinance should be passed to bring laws and practices into conformity with most of the rest of the country. The report criticized in particular the local practices of using stop signs in combination with flashing yellow lights at intersections at night to make traffic on the minor streets stop (the conventional procedure was to have no stop signs and to flash red for the minor street and yellow for the major street) and of using octagon-shaped signs for both "STOP" and "SLOW" (most of the country had a different shape for "SLOW" signs). And finally, the report recommended the adoption of a major street plan proposing the development of more main arteries to carry the traffic to and from the downtown area and the construction of more bridges and underpasses to cross the Rio Grande and the Santa Fe Railroad, the chief obstacles to east-west traffic.[203]

The report by the experts from the Automotive Safety Foundation had a huge impact. Over the ensuing years most of the major recommendations were adopted and integrated into the city government's structure of ordinances and bureaucracies. Two weeks after the report was publicly issued, the City Commission established a Traffic Commission to be composed of the city manager, the police chief, the city engineer, the city attorney and the city traffic engineer, yet to be hired. At the same meeting an eighteen-page uniform traffic ordinance passed on the first of three readings.[204] The Traffic Commission did not begin to function that year, but the recently established Planning Commission, with the help and advice of the new planning department under Edmund Engel, studied and conducted hearings on the major street plan.[205] In early September the City Commission approved this master plan for traffic,[206] and a week later it gave final passage to the uniform traffic ordinance.[207]

On December 1, 1950, traffic control and planning was given a boost when the city hired its first traffic engineer, David Dabney, who had worked for three years in the municipal traffic engineering department of the City of New Orleans.[208] An energetic and forceful personality, Dabney immediately set about the task of rationalizing traffic control and implementing the master plan, and his enthusiasm soon carried him far beyond the recommendations of the traffic survey report. Before the year was out the city began altering the system of stop signs and flashing lights at intersections in accordance with the new traffic ordinance.[209] In January the first parking meters—1700 of them— were installed downtown with half of the take to go to the traffic engineering department.[210] The next month the first of many changes of downtown streets to one-way was implemented.[211] And Dabney was just getting started.

Not all of the work being done at this time to improve Albuquerque's street system was conducted through the traffic department, however. In April of 1950, before the results of the traffic survey had been announced, the City Commission inaugurated the first paving district program in twenty years. Owners of property along streets which the commission declared needed paving or otherwise improving were assessed the cost of the improvements.[212] In some paving districts the property owners protested loudly, and in at least one case a compromise was worked out whereby proposed improvements and costs were substantially reduced.[213] But by the end of 1951, the equivalent of seventy-eight miles of city streets had been paved under the new program,[214] and thenceforth the city actively promoted the paving of streets and expanded its operations in that area.

Another change that took place in this period was the systemization and rationalization of street designations. Starting in February 1951[215] and going through July 1, 1952, when all the name changes became finally effective, the city altered the names of about three hundred streets, in most cases to ensure that the different segments of what was clearly the same street would all have the same name. Sometimes the residents objected, and occasionally their objections prevailed. Some of the more unimaginative and colorless of the proposed changes were thrown out, such as the proposal to switch the name of Lomas Avenue, an important street several blocks north of Central, to North Avenue. Commissioners Tingley and O'Bannon were unenthusiastic about the program, but they and the other citizens who felt as they did were unable to stop this new surge of orderliness.

At the same time, the city designated streets which ran east and west as "avenues" or "roads" and those which ran north and south as "streets" or "drives." Most of the thoroughfares became "boulevards" regardless of their direction. Short streets were called "places," "courts," "lanes" or "circles." The city was split into four quadrants—NE, SE, NW and SW—with the Santa Fe Railroad and Central Avenue serving as the dividing lines, and the new quadrant designation became a part of every street address replacing the old directional prefix of the street names. An East Central Avenue address, for example, got the more precise designation of Central Avenue NE or Central Avenue SE. In this manner the city map became easier to follow and more predictable.

Meanwhile Traffic Engineer David Dabney pressed on with plans to improve the traffic situation. It probably surprised few political observers that this man, an outsider with strong views, began to clash with Clyde Tingley, who was used to running the show in his own colorful way. At a commission meeting on January 22, 1952, the break between the two became public when the commissioners voted three to two—with Wilson, Batsel and Gilbert for and Tingley and O'Bannon against—to approve routing North Third Street diagonally through Coronado Park to join North Second. Dabney had authored the proposal, and immediately after the vote Tingley launched into a cross-examination of Dabney concerning the latter's personal use of city facilities and employees. In the exchange it was brought out that the traffic engineer had paid municipal employees out of his own pocket at "double the city rate" to do work for him after hours. He invited the commission to conduct an investigation of his department if there were any complaints, whereupon that body gave him a vote of confidence of four to none, with Tingley keeping his silence.[216] The war of attrition was not over, however. Two months later Dabney lodged a formal protest against Tingley's interference with his department's work, alleging that the commissioner had told his men to stop work on a paving project.[217]

In the months ahead Dabney retained the support of Tingley foes Gilbert and Batsel and also that of Wilson. During his tenure as traffic engineer he managed to persuade the city to adopt a remarkable number of changes. Besides those already mentioned, they include the construction of a traffic divider along East Central, the installation of prominent street signs along Central Avenue, the replacement of a number of "STOP" signs with "YIELD RIGHT-OF-WAY" signs, and the removal of walls and shrubs causing blind intersections. His proudest accomplishment was having more street lights installed. East Central and the downtown area were lighted up, and a program was approved to increase the 534 residential street lights by some 8,000, the first of which were to be put up in such high crime districts as Barelas. Light and safety would shine throughout nighttime Albuquerque. If his department had had more money, Dabney believed, he could have accomplished more. He also managed to gain some grey hair and ulcers.[218]

In the long run Tingley's opposition proved too much for the traffic engineer, although not for the program of traffic control and traffic planning. On November 13, 1952, David Dabney submitted his letter of resignation, effective three weeks later. He wrote that he had "made every effort to overcome Mr. Tingley's objection to the traffic improvement program." "I am sorry to admit, however," he went on, "that I have been unsuccessful and that Mr. Tingley's objections have grown to a feeling of personal animosity which makes a bad situation unbearable." In the aftermath the limits to Tingley's triumph soon became apparent. He narrowly escaped being ousted again from his chairmanship, and the other four commissioners voted against him when he attempted to have the department of traffic engineering abolished.[219] In May 1953 a new traffic engineer was appointed, Francis Burton, a graduate of the University of New Mexico. [220] More of the work of that department came to be overseen by citizens' boards. In June an ordinance was passed establishing the Parking Board,[221] and in January 1954 the Citizens Traffic Commission composed of independent citizens was formed to advise the city on traffic matters.[222] By now most of city government and most of the people of Albuquerque had embraced the principle of rational control and planning of traffic, and these functions were deeply enough entrenched in the governmental structure to be insulated from the whims of the powerful few.

The Albuquerque Citizens' Committee

As a result of growing dissatisfaction with city government on a number of fronts, many people were looking forward to the upcoming election in April 1954. The largest newspaper in town, the *Albuquerque Journal*, was becoming increasingly critical of the actions of the City Commission but was throwing its support to none of the announced candidates. Municipal employees at every level were showing signs of restiveness. The mounting pressure for change suffused the air.

One of the first candidates to declare for the race was Dorothy I. Cline, who had taught government at the University of New Mexico since 1946 and had recently been active in the political struggle with the Albuquerque Bus Company. "I can't throw my hat into the ring," she said, "because I seldom wear a hat." She went on, "I am in the race to stay and to win. It's about time we had some action on city services. While the city has been bursting at the seams, we've had a do-little city government. A woman with courage and a knowledge of city affairs can do something practical to bring city services up to date."[223]

Meanwhile, a small group of people which called itself the Citizens' Committee was looking around for a slate of candidates to back. This organization had earlier been the steering committee for a larger body, the Citizens' Council, which devoted its energies to making recommendations on political matters. Coming to the conclusion that a more direct course was needed, the committee broke away and prepared to enter the political arena as an active participant. It organized itself into a three-tier structure, with a chairman at the top, an executive board and the membership at large—the same kind of structure that had been adopted by the Citizens Committee for a Fair Bus

Franchise, among other groups. By early 1954 it included about twenty members;[224] in later years it grew to several hundred. A large proportion of the membership worked at the defense-related complex on and around the military bases, and the overwhelming majority lived on the eastern side of the city.[225] More than any previous political organization, the Citizens' Committee represented the rational and disciplined impulse which had been surging into Albuquerque ever since the end of World War II.

On February 9 it announced its support for Maurice Sanchez, Richard A. Bice and Lars Halama. Sanchez, former U.S. attorney for New Mexico, had been born in Socorro County but had resided in Albuquerque most of his life. He had practiced law locally for the past fifteen years. Bice, who was originally from Colorado, was a manager of one of the engineering departments of Sandia Corporation. Halama had been born in California but had lived in New Mexico off and on since he was one year old. He was general agent for the Ohio National Life Insurance Company as well as president of the New Mexico Junior Chamber of Commerce. All three had addresses in the northeast heights.[226]

Three days later Clarence Forsling, chairman of the Citizens' Committee, issued a four-point platform:

1. Put an end to government-by-crisis.
2. Stop commission meddling in day-to-day operations and give the city manager form of government a chance to work.
3. Clean up the mess in public works construction.
4. Plan ahead for city requirements and facilities and for finances to meet them.

He emphasized that the committee was not attacking City Manager Edmund Engel or any other city employees.[227] In addition, the Citizens' Committee leaned toward running the city in the same rational and efficient manner that might characterize a successful business enterprise. In an earlier statement Don Johnstone, member of the group's executive board, declared that Albuquerque needed leadership with "the competence and willingness to put sound management practices into effect in city government. . . ."[228] Much of the essence of the committee's thrust was summed up several years later by Richard Bice in a campaign speech, when he compared organization of a city government to that of a big company and said that the development of "pyramid organization" was one of the reasons for America's progress.[229]

Maurice Sanchez, Richard Bice and Lars Halama opened their well-orchestrated campaign with speeches at the Knights of Columbus Hall. Sanchez blamed city service inadequacies on "a seizing of the city administrative officer's duties by the commission—especially by the chairman." Further referring to Tingley, the lawyer said it "is too bad we have to fight these sidekicks because the real enemy has not come into the open, but he will, and we will fight him. . .there will be a lot of false candidates." Alluding to a charge made by candidate Dorothy Cline that the committee's platform was a "review" of a pamphlet she had written five years ago, he called it "the biggest laugh of the campaign." Bice focused on a controversy which had developed over a leaking Rio Grande sewer and said the problem had been caused by "political meddling." "We are pledged not to allow this kind of a situation to develop by taking the public works program out of the sphere of political influence and putting it in the air of technical thinking, where it belongs," the engineer declared. Halama followed by citing statistics on the declining number of policemen per thousand city residents. Juggling figures with effortless wizardry, the insurance man brought down the house saying that if the present trend continued, "By 1963, we'll have 110 gone out of the present force of 94—we can't afford that." He remarked that "what you hear around Albuquerque is, 'Let's go down to the City Commission meeting, it's better than a three-ring circus.'"[230]

In contrast, Clyde Tingley, whose commission term was not yet up but who was expected to back a slate of candidates of his own choosing, waged an uncharacteristically restrained campaign. He was suffering an eye ailment at the time—perhaps that was the reason for his lack of vigor and vehemence, or perhaps it was that he sensed popular sentiment was no longer with him, or maybe he just felt himself growing old. He challenged Maurice Sanchez to a television debate, then backed down when his opponent took up the gauntlet.[231] In mid-March he threw his support to the United Albuquerque ticket consisting of William J. Bingham, an attorney; Homer Latham, a real estate man; and Shelby Hogan, an accountant; and these three declared they would vote to keep Tingley as chairman.[232] But two weeks later he said he was ready to give up the chairmanship to a younger man.[233] Much of his campaigning consisted of denying charges made against him by the Citizens' Committee and their candidates, as he himself was the main issue. City Manager Engel stated that Tingley had directed him in 1952 to fire four city employees, including Police Chief Paul Shaver, but that he had refused; Tingley called the statement a "lie."[234] In a television talk he asserted he had "lived up one hundred per cent to the city charter and the commission form of government."[235]

On April 6, 1954, the Citizens' Committee candidates swept into office on a record turnout of voters. Sanchez came in first with 12,799, then Bice with 12,020, followed by Halama with 11,599. The runners-up got substantially fewer: Professor Dorothy Cline with 4,791, Bingham with 4,402, and Wilson, the only commissioner to seek reelection, with 4,143. Then came the other two candidates of the United Albuquerque ticket, and a host of independent candidates trailed behind with a handful of votes apiece.[236] This was the first time since the commission election of 1946 that a Tingley-backed slate had been clearly defeated, and the defeat this time was more overwhelming. Furthermore, as the developments of the next several years were to demonstrate amply, it was a much more decisive turning point in city politics.

A few days later the commission meeting was held during which the victors were sworn in. In the early part of the meeting Tingley yielded the chair to one of the outgoing commissioners, Paul Batsel, saying he believed Batsel's grandchildren would like to see pictures of him in the ceremony which marked the changeover. Tingley also made reference to the rupture of a blood vessel in his eye: "I can't see you out there very well," he told the crowd. After the swearing in, Maurice Sanchez was elected chairman. Throughout the meeting the intermittent flash of cameras could be seen, and movies were made for later telecasting.[237]

Few if any of the commission meetings over the next five years were as memorable as that one, but what the new City Commission gave up in warmth and color it gained in orderly efficiency. Holdover Commissioners Tingley and O'Bannon served out the remainder of their terms with little impact on city government, frequently not even attending the commission meetings.[238] The following two City Commission elections saw a decline in controversy and in voting as the Citizens' Committee consolidated its grip on local government. In September 1955 the committee selected and the people voted in William Atkinson, a prominent lawyer who had come to town as a boy in 1922, and Charles Lanier, a native of Aztec, New Mexico, an Albuquerque resident since 1939, and presently the manager of a golf club.[239] For the election of April 1958 Commissioners Sanchez and Bice chose to run again, and Clarence Davis, the operator of a variety store, was tapped to take Halama's place. The Citizens' Committee candidates again swept to easy victory.[240]

The well-mannered tone that city government took on contrasted sharply with the earthy flamboyance of the Tingley years. Referring obliquely to Clyde Tingley and Dan O'Bannon, Commission Chairman Maurice Sanchez told a group of young Albuquerque citizens, "We've had a little trouble with decorum at times. We want to assure the people that we won't have any trouble with decorum so long as Mr. Halama, Mr. Bice and myself are here."[241] And decorous the Citizens' Committee commissioners were, often to the point of being dull and grey. At one meeting in September of 1956 they amended the minutes of the previous meeting in order to make the language milder. According to the record, the commission had "ordered" the City Personnel Board to study procedure dealing with personnel; the word was changed to "asked." What had been "asked" for, according to Commissioner Lanier, was a "review," not an "investigation," as had been reported.[242] With the lowering of voices and the trimming of epithets it seemed that city politics was losing its theatrical aspect and was becoming more and more a matter of day-to-day administration and long-range planning.

In their low-keyed fashion the new commissioners were tough disciplinarians. They believed that if municipal government were to operate more cleanly, efficiently and responsibly than in the past, and on a wider scale, every government employee would have to take his job seriously and follow the rules. A few months after winning the chairmanship of the City Commission, Maurice Sanchez issued a directive reprimanding firemen for "horseplay" on the job.[243] Discipline was a particularly crucial concern in circumstances where city officials might be or appear to be susceptible to outside influence. In May 1955 Clyde Tingley went on a fishing trip to Guaymas, Mexico, and there he saw E.O. Betts, director of public works, in the company of two friends who were also city contract holders. These two, it turned out, were picking up Betts's tab.[244] As a result of the ensuing publicity, the City Commission issued a policy forbidding city employees to accept gifts, favors or money from anyone having "any business relations with the City of Albuquerque." The penalty for violating the rule would be a thirty-day suspension at the minimum and could be dismissal.[245] A year later the City Commission went so far as to order all city workers to resign from any positions of responsibility they might hold in political parties.[246]

Equally important to city government as the discipline was a reorganization of the administrative structure. Commissioner Bice's term "pyramid organization" is indicative of the type of centralization of authority which took place. At the lower end of the scale employment practices were made more rigorously systematic: in late 1954 laborers were put under the merit system,[247] and all city personnel records were standardized in 1958.[248] City staff increased rapidly during these years, and the power of making decisions was dispersed throughout the bureaucracy in such a way that strong individuals at the top had less opportunity to make important unilateral moves on their own. Before the 1954 election there had been sixteen departments reporting directly to the city manager, so this individual, or whoever was in a position to influence or control him, had concentrated power. By 1958 all city departments had been placed under five directors, each of whom controlled a "superdepartment," and these five, along with three staff members, were the only ones who reported to the city manager.[249]

Like an efficiently run business, city government began to draw in substantial revenue increases. The biggest came from a one-cent city sales tax added in 1955 to the two-cent sales tax of the state—Tingley had claimed the city did not need the money and had fought it gamely.[250] Property taxes were another important source. In 1953 the New Mexico Legislature had ordered Bernalillo County to put into effect a single-unit system according to which tax accounts were to be kept by properties rather than owners; the local tax commission spent several years on the process of coding and listing the parcels of land;[251] the Citizens' Committee criticized that body in 1956 for taking so long;[252] the task was completed the next year;[253] taxes were then raised and again three years later.[254] Other sources of additional revenue included tightening collection procedures for the occupation tax and for sewer charges, raising parking meter rates, and obtaining a slice of the state cigarette tax. In conjunction with their efforts to encourage development of vacant city land, the commissioners came up with still another source of money—a standby sewer and water tax.[255]

Most of the increase in the city's budget went for a rapid expansion in services for the public, and as far as most of the citizens were concerned, this expansion was the greatest overall accomplishment of the new commission. From 1954 to 1958 the city government built four new fire stations, two new libraries, an off-street parking garage in the downtown area, and a new community center. Two other community centers were established in already-existing buildings to raise the total in the city to four. Over this period 157 miles of Albuquerque streets were paved, and many new street signs and traffic signals were put up. Water facilities were expanded six million dollars' worth; some of the money paid for 190 miles of new water lines and for automating operations to such an extent that manpower in the water department could be cut. The number of police department personnel grew from 118 to 208 and fire department personnel from 89 to 179; both departments also added much new equipment. Furthermore, these two departments expanded their field of operations: a juvenile division and a laboratory were added to the police department, and the firemen gained a fire prevention bureau.[256] According to the standards by which civic achievement was measured in the late 1950s, Albuquerque had much to be proud of.

In several instances city government extended its reach into areas that had heretofore been the province of private citizens. In May 1955 the parks and recreation department took control of the old Barelas Community Center,[257] and it ran the more recently established community centers as well. In early 1957 a controversy erupted concerning the running of the City Animal Shelter, which the city supported financially but the Humane Association controlled. The newly organized health and welfare directorate took over the shelter and replaced the manager in May.[258] An ordinance was passed in 1959 providing for industrial bonds—a variety of revenue bonds but supported by the assets of the company involved—in order to build facilities for private companies considering moving to the city.[259] . . . As a result of the energy and ambition of the City Commission in these areas and others, over the four years following the election of 1954 the number of ordinances on the books jumped from 935 to 1325.[260]

Although most of the work carried out by these City Commissions involved unspectacular matters, from time to time their actions affected issues of widespread public concern. One such issue was union representation of city workers, which had been granted earlier but which the new commissioners opposed. It was not that they were unsympathetic to the lot of the working man; rather they were opposed on principle to any sort of special interest pressure group, and they believed wages should be determined on the basis of impersonal analysis of the city's priorities and available funds. In their first year of office the Citizens' Committee commissioners granted laborers a raise of ten cents an hour,[261] extended to them such new benefits as paid vacations and holidays,[262] and yet refused to sign a union contract. The Albuquerque Central Labor Union joined with Commissioner Clyde Tingley in denouncing the refusal, but the commission majority held firm.[263] More raises were budgeted for city employees at all levels, and worker resentment seemed to subside.[264]

Another controversial issue with which the commission had to contend was the continuing problem of bus service. Many had thought that the new bus franchise would take care of bus transportation for the twenty years it would presumably be in force, but the growing public concern with traffic and urban transit coupled with declining use of the bus system was changing the picture. In May 1954 the Albuquerque Bus Company cut seven night lines in the eastern part of town to save money.[265] A few days later the City Commission ordered Engel to have a survey made of the bus service,[266] and around the end of the month City Traffic Engineer Francis Burton made a report. He said that bus patronage had been declining locally since the spring of 1952, following a national trend.[267] Evidently the rising affluence of the people and the suburban sprawl of their residential patterns, particularly in the eastern heights, were leading to more use of private automobiles. Clearly the bus company had its problems, but the influence of city government was stronger than in earlier years, and maximization of profit was not to be the only consideration. Two days later the company reinstated four of the discontinued lines.[268]

Bus finances became tighter in July 1955 when drivers started getting a guaranteed hourly wage instead of a percentage of the profits.[269] This change provided the employees with greater security, but it put the company in more of a bind. Company representatives informed the City Commission that costs and revenues were cancelling each other out. The commissioners felt a responsibility to ensure that the owners got a decent return on their investment, and another rate hike was approved. Student fares went up to ten cents. A plan was inaugurated according to which the city was divided up into zones and any passenger who crossed a boundary would have to pay an additional nickel. To further help the company, the commission waived the 2 percent franchise tax on gross profits.[270] Slowly but surely, the bus company was moving toward the status of a publicly controlled utility.

One of the greatest triumphs of the new city leaders was the resolution of the long-standing question of a civic auditorium. The month after the Citizens' Committee's first victory at the polls, the commission acted on a recommendation by the Auditorium Board calling for a survey by experts available through the National Association of Auditorium Managers to determine the best site and the best type of building.[271] In August they announced plans for a huge civic center, preferably in the downtown area, to include both the auditorium and a new city hall,[272] but it soon became apparent that the available funds could not match their vision. Early the next January they settled for a twenty-acre tract just north of St. Joseph Hospital and roughly midway between the University of New Mexico and the central business district. The same site had been considered by an earlier commission and then rejected because of difficulties in acquiring the land; now, however, the titles had been cleared and the owners were willing to sell or trade.[273] Then came much sifting through of prospective designs; the one finally selected consisted of a structure with a huge low dome to be constructed by pouring concrete over a built-up mound of earth. Construction got underway in 1956,[274] and in early 1957 the city's new civic auditorium, completed at a total cost of around a million and a half dollars, was ready for use.

On Friday night, April 26, 1957, came the grand opening. Maurice Sanchez delivered a short speech; then followed two prayers and a mass singing of the national anthem by all the performers and some four thousand in the audience. The Albuquerque Civic Symphony Orchestra, the Albuquerque Civic Chorus and pianist George Robert from the university entertained the crowd with several popular classics; one of the favorites was Tchaikovsky's *Nutcracker Suite*. The dignitaries seated on the main floor enjoyed excellent listening, but for the general audience in the balcony sections the brass and woodwinds boomed across with exaggerated volume and the stringed instruments gave off whispers.[275] Most of the citizens, however, were very glad to have the auditorium at long last. Over the following year it hosted operas, ballets, ice shows, wrestling matches and rock and roll shows.[276] With its capacity to accommodate large numbers of people and a large variety of entertainment, the auditorium matched the dream which Clyde Tingley had stubbornly held out for, but it was the teamwork, the careful planning, the diligence and the discipline of the new commission and all the people they consulted and worked with along the way that made the fruition of the dream possible.

Management Relaxes Its Reins

The systematic changes which took place in Albuquerque city government during the late forties and the fifties were paralleled by shifts occurring in other local institutions, businesses and professions. Such trends as increased size of groups, decreased dependence on strong leaders who made all the decisions themselves, greater emphasis on cooperation, and exaltation of technical expertise manifested themselves in almost every type of work place. They seemed to be part of broad shifts taking place throughout the society.

Among the institutions most sensitive to the breezes of change were those established primarily to serve the public, such as the schools. Right after the end of World War II the University of New Mexico underwent a period of turbulence which eventually resulted in a change of administration. The enrollment was jumping wildly, from 1009 in the spring semester of 1945 to 3653 in the fall of 1946 as veterans came back to take advantage of their G.I. Bill education benefits;[277] and the strong-handed Dr. John Wernette, recently appointed president of the university, was not getting along with his faculty. In 1946 the university lost a research project funded by the navy and the chairman of its physics department to the New Mexico School of Mines as a result of Wernette's opposition to using university building space for purposes not connected with teaching. Later that year he appointed Dr. John Robb dean of fine arts, drawing more protests from faculty and students. In April of 1947 a controversy arose for which Wernette was not responsible but which further inflamed emotions. Three students had burned a building belonging to Pi Kappa Alpha Fraternity and had been suspended by vote of the faculty. The regents overturned the suspension, whereupon the dean of men resigned from the university and every member of the University Student Affairs Committee quit the committee.[278] The dean's resignation was just one of many recent faculty resignations at a time when the university needed all the teachers it could get. The following month Wernette made his annual report to the regents and complained of the opposition he had met. "I have been somewhat astonished to discover the inertia, and even downright hostility, which oppose a drive for quality and which conceal their true objections to phases of a quality program behind vague or general criticisms," he stated.[279]

The tension was growing intolerable, and matters headed for a showdown. The regents held a two-day meeting in June and then announced they had decided to reappoint Wernette as president and give him a thousand-dollar-a-year raise. But everyone knew the settlement had not been an amicable one; unofficial reports reached the public that the regents had been unanimous in asking Wernette to resign but that he had countered with pressure of his own. Apparently he had pointed out that it was too late for him to look for another position, and if forced to do so, he would bring charges against the regents for political interference for their actions in reinstating the three suspended students. The North Central Association of Colleges and Universities, he allegedly said, would look askance at the reinstatement. So the regents knuckled under, but not for long. In January 1948, five months before Wernette's contract expired, they met and announced that Tom Popejoy, comptroller of the university, would be the president in June. Another autocrat had been replaced.

The new president was ready to exert strong leadership, but he was more inclined than his predecessor to work with those around him. His background and experience provided him with an abundance of local contacts and good will. Born in Raton, New Mexico, in 1902, he had studied at the University of New Mexico and gained bachelor's and master's degrees there. In his undergraduate days he had been a star halfback; he was still a very good amateur golfer. In 1925 he had joined the economics department as an instructor, and ten years later he had been promoted to assistant to the president. He had been made comptroller in 1937, a post he had held ever since except for several leaves of absence to serve in federal government positions. In addition to his university responsibilities, he was a member of the Chamber of Commerce Board of Directors, the Rotary Club and the Albuquerque Country Club,[280] and his gregariousness was to serve him and the university well in later years.

The Albuquerque Public Schools system was considerably more placid during these years, but in 1956, when John Milne, the superintendent for the past forty-five years, stepped down, he too was replaced by a slightly less forceful leader. During his long tenure in office he had exercised almost dictatorial authority over his underlings, and in 1949, when the city and county systems had consolidated,[281] he had expanded his hegemony. When he retired, he left to Dr. Charles Spain, the new superintendent, a staff and administrative structure accustomed to looking to the head man for all important decisions.

Dr. Spain had a more educated and cosmopolitan background than Milne. Born in Huntingdon, Tennessee, he had attended George Peabody

College for Teachers and Columbia University, where he got his doctorate. He then taught at several universities and was president of Morehead State College in Kentucky. In 1955 he was appointed dean of the College of Education at the University of New Mexico.[282] After becoming superintendent he continued his university contacts and made new ones, frequently socializing with President Popejoy, Dr. McRae, president of Sandia Corporation, and other leaders of the local intellectual and scientific establishment.

Charles Spain cultivated the appearances of democratic processes and was probably more subject to outside influences than Milne, but like Milne he liked to make decisions unilaterally. Often he would set up committees of teachers and other interested citizens to advise him on matters pertaining to allocations and then use his persuasiveness to influence these bodies in the direction he already had in mind, or, if he did not agree with the advice they gave, he would simply ignore it. One Albuquerque Public Schools principal summed up his views of Dr. Spain's method:

> Spain liked to give the teachers and the public the impression that he ran a democratic school system, but we principals knew better. Despite all of his committees and all of his talk about consulting the principals, we were all informed that when any important question arose we were to call the Superintendant. When we didn't all hell broke loose.[283]

Nevertheless, the sheer number and variety of Dr. Spain's contacts with other people made him more susceptible to public pressure than Milne. Perhaps more important, the establishment of democratic-appearing structures prepared the way for more genuinely democratic processes in later administrations.

Most of the local businesses, run by vigorously competitive entrepreneur-owners, did not alter their style of management so extensively as the public sector, but changes in the persons they did business with, in their employees, and in the regulations they had to adjust to all left an impact. One fairly representative example is the Springer Transfer Company, founded in Albuquerque in 1902 by William Springer and run with a tight hand from 1925 to 1957 by L.C. Bennet, president and one of the principal stockholders. The main activities of the company were moving, storage and providing ready-mix concrete. Bennet was adamant against unionization; to build loyalty to the company he followed such practices as bailing his employees out of jail when necessary, giving them advance pay on request, and always finding work for them in slack times. His stance lost the company many jobs requiring union labor during the postwar construction boom in Albuquerque. A competitor, Albuquerque Gravel Products, was founded in 1947, became unionized and soon passed Springer as the leading local supplier of concrete. In 1952 the company was moribund and plans were being considered for partitioning it off, but then Emmanuel Schifani was promoted to vice president. Energetic, outgoing and optimistic, Schifani influenced the firm to undertake a program of expansion. The expansion accelerated in 1957, when Schifani took over the presidency. The increased work force, however, included more union sympathizers, and the National Labor Relations Board conducted an election in 1959. The Teamsters Union and the Operating Engineers won representation. The benefits which the company had traditionally extended to its employees were immediately withdrawn, but they, glad to have their newly won power, stuck with their unions. And very likely everyone connected with the firm benefitted financially from the expansion and unionization, for now the Springer Transfer Company could bid on union jobs and further augment its slice of the market.[284]

Still another current of the times which was flowing through the workaday world, especially the professions, was the emphasis on merit and expertise. The persons with the most prestige in their professions were no longer the fighters who carved out for themselves places in the landscape and society and who left behind monuments for posterity to wonder at; rather they were the achievers who advanced human knowledge and helped make society more humane. Two figures widely admired for their accomplishments and for their humanitarianism were Dr. W.R. Lovelace and his nephew Dr. W.R. Lovelace II.

Although the two men were close and had much in common, the elder Lovelace fit more into the mold of the hardy frontiersman. Born in a log cabin on a farm near Dry Fork, Missouri, in 1883, he grew up to study at St. Louis Medical School and perform his internship at a hospital nearby. But like so many others at the time, he contracted tuberculosis, and he moved to New Mexico in 1906. Unable to find work in Albuquerque, he went to Sunnyside, New Mexico, and became a surgeon for the Lantry Sharp Construction Company and the Santa Fe Railroad. Seven years later Lovelace moved to Albuquerque, still working for the Santa Fe and joining the staff of St. Joseph Hospital and Sanatorium. He performed a delicate operation on Clinton P.

Anderson, and the two became lifelong friends. In 1922 he and Dr. Edward Lasseter, his brother-in-law, formed a partnership; the following year another surgeon joined the association and Lovelace Clinic was formed.[285]

Meanwhile his nephew Randy was growing up on his father's New Mexico ranch. As a boy he had two consuming interests, medicine and flying. During winter visits with his uncle in Albuquerque, he would accompany the doctor on his medical rounds. But aviation also attracted him; in later years he remembered vividly going to an air circus in Albuquerque while he was still in the seventh grade and trying desperately to get a ride in one of the planes. His family thwarted him then, and they exerted constant pressure on him to finish his education and get his medical degree, which he did. Nevertheless, he learned to fly and managed to combine his twin passions by specializing in aviation medicine. In 1936 he became a fellow in surgery at the Mayo Foundation at Rochester, Minnesota, and for the next several years he expanded his medical experience and horizons. When the war came in 1941, he joined the Medical Corps of the Army Air Force and made numerous combat flights over Europe to test lifesaving equipment. His most outstanding feat during the war took place while he was working with a team to develop oxygen equipment for pilots who had to bail out at high altitudes. He tested it himself by jumping out of a plane eight miles up. On the way down he lost consciousness; luckily, he recovered at about ten thousand feet and had time to open his parachute. The force of the chute popping snapped off his gloves, and his left hand was badly frostbitten. The mission was a complete success: not only had the oxygen equipment worked perfectly, but Lovelace's blacking out led to a new technique in parachute jumping, that of delaying pulling the rip cord until reaching nearly normal atmosphere. For this achievement Dr. Lovelace II was awarded the Distinguished Flying Cross.[286]

In 1946 the younger Lovelace moved to Albuquerque and joined his uncle at Lovelace Clinic. In 1947 they founded the nonprofit Lovelace Foundation for Medical Education, and they reorganized the clinic into a voluntary association of sixteen physicians. Two years later they built new clinic facilities in southeast Albuquerque near the military bases and the Veterans Administration Hospital. The clinic, the foundation and Bataan Memorial Hospital, erected a few years later, were all on land donated by the elder Lovelace. In subsequent years this medical complex included some of the outstanding facilities in the nation for treatment and research in the fields of aviation and nuclear medicine. Dr. W.R. Lovelace provided most of the administrative leadership, serving as chairman of the Board of Governors for Lovelace Clinic and as a member of the Board of Trustees for Lovelace Foundation,[287] while Dr. W.R. Lovelace II spearheaded the research. It was the nephew whose achievements and vision gave the medical complex most of its vitality. In 1951 he was appointed chairman of the Armed Forces Medical Policy Council,[288] and in 1955 he was given the Exceptional Service Award by the U.S. Air Force for his wartime service and for "exceptionally meritorious service to the United States from 1946 to 1955."[289] His growing list of honors reflected glory on the discipline, dedication and expertise his career exemplified.

As occupational practices shifted, so did the ideologies by which working people justified what they did. In the 1953 commencement address at the University of New Mexico, Walter R. Bimson, a prominent Arizona banker, presented what he called the new American business philosophy, a change from one of "take" to one of "serve." Speaking in pleasant weather to a crowd of more than five thousand at Zimmerman Field, he told of the increasing social obligations of management and ownership. "An important point in all this change," he said, "is that by use of traditional democratic processes we have almost done away with the old concept that the owner of property and wealth has a right to use his property any way he pleases." Bimson then enumerated seven new factors which he regarded as characteristic of contemporary American business. First was its voluntary nature: the businessman could no longer force his employees to work for him on his terms alone, nor could he use monopolistic practices to force customers to buy his product. Second, free competition was the rule. Third, there was the "watchful eye of government" to regulate business. His other points included the growth of scientific research, of wide ownership of business, of free exchange of information, and of wider distribution of income. He closed, however, by telling his audience to hold fast to the traditional values of self-reliance, resourcefulness and adventure in their pursuits. Perhaps there were conflicts which Bimson did not recognize between these old values and the new code, maybe what he was describing was truer for other places than for Albuquerque, possibly he was presenting a slightly utopian view of American business, but his speech struck a resonant note among the graduating seniors and their guests.[290]

Albuquerque's Postwar Building Boom

Even the industries which were inherently fragmented, competitive and risky were affected by the new trends in the business world and society at large. In the years following the Second World War the construction industry was booming lustily, and hundreds of small operators vied energetically with one another for the large profits they could see in their minds' eyes. But as the rigors of competition weeded out the less capable businessmen, as the builders undertook bigger projects requiring greater capitalization, as the hand of government regulation grew more forceful, and as the appearance and nature of the urban landscape altered, this segment of the private sector also changed. The roughhewn individualists of the early postwar years had to work with larger numbers of people and to be sensitive to the increasing interrelatedness of modern urban society if they were to remain successful.

Throughout these years the builders were blessed with an expansive market. The swelling population made the demand for new homes intense, and miles of empty mesa land were available to be developed. The vast majority of the new houses was erected in the eastern side of the city, particularly the northeast quadrant, for not only were thousands of jobs opening up around there—at the University of New Mexico, at Sandia Corporation, at the military bases and at related businesses, but also the area included large tracts of land to which the owners had clear title unfettered by the complications of multiple ownership and land grant tangles. Rising costs and expectations pushed the prices steadily upward. A typical new five-room house, the kind of home that was the most sought after at this time, had sold for $4,000 to $4,500 before the war; in 1947 the going price for such a home was $7,500 to $8,500.[291] By the late fifties the market was more diversified, but fairly representative was an addition to Princess Jeanne Park announced in 1958 with three- and four-bedroom houses to sell for $10,900 to $16,000.[292] The FHA interest rate edged up more slowly—from 4 1/2 percent in 1945 to 5 3/4 percent in late 1959.[293] The rising expenses discouraged few from pursuing the attainable dream of owning their own homes, and the increased costs and prices meant greater profits for the builders.

Of the many builders who plunged into the market to take advantage of the ripe conditions and to seek their fortunes, a few met with outstanding success. Overshadowing all the others and exemplifying to the highest degree what it took to thrive in this milieu were three men—Dale Bellamah, Ed Snow and Sam Hoffman.

Dale J. Bellamah, a man of enormous energy, was born in a tiny New Mexico town, San Juan (since renamed Veguita), in 1915, the son of Lebanese parents. When Dale was four, his father, having trouble getting a teaching position because of language difficulties, moved the family to Barelas, a poor community in the Albuquerque area, and became a grocer. The mother died, the father became an invalid, and so at the age of twelve young Dale left school to deliver telegrams for Western Union. After a few more odd jobs he went to work, at age fourteen, at the Santa Fe Railroad shops. His father soon died, but Bellamah always remembered the fact that he was descended from Lebanese royalty, and pride fueled his drive for success. He took correspondence courses and gained a high school diploma when he was twenty-two. Then on to the University of New Mexico, where he majored in political science, made high grades and took honors in debate. Into his junior year he supported himself by working nights at the railroad shop, but then, in 1939, he married his wife Jeanne and bought a small retail liquor store, Dale's Liquors. (Not at all shy about advertising his name, in later years he named a huge tract of housing Princess Jeanne Park in honor of his wife and his own royal antecedents.) The following year he graduated.

At this time Bellamah was planning eventually to go on to law school, but the war changed his career. He entered the armed services in 1943, leaving the store for his wife to manage, and gained experience in organizing and supervising people. After the war he became convinced that Albuquerque would grow rapidly and that there was a vast market for low-to-medium-priced homes. So he sold his business in 1946 and embarked on his building career in 1947.

His start was slow, but his persistence, industry and vision sustained him. "Look at a piece of land," he was to say in later years at a national conference of home builders and land developers; "see how it is today; dream of how it could be tomorrow. If the dream is right, buy it." The first year he built three houses in the southeast heights, the next year he built twenty-four, and the next over a hundred. Then in 1950 he purchased a substantial acreage in the northeast heights from Oscar Love, vice president of the Albuquerque National Bank, and established the Bellamah Addition. By now the biggest housing boom in Albuquerque history was well underway.[294]

The youngest of these three builders was Edward H. Snow, born in Ottumwa, Iowa, in 1923. While he was still an infant, his father, a home builder himself, moved to Albuquerque. The elder Snow died when the son was fifteen, but Ed went on to graduate from Albuquerque High School and to enroll at the University of New Mexico. When the war came he quit school and enlisted, fighting with the infantry in France and Germany. Afterwards he resumed his college studies and graduated with a degree in engineering. Then in 1947, at the age of twenty-five, he launched his career as a builder and in the next few years became a dominant figure in the Albuquerque housing industry.[295]

The third of the big Albuquerque builders, Sam Hoffman, was the oldest and had come from the farthest away. Born in 1900 in Polish Russia, he emigrated to this country following the Russian Revolution and worked as a plasterer in Detroit. A few years later he moved to Chicago and operated a truck line. In 1946, tired of the cold weather, he borrowed five hundred dollars, bought a truck, loaded up his family and belongings and headed for Phoenix, Arizona, looking for work and sunshine. There he bought a lot and built himself a house, only to sell it when a buyer offered him a good price. He repeated the process, his enterprise mushroomed into a full-scale building and real estate operation, and thus was born F & S Construction Company. The initials refer to father and son, for his son Jack, an accountant, was in business with him. Keeping his central office in Phoenix, a small, bare room which he shared with his son, two desks and a few chairs, he began constructing houses in Albuquerque in the late forties and straightaway became a force to be reckoned with.[296]

From the time of their entry into the local housing market, Hoffman, Snow and Bellamah competed vigorously among themselves and with the lesser builders in the race to be preeminent in the industry. Thousands of houses were put up each year; space in these pages, far less bountiful than the undeveloped land in Albuquerque at this time, permits treatment of only a few of the highlights. In 1950 Sam Hoffman's Hoffmantown in the northeast corner of the city was being developed. By early 1952, it was the largest suburban community in New Mexico, including about 800 new homes and 2,800 residents.[297] In 1953 Ed Snow bought a quarter section from the university just east of Hoffmantown, built 500 houses on the land, and called it Snow Heights. The same year he bought 640 acres just to the northeast from Dr. W.R.

Lovelace for a price estimated at over one million dollars in what was probably the largest single land transaction in the city's history up to that time.[298] Within a few months he got underway on a $10 million building project, subdividing 320 acres of his new acquisition and calling it Snow Heights Addition Numbers 2 and 3.[299] Not to be outdone, in 1954 Dale Bellamah started Princess Jeanne Park, a 1600-home, $15 million project on a 327-acre tract. The development would include its own recreation area with a large swimming pool, bathhouses, a full-time lifeguard, tennis courts, picnic grounds and over three hundred shade trees. Buyers had only two styles to choose between—Pueblo and Colorock—and three sizes in each style—two, three or four bedroom—for a total of six models, but each house had its own garbage disposal.[300]

As the residential areas of the city expanded, the distribution of businesses also shifted. In the late 1940s business activity was still very much centered in the downtown area, and various firms jostled for advantageous locations. Because of the limitations of space in the district, there was a tendency for big businesses to expand and push out smaller ones. In 1947 the State Theatre was built, displacing the Mesa Theatre and Owl Drug Company, and Stromberg's Men's Store expanded its facilities to take over an entire building and push out Everitt Jewelry Store.[301] Two years later Penney's opened a new four-story store on the same site its old building had occupied.[302]

Gradually, however, greater numbers of businessmen came to see the advantages of moving east to where the people were. With the increasing dispersal of the population and the worsening traffic congestion, the central business district was becoming less accessible to most of the citizens. Several miles eastward land was cheaper and more easily available. An entrepreneur or group of entrepreneurs could even, if it had the resources, obtain a substantial piece of land and locate on it businesses of its own choosing; such flexibility was harder to come by in the crowded downtown.

The main roads of the city, especially the eastern part of Central Avenue, began rapidly to accumulate clusters and strips of all kinds of commercial establishments. For some years there had been a flourishing group of businesses just east of the university, about two miles up Central from the downtown area. Then in 1947 R.B. Waggoman opened the Nob Hill Center, a one-story U-shaped building a few blocks to the east. This first of all shopping centers in Albuquerque was dubbed "Waggoman's Folly" by its early detractors, and it was small by later standards, including only forty-four thousand square feet and twenty-one businesses.[303] In quick succession more businesses began to line up still further eastward.

The strip commercial development along the chief thoroughfares, however, suited the convenience of the average retail shopper little better than did the congested downtown. Shopping centers like Nob Hill combined easy access with the handiness of a central location for one-stop shopping, and their success prompted the builders to include similar centers in the new housing developments. In 1949 a ten-store center was established in the Bel-Air subdivision, begun two years earlier.[304] In 1951 a 450-foot-long building was erected in the heart of Hoffmantown to serve as a shopping center for that community, and it was later expanded.[305] Neighborhood shopping centers were soon under construction to serve several other large developments, including Bellamah's Princess Jeanne Park.[306]

At the same time that the builders were influencing and being influenced by the evolving residential and shopping patterns, local government was extending its authority into the industry. From the beginning of the housing boom, civic leaders had shown concern about protecting the city and the people from the more glaring of the pitfalls of unregulated building; and as some of the construction companies and the subdivisions they were developing got bigger and bigger, city government took steps to counteract the growing power of the big builders. In September of 1948 Erna Fergusson proposed in a talk before the Downtown Lions Club long-term planning for the cities of New Mexico.[307] In December the City Commission established a seven-member Advisory Planning Board with instructions to prepare a master plan.[308] At this point the building interests wielded considerable influence at city hall: the first members of the board included Hugh B. Woodward, an attorney and the president of a real estate management corporation; Marvin C. May, an engineering professor at the University of New Mexico who also did private engineering work; S.Y. Jackson, head of the Albuquerque Public School Board (the Albuquerque Public Schools had extensive land holdings); and Dale Bellamah.[309] At the first meeting S.Y. Jackson was elected chairman,[310] and Edmund Engel was soon hired as city planning engineer.

The Planning Board gradually accumulated more power. In 1949 it questioned the lack of playgrounds in a proposed subdivision submitted by W.J. Wagner of Reliable Homes, Inc., and the City Commission demanded and received a gift to the city of five acres for a park before it approved the subdivision plat.[311] This requirement of a portion of land for parks before a subdivision would be approved became city policy from then on. In April of the next year the Planning Board issued a "tentative guide for subdivision design," consisting of minimum specifications for new streets and residential lots.[312] In June an ordinance was passed giving the City Planning Commission initial jurisdiction over the subdivision and platting of land in the city; its powers were now no longer merely advisory.[313] The Planning Commission required topographical maps for every proposed plat of more than five acres, and the planners checked to determine whether the drainage would be adequate and whether residential lots had been placed in arroyos or drainage ways.[314]

The members of the Planning Commission were committed to improving the minimum standards for subdivisions, but with their ties to the real estate and construction industries they were reluctant to impose heavy financial burdens on the developers. In 1952 they unanimously disapproved a proposed ordinance amendment requiring builders to pay for the installation of utilities and paving in new subdivisions. Professor Marvin May called the measure "an infringement on a man's right to develop his own property."[315] The City Commission, however, painfully aware of the shortfall of money in the city coffers and of water for the people, did not hesitate to move in that direction. In December of the same year, it temporarily adopted the policy of requiring developers to pay for block-to-block water and sewer extensions within subdivisions, and a few months later it made the policy permanent.[316] Further on into 1953 the City Commission passed an ordinance forcing builders to pay part of the cost of extending the large water and sewer mains out to the new housing developments, and Clyde Tingley pointed out that this would make it more advantageous to develop land closer to the city's center and would reduce "checkerboard" expansion.[317] The commission voted in 1955 to require builders to foot the bill for paving side streets as well as frontage streets in their new subdivisions.[318] These regulations had the cumulative effect of making new homes more expensive to build and to buy.

With the urban and suburban growth in Albuquerque came the demand for a different kind of regulation, zoning. The City Planning Department inaugurated a land use survey in 1950;[319] in 1953 a comprehensive zoning ordinance was drawn up. Speaking at a public meeting sponsored by the League of Women Voters, Irvin Esenwein, member of the Zoning Commission, declared, "Zoning is necessary because persons owning land in residential areas can be hurt if there is no organized method of protecting them against undesirable developments on adjacent land."[320] The ordinance, which specified various classifications of rural, residential, commercial and manufacturing zones, was passed. Meanwhile, special treatment was in store for Old Town; that same year the City Commission voted to exclude heavy trucks from the area.[321]

As city government took a more active part in regulating land development and as the builders strove for ever more gargantuan projects, it was inevitable that new conflicts would arise. In the late 1950s several developers submitted plans for regional shopping centers considerably bigger than the neighborhood shopping centers that had up to then been built. Competition among them was keen, and it extended into the upper reaches of city government.

In early 1955 the Tijeras Place Improvement Company requested a zone change and street vacations for a proposed center near the state fairgrounds. (This area had been on the eastern edge of town in 1945, but was now well inside the city limits.) The City Commission turned the company down in September and told it that it might apply again after a shopping center ordinance had been drawn up.[322] In the meantime, Dale Bellamah entered the race. He bought 160 acres near Bel-Air, in the heart of the northeast heights, for $450,000 in May, at that time intending to use the land for another housing development.[323] But in December he announced plans to build a $6 million shopping center on the northern half of the tract. The center would include a department store. Of the 3,500,000 square feet in the area, about 600,000 would be taken up by buildings and the rest by parking, service and landscaped areas.[324] Less than a month later, Ed Snow announced he would build a $5 million shopping center in Snow Heights, also on an 80-acre tract of land. Among the businesses already committed to occupying the center were a Furr's Supermarket and a Woolworth (it would be the only Woolworth store in New Mexico outside a central business district).[325] The heat was on.

A few days later the City Commission tentatively approved the zone change for Bellamah's shopping center and instructed him that the center would have to meet the requirements of the shopping center ordinance yet to be passed. Representatives of the Tijeras Place Improvement Company were quite upset, as they had begun their negotiations a year earlier and were still awaiting approval. (The Tijeras Place shopping center was never built.) The *Albuquerque Journal* charged that little action on the proposed ordinance had been taken until Bellamah, a member of the City Planning Commission, had announced his projected shopping center. Snow needed no zone change for his center, but he too would have to abide by the requirements of the new ordinance.[326]

In the first six months of 1957, two incidents took place which were early signs of a decline in the power of the big local builders to get their own way. In March the regents of the University of New Mexico granted an 18-month option to Winthrop Rockefeller's Winrock Enterprises Inc. to lease 160 acres of university land in order to build a $7 million shopping center.[327] The land happened to be across Louisiana Boulevard, one of the main north-south streets in the northeast heights, from Bellamah's proposed center. The combined resources of a large public university and vast quantities of outside money had entered the tug of war. And in June Dale Bellamah lost his seat, which he had held for nine years, on the City Planning Commission. The Planning Commission had recommended his reappointment, but the City Commission, now dominated by the Citizens' Committee, replaced him with one of their own men.[328] The picture was getting more complicated and less susceptible to control by individuals.

The local developers did not give in easily. At a meeting of the Planning Commission, Bellamah, Snow and representatives of the Tijeras Place Improvement Company protested that it was unfair for a public institution to compete in private enterprise.[329] Several months later the Planning Commission approved the zone change for Winrock by a vote of four to two. One of those dissenting was Robert Nordhaus, who owned an interest in two other shopping centers.[330] In October 1957 the City Commission gave the zone change full approval.[331] The battle was not over, however, until eight months later, when district court ruled against a suit filed by Snow and others to block the zone change.[332]

Along with the widening range in the size of shopping centers to be found in the city came an increasing diversity in the housing market. For as Albuquerque grew, significant numbers of people with different incomes flocked in wanting new homes. Gaps appeared in the market which the mass-production building techniques of such giants as Bellamah, Snow and Hoffman could not easily reach. As a result the small builders were not swallowed up by the big to the extent that might have been expected; instead the small operators turned increasingly to whatever slices of the market they could make their own.

Two of the low-income projects were a 1,000-house enterprise on the east mesa by Horizon Homes and Adobe Acres, a smaller venture in the south valley built by San-Bar Construction Company. The Horizon Homes project, set in the northeast heights east of the more expensive Snow Heights area, was begun in 1954 and featured two- and four-bedroom houses to cost from $5,900 to $6,500.[333] By 1958, when Adobe Acres was announced, prices had risen; the houses in that tract were to fall in the $9,000 range. The land had been part of Clinton P. Anderson's farm, bought by Snow three years earlier, but that builder had decided not to develop it himself and had sold it to San-Bar.[334]

There was greater activity in the upper-income part of the spectrum, particularly toward the end of the 1950s. One of the firms that concentrated on more-costly-than-average tract housing was Broad Acres, Inc., which in early 1958 announced a 40-acre subdivision of houses most of which would cost more than $25,000.[335] Later that year Don Pravitz, vice president and general manager of the two building corporations involved, announced two projects near Four Hills Country Club, far to the east but south of Central Avenue. One would consist of 600 homes and sites to be priced from $14,000 to $25,000; the other would have 1,100 homes and sites, and each would cost more than $30,000.[336]

The ever-active Dale Bellamah hastened to join in this lucrative market. In 1958 his building firm was the sixth largest in the world,[337] but he saw no reason to slow down. Early the next year he started Bellehaven, a 160-acre project in the northeast featuring four styles to choose among, price tags ranging from $18,000 to $25,000, intercom systems in each house and an architectural control board to oversee future additions.[338] A few months later he announced plans for a development along both sides of the Rio Grande just north of the city limits. The 150-acre farm he had bought from the Dietz estate would be divided into lots from one-third acre to five acres, the prices of lots and homes would be from $25,000 to $85,000, and an architectural control committee would formulate restrictions to be followed by prospective buyers who wanted to build their own homes.[339] . . . In his quest for exclusivity and quality the builder was utilizing a private-enterprise equivalent to building codes and zoning ordinances.

The end of the decade also saw the construction of more specialized types of housing. In 1958 El Encanto of New Mexico, Inc., a nonprofit corporation organized by the New Mexico and Southern Colorado Council of Lumber and Sawmill Workers and Allied Products, started a $5 million housing project for persons sixty years of age and older. The group of buildings, including 530 dwelling units, dining and recreational facilities, and a chapel, was constructed under provisions of Title 207 of the Federal Housing Act, which had been passed to stimulate the building of housing for the elderly.[340] The following year C.R. Davis Construction Company began developing a 400-unit mobile home park.[341]

As the range of residential housing and places for shopping widened across the city and the downtown district lost some of its traditional importance, the physical layout of Albuquerque changed. To some observers it took on an aspect of sprawling chaos, yet a loose pattern was spontaneously emerging which reflected the growing interdependence of the people. Although fewer people actually went downtown very often, it remained the central focus of the city and became more a center of governmental and financial power than a shopping district. The shopping centers dispersed throughout the metropolitan area served as lesser foci, and the important streets provided for circulation from one cluster of businesses and residences to another. This gradually evolving form was natural and organic: the civic leaders and the big builders might accentuate a facet of it here and there, they might stall it in places from time to time, they might profit from it or suffer from it, but they were by no means in control of the overall phenomenon.

Early signs of the transformation of the downtown area were already in evidence. The part north of Central was still primarily a retail district, yet just to the south new office buildings were going up.[342] In 1952 John and Albert Simms announced plans to build a new Simms Building, a twelve-story skyscraper and the tallest in town, to replace their old sandstone structure erected by the Commercial Club in the 1890s.[343] In 1955 the telephone company announced it was building its new headquarters in the area.[344] And in 1957 the Bank of New Mexico, which for a long time had had its only branch on Central east of the university, made public its intention to build its main office downtown. The new edifice would be fourteen stories high and would look down at the Simms Building across the street.[345]

Outside the central business district the variety of business centers was further increasing. Some of these were simply clusters of allied business or offices which located together for convenience and mutual benefit; others were planned complexes built and owned by a single individual or group of individuals. An area about halfway between the downtown and the University of New Mexico had been for years a medical district, including St. Joseph's Sanatorium, Lukens Hospital and Regina School of Nursing north of Central and Presbyterian Sanatorium to the south. In 1950 Medical Arts Square opened up in this neighborhood; this complex of offices was owned by a corporation formed by the physicians themselves under the leadership of Dr. James Hannett, brother of the former governor A.T. Hannett.[346] That same year Lovelace Clinic moved from the First National Bank Building in the central business district to a new building of its own on the southwestern edge of town near the Veterans Administration Hospital, thereby giving impetus to a new medical district further out.[347] Bataan Memorial Hospital, built on adjoining land, opened two years later.[348] In a somewhat similar fashion, automobile dealers began to relocate in newer parts of town, where they could expand their lots and be closer to their customers. Eventually, the tendency toward clustering began to operate in areas where the convenience of the individual consumer was not a consideration. In 1957 Albuquerque got its first industrial park; another opened up the following year.[349] Wholesale outlets and manufacturing firms were beginning to avail themselves in an organized way of the same advantages of shared facilities and easy accessibility that had long been available to retail stores. The urban landscape was beginning to mirror the complexity of the levels of interaction and organization in the society at large.

Rising Affluence

Accompanying the headlong growth in business and government during this period—both making the growth possible and also being fed by it—was a leap in personal income on a scale rarely seen. Although the expansion of income had a substantial impact on the institutional structures in Albuquerque, it most directly affected the individual persons receiving it. Their levels of material welfare were abruptly boosted, and gradually their attitudes and perceptions were nudged in new directions.

Sheltered by the government money pouring into the defense-related industries, the Albuquerque economy boomed more spectacularly during the late forties and the fifties than most of the rest of the country. The seeds of the expansion had been planted during the war years, when the local economy was heated by the military bases located just outside the city limits, but scarcity of consumer goods and rationing had kept spending somewhat in check. With the advent of peace the stops were pulled out; most price restrictions were eliminated in 1946 and 1947, and pent-up capital was available at low interest rates to add to the spree. As the money poured out and recirculated at a faster rate, income and buying power shot up. From 1950 to 1960 the annual median family income in Bernalillo County rose from $3,260 to $6,252; corrected for inflation, this was a jump of 54.4 percent. And almost everyone in the society shared in this windfall: the annual median family income of those in the bottom tenth percentile rose from $922 to $2,217 during the fifties for a 93.6-percent increase in real income.[350]

How did the people of Albuquerque spend their newly acquired cash and credit? Scrutiny of retail sales statistics in the county reveals a leap in the purchasing of tangible goods which expressed their deeply rooted individualism and their drive for success. As time went on, however, and they grew more accustomed to their heightened incomes, they directed more of their spending to entertainment and creature comforts.

From the early postwar years consumers were fascinated with private automobiles. From 1948 to 1958 the automotive sector of retail sales climbed from 15.6 percent of the total to 20.2 percent, and the proportion spent at gasoline service stations from 6.0 percent to 7.6 percent.[351] New cars seemed to promise increased freedom of movement, heightened power and stylish abandon. In 1952, a representative year, the newspapers rang with phrases like "The most challenging new car you'll see for years—and years!" (Mercury), "Styled to be your pride and joy . . . powered to spoil you for any other car" (Hudson), and "Here's the big new '52 Ford . . . most powerful car in its class!"

Still more evident was the growing demand for homes—we have seen how the housing and real estate market was expanding. The percentage of occupied living units which were owned by their inhabitants rose from 56.8 in 1940 to 62.0 in 1950 to 68.3 in 1960.[352] This surge in home buying made most of the townspeople quite proud; they felt it demonstrated the strength of traditional values. "As home ownership grows," proclaimed a 1958 editorial in the *Albuquerque Journal*, "so is our democracy strengthened. A nation of home-owners won't ever do much flirting with any of the 'isms' including Communism."[353] As might have been expected, those who profited from the boom were especially enthusiastic. In 1957 the National Institute of Real Estate

Brokers set forth what it considered the reasons for buying a home rather than renting one, and the local realtors publicized these reasons. Foremost was the financial advantage of building up equity in an investment. Among the others:

> Independence: More people have started on the road to financial independence through home ownership than any other way.
>
> Thrift habits: The purchase of a home imposes beneficial obligations which encourage systematic saving.
>
> Development of Responsibility and Character: The home owner feels greater responsibility toward his dwelling and the neighborhood. Such responsibility makes the home owner a better citizen by increasing his interest in civic matters.[354]

Owning one's home also tended to reinforce a sense of self-sufficiency and rugged individualism, although on a deeper level the mass production by the big builders of vast tracts of nearly identical houses on uniform streets may actually have been an early sign of the erosion of traditional individualism.

Most of the early houses were small and austerely furnished, but the residents sought out more lavish living conditions as soon as they could afford them. In 1940 63.6 percent of all the occupied living units in the county housed one or fewer persons per room; the figure was 82.9 percent by 1960.[355] The median number of rooms per unit grew from 3.6 to 4.7 over these twenty years.[356] The amenities grew at a faster rate than the space: the proportion of dwelling units with a private bath went up from 47.5 percent in 1940 to 83.8 percent in 1960,[357] and the proportion with a telephone rose from 48.1 percent in 1945 to 75.8 percent fifteen years later.[358] In the light of the flourishing demand for more and better housing, it should be no surprise that the costs skyrocketed. The median monthly rent rose from $21 in 1940 to $80 in 1960 for an increase of 84.8 percent adjusted for inflation, and the median value of privately owned homes shot up from $1,996 to $13,000, an increase of 216.3 percent in real money.[359]

Improved material welfare and the celebration of it pervaded almost every crevice of Albuquerque life. It was even felt in such apparently unworldly spheres as religion. New and splendid church buildings were erected, and newspaper accounts described them in radiant tones.

There is a comfort and convenience about the new Temple Albert that makes it a home . . . as well as a house of God. The comfort is found in pushback chairs, soft rugs, tasteful furnishings and kindly lighting. Convenience is typified by a relationship of rooms that allows the synagogue to be expanded to suit any crowd size. [1951][360]

Dedication services for the new $75,000 Christ Methodist Church at 6200 Gibson S.E. have been set for Sunday with a key ceremony at 9 a.m. opening a full day of events. [1957][361]

Albuquerque Turns Inward

As the decade of the 1940s gave way to the 1950s, the people of Albuquerque came to devote more of their attention to individual concerns, less to social and political matters. We have seen how local politics was losing much of its drama and color, how the flamboyance of the Tingley era was supplanted by the decorous efficiency of the Citizens' Committee commissions. This atmosphere of quietness and orderliness seemed to be pervading the whole society, as the residents concentrated their energies on their jobs, their homes and their recreation, as they divided their lives into neat compartments which interfered with one another only minimally, as they turned all the more inward. Yet the people were not losing their capacity nor their appetite for emotional color, they were just finding different outlets. The worlds of the large institutions might be blandly systematic and efficient, but away from them lay rich channels for satisfaction on a more personal level.

One of the earliest signs of the inward orientation was the recrudescence of traditional values. Even though the Second World War was over, patriotism and the American way of life became all the more popular rallying points. In 1948 the Freedom Train, sponsored by the American Heritage Association, came to Albuquerque for its 123rd stop. A party of civic officials, a delegation of disabled veterans and a crowd of over seven thousand onlookers streamed through the red, white and blue cars and admired the cargo of historic documents and flags.[362] When the Korean War opened in 1950, the patriotic fervor intensified. In August the City Commission unanimously passed a resolution "asking" all city officials and employees to sign non-Communist affidavits.[363] The following month leaders were picked to spearhead the local efforts on behalf of a nationwide campaign to get signatures on a Freedom Scroll, which was inscribed as follows:

> I believe in the sacredness and dignity of the individual.
> I believe that all men derive the right to freedom equally from God.
> I pledge to resist aggression and tyranny wherever they appear on earth.
> I am proud to enlist in the Crusade for Freedom. I am proud to help make the Freedom Bell possible, to be a signer of this Declaration of Freedom, to have my name included as a permanent part of the Freedom Shrine in Berlin and to join with all the millions of men and women throughout the world who hold the cause of freedom sacred.[364]

The spirit soon filtered down to the young. At a preschool meeting of the staff of Albuquerque Public Schools in 1952, Superintendent John Milne told his people, "Do not be afraid to teach Americanism. . . . In Albuquerque we expect a good teaching job on fundamental work. . . .We also believe that the schools should take a very solid stand for our American way of life."[365] And Americanism was taught, sometimes at the request of the students themselves. In 1953 at Ernie Pyle Junior High School the students asked the ladies auxiliary of the Hugh A. Carlisle Post of the American Legion to start such a program. The ladies presented an American flag for each homeroom and some four hundred copies of the U.S. Constitution, and they initiated a series of outside speakers to talk before the Student Council. Homeroom representatives would then give fifteen-minute reports on the speeches to their classes.[366]

A related aspect of the reassertion of old values was the growing interest in religion. Organized religion was on the move: in the years following World War II religious activity and pronouncements took on the same aggressive and militant tone that characterized much of the rest of society, and as the social climate became more temperate and orderly, religion shifted in this direction. Church attendance swelled, elaborate religious buildings were erected, and Catholic parochial schools boomed—from 1948-49 to 1958-59 the enrollment in the Albuquerque area jumped from 3013 to 7743.[367]

In 1950 the Catholic Church started building a new college in the city, St. Joseph on the Rio Grande. At the ground-breaking ceremonies Archbishop Edwin V. Byrne declared that a "Godless heresy has made its diabolical way across Europe, across Asia and down to the heart of Africa." This institution, he said, would help combat the menace. Its primary objective would be to "give the students a philosophy of life based on the best thought of the greatest men that have ever lived. . . . The student [of a Catholic college] at graduation knows what is right and what is wrong, and almost as important, why certain things are right, and why certain other things are wrong. . . ."[368] Two years later the buildings were dedicated,[369] and the College of St. Joseph was ready to fill a need that many believed the University of New Mexico could not meet.

As far as the Protestants were concerned, the local religious resurgence got going in a big way when Billy Graham brought his crusade into town in November of 1952. Thousands thronged to a specially built tabernacle on East Central to hear him night after night. On one Friday night about six thousand people converged there for the largest indoor crowd in the history of Albuquerque up to that tine.[370] In the wake of that crusade many other evangelists held meetings and services, and religious columns began to appear in the newspapers. Religion became a favorite topic at luncheons and casual conversations.

Powerful as the religious impulse was during these years, it did not go unchallenged. One of the more important perceived functions of religion is to keep the people from straying too far from the accepted conventions of behavior, and behavior, especially sexual activity, was undergoing changes. During the fifties the whole society seemed to be increasingly preoccupied with sex. In 1953, for example, when Dr. Alfred Kinsey's *Sexual Behavior in the Human Female* appeared, a dry and tame treatise by later standards, it became a best seller. The local pillars of respectability counterattacked as best they could. One of the most extreme reactions came from Dr. William Wyatt, pastor of the First Baptist Church, who delivered a sermon one Sunday morning that year asserting that the book would bring about numerous divorces, undermine the American home, destroy a married couple's trust in each other, produce orphans, instability and insecurity, lead to extramarital immorality, cause juvenile delinquency, influence young people to throw away moral teachings, cause a wave of sex crimes, add to the load of social and welfare workers, help the Communists and reap a horrible harvest. He admitted he had not read the book, but he had perused a number of published reviews. His sermon was not all denunciatory, however; he told the women of this audience, "We believe in you—in your chastity, your goodness."[371]

The Catholics in the city also took stands against sexual openness. A Miss Duke City beauty contest at Ernie Pyle Beach was about to be sponsored by the Chamber of Commerce in 1952 when Archbishop Byrne sent out a pastoral letter condemning the event. The heart of the letter went as follows:

> Such beauty contests are an appeal to the baser instincts of mankind and an incentive to uncleanness in thought and action. At a time when our nation needs all the inspiration deriving from purity and morality, it is tragic that our citizens are debased and humiliated for commercial ends. Any Catholic that does participate or assist in the bathing beauty contest will not be allowed to receive the sacraments of Penance and of Holy Eucharist, and their parents or guardians fall under the same punishment.

The contest was cancelled.[372]

The sexual content of movies, though mild by later standards, was on the increase, but Catholic and Protestant spokesmen alike strived hard to stem the tide. In early 1950 the Swedish actress Ingrid Bergman precipitated a scandal when she announced she had given birth to a baby boy, and the Italian director Roberto Rossellini, to whom she was not married, was the father. The Albuquerque Ministerial Alliance asked the local movie houses to refuse to show Bergman-Rossellini pictures because such showing would "glamorize and sensationalize adultery."[373] In May 1955 the Albuquerque Committee for Juvenile Welfare was formed to campaign against movies and comic books the Catholic church considered indecent, and it acted as a local arm of the Legion of Decency.[374] A week and a half later, the showing of the Howard Hughes movie Son of Sinbad was cancelled at a downtown theater because the Legion of Decency had condemned it for containing "grossly salacious dancing and indecent costuming."[375] For the next several years that organization continued to bring pressure against local movie houses which showed films with what it regarded as an undesirable emphasis on sex.

Most varieties of behavior, however, remained relatively orderly throughout the period. As the population grew, so did the crime rate, but not enough to disturb the social foundations. Vandalism by the young was neither widespread nor costly.[376] Drug abuse was rare: in 1950 there were only twenty-three adults arrested for possession of marijuana and just six convicted,[377] and the first recorded death from a heroin overdose in Albuquerque did not occur until 1954.[378] That same year a local policeman, Frank Sjolander, was killed in a gunfight with a robbery suspect, but the entire community rallied to the side of the law. While Sjolander's killer fled on foot and joined another suspected criminal, two of his friends at the boarding house lent aid to the dead policeman's wounded partner, one of them summoning more help on the police radio. The next day six citizens applied for jobs on the police force, more than usually did so in a month; City Personnel Manager William McHugh compared the situation to the tremendous outpouring of enlistments in the armed forces immediately after the bombing of Pearl Harbor. Funds were raised for the dead officer's family, and the two fugitives were captured shortly thereafter near Isleta Pueblo as a result of a tip from an alert woman who refused to sell them food at a grocery store.[379]

Part of the reason why the people were embracing order and traditional values so fervently was that they felt they had much to be afraid of. Shortly after the outbreak of the Korean War the City Commission authorized a civil defense program for Albuquerque, to be paid for by utility companies operating locally.[380] Several women's clubs volunteered to raise money to buy equipment for air raid warnings,[381] and a number of new homes were built with sturdy basements made of steel and concrete—to serve as bomb shelters.[382] Coincidentally or otherwise, a number of unidentified flying objects were sighted over the following months, adding to the anxiety. Dr. Lincoln La Paz, head of the Meteoritic Institute at the University of New Mexico and an acknowledged authority on the subject, declared,

> Three possible explanations . . . come to mind at once. First, they may simply be an unconventional kind of fireball. Second, they may be guided missiles undergoing tests in the area which they are designed to defend. Third, they may be guided missiles of foreign origin.[383]

However most of the people regarded the mysterious objects, the sightings continued to remind them how frightened they were. A 1952 editorial in the *Albuquerque Journal* discussing the pervasive fear of another global war ended on a somber note. "We are all tired of being afraid," it went, "but fear promises to be with us for a long time."[384]

Such waves of anxiety and of emphasis on social order were by no means unprecedented in Albuquerque or in other parts of the country. They seemed to recur periodically, yet each time striking with the fresh impact of new experience and insight. One feature of the growing concern for security which actually was new, though, in degree if not in kind, was the increasing interest in looking after the poor and the infirm. If one can judge from the content of the mass media, the members of the community were becoming more sympathetic for the downtrodden and going more out of their way to help them. The newspapers carried hundreds of articles illustrating this rising feeling. In 1949, for instance, the service fraternity Alpha Phi Omega began an annual practice of holding a Toy Dance at the University of New Mexico each December to collect Christmas presents for indigent children. The price of admission was one toy, which could be bought at wholesale price in the lobby of the Student Union.[385] In 1951 airmen at Kirtland "adopted" for Father's Day boys from St. Anthony's Home for Boys. The boys to be treated were selected on the merit system.[386] The following year the Sigma Chi Fraternity at the university changed their tradition of a "Hell Week" for their pledges to a "Help Week." The freshmen spent the Saturday before their initiation doing miscellaneous odd jobs and repair work at St. Anthony's and the Good Shepherd Refuge.[387]

With the passage of time, however, more of the charitable activity was taken over by organizations set up specifically for that purpose. And as welfare activities were installed on a less personal basis, those being helped gained a little more direction over their own lives. In 1950 the Legal Aid Society was formed to provide the poor and unemployed with legal counsel. Most of the early cases involved family matters, primarily the failure of a divorced father to provide support money, and small claims. The society was financed through the Community Chest and given free office space in the county courthouse.[388]

As the city grew and more demands arose for funds for the needy, charitable organizations became more bureaucratic in order to handle the increasing load. Too many different organizations were conducting competing drives for money, and the harassed citizens were tightening their grips on their wallets and pocketbooks. In 1954 the president of the Community Chest asked City Commission Chairman Maurice Sanchez to appoint a committee to develop an Albuquerque United Fund which would make a single drive for all charitable, recreational and welfare organizations, and Sanchez agreed.[389] The committee was largely successful; an umbrella group of twenty-four participating organizations was formed by the coming together of the Community Chest and the Red Cross. On the night of November 10, 1955, twenty-five hundred Albuquerque mothers marched to collect for a mammoth fund drive.[390]

The concern for the well-being of others was not limited to the unfortunate of society; it was hoped that everybody would stay safe and sound. And with the rapid increase in the number of automobiles, especially those available to young people, traffic safety was particularly important to the citizenry. In 1951 the Junior Chamber of Commerce sponsored a series of articles in the *Journal* entitled "Safe Driving Habits." The following year the city police inaugurated an accident investigation squad,[391] and City Manager Edmund Engel organized safety committees in every city department to help reduce accidents.[392] Juvenile Court Judge Edwin Swope established a Teenage Traffic School in 1953 for young offenders to attend on Saturdays.[393] National Safe Driving Day was observed; in 1954 police with loudspeakers teamed up with girls from the public high schools handing out pamphlets donated by the Elks Club and the Junior Chamber of Commerce, and they patrolled the streets spreading their plea that the city not have a single accident that day.[394] As the decade wore on and the accident rate continued to mount, the efforts became more bureaucratized. In 1956 City Safety Director George Thompson set up a driver clinic to test employees for such individual limitations as poor reaction time and faulty vision,[395] and two years later the traffic safety committee of the Chamber of Commerce organized the Greater Albuquerque Safety Council.[396]

The declining appetite for taking risks and the overall inward orientation of the people led them to center more of their attention and activity around the home. The increase in home ownership and in the spaciousness and elegance of most residences was one indication of the heightened emphasis on home life. Another was the shifting tastes in entertainment. Movie attendance sagged, particularly at the stately downtown theaters, but the less formal neighborhood movie houses and the still more casual drive-ins became more popular. Watching television at home, however, where one could relax without worrying about impressing strangers, grew to be the favorite visual recreation. When Station KOB began making regular telecasts in 1948, the fare consisted solely of tele-transcriptions flown in from New York, and there were only about one hundred television sets in the Greater Albuquerque area.[397] Enthusiasm for the new medium grew like wildfire. Many telecasts originated locally, and in 1953 two more commercial stations took up television.[398] In

1958 even education got into the act when the University of New Mexico and the Albuquerque Public Schools undertook the joint venture of establishing and running KNME-TV.[399]

Other burgeoning activities for the stay-at-homes included listening to high-fidelity sound equipment and taking up do-it-yourself home improvement projects. The popularity of recorded music increased at all age levels. The tastes and pocketbooks of the youngsters came to dominate most of the radio music shows and the lion's share of the 45 rpm discs, but their more affluent elders also spent heavily on music. High-fidelity long playing records were developed and sold, as were better quality phonographs and components—one local hi-fi dealer estimated that his sales almost doubled for several consecutive years in the early fifties.[400] So jazz music and Broadway show tunes might compete with rock and roll blaring forth from the next room. Many of the hi-fi enthusiasts prided themselves on putting together their own equipment, and others shared in this do-it-yourself craze. Home carpentry, amateur landscaping, small-scale masonry and many other well-intentioned and often constructive activities flourished. An addition might be built onto an already-existing house; a piece of furniture might be varnished. All over America armies of husbands brandished their tools while their wives checked their first-aid kits.

Along with the increasing significance of the home in the lives of the residents came more prominence for women. During these fairly conventional years few of them were making news by breaking into previously male-dominated areas; in fact, they seldom made the headlines at all. But the quietness, the domesticity, and the interest in charity which characterized the period made it particularly amenable to the influence of women. Some observers, like the writer Philip Wylie, reacted fearfully to what they perceived as "momism" on the rampage. Their impact, however, continued to grow, particularly in the area of making institutions and people more concerned with the weak and the helpless and the ignored. Newspapers featured an increasing number of articles on subjects traditionally appealing to them, including homes, fashion and culture. More and more movies highlighted their female stars, especially in the second half of the fifties. Women as light romantic leads—Debbie Reynolds in *Tammy and the Bachelor* (1957) and Doris Day in *Pillow Talk* (1959)—as passionate and sultry sex queens—Elizabeth Taylor in *Cat on a Hot Tin Roof* (1958)—as complicated human beings with serious problems—Susan

Hayward in *I'll Cry Tomorrow* (1956) and Joanne Woodward in *The Three Faces of Eve* (1957)—and as many other notable types captured a large share of the public vision. Tame though these years were in many respects, they endowed the females of Albuquerque and elsewhere with substantial attention and glory.

The Arrival of the Youth Culture

The lives of the young people of Albuquerque were undergoing much the same sorts of changes as those of their elders. The growing emphasis on rationalism and expertise was leading them to take their studies very seriously, especially mathematics and science. But like their parents they were also coming to compartmentalize their lives: away from their classrooms and books they were developing a world of informality and entertainment. And as the decade of the fifties stretched on, this young world began to separate itself all the more from the culture of the adults.

Throughout the postwar years the whole community put a high priority on education. In 1946 the citizens approved a county school bond issue with only three votes opposing,[401] and subsequent school bonds always passed easily if not quite so overwhelmingly. The voters also gave the nonpartisan members of the school board their solid support, turning away candidates backed by political figures and special interest groups.[402] And partly as a result of the devotion to the cause of education, the educational level in the area steadily climbed. In 1940 35.2 percent of the residents of Bernalillo County twenty-five years old or older had graduated from high school; the figure was 48.6 percent in 1950 and 57.1 percent in 1960.[403] The number of students increased faster than the general population. During the 1944-45 school year there were 15,394 persons enrolled in city and county public schools grades one through twelve, and the January 1945 enrollment at the University of New Mexico Was 1,009.[404] The respective numbers for 1959-60 were 64,660 and 7,284.[405]

The fervor of public exhortations on the subject rose at a similar pace. In an article written in 1955, Eldred Harrington, director of secondary education for Albuquerque Public Schools, expressed a widely held double motivation for education—economic betterment and national defense. "People strive for economic improvement and they should do so. . . . The man must train the eye, the brain, the hands so that the horse is the servant of man rather than his

127

competitor." He went on, "Every citizen has responsibilities to his society. . . . The state and the nation also depend upon their junior citizens. Such citizens are in the great potential army upon which the nation's survival depends. When a person deserts the field of education and hides out from it he is harming his country and himself."[406] At a meeting of the Stronghurst Elementary School PTA in February 1958, R.B. McIntosh, a mechanical engineer for Sandia Corporation, emphasized the economic advantages. He said that interest in science had been hurt by the way scientists had been depicted as living in cold water flats with frosty windows, hungry, and with test tubes on the table. "They're not like that," he protested. "They dress well and get good money."[407] Most people who aired their opinions on education, however, gave national defense more emphasis than material betterment, for the students could generally be expected to look after their individual welfares. In 1956 Rear Admiral Frank O'Beirne, Commander, Air Force Special Weapons Project at Sandia Base, delivered an address in which he warned that Russia was ahead of the United States in turning out scientists and he declared that parents and teachers should encourage more high school students to take mathematics and science courses as a safeguard to the nation.[408] In January 1957, when Dr. Charles Spain was formally installed as the new superintendent of Albuquerque Public Schools, he said the schools must not lose sight of their fundamental goals, but they "should develop an educational program reflecting the need for technical, scientific and specialized skills needed in the state and nation."[409] In April the American Association of University Professors held their state meeting and came up with a specific recommendation for tightening standards, as other organizations and persons had been doing from time to time. They advocated ending athletic scholarships as a step "to restore a reasonable balance among a University's total objectives."[410] But perhaps the strongest stand for education heard in the Albuquerque area thus far came from the 1957 commencement speaker at the University of New Mexico. Dr. John W. Gardner, president of the Carnegie Foundation, announced that "the race today which does not value trained intelligence is doomed."[411]

With such pressure on them to attain academic excellence, it was no wonder that the young people came to create their own culture well insulated from the stresses of adult demands. Teenage society could offer the conscientious student the same type of retreat that a home nestled in the suburbs could provide his parents.

This world of the young took a number of years to evolve. In the late forties and early fifties the youth of Albuquerque seemed to adhere to discipline and follow authority nearly as much as the rest of the society, a few lawbreakers and other rebels notwithstanding. In 1948, for example, students at the University of New Mexico approved universal military training and the selective service by a vote of more than two to one.[412] Girls looked to their elders for advice about how to win men. The nationally syndicated column "Secrets of Charm" ran in the *Albuquerque Journal* in 1950 giving tips on grooming and behavior. A sample lead sentence: "Great charm redounds from looking natural at all times and in any situation, but it takes practice, practice, practice!"[413] At a Pan-Hellenic Luncheon for sorority members attending the University of New Mexico in 1953, authoritative counsel was issued by Michael of New York, member of the National Hairdressers and Cosmetologists of America, and Miss Jane Donnelly of the Robert Watkins School of Modeling in Old Town.[414] Even courtship was something that had to be approached with much conscientiousness and self-control.

When young people were selected for honors, the ones who made the selections were often celebrities who had no particular expertise in the field or acquaintance with Albuquerque. In 1950 the baseball pitcher Bob Feller picked Henry Whately, age twelve, as the "Outstanding Youth of Albuquerque," the winner of a contest sponsored nationally by the Popsicle Company and the Bob Feller Youth Foundation and locally by the Junior Chamber of Commerce. For his heroism in saving the life of a friend whose clothes had caught on fire, Henry was awarded a hundred-dollar savings bond, a gold medal, a certificate of merit plaque and a baseball autographed by Bob Feller.[415] Local beauty contests were frequently judged by Hollywood stars by means of photographs sent to them. The 1952 Fiesta Queen at the University of New Mexico, for example, was chosen by John Wayne from afar.[416] Great honor had to be validated from on high.

It was around this time, however, that the discipline and respect for authority began to show cracks, and the young people looked more to each other for guidance. One early signal of this trend was a panty raid at the University of New Mexico in May of 1952. Some five hundred young men swarmed around Hokona-Marron Hall and Bandelier Hall, two women's dormitories, and were met by large contingents of city, state and military police and deputy sheriffs. Rocks were thrown, tear gas was fired back and a handful of the malefactors captured, and girls crowded to the dormitory windows. "Why don't you get the militia out, you damn dogs," one of them yelled. The crowd split the police attention between the two buildings and then a few male students got into Hokona-Marron and gathered a few trophies. In the midst of all the milling around, shouting, stone throwing and raiding, a sandwich salesman was seen enthusiastically hawking his wares. City Commission Chairman Clyde Tingley was on hand too, along with a number of other officials. "I think the girls are enjoying it," he said. It reminded him, he added, of the goldfish gulping college craze of a bygone day. Finally, after the uproar had gone on for an hour and twenty minutes, Dean of Student Affairs Sherman Smith worked out an agreement by which the police would release their captives if the raid ended. An honorable truce having been reached, the excitement subsided and the crowd melted. Only the girls were disappointed at the settlement; "Chickens!" one of them called out in disgust.[417]

Over the following days disgust was also expressed from the opposing corner. Typical of most of the adult reaction was a *Journal* editorial, represented by the following excerpts:

> Have college men lost their good sense or respect for the feminine sex, or how can their behavior be explained?
>
> College administrators owe it to the people to investigate and then let the public know what is responsible for the breakdown in propriety that the nation is witnessing. . . .
>
> The director of student affairs, we fear, showed an amazing softness and lack of judgment. The rowdies should have been jailed and booked just like any other law violators and peace disturbers.[418]

University President Popejoy supported the on-the-spot agreement arrived at by Dean Smith, but otherwise his reaction was no less indignant. He issued a statement calling the raid a "disgraceful outbreak." Portions of his statement read as follows:

> The "raid" was a serious breach of the trust which the university has placed in its students. It reflects on the integrity of the entire student body. . . .
>
> The students I have been able to interview in the time at my disposal

130

have expressed deep regret that they took part in the "raid." They have been advised that any similar disturbance in the future will be dealt with severely. . . .

It is my belief that a recurrence of this deplorable incident is extremely unlikely.[419]

Nevertheless, panty raids did recur, and other signs of self-assertion by the young cropped up as well. In 1953, for example, the students at the University of New Mexico selected their own beauty queens by vote, inaugurating a practice that continued for as long as they had beauty queens. And gradually, the adult population came to be more tolerant of emerging patterns of distinctly youthful behavior.

One such pattern was their way of speaking. Youth has had its store of favorite words and phrases for a long time, but in the fifties its vocabulary was becoming more distinctive and cryptic. In 1953 a newspaper article described and translated some of the current slang. Many of the terms reflected the frenetic and unstable social environment in which the teenager found himself. If something or someone was very good, he was "nervous," "crazy," "rare," "fabulous," "cool" (extremely cool was "frozen"), or "the greatest." Suffering misfortune was being "out with the gout" or getting "the purple shaft." As a result, the teenager would be "all shook up." The opposite condition was "made in the shade." Other phrases referred to hurrying up, such as "tool it," and continuing energetically with one's present activity, "go, dad." The influence of the automobile was prominent in their speech: a car was a "mill," somebody important was a "wheel" (a popular song of the fifties contained the line, "I'm gonna be a wheel someday, I'm gonna be somebody"), and drive-in theaters, which had only come to Albuquerque since World War II, were "passion pits." The words tended to be imprecise and widely used to cover a variety of vaguely similar situations, and they acted as a kind of code to distinguish the cool teenager from his inept and unfortunate acquaintances.

Manner of dress was also important to the young, and like their language it was more informal than that of the adults although no less conventional. A teenage boy of 1953 might be a "cat" decked out in suede shoes, yellow corduroy peg pants, a narrow suede belt, sunglasses and a golf hat, or he could be a "stomper," wearing a uniform of low, western-cut blue jeans, a western shirt with the top three snaps open, a western hat and a wide tooled-leather belt with his name on the back and a big silver buckle. Girls generally wore blue jeans or frontier pants, although fiesta dresses were also popular. The nonconforming young person could be isolated at a glance.[420]

Probably the most dramatic manifestation of the development of a separate society and culture for the young during these years was their music. Right after World War II the most popular recorded songs were such all-age types as "Let It Snow, Let It Snow, Let It Snow" by Vaughn Monroe and "On the Atchison, Topeka and the Santa Fe" by Judy Garland, but every year thereafter the list of top songs became more infiltrated and dominated by teenage favorites. 1955 was a pivotal year in Albuquerque and across the country; that was the year "Rock Around the Clock" by Bill Haley and the Comets was the number one song and rock and roll was introduced. (The Albuquerque Police Department also opened its juvenile division that year.[421]) The next year Elvis Presley, the young ex-truck driver from Memphis, gyrated onto the music scene with such blockbuster hits as "Don't Be Cruel" and "Heartbreak Hotel," leaving a wake of duck-tail haircuts and sideburns to the sorrow of every parent.

Rock and roll music elicited varying responses from the people of Albuquerque, but nearly everyone had strong opinions. According to Sleepy Eyed John, a premed student, former night club operator turned disc jockey, "Rock 'n' roll does lend itself to a rather exuberant style of dancing . . . befitting a teenager . . . that allows for a letting off of steam. I don't see any evil connotations about rock 'n' roll unless you come from a family where sex is a dirty word." Youth Center Director Virginia Bedford opined, "I don't think there's anything wrong with the music, although, unfortunately, some of the lyrics are suggestive." An unidentified social worker was more negative. "The beat excites the youngsters to the point where they lose their inhibitions and sometimes their restraint," she said. "They stick in groups—and outlaw the rest of the world. The only thing they ask is that their partners—regardless of other qualifications or standards of decency—be able to rock and roll."[422] U.S. Judge Waldo Rogers was the least enthusiastic of all. On sentencing four California teenagers to eighteen months in jail apiece for interstate transportation of a stolen car, he told them, "If you have a hero, it's probably someone like Elvis Presley." He went on to say that the singer was the type "that all juvenile delinquents admire and look upon as a god."[423]

Eventually, however, most of the adults gave in and accepted the new music. In 1957 the City Recreation Department began a weekly series of Duke City Hops at the Civic Auditorium. The first was held from two to five one Sunday afternoon in late August, and it featured Al (Hurricane) Sanchez and his Night Rockers. City Commission Chairman Maurice Sanchez took part in the opening ceremony, and Rev. Charles Thigpen from the First Methodist Church gave the invocation. Teenagers were charged fifty cents admission, but parents were admitted free and encouraged to attend.[424]

Albuquerque's 250th Anniversary

In spite of the people's tendency during this period to compartmentalize their lives and to turn inward, on one occasion almost the whole of Albuquerque united in a civic festival on a scale to rival the most extravagant of the Hollywood spectaculars that were so widely popular. The year 1956 marked the 250th anniversary of the founding of the city, and the elected leaders were determined that it be celebrated in an appropriate manner. The celebration was planned for the fourth of July through the fourteenth; as the time of the festivities drew near, civic pride and enthusiastic anticipation welled throughout the metropolitan area.

Months before the actual celebration the city began getting into the spirit of the occasion. On April 13 City Commission Chairman Maurice Sanchez issued a proclamation ordering all males of shaving age to start growing beards, moustaches and sideburns in order to make the city look the way it did two hundred fifty years ago. The Dukes of Albuquerque was organized, and any beard-growing male could join and get a souvenir certificate and a large orange membership button by paying a dollar.[425] Two weeks later the women were ordered to cease wearing makeup until the end of the events.[426] The enthusiasm was dampened not at all when a researcher discovered that the men of the early 1700s were clean-shaven and grew their hair long and that the women indulged in cosmetics.[427]

After exhaustive preparation the festivities began on the night of July 3 at the fairgrounds. At seven the anniversary committee opened with speeches, and half an hour later the San Diego Naval Training Station drum and bugle corps drill team performed. Then at eight a pony express rider dressed in black and white western clothes galloped in from Santa Fe (most of the trip had been made by truck) bearing an official message from the governor. A two-hour fireworks display put on by the Hugh A. Carlisle Post of the American Legion followed.[428]

The next morning a huge Fourth of July parade marched down Central Avenue. It included elements from every period of Albuquerque's history: a horse-drawn cart with solid wooden disc wheels, a horse-drawn express wagon, Wells Fargo stage coaches, miniature Santa Fe trains, surreys, ancient cars, a nineteenth-century baby buggy and unicycles. Military color guards and bands from all over the state added pomp and color. The most elaborate floats of all carried La Reina de Albuquerque and her court and La Princessa and her attendants.[429]

That night at Zimmerman Field was presented the first showing of Enchantorama, a ninety-minute pageant of Albuquerque's past in sixteen episodes using about two thousand actors, more than fifteen hundred costumes, fifty horses and countless props. It opened with a prologue in which La Reina and La Princessa de Albuquerque, surrounded by the ladies of their courts, cadets, trumpeters, majorettes, boy scouts, girl scouts and others, welcomed visitors from all over the country. Then the Albuquerque story opened with depictions of Indian life. The Spanish Conquistadores came next on the stage, gaily bedecked and seeking gold and adventure. Colonization and Indian rebellion were presented. The audience watched spellbound as the Spanish governor and his council planned the founding of the little villa of San Francisco Xavier de Alburquerque on a shallow stretch of the Rio Grande. Then came the mountain men and the traders from the East, United States territorial status for New Mexico, and the Civil War. Early religious life and school scenes were depicted. The pace picked up again with the coming of the railroad in the 1880s, the booming of New Town, the First World War and the building of the Franciscan Hotel in the twenties. Then the Second World War and atomic research. The extravaganza concluded with a salute to the children—the hope of tomorrow—and a display of fireworks. On succeeding nights of the festival Enchantorama was again performed.[430]

The enthusiastic festivities continued. An almost continuous sequence of events occupied the city, including daily judgings of the beard-growing contest, a national baton-twirling contest, and art shows. On Saturday, July 7, the eighteenth Duke of Alburquerque, Don Beltran Osorio y Diez de Rivera, flew in with his wife from Madrid, Spain, by way of New York,[431] and the pair was greeted by a crowd of some thirty-eight hundred persons waiting in the

134

blazing sunlight. Maurice Sanchez read a proclamation making the descendent of the man for whom the city was named and his duchess honorary citizens of Albuquerque.[432] The next evening the two were special guests at a gigantic Catholic mass held at Zimmerman Field. Archbishop Byrne of Santa Fe and others conducted the service, but the principal attraction was James Francis Cardinal McIntyre from Los Angeles.[433] "Albuquerque's celebration is magnificent because it is typically American, and revival of the true American spirit is the most powerful front against Communism," he proclaimed.[434] Not to be outdone, sixty Protestant churches followed the mass with a "Procession of Faith," highlighted by tableaux, hymns and prayers. The ceremony took place beneath a ten-foot white cross and in front of a huge white replica of a Bible.[435]

Religion, patriotism, tradition; Anglo and Spanish-American; youth and age; men and women; exuberance, bigness and spectacle—all these elements and more seemed to converge in Albuquerque's biggest celebration in history. The townspeople pulled together for their anniversary festivities as perhaps they never did before or since. It was the culmination of what was happy and optimistic in Albuquerque during the period, and the enthusiasm and euphoria continued for many months afterwards.

The Natives Grow Restless

From the end of the Second World War to around the time of Albuquerque's 250th anniversary celebration in 1956, the spirit of harmony and unity had been growing stronger. The conflicts on the City Commission, citizen political activism and contentiousness in general had steadily waned. The tone of discourse in the community had become quieter and more reasonable, security and domesticity had assumed increasing importance, and people had steadily turned all the more inward. But this broad trend in the shifting mood of the people could not last forever, and soon indications began to appear of the beginnings of a reversal in the movement of the atmosphere.

How can such mood shifts by a community or a nation be explained? The underlying cause or causes lie beyond the bounds of this historical account, perhaps even outside any study limited to the examination of past human events. But we can perceive similar cyclical fluctuations extending many decades back into the past. Before the well-behaved fifties there were the intense and aggressive forties. For all the privation of the years of the Great

Depression, they were a time of reassertion of traditional values. And before them was the adventurousness of the roaring Twenties . . . the sequence of alternating moods continues. Another testimony to this pattern is the folk wisdom that this country gets involved in a major war about every twenty years. Other significant phenomena that follow a cycle of approximately twenty-two years are the sequence of drought and heavy rainfall, certain large-scale business cycles, and sunspots (actually, sunspot activity peaks twice every twenty-two years; a complete cycle lasts only about eleven). A determination of why the people seem to turn inward and then outward in such a regular periodic progression would require, at the very least, a separate study. What concerns us here is that the cycle affects the manifestations of the overall social and cultural transformation which is the subject of this work. The causes of the transformation as they have been analyzed in these pages are not related to the cycle, the transformation proceeds during both the inward-looking and the outward-looking phases, but the types of long-term changes which reach the surface and their appearances are very much influenced by the tone of the times.

The atmosphere began to shift in a new direction sometime around Albuquerque's anniversary festivities. Within a few months news events—some of them trivial, some substantially significant—began to indicate a slight rise in social turbulence. Judging from what was being carried by the news media, not only were the people slowly becoming more assertive and adventurous in their behavior, they were also growing more interested in reading and hearing about such activity. This changing mood in the community was so gradual as to be almost imperceptible, for a while at any rate, yet over the years it gathered force. The late 1950s were still relatively quiet, but they afforded glimpses and flashes on an increasingly frequent basis of the spirit of the decade to follow.

One of the most unsettling developments of the period came from the other side of the world—the Russian launching of Sputnik, the first man-made satellite to circle the earth, on October 4, 1957. The news sent shock waves across the United States; the reaction was particularly intense in Albuquerque, as a large contingent of the population worked for defense-related industries. A few days after the event Dr. Lincoln LaPaz announced that the Russian triumph posed a danger to the free world.[436] A rash of new flying saucer sightings was reported. The struggle to catch up with Russia became a common topic of anxious conversation.

Much of the local anxiety was channeled into efforts to make education more rigorous, especially scientific education. The chorus of criticism of the present educational practices, which had already been growing, rapidly intensified. Responding to the building pressure, the State School Board passed in December regulations requiring science teachers to take more science courses effective for the 1960 school year.[437] The following April the graduation requirements for the Albuquerque high schools were amended to include more mathematics and science courses.[438] Toward the end of the spring of 1958 the elementary schools adopted competitive grading systems.[439] And a number of smaller changes were made as well, including boosting faculty salaries at the University of New Mexico[440] and making the prizes at the New Mexico Science Fair bigger.[441]

How did the students take this increased pressure and limelight? Ambivalently. The competition to beat out the Russians and each other was exciting, and it gave the brighter students the opportunity to bask in the same public attention as the standout athletes. Some entered enthusiastically into the spirit of scientific inquiry. Shortly after the launching of Sputnik, for example, a rocket club was organized at Albuquerque High School, and the students fired a test shot on a nearby mesa.[442] On February 11, 1958, the 111th anniversary of the birthday of Thomas Edison, one hundred of the outstanding science and mathematics students from the Greater Albuquerque area went on a tour of Sandia Corporation. Exclaimed Mary Jo Nabors, a junior at Highland High School, "The talk was on a much higher level than what we were used to, but we understood most of it. It was just wonderful." Some other students attempted to beat a giant computer at a mathematical game. When one of the visitors tried to cheat, the machine typed back, "Okay, wiseguy," and proceeded to lecture him on the rules of the game.[443] Exhilarating as investigation into science could sometimes be, however, the pressure sometimes became a little too intense for even the most capable students, and their less well endowed compatriots had to suffer the ignominy of being overlooked. The darker side of the new developments was attested to by the widespread popularity of cruelty jokes in the schools during these months. Example: Johnny—"Mrs. Smith, can Bobby come out and play?" Mrs. Smith—"Why, you know he's a quadruple amputee." Johnny—"That's all right, we'll use him for third base."

While the residents were still worrying about Sputnik, rivalry between businessmen headquartered in the heights and those in the downtown came to a head. Ever since the Second World War a certain degree of latent antagonism had existed between these two groups, as each had wanted more attention paid to its area of the city, but most differences had been patched up in a spirit of accommodation. In August 1953 the Heights Businessmen's Association had joined the Chamber of Commerce as an affiliate, and the North Albuquerque Association had done likewise.[444] This move was in line with the general expansion of government and other institutions taking place over these years; it seemed to be part of the wave of the future. But increasing traffic congestion downtown and continuing expansion of the city to the east aggravated the differences among the groups. A formal break was made on February 7, 1958, when the Board of Directors of the Heights Businessmen's Association voted unanimously to sever ties with the Chamber of Commerce. They announced that they felt they could best serve the six hundred businessmen members east of University Avenue if the organization was independent. Moreover, they asserted, "The chamber never lived up to its agreement to give a small percentage of its dues funds to the Heights Association. The chamber never lived up to its agreement to permit the Heights Association to use a chamber employee part time."[445] In September the heights group heartily endorsed a city and county plan to move the government offices from the downtown to a site next to the civic auditorium.[446]

Early in the morning of October 7, 1958, ten girls staged a small riot at the New Mexico Girls Welfare Home, the worst such disturbance in recent years. After supper the following night, seven of the girls plus four more started running around the halls, shouting and smashing furniture, flower pots and windows. Using slivers of glass for weapons, they forced an attendant to unlock the main entrance, and they escaped.[447] All were soon captured, but the New Mexico Girls Welfare Home, which had quietly been taken for granted for years, became the object of intense public scrutiny.

On November 26 the State Fair Board, under the influence of Chairman Clyde Tingley, ousted Fair Manager Leon Harms, who had held the post ever since the first state fair in 1938, which he had helped produce while Tingley was governor. Harms said that Tingley had grown cool to him ever since some ranching and farming organizations had suggested that the new coliseum on the fairgrounds be named after the manager. As a matter of fact, the motion to accept Harms's resignation was made and passed immediately after the board voted to name the building for Tingley. The chairman was absent from the meeting because of illness, but he said he would have gone along with the majority of the board on all its decisions had he been present, and it was an honor to have the coliseum named after him.[448]

Around the middle of the next month it was announced that Tingley had ordered a red neon sign with three-foot-high letters spelling out his own name for the coliseum. The purchase, which had been authorized by the Fair Board, had been made without bids and cost $1,905. The contract specified that delivery and installation be made before December 31, the day Governor John Burroughs was to take office.[449] In March 1959 the new governor replaced Tingley on the board. On hearing the news, Clyde Tingley, who had been a member of the State Fair Board off and on for eight of the past twenty years depending on whether one of his allies held the governorship, commented, "I was fired by Tom Malry, Democrat, and by John Simms, a Democrat, because I wouldn't work politics on the fairgrounds—but I never thought I would live to be fired by a peanut vendor."[450]

Earlier that month Civic Auditorium Manager Jack Baker announced he would attempt to cancel the contracts for the remainder of the monthly teenage dances scheduled there. He said he could not control the use of liquor and narcotics at the dances "because we can't search the teenagers as they come in." Consultations with other city officials had convinced him that twenty to twenty-five policemen would be needed to patrol the dance area. "We're sitting on a keg of dynamite and some kid is going to be killed if we don't do something," he said.[451]

Late in the spring of 1959 and on into the summer, disputes raged within the County Commission, gaining that body more attention than it had had in years. Toward the end of 1958 two Democrats, Dorothy Cline and Manuel Armijo, had been elected to the commission. Dorothy Cline was made chairman, Charles Brunacini was named county manager,[452] and it looked as though Edward Balcomb, the holdover commissioner and a Republican, would have very little influence. But friction mounted that spring. In late May an apparent alliance developed among Armijo, Balcomb and Brunacini, isolating Chairman Cline. Armijo and Balcomb voted to raise Brunacini's annual salary from $9,000 to $12,000, and they praised his work enthusiastically. Miss Cline abstained from voting, saying she had not been consulted about it and questioning the wisdom of giving Brunacini the extra three thousand instead of spending it on county planning and zoning.[453] A few days later the tension seemed to abate as Miss Cline started to resign from the chairmanship and then reconsidered and Brunacini turned down the raise.[454]

The next month, however, matters became all the more roiled. The county recreation program had been one of Miss Cline's pet projects, but the district attorney questioned several purchases by the recreation department as being apparent violations of the state bidding laws. The Parks and Recreation Board defended their department, but the director, Margaret Butler, was demoted as of July 1, and she resigned effective August 15. Four of the five members of the Parks and Recreation Board resigned. At a commission meeting on June 25, Armijo and Balcomb terminated Miss Butler's employment "immediately," and Miss Cline charged the recreation program was "going down the drain." Miss Cline then demanded that Brunacini tell her what the county's personnel policies were, whereupon the manager reminded her that the county had a personnel committee, which had never made a report, and that she had appointed all the members of the committee without consulting the other commissioners. A lengthy clash between the two ensued. Armijo and Balcomb voted to reaffirm Brunacini as manager for the remainder of the commission term, and they asked Miss Cline to resign as chairman. Under a peculiar wording of the state law, they could not vote her out, and Miss Cline said she would take the request under consideration. The meeting ended on this frustrating note,[455] setting the tone for much of the rest of the term. On the last day of the month the budget was passed over Dorothy Cline's objections that it contained too little for recreation.[456] She continued as chairman, but her power was effectively thwarted.

In July another episode involving conflict between the sexes hit the news. Sue Ingersoll, a twenty-year-old beautician with red hair and brown eyes, was New Mexico's entry in the Miss Universe contest at Long Beach, California. She was also a Catholic, and while waiting in California for the contest to open, she heard from a newspaper reporter that if she participated in the contest, which involved appearing in public in a bathing suit, she and her family would be excluded from the sacraments for a period of time later to be decided. She declared she was determined to stay in the contest,[457] and a minor controversy erupted. Protestant ministers criticized the Catholic church,[458] and many people wrote Miss Ingersoll letters praising her stand.[459] But on the eve of the contest she withdrew, leaving an alternate to take her place.

Back home in Albuquerque, Sue Ingersoll explained her actions. "My main reason for staying in the contest after the controversy arose was to clarify this issue as best I could. I had a statement which I wanted to release to everyone interested . . . then when it was impossible for me to stay in the pageant and take care of this at the same time, I knew what I had to do." She then presented her prepared statement, which read as follows:

> In areas that are not clearly defined by the laws of the Church, a Catholic must in the last analysis use his conscience as his guide. A person can disagree with a bishop, realizing at the same time the necessity for the bishop to do as his own conscience bids him. I realize that in matters of church law, there is no variation. But in matters outside these absolutes—areas such as politics and bathing beauty contests—I think an individual must be guided by his own conscience.

She went on to criticize the archbishop for the way the penalty was imposed but praised him for past work he had done for the church in New Mexico.[460]

Such incidents slipped to the back of the people's minds as Albuquerque began to prepare for a very important city election that fall. Among the matters to be decided were several bond issues, including one for a proposed joint city-county government building to be constructed beside the civic auditorium. Also on the ballot were a proposal and a charter for consolidation of city and county government, an issue which had been under public consideration for at least a decade. And overshadowing these questions were the races for the City Commission and for the directorships of the Sandia Conservancy District.

The campaign over the conservancy district was highly controversial, and it did much to set the tone for the election as a whole. The main issue was what kind of flood control the citizens wanted and how much they were willing to pay for it. Flash floods struck Albuquerque every year, and they had rampaged in the area for as long as history had been recorded. The existence of floods in a region as dry and as prone to drought as central New Mexico may seem surprising, but the explanation lies in the unusual climate and geography. Although the annual rainfall was generally slight, torrential cloudbursts were not uncommon, dumping more water on the barren ground than could readily be absorbed. The Sandia Mountains to the east got much more rain than the city did; often water would rush down natural gullies or arroyos and run across the mesa toward Albuquerque, which had grown up mainly between the mountains and the river. Even the Rio Grande, somnolent most of the time, provided a threat. Once called Rio Bravo del Norte (Fierce River of the North), it had a history of dumping convulsions of water from the melting snow or sudden rainfalls in the northern part of the state into the valley which stretched through Albuquerque. Furthermore, the river had a tendency to change its course in flood times: for most of the year the slow-moving water would deposit silt, gradually raising the river bed, but when the raging current rose out of its banks it might seek a newer, lower path in which to flow.

The postwar population boom in the area had reduced the danger of floods from the river while making the arroyo floods worse. More irrigation lowered the level of the Rio Grande; more wells reduced the water table and made the land more absorbent. But the huge surge in home building led to the utilization of low-lying, flood-prone land that had earlier been left vacant. Some of the early subdividers, in fact, put up homes straddling arroyos. The growth of regulation ended most of these abuses; some problems, however, proved more stubborn. As more of the east mesa was covered by paved streets, flood waters were absorbed less and they flowed faster. The only easy alternative to using the roads for drainage ditches was to let the water back up in people's yards.[461]

It had soon became evident that an involved and expensive system of drains, drainage ditches and dams would have to be constructed to take care of the flood waters. The evolution and implementation of this ambitious project, however, was slow. The Middle Rio Grande Conservancy District had been formed in 1925[462] to handle irrigation, land reclamation, drainage and floods in the central section of the Rio Grande flood plain, but its directors disclaimed responsibility for arroyo flood control. In August 1951 the members of the City Commission, conservancy officials and representatives of several federal agencies met and decided that the problem was up to the city,[463] and later that month the City Commission voted in favor of a special conservancy district to deal with the matter.[464] The ponderous machinery for the formation of the new Sandia Conservancy District was set in motion in accordance with local political procedures and state law; the stages included a favorable report by the city's Special Arroyo Flood Committee, formal approval by the City Commission, petitions by property owners to district court, court approval, court appointment of five directors whose first job was to formulate a master plan, court approval of the plan, court naming of appraisers to determine "benefits"—amounts properties would be benefitted by the flood control construction—and to levy assessments, and, finally, actual construotion.[465]

The process had been given a boost in 1954 when the United States Congress enacted a flood control act which set aside funds for the construction of two large ditches designed by the Army Corps of Engineers for the western part of the Albuquerque heights. The new law required that a local sponsoring agency contribute part of the building cost, that it provide the necessary rights-of-way, that it make the needed alterations to existing improvements such as building bridges for roads crossing the ditches, and that the agency maintain the ditches after construction.[466] The larger of the two ditches was to begin a few blocks north of Central, at the intersection of Lomas and Stanford, where the Campus Boulevard storm sewer ended, and extend northward for about nine miles before twisting to the west to run into the Rio Grande near the community of Alameda. Over its course it would catch the water from nine different arroyos coming down from the eastern heights. The huge concrete-lined ditch, ten to twenty-five feet wide at the bottom and around six hundred feet wide at the top, was designed to carry off as much water as had been dumped by the biggest storm ever recorded in New Mexico.[467] The other ditch would begin about a mile to the west of the starting point of the north ditch and several blocks south of Central, near Roosevelt Park. It was slated to run south for about five miles, at which point it would be joined by a branch bringing in the flow from Tijeras Arroyo, and the channel would then swing west and empty into the Rio Grande south of the city. Along its course it would also catch the water from numerous gullies in the southeast heights.[468] The court-appointed directors of the Sandia Conservancy District had made these two proposed ditches the cornerstones of the overall program for flood control, which included as well such lesser projects as the construction of pumping stations and the enlargement of existing drainage ditches.[469]

Everything had gone smoothly, although more slowly than anticipated, until the appraisers made their report in September 1957.[470] Property owners in the Albuquerque heights were furious over the increased taxes they would have to pay, and most, living on the high ground themselves, saw few direct benefits to be gained. They were not impressed by the argument that subdivisions in their area had increased the runoff and therefore the flood danger to the lowlands. If flood control was a community-wide responsibility, they asked, why had not the residents on the west mesa been proportionately taxed? And almost no one liked the system of the conservancy district holding liens on their land. At a protest meeting on October 18 held at the Monroe Junior High gymnasium, thousands more showed up than could be packed in.[471] More meetings were held all over town. Clyde Tingley, chairman of the State Fair Board, attacked the levy to be charged the fair saying that he doubted the tax was constitutional since the fair was a nonprofit organization and the fairgrounds were owned by the state.[472] The worst flood of the year came on October 20[473] and dampened the uproar, but formal protests continued to be filed and court hearings were held.

When disgruntled property owners formed the Property Owners Protective Association (POPA), they made the conservancy district an important issue in local politics. This heavily financed organization ran a slate of candidates in the City Commission election of April 1958. Their three hopefuls finished right behind the three victorious Citizens' Committee candidates but garnered only about half as many votes.[474] POPA gained a significant triumph in August, however, when district court ruled that the Sandia Conservancy District would have to make a new assessment and revise its engineering plan (its current master plan had been approved by a previous district court). The court hinted that new legislation should be passed to make the directors more responsive to the will of the people. So the program of the conservancy district was delayed again.[475]

The New Mexico Legislature amended the law to make the directors of the Sandia Conservancy District elected by the people, and the stage was set for the next city election. POPA announced a full slate of candidates for the five directorships, and the Citizens' Committee, now called the Albuquerque Citizens Committee (ACC), backed a competing ticket. For the City Commission race the ACC supported its incumbents William Atkinson and Charles Lanier; POPA countered by campaigning for two men running on the Good Government ticket, James O'Toole and Orlando Ulivarri. The Property Owners Protective Association had more money, and the Albuquerque Citizens Committee had five and a half years of incumbency. The campaign was the most heated in years.

On October 6, 1959, the election was held, and the ACC suffered its first setback. POPA candidates won all five positions on the Board of Directors for the Sandia Conservancy District by margins of about two thousand votes each.[476] The City Commission race was closer, with Atkinson winning reelection but O'Toole, a practicing lawyer and retired naval commander, edging out incumbent Lanier.[477] For the first time in years a dissident voice would be heard on the commission. The city-county merger was resoundingly defeated 13,506 to 5,777; the bond issue for the proposed city-county building was voted down even more overwhelmingly.[478] The voters were restless, and they were particularly resentful of taxes and liens imposed on them against their will. Increasingly they were willing to clash with established authority.

The people's bold and tense mood was apparent in thousands of other signs of the times as well. Movies were beginning to be less conventional, especially in their treatment of sex. The nude scenes in 1958's *La Parisienne* helped make Brigitte Bardot a star and pave the way for her later, more explicit pictures. Many local citizens became concerned with the deteriorating condition of the downtown area, where once-proud structures had become dilapidated as business had fled to the suburbs and occupancy had dwindled. The *Albuquerque Journal* ran article after article every day for more than a month in late 1959 on the problems of the downtown and on how other cities were revitalizing their cores. And throughout the waning years of the fifties the young people, perhaps more sensitive than their elders to the shifting atmosphere, were taking on new interests. High school and college students were listening avidly to popularized versions of folk music, such as sung by the Kingston Trio. A vague longing for something meaningful and exciting beyond their circumscribed world was beginning to emerge.

San Felipe de Neri Church, originally built in 1706, on Old Town Plaza, Albuquerque, New Mexico, ca. 1955. Created by New Mexico Tourism Bureau. Courtesy Palace of the Governors Photo Archives (NMHM/DCA), negative number HP.2007.20.553.

Fiesta Queen and her court in procession, Old Town, New Mexico, ca. 1945. Bill Lippincott, photographer. Courtesy Palace of the Governors Photo Archives (NMHM/DCA), negative number 008608.

Exterior of Castle Huning, 1954, built in 1883. Walter Haussaman, photographer. William A. Keleher Collection (000-742-0485.tif), Center for Southwest Research, University Libraries, University of New Mexico.

Alvarado Hotel, 1970 (shortly before being razed via Urban Renewal), built in 1902. Courtesy The Albuquerque Museum Photo Archives, PA 1970.18.7.

Car and bus on Second Street, ca. 1940–1945. Cobb Memorial Photography Collection (000-119-0694.tif), Center for Southwest Research, University Libraries, University of New Mexico.

Looking west on Gold Ave. from Third St., ca. 1940–1945. Cobb Memorial Photography Collection (000-119-0696.tif), Center for Southwest Research, University Libraries, University of New Mexico.

Clyde Tingley at his desk, 1945.
Courtesy The Albuquerque Museum
Photo Archives, PA 1986.4.11.

Mrs. Clyde (Carrie) Tingley, ca.
1940–1950. Photograph by Gunion
photo studio, Albuquerque. William
A. Keleher Collection (000-742-
0332.tif), Center for Southwest
Research, University Libraries,
University of New Mexico.

Commencement. Honorary degree recipient William A. Keleher, 1946. University of New Mexico Commencement Records, 1898. (Commencement photos_12), Center for Southwest Research, University Libraries, University of New Mexico.

Commencement. Earl Lake Moulton, two unidentified women and President John Wernette, 1946. University of New Mexico Commencement Records, 1898. (Commencement photos_14), Center for Southwest Research, University Libraries, University of New Mexico.

Erna Fergusson portrait late in life. Huning-Fergusson Family Photograph Collection (000-194-0003.tif), Center for Southwest Research, University Libraries, University of New Mexico.

Nob Hill Business Center, 1950. Albuquerque Photograph Collection (986-038-0004 in Abq GF folder 5.tif), Center for Southwest Research, University Libraries, University of New Mexico.

Albuquerque Municipal Airport, Continental Airlines DC-3, 1950. Courtesy The Albuquerque Museum Photo Archives, PA 1982.180.37e.

Arrival of Duke and Duchess of Alburquerque from Spain at Albuquerque Municipal Airport for "Enchantorama" celebration, 1956. Courtesy The Albuquerque Museum Photo Archives, PA 1994.12.4.

250th Year Anniversary of Albuquerque: 1706–1956, 1956. Photograph courtesy of the Los Lunas Museum of Heritage & Arts, Montoya Family Photograph Collection.

Commencement. President Tom Popejoy awarding degree, ca. 1968. University of New Mexico Commencement Records, 1898- (Commencement photos_34), Center for Southwest Research, University Libraries, University of New Mexico.

Man with a Mission (Reies Tijerina), 1966. Nancy Tucker Pictorial Collection of Southwest Materials (000-885(3)-0003), Center for Southwest Research, University Libraries, University of New Mexico.

President Ferrel Heady walking with students, 1968. University of New Mexico Student Publications Board Records, 1939-1987 (CAMPUSSCENE_1968), Center for Southwest Research, University Libraries, University of New Mexico.

1970 student strike, group on Cornell Mall, 1970. Calvin Horn Collection (UNM student demonstration_01), Center for Southwest Research, University Libraries, University of New Mexico.

1970 student strike, Allen Cooper and William Orzen, 1970. Calvin Horn Collection (acc 108 002 001 005), Center for Southwest Research, University Libraries, University of New Mexico.

1970 student strike, National Guard troops advancing, 1970. Calvin Horn Collection (UNM student demonstration_12), Center for Southwest Research, University Libraries, University of New Mexico.

City riot in Roosevelt Park, 1971. Courtesy The Albuquerque Museum Photo Archives, PA 2012.6.2.

College of Education complex, panoramic view, 1960s. Department of Facility Planning Records, 1889. (COLLEGEOFED_27_19XX), Center for Southwest Research, University Libraries, University of New Mexico.

Health Sciences Services Building seen through bare trees, 1971. Created by Van Dorn Hooker. Department of Facility Planning Records, 1889 (HEALTHSCIENCESCENTER_1971), Center for Southwest Research, University Libraries, University of New Mexico.

Ortega Hall exterior looking southeast from Yale Mall, 1971. Department of Facility Planning Records, 1889. (ORTEGAHALL_1971), Center for Southwest Research, University Libraries, University of New Mexico.

4

YEARS OF TURBULENT CHANGE, 1960–1972

Friction in City Government

During the first half of the sixties the restless breezes of change were felt in the upper reaches of city government. Some of the city commissioners were asserting themselves into areas that had earlier been considered off limits. Ordinary citizens were also becoming more assertive, sometimes grouping together to overturn the decisions of their leaders. And in the middle was the municipal bureaucracy, ever increasing in size and becoming less susceptible to control by the pyramidal type of organizational structure long espoused by the Albuquerque Citizens Committee. A misunderstood order or an irresponsible administrator somewhere along the chain of command could create substantial havoc and resentment before word of the damage got back to the commissioners. So adjustments were made in style and procedure, and the impersonal efficiency of the middle and late fifties gave way a more spirited approach to government.

Early in 1960 newly elected City Commissioner James O'Toole showed his readiness to buck prevailing policies. In March Municipal Judge John E. Brown drew criticism from the other commissioners by openly campaigning for the Democratic nomination for the State Supreme Court. Because Brown was an elected official, he was not covered by the ordinance forbidding political activity by city employees, but the ACC commissioners felt his actions were undermining the spirit of impartiality which ought to pervade government. O'Toole, however, saw nothing wrong with the campaigning.[479] A couple of months later he clashed heatedly with Commission Chairman Maurice Sanchez over the placement of a pump site in a new subdivision. O'Toole questioned the soundness of locating the pumphouse at a point lower than the reservoir elevation, whereupon Sanchez retorted, "If we're going to engineer reservoirs and pump stations right here we might as well do away with engineers." As usual, the majority followed established procedure and supported the chief water engineer's recommendations.[480]

O'Toole got frequent support from Commissioner Clarence Davis, who had been elected in 1958 on an ACC ticket. Davis, the owner of a variety store, began to take on the role of spokesman for the small businessman.[481] In June the commission had to award a contract for eleven new trucks for the garbage department. Among the bidders were Oden Chevrolet, whose trucks had thirteen-inch clutches, which were specified by the City Purchasing Department, and Frontier Ford, which offered vehicles with twelve-inch clutches but guaranteed it would replace any clutch that failed within a year if the city could prove the failure resulted from the smaller size. When the commission majority voted to adhere strictly to the purchasing department's specifications and buy from Oden Chevrolet in spite of the fact that Frontier Ford's offer was less expensive, O'Toole and Davis protested. Davis went so far as to accuse the city staff and indirectly City Manager Engel of giving the commission false information and rigging bids.[482] Over the next several months these two commissioners continued to be openly critical of the city manager and of certain city operations, in particular the traffic department.[483]

Being skeptical of the quality of information which the city manager supplied to the City Commission, O'Toole and Davis sought out additional facts and opinions from various municipal employees. In late 1961 a scandal erupted which seemed to vindicate their suspicions. It came to light that 2,750 gallons of yellow and white traffic marking paint had been purchased for $7,782 without bids being submitted, in violation of state law. In November City Purchasing Agent W.R. Rockafellow was dismissed for "grossly irregular procedure" and charged with embezzlement.[484] (He was acquitted the following May.[485]) At a December meeting of the City Commission Bice and Sanchez called for a tightening of city purchasing procedure, Davis called for a new traffic engineer, and O'Toole asked, "If the people concerned didn't know what was going on, why didn't they know—and if they did know, why did they keep it from us?"[486]

Over the next two months repercussions from the affair led to further shake-ups in the city administration. On December 17 City Finance Director Harold Kious, who was in charge of the city's investigation of the matter, resigned under pressure. Reports circulated that Engel had charged him with "disloyalty" for supplying O'Toole and Davis with information which they had used against the city manager; Engel stated publicly that Kious had "failed in proper supervision" of his department.[487] The investigation was eventually taken over by the state auditor.[488] At an early January meeting of the City Commission City Manager Engel came up with a directive forbidding city employees to furnish individual commissioners with information. Richard Bice stressed the need for employees to be loyal to the city manager, whereupon Clarence Davis countered by saying that Engel owed the commission loyalty. Later that month Engel issued a revised directive, less stringent than the earlier one. It went as follows:

> Commissioners generally will channel offers of advice or requests for information through the city manager. It is recognized, however, that commissioners will from time to time contact employees directly. When this happens, employees should give any information requested as quickly and accurately as possible. If the advice given or the information sought by an individual commissioner relates to a matter on which the commission or the city manager may be required to act, if it could result in interruption of normal activities, or if it would be helpful to the other commissioners or the city manager, the employee should inform the city manager of the contact.[489]

Around the end of the month Curry A. Long, the head of the embattled traffic department, resigned,[490] and he was soon replaced by a former head of that department, Edwin L. Beck, who had recently become a registered engineer.[491]

It seemed that the businesslike management procedures proclaimed so enthusiastically by the ACC in the middle and late fifties were subject to breakdown. That orderliness and a scientific outlook were not enough to cope with the rising problems of Albuquerque at this time. One afternoon in late 1960 the computer which controlled the traffic lights in the downtown area went haywire, jamming traffic for about an hour. At some corners the green "WALK" signals stayed on, and obedient pedestrians freely crossed the streets at those points, the efforts of whistle-blowing police and frustrated motorists notwithstanding. One driver travelled only seven blocks in half an hour. Meanwhile electricians in the traffic engineering department were working feverishly to find out what had caused the mess, unwinding miles of wiring and removing myriads of flashing tubes and dials. They finally determined the source of the trouble—a blown-out fuse about an inch long and no wider than the diameter of a cigarette. The fuse was quickly replaced and order restored,[492] but the memory of the vulnerability and fallibility of complex systems lingered on.

Responding to recent challenges to its power and changing political conditions, the Albuquerque Citizens Committee began to alter its nature. In November of 1960 its chairman, Harry Stowers, announced that new policies and a revised constitution would be forthcoming. "Our basic principle remains unchanged," he stated. "We will continue to work for a better municipal government and to back qualified men to carry out our ideas. But we no longer will operate as a reform committee—more as a non-partisan municipal political party, following basic political activities that apply to any party. This city is growing to such a size that we know that from now on there will be organized opposition of one kind or another. The concept of a reform committee can't fill the need to fight the organized opposition." The ACC took up the practice of declaring its stands on city issues as they arose, and its membership was opened up in order to gain a wider base of popular support.[493]

In some ways the new orientation of the ACC marked a return to the political approach followed by Clyde Tingley, who had been highly adept at building and utilizing power bases. But Tingley's influence had also been based on the force of his personality, and that aspect of politics continued to wane. The former commission chairman's physical health declined as well. A little over a month after Stowers' announcement, on Christmas Eve, Clyde Tingley died of multiple causes at Bataan Memorial Hospital at the age of seventy-nine.[494] Just a few days earlier he and his wife Carrie had had sent two loads of toys to the Carrie Tingley Hospital for Crippled Children in Truth or Consequences, New Mexico, as they had done every Christmas season since its founding more than twenty years back.[495] With Tingley's death a large portion of the earthy flamboyance and style that had characterized Albuquerque politics in earlier decades left the city.

The next city election gave the ACC the opportunity to try out its new approach, and it gave the voters the chance to settle the conflict on the City Commission. The ACC candidates were Archie Westfall, operator of the University Book Store; Sam E. Brown, a real estate broker; and Luther J. Heilman, director of programming for Sandia Corporation and a civil engineer. All three had been active in community affairs, and Westfall and Brown had both served as president of the Albuquerque Chamber of Commerce. The opposition consisted of a slate led by Clarence Davis, who had split with the organization which backed him four years earlier.[496] In the course of the campaign the reorganized and enlarged ACC systematically went about tapping into long-established political alliances. Director of Maintenance and Services G.B. Robertson, who had been building up influence for years while taking care not to violate the letter of the city merit ordinance, actively supported the ACC ticket, as did such well entrenched powers in valley politics as Manuel Sanchez and Rudy Ortiz. On the other side, holdover Commissioner James O'Toole backed his ally Davis and his running mates.[497] On April 3, 1962, the three ACC candidates swamped their opposition at the polls by a margin of more than two to one. Again most of the votes for the victors came from the heights precincts,[498] and again the citizens seemed to signal that they preferred more or less orderly and efficient government.

The conduct of the new commission, however, amounted to more of a compromise between the stances of the old opposing factions than a triumph of one over the other. The commissioners moved further away from the policy of noninterference with city administration, which had been a devoutly held ACC tenet, when they established a liaison system whereby each commissioner was given the responsibility of keeping abreast of developments in different departments. Significantly, O'Toole embraced the liaison system more enthusiastically than Atkinson, the other holdover, who felt it undermined the authority of the city manager.[499] As a matter of fact, O'Toole functioned more cooperatively in the new commission than he had in the old—perhaps because of his liking for this new system, perhaps because the new chairman, Archie Westfall, was less domineering than Sanchez had been, or perhaps simply because he recognized the futility of being a lone voice of dissent.

When the time came for another city election, only two of the ten candidates for the City Commission had the backing of an organized group, and it looked as though the political harmony would continue. The ACC tapped Emmanuel Schifani, president of Springer Transfer Company, and Ralph Trigg, president of Western American Life Insurance Company, for its standard bearers.[500] Both men were active Democrats, but both took pledges to conduct themselves as commissioners in a nonpartisan manner as prescribed by the ACC. On October 8, 1963, they won handily, and once more the Albuquerque Citizens Committee had a monopoly on the City Commission. All the voting that day did not go to that organization's liking, however, for bond issues for streets, a museum and a convention center met defeat.[501]

The new commissioners lost little time making their influence felt, much to the consternation of some of their backers. While serving as master of ceremonies at a Disabled American Veterans banquet on December 10, Schifani introduced U.S. Congressman Joseph M. Montoya, who was running for the United States Senate, and the commissioner proclaimed that the people were "very fortunate" in having Montoya as a candidate.[502] Over the next several days many protested Schifani's remarks, but he issued an apology stating that he had not endorsed the candidate and he regretted that his words had been so construed.[503] This controversy died down; much more significant was the activity of Schifani and Trigg in the meetings of the City Commission. In 1964 they emerged as a minority faction, sometimes clashing openly with the other three commissioners, sometimes merely bringing a distinctly different point of view to the deliberations. In general, the newcomers seemed more concerned with the rights of the individual than the holdovers were and more ready to rock the boat. In September, for example, Ralph Trigg made the suggestion that the city garbage workers, who made $1.46 an hour, be given raises of $0.10 an hour and that, if necessary, the monthly garbage fee be hiked by $0.75. Emmanuel Schifani pointed out that local union wage scales were more than $2.00 an hour. Commissioner Sam Brown called the idea "ridiculous," said the city budget could not stand it, and implied Trigg was "grandstanding." No wage increase was passed.[504]

This term of the City Commission was marked by increased participation by the members in hiring of city personnel, an activity traditionally and legally the exclusive province of the city manager. The positions of personnel director, public works director and assistant city attorney were filled after some of the applicants had been interviewed by the commission. Said City Manager Edmund Engel, "When department heads are to be employed, I think the city commissioners should meet them," and he added that he was "definitely not" abrogating his own authority. These words of assurance did not stop some city employees from wondering whether the commission might also participate in the firing of unpopular personnel for political reasons.[505]

However, the growing assertiveness of the city commissioners did not bring them more power than before, for the voters were acting with greater independence. In an effort to increase revenues to make up for the bond issues defeated in the 1963 election, especially the bonds for new streets, the commissioners voted on December 15, 1964, to raise the city gasoline tax by half a cent a gallon effective January 1. The money would finance new road construction, mostly in the heights areas, and many citizens, in particular those who lived elsewhere and who were connected with the petroleum industry, vehemently opposed the measure. The Fair Gasoline Tax Committee was formed to conduct a drive for signatures on a petition to force a referendum. According to state law, the protesters had thirty days to collect valid signatures of at least 20 percent of the city's registered voters, and the thirty-day period would start five days after the publication of the ordinance. Thus assured by City Attorney Frank Horan that the deadline was January 22, 1965, the Fair Gasoline Tax Committee speedily went about its business of collecting names.

The number required was 21,724. On January 18 petitions containing more than 24,500 signatures were filed with the city clerk. The next day the commission met and, acting on the advice of City Attorney Horan, voted to ignore the petitions. According to Horan, he had reread the city charter over the past weekend and concluded that the thirty days had started immediately after the passage of the tax ordinance rather than five days after its publication. The deadline, he belatedly reported, had been January 15; therefore the petitions were "untimely filed."[506]

Legal action instigated by the Fair Gasoline Tax Committee quickly followed. On January 29 District Judge John McManus ruled that the referendum petitions had indeed been "timely filed," and so the city was required to proceed with the task of checking the signatures against the list of registered voters and to make plans for the referendum election. The same day Assistant City Manager Arthur Jones disclosed that he had asked representatives of the Fair Gasoline Tax Committee to watch the city people screen the petitions in order to eliminate signatures of unregistered voters.[507] The people of Albuquerque, then, had the assurance that city officials would not highhandedly throw out valid signatures as Clyde Tingley had been accused of doing in 1952, when the Fighters for Fair Fares had vainly tried to get a referendum on a bus fare increase.

More legal battles ensued, but the city was finally forced to hold the election on November 16, 1965. The voters turned out in substantially greater numbers than for the last City Commission election and ended the half-penny-a-gallon tax increase 11,734 to 10,943. Its narrow margin of defeat came from valley precincts. City Manager Engel and all the city commissioners expressed their disappointment. Showing his continuing disapproval of Engel, Commissioner Trigg said that the vote might not indicate dissatisfaction with the tax so much as with the administration at city hall.[508]

New Energy in City Politics

In the latter part of the decade of the sixties, the local political leaders strove to adjust to the changing conditions and to take advantage of them. In important ways they had less independence than their predecessors, less room for forceful action. They had to be more responsive to the demands of the ordinary citizens, who were not so docile as in earlier years. At the other end of the spectrum, the federal government was extending its funds and regulations; the city leaders also had to pay more heed in that direction than before. Nevertheless, there was still much need for leadership on the local level and much opportunity for people with the requisite abilities.

Since the most important political body in Albuquerque was the City Commission, the city election coming up in the spring of 1966 gave the people a chance to indicate what kind of leadership they preferred. It also allowed them to resolve the split on the commission, which had been growing ever since the election of Ralph Trigg and Emmanuel Schifani. The Albuquerque Citizens Committee nominated for its candidates two of the incumbent commissioners, Archie Westfall and Luther Heilman, as well as William F. Whitfield, a ranch owner and investment man.[509] The most formidable opposition consisted of the slate backed by the People's Committee for Better Government (PCBG), a group which included a number of former ACC members. Their candidates were Pete Domenici, a thirty-three-year-old lawyer with six children and an Albuquerque native;[510] John Gurule, a Spanish-American who had been born in Bosque Farms, New Mexico, was presently a foreman for the Santa Fe Railroad, and took an active part in several veterans' organizations;[511] and Harry Kinney, an engineer for Sandia Corporation and a three-time county commissioner.[512] During the campaign the ACC standard bearers were content for the most part to point to what they regarded as their successful record, and they sounded their traditional themes of continuing nonpartisan government, the merit system and the city manager system.[513] The People's Committee for Better Government ticket seemed more dynamic and progressive: they claimed they better represented the various sections of the city, they advocated more openness in government and rotating the post of chairman, they pledged they would raise the wages of the city employees, and they criticized City Manager Edmund Engel for failing to keep the commission informed on city operations. They also declared they could work better with Commissioners Trigg and Schifani,[514] and less than a month before the election the two holdovers, whose stands agreed with the PCBG candidates positions on a number of points, formally broke with the ACC and supported the opposition.[515] Around the first of April most of the labor unions in Albuquerque came out in favor of Domenici, Gurule and Kinney, the first time the locals had ever publicly endorsed candidates in a race for the City Commission.[516] The momentum of the insurgent candidates and the breadth of their support, particularly in the valley precincts, proved unstoppable: on election day, April 5, 1966, all three won easy victories, and Domenici's 14,208 votes led the pack.[517] For the first time since its founding, the Albuquerque Citizens Committee had been decisively defeated and was out of power.

The new commissioners worked as cooperatively with Trigg and Schifani as they had predicted they would, but since the holdovers had been a vociferous minority in the previous commission, the effect was the biggest change in a city administration since the ACC had taken over in 1954. Ralph Trigg was elected chairman unanimously. Six of the seven members of the Planning Commission resigned, to be replaced by citizens more in tune with the new leaders.[518] A number of important paid city officials were also ousted, including the planning director,[519] the personnel director,[520] the publications Officer,[521] and City Manager Edmund Engel, whose performance during his fourteen-year tenure in that position had been a campaign issue. Engel's removal and replacement by Maintenance and Service Director G.B. Robertson came without specific advance warning a few weeks after the election. Surprised but philosophical, the departing city manager wrote out a brief note of resignation, gathered up his ashtray, his coffee cup, his wall barometer and his other personal belongings and went home.[522] Shortly thereafter he obtained the position of special assistant to the president of New Mexico State University at Las Cruces, and a few days into his new job he was presented with a gift of appreciation from his former employees—an abstract painting by Henry, an orangutan at the Rio Grande Zoo.[523]

Commission Chairman Trigg moved energetically to impose his stamp on city government. The previous year he had declared himself in favor of a mayor system;[524] now he seemed ready to act the part even though the city charter had not been amended. Less than a month after the election he took over a carpeted office in the city hall next to City Manager G.B. Robertson's, and some nervous employees began to refer to him as "Boss Trigg."[525] They may not have needed to worry about their welfare, for the new commission soon made good its campaign promises to raise the city workers' wages.[526] Indeed, Trigg could not be faulted for penny-pinching; one of his favorite themes was that the city had to be ready to pay high salaries to attract talented people to key positions. Over the next year and a half Rex Allender was brought in to run the urban renewal program at an annual salary of $16,500;[527] Richard Wilson was hired as the new assistant city manager for $17,000, $3,000 more than his predecessor had been paid; and Reuben Ramirez was made planning director for $18,500 a year, a salary equal to that of the city manager.[528] Seeing Albuquerque's potential for impressive change, Trigg stated that, unlike the previous chairman, he would not hesitate to seek out all available federal funds to aid city development.[529] But his ambitions for the city did not meet with the success he dreamed of. An early plan for a committee of one hundred prominent businessmen to work to attract new industry to Albuquerque received an apathetic response and never got underway.[530] A year after taking over the chairmanship, Ralph Trigg admitted that the city was not moving forward as fast as he would have liked.[531]

As the time drew toward another city election, the People's Committee for Better Government was not in as strong a position politically as it had been before. For all Trigg's forcefulness, he was not overwhelmingly popular, and the United States government had not yet acted on the applications for federal funds.[532] Furthermore, little had been done to implement the pledge of making city government more responsive to all the people. The PCBG candidates for Trigg's and Schifani's positions on the City Commission were James Murphy and Howard Phillips; the ACC nominated Charles Barnhart and Word Payne. The campaign was restrained and the voting on election day, October 3, 1967, was light, but the better organized ACC carried the day. Barnhart, a lawyer-engineer, and Payne, a masonry contractor, declared they would try to work smoothly with the PCBG commissioners.[533]

Pete Domenici was elected chairman of the City Commission, and he immediately set out to make more people involved in the workings of government. At a breakfast meeting with the Chamber of Commerce two weeks after the election, he announced the creation of an Albuquerque Goals program to get the citizens' ideas on where the community should be heading and of an Airport Advisory Board, and he said a team of three city aides would work with the Chamber of Commerce and two other business-oriented groups—the Albuquerque Industrial Development Service and the Albuquerque Industrial Foundation—to help coordinate plans for bringing in new industry. His presentation was smooth and effective. He told the people present that the city commissioners "can assure you that you can look for great things for the city."[534] Indeed, good things seemed to be ready to break for Albuquerque, whether through the efforts of this commission, the previous one or the ponderous machinery of the federal government. The following month came the announcement that the metropolis had been selected to be one of the "Model Cities" as part of the national "War on Poverty," as well as the news that federal funds would also be available for leased housing for the poor.[535] In late June of 1968 the federal government approved urban renewal funds for the city amounting to around $25 million.[536] All such announcements were made with great fanfare and met enthusiastic reactions. Ever concerned with presenting the actions of city government in the most favorable light, Domenici and the other commissioners had the position of publications officer, which had been left vacant since the beginning of Trigg's chairmanship, filled in July 1968.[537]

For several years relations between the poorer neighborhoods and city government had been uneasy, and Domenici resolved to try to improve them. In August he announced a plan for the commissioners to hold gripe sessions with the various neighborhood associations in order to improve communications and to cut through the bureaucratic red tape and promise quick relief from such minor grievances as chuckholes and faulty traffic signs.[538] Sometimes the sessions were volatile as militant spokesmen tried to provoke hostile confrontations, but for the most part Domenici remained cool and articulate.[539] At a meeting at the San Jose Parish Hall in June 1969 to deal with flood problems, however, the youthful chairman showed his temper. After residents Max Carmona and Gloria Tolan read statements accusing the city of neglecting their area, Pete Domenici snapped, "I want to thank Gloria Tolan for her speech, although I know she's not bright enough to write it." Stabbing the air with a finger, he declared, "I'm not going to drop down to these meetings to discuss your problems if we're going to hear what the terrible old city hasn't done." He told the people in attendance that over the past year the city had spent $70,000 on dams and $90,000 on cleaning out drains, and that the flooding in the area had been reduced to one-sixth of what it had been the previous year. As he left to attend another meeting, many of the residents cheered him.[540]

Meanwhile, Domenici was also persuading large numbers of citizens to work on new projects which caught his imagination. Six months after it was begun, the Albuquerque Goals program was rolling along with numerous committees and subcommittees under the overall direction of former University of New Mexico President Tom Popejoy. More than three hundred people were direct participants, and plans were underway to seek out the opinions of thousands of residents across the city.[541] Ties with the university community were further strengthened when Albuquerque was awarded federal funding in January 1969 for an urban observatory, an institutional arrangement for the purpose of bringing academic expertise to bear on selected city problems.[542] In July of that year Domenici launched ACTION (All-Out Clean-Up Trash In Our Neighborhood), an intensive citywide drive to pick up debris not normally handled by the garbage department. With several businesses and other organizations donating food and the use of their equipment and with G.P. Reyes, manager of Coronado Shopping Center, coordinating the efforts, hundreds of volunteers and city workers collected almost a thousand tons of refuse over two Saturdays.[543] In these heady times, with so much energy and adventurousness at every hand, much of the citizenry was eager to follow the chairman's lead in the striving to make the city greater than it had ever been before. The City Commission approved in February 1970 the establishment of Advanced Urban Systems Corporation of Albuquerque, a nonprofit corporation funded jointly by the city and by the Albuquerque Industrial Development Service to develop new systems that might range anywhere from improved methods of garbage collection to recreation. No one knew what the corporation might accomplish, but many were hopeful that Albuquerque would pioneer broad techniques that more staid communities would eventually emulate.[544]

Over the same months that these ambitious projects were being launched, some high positions in city government were shifting. In December 1967 John Gurule relinquished his post on the City Commission to take a job out of the state,[545] and Louis Saavedra, a Spanish-American who was principal of the Albuquerque Technical-Vocational Institute, was appointed to take his place.[546] Over the next year and a half a dark side of city life and politics was exposed when Gurule and Harold K. Baker, an Albuquerque businessman, were indicted and convicted for using the U.S. mails to defraud the Santa Fe Railroad of more than $240,000 during 1966 and 1967.[547] In 1968 City Manager G.B. Robertson announced his retirement, and Richard Wilson, his assistant, was promoted to the position.[548] And in March of 1970, just about a month before the next city election, Pete Domenici turned the chairmanship of the City Commission over to Charles Barnhart. His ambition keeping apace with his growing power base, Domenici was running for governor.[549]

The Complications of City Projects

Successful as Pete Domenici and certain other leaders were in winning the support of the people, the most significant activities of local government during the 1960s were large projects beyond the control of any single person or small group. Such matters as reacquiring the airport, taking over the operation and ownership of the bus service, building a new city hall, resolving the problem of flood control and launching urban renewal took years to unfold, and along the way they involved various levels of government and numerous formal and informal groups of interested citizens. These long-term projects further extended the influence of government into areas which it had previously left alone—a trend which had been underway at least since the end of World War II. But the lengthening reach of local government was accompanied by shrinking independence. Just as the political leaders had less opportunity than before for independent forceful action, so did the local government become more dependent on the favor of outside groups and individuals. And as the political processes grew more complicated and interdependent, people came to perceive them differently. The development of an urban renewal program, for instance, was seen less as the product of a few pivotal decisions made by powerful men, more as an evolving complex of ideas, persons, bureaucratic structures and tangible accomplishments tugged to and fro by massive social forces.

One of the simpler of the city development activities of these years was getting airport land back from the U.S. Air Force. In 1949 the City Commission, its available funds depleted by the rapid expansion of municipal government in other areas, had cut back expenses by turning all but fifty-three acres of the airport land to the Air Force in return for one dollar and that branch of the service's agreement to maintain the facility. The arrangement had seemed quite satisfactory for a number of years, and the Air Force had built a new runway which served military and commercial planes alike.[550] By 1960, however, the local demand for commercial aviation had outgrown the number of nonmilitary flights permitted in the original agreement. Furthermore, city authorities wanted to build a new terminal, but without title to the land they could not qualify for a federal grant to help pay for the proposed construction. Over a number of months the City Commission and the Airport Advisory Board investigated possibilities of establishing a new airport elsewhere; all such alternatives looked prohibitively expensive. The most economical solution seemed to be to renegotiate the agreement with the Air Force, which apparently was well pleased with the way the terms presently read.[551]

Over the next two years, more as a result of luck than of good management, the matter was resolved to the city's satisfaction. Military flights were declining, and in 1961 President Kennedy decreed that a portion of Kirtland Air Force Base would be deactivated.[552] After prolonged haggling, a new agreement was reached. In December 1962 the city aviation director flew to Washington to get a quitclaim deed to approximately twelve hundred acres comprising the northwest quadrant of Kirtland Field and amounting to slightly more than half of the land earlier ceded to the military. The U.S. Air Force, now a tenant rather than an owner of this parcel of land, committed itself to pay lease money for the use of the runways and also to provide them with fire protection and crash barriers. The grant that had been sought from another branch of the United States government on numerous occasions was never obtained, but the way was clear for the city to sell $3.5 million in revenue bonds to finance construction of the new terminal and related facilities.[553]

Bus transportation in Albuquerque presented a thornier problem, since it was affected by long-term trends on which government action had little impact. As the people had grown more affluent, they had turned more to riding in private cars. As the city had grown and its central focus had become less pronounced as a result of the burgeoning shopping centers and other business areas outside of the central business district, the bus system, with its runs still going for the most part to and from the central core, had become less suited to the people's needs. Every year since the early fifties patronage had been on the decline; to keep turning a profit the Albuquerque Bus Company officials raised the fares and cut some of the emptier runs. Permission from the city, however, was required before such changes could be made, and it was not always forthcoming. Moreover, such measures tended further to reduce patronage. And still another factor eroding the company's margin was the rise in drivers' salaries during these years.

The plunging earnings soon brought the company to a desperate financial condition. For the fiscal year ending on January 31, 1960, it earned more than $81,000 in net profits; the figure sagged to less than $18,000 the next year, around $13,000 the next,[554] and a loss of nearly $24,000 in the year ending January 31, 1963.[555] In November 1963 the company gave the city notice that it would cease operations at the end of that fiscal year,[556] and the city began looking for a new proprietor to take over. When the deadline arrived and no replacement had been found, the company agreed to continue "for a reasonable time." The past fiscal year had brought a net profit of $2,386—an improvement over the preceding year but hardly a decent return on an investment of around a million. In April of 1964 the city took a six-month no-cost lease on the Albuquerque Bus Company, thus saving the firm about $17,000 in state motor vehicle license fees.[557] Finally, with no other avenue in sight, the city decided to operate the bus system on a permanent basis. On December 15, 1964, the City Commission voted to buy the buildings, buses and equipment of the company for the appraised value of $931,002 less $42,000 credit for outstanding tokens and employee vacation time, a total price of $889,002. Commissioners Trigg and Schifani voted against the measure, contending that it was unwise to buy the old equipment, but the majority felt that new buses were too expensive and that the company, which had "been gracious in allowing us time," should be treated graciously. [558]

Financial problems were not yet over, however. To pay for the transaction the city applied for a federal grant, but the U.S. Department of Labor decreed that funds could be obtained only if the City of Albuquerque agreed to enter into collective bargaining with the bus drivers, who had been unionized for years and had previously bargained with the privately held Albuquerque Bus Company. Ever since the first Albuquerque Citizens Committee city commissioners had been elected in 1954, city government had been unfriendly to public employees' unions, and a state attorney general had issued an opinion prohibiting municipalities from entering into collective bargaining agreements. Now, still reluctant to open the door to such labor negotiations but bowing to the pressure, the city obtained permissive legislation from the State Legislature.[559] In September 1965 the City Commission authorized City Manager Engel to begin collective bargaining talks with representatives of the bus workers' unions,[560] and an agreement was reached in January 1966.[561] The way was clear for getting the money for paying off the purchase of the facilities and equipment, and this time the United States government came through.[562]

Another issue that preoccupied the city fathers during the early 1960s was government office space, for fast as the metropolitan area had been growing, the city administration had expanded more swiftly. Deciding on a location for the new city hall, gathering the money to pay for it, and then building the structure proceeded much more rapidly than had been the case with the civic auditorium. But within a fairly short period of time more government bodies and citizen groups made their influence felt on the final decisions than had happened with earlier civic building projects, when a limited number of prominent citizens were able to determine the final outcome.

The biggest question regarding the proposed new city hall was where to build it. In general, persons with a power base in the heights favored a location near the civic auditorium for reasons of convenience and economy (the land there was thought to be relatively cheap), and downtown businessmen and others who favored strengthening the city's core wanted to keep it in the downtown section. After giving some consideration to a plan proposed by the architectural firm of Flatow, Moore, Bryan and Fairburn to put it in the eastern part of the downtown,[563] the City Commission voted in August 1960 for the civic auditorium area about a mile further to the east.[564] But when the city commissioners held a series of meetings with the county commissioners in order to work out plans for a joint city-county building, the members of the County Commission declared they would have nothing to do with the project unless it was built downtown. Said County Commission Chairman Gerald Cornelius, "Downtown Albuquerque is the core and the heart of the city . . . a city must have a core to have a personality."[565] The planning stalled until December 1961, when the City Commission appointed Emmanuel Schifani to head a citizens improvement committee. Over the next two months the group, which took the name the Albuquerque Growth Committee, expanded to around two hundred members, became convinced that a downtown location for the city hall was the best answer, and made recommendations for a set of bond issues totaling $18.5 million, including $1.7 million for construction of the building. The City Commission adapted all the recommendations exactly as submitted,[566] and so did the voters in the April 1962 election.

No specific site had yet been found for the city hall, and no money had been allocated to acquire the land. Those who had faith were vindicated, however, for in June an unofficial downtown group led by A.F. Potenziani, president of Mountain States Investment Corporation, pledged $100,000 to buy the property provided that it would be located in the core area.[567] A few weeks later four property owners offered the city a large downtown lot fronting on Marquette NW and extending from Fourth to Fifth; their price was the $100,000 that had been raised plus 54 acres of city-owned land in the northern heights, on Montgomery Boulevard between San Mateo and Louisiana. The city commissioners accepted the terms.[568] Meanwhile, some people were still pushing for a single structure for both the city and county. In July Dr. W.R. Lovelace urged the City and County Commissions to agree on a joint building,[569] and a week later a Chamber of Commerce committee led by Emmanuel Schifani, who was also vice president of the chamber, did likewise.[570] The County Commission gave the idea its final rejection the following month.[571] In May 1963 the county voters approved a supplemental courthouse bond issue of $725,000,[572] and soon thereafter work began on the new city hall and on renovating the old county courthouse. The two structures were separate but located near one another; soon more new buildings would rise in the area, making it in appearance and function very much the vital core of the city.

Although the city hall project followed a circuitous path and required the cooperation of a large number of people, it ran into few pitfalls along the way. Considerably more plagued with troubles was the implementation of the twin-ditch flood control system, which already had a contentious history. Some observers thought that the victory of the Property Owners Protective Association in 1959 would bring an end to the discord, for the new Board of Directors for the Sandia Conservancy District was composed of the very people who had been least happy with the system of benefits and liens. But POPA was not so sensitive to the community as one might have imagined: from the time of its founding in 1957 there had never been another meeting of the general membership,[573] and the leaders lost touch with many of the rank and file. As a result of the isolation from their constituency of the persons responsible for flood control and their continual bickering, the program was very slow getting underway.

Serious conflicts erupted shortly after the election. In December 1959 the president of POPA and five other directors resigned,[574] and less than a week later the new president resigned to be replaced by Fred Poorbaugh, the organization's first president. The losing faction maintained that the purpose of POPA had already been achieved with the election of its slate of directors to the conservancy board, whereas Poorbaugh and his backers contended that further changes were needed. "The backbone of the POPA campaign and fight," he declared, "was to keep this lien off the property. We shall continue to fight for that." Poorbaugh added, "The function of the POPA is to change the conservancy law to allow property owners the right to vote on the amount of money to be spent in any conservancy."[575] While the directors of the Sandia Conservancy District and most of the directors of POPA were pushing for these changes, a new issue of controversy arose. The district, which had been empowered since 1953 to levy a tax of six mills on property within the district, had already collected the first five mills, raising about $400,000, but by early 1960 only around $26,000 was left, so the newly elected directors voted to levy the remaining mill. The ACC denounced the move,[576] as did many of the POPA directors. Dick Smith pushed an unsuccessful move to force Fred Poorbaugh, who was also a conservancy district director, to resign from the presidency of POPA.[577]

During the course of 1961 the Sandia Conservancy District and POPA moved apart. In January the conservancy board ceased its efforts to remove the lien provision from the law and asked only for a public election on any proposed bond issue. The State Legislature soon incorporated this change into the law.[578] The directors of the board began openly to endorse the twin ditch proposal and the system of benefits assessed against property in the district, both of which plans they had opposed before their election.[579] In late July a group of POPA board members met and decided that no director of the flood control agency would be allowed to serve on the POPA board "due to the diversity of interest between the two groups." The Property Owners Protective Association was now "in favor of drainage control" but opposed to the Sandia Conservancy District.[580]

While this internecine bickering was going on, much of the responsibility for protection against arroyo flood control was gradually being shifted over to other public agencies. In April 1960 the conservancy board began negotiating with the City and County Commissions to turn over maintenance of the twin ditches, when and if they were constructed, to local government.[581] That fall the Board of Directors began the process of requesting district court to strike all proposed works except for the twin ditches from their program, and the court complied in March 1961.[582] Later that year the city government began work on several of the projects dropped from the district's program,[583] and the Small Business Administration offered low-interest loans to flood victims.[584]

On January 5, 1962, the district court stepped in and brought an end to the foot-dragging by ordering the dissolution of the Sandia Conservancy District because its plans were "not suited to the requirements" of the area. In their written opinion the judges urged the city and county to prepare an alternative plan for flood control.[585] The directors of the Sandia Conservancy District decided not to appeal the ruling, and later that month they began to wind up their official affairs.[586] For the rest of that year and most of the next, government officials scrambled to enact a viable plan in time to beat the deadline written into the 1954 Flood Control Act—November 22, 1963—after which the offer of federal money would be withdrawn if nothing had been gotten underway.[587] The New Mexico Legislature enacted a law creating a new agency, the Albuquerque Metropolitan Arroyo Flood Control Authority, and the governor appointed five temporary board members—Reginald Garcia, attorney and chairman of the board; Marvin May, civil engineer, professor at the University of New Mexico, and former member of the City Planning Commission; Mrs. J.B. McCoy, wife of a state representative; W.C. Scrivner, director of personnel at Sandia Corporation; and Bernard Swinburne, manager of a branch of the First National Bank. The new agency was empowered to impose property taxes on the land within its district in order to pay the principal and interest on bond issues to be submitted to the voters, but unlike the Sandia Conservancy District it could not place liens on the property. A special election was scheduled for August 27, 1963; at stake were the five positions on the board and a bond issue for the local share of the twin ditch construction costs, about $2.7 million. If the bonds failed, the new agency would be dissolved.[588]

The citizens turned out in record numbers for a special election and supported the bonds 15,575 to 8,009. They gave the five appointed directors margins over their opponents of more than eleven thousand votes apiece.[589] Work on the twin ditches could soon begin. The date of completion for the mammoth project was still years away, but secure in the knowledge that the overall problem of flood control was being taken care of, the City Commission could order stopgap projects, such as retention dams on arroyos, in places where there was the greatest danger of overflow. The sequence of developments which was nearing culmination had been long, circuitous and often frustrating, yet the various levels of public authority involved along the way—grass-roots citizen activism, pressure groups, municipal political parties, public elections, bodies of appointed officials at several levels, and bodies of local, state and national elected representatives of the people—had managed through their interaction to resolve the matter.

More complicated still was the evolution of urban renewal in Albuquerque. In the case of this variety of development activity, the actual meetings, votes and decisions represented only the easier part of the process. Harder to attain yet fundamentally more significant was the slow shift in values which made such a program possible.

The local beginnings of urban renewal were spearheaded by a young city employee, Vernon Doaks, who had been working in the City Health Department since 1954, the year the Federal Housing Act had been revised to provide for planning assistance and mortgage insurance. In 1959 Doaks had prepared the first housing code for the city;[590] among other strictures, it outlawed outdoor toilets.[591] The same year the New Mexico Legislature had passed enabling legislation to allow the city to begin urban renewal, the Planning Commission had established the Neighborhood Development Commission, and Doaks had been made its coordinator.[592] In 1960 the City Commission took the step of setting up an urban renewal committee.[593] Doaks and the new committee developed a program to qualify the South Broadway area—a poor residential district some six blocks long and twenty blocks deep—for federally insured mortgage loans, the City Commission approved the program,[594] and late in the year so did the Federal Housing and Home Finance Agency.[595]

From the outset enthusiasm and energy abounded. People talked as though the neighborhood were to be cured of a disease and the unwholesome structures in the area to be amputated—a typical newspaper phrase was "slum and blight clearance and prevention."[596] A clean-up drive in 1960 garnered eight hundred tons of trash. Whole buildings were ripped down. Vernon Doaks and other city workers toured the area frequently and got to know the residents on a first-name basis.[597] In the upper reaches of city government the red tape holding up the loans was being cleared away. Acting to comply with federal and state regulations requiring a local authority to administer the program, in the summer of 1961 the City Commission established an independent Urban Renewal Board with five members appointed to one-year terms.[598] Then the loans came, and houses were painted and remodeled. The city bought six acres in the neighborhood for a new park, and Piggly Wiggly purchased an entire block for a new supermarket. Fire calls in the area declined 19 percent in 1960 and another 49 percent in 1961.[599] By later standards of measurement, the effort and the expenditure in the neighborhood were quite modest, but success seemed to be at hand.

Over the next several years, however, the conservatism of the city commissioners and the suspicion with which the businessmen, particularly those in the housing and real estate industries, regarded anything they felt might reduce private initiative kept the city from undertaking more ambitious projects. In late 1961, when the Urban Renewal Agency recommended that federal funds be sought for a survey of the downtown district and the fringe residential sections, Commissioner Richard Bice declared himself in favor of deferring action until private interests had the opportunity of coming up with a redevelopment plan, and the rest of the commission agreed.[600] The election of Westfall, Brown and Heilman in 1962 tilted the City Commission decisively against extending urban renewal;[601] in July of that year the commissioners decided not to reappoint the five members of the Urban Renewal Agency to a second term, thus letting the body become defunct.[602]

The downtown still had an overabundance of old, dilapidated buildings, and the city commissioners and the businessmen of the area worked to bring them down. Fire Chief Simon Seligman, City Health Director Larry Gordon and Supervisor of Building and Inspection A.P. Garland, accompanied by their assistants, were sent on inspection tours of buildings along First Street and nearby areas. Announced City Manager Engel, "We want strict enforcement of the fire, housing and building codes." Structures were checked to determine the extent of their deficiencies, and in extreme cases the three city officials passed along recommendations of condemnation to the City Commission.[603] Economic forces also contributed to the clearance: according to one realtor in early 1963, downtown property had declined in value 50 percent over the last three years.[604] The centrifugal pull of the outlying shopping centers was hurting business. Another significant factor was the preference the professional people had for new structures, such as the Simms Building and the Bank of

New Mexico Building, where office space was at a premium, over the older structures, where occupancy sank to such low rates that it often became more profitable to demolish them. By the end of 1963, about sixty of the old buildings had come down, most without having been condemned.[605] Gaping holes emerged in the district where, not many years previously, throngs of shoppers and festive parades had enlivened the streets, and political and business alliances had been forged and broken in the once-grand hotels. Space for parked cars, woefully scarce in the late forties and fifties, became abundant as vacant areas were transformed into parking lots.

The demolition of decrepit buildings had been accomplished with a minimum of public turmoil; erecting a new complex of structures to serve the city promised to be more difficult. Undaunted, the City Commission pressed on with its efforts to get the downtown businessmen to work together to improve the district. At a commission meeting in January 1964, Chairman Archie Westfall told of his hopes and concerns for the downtown and its position in the whole metropolitan area:

> For the past year and a half or so a number of people in Albuquerque have become keenly and greatly concerned over our little condition of "sprawlitis." While we on the commission like to see the city grow and vast shopping areas spring up on the outskirts, we have always believed that the core area is, and will remain, the core area. That is what prompted us to keep our new city hall downtown where it belongs.
>
> We believe the future holds great things for us. Our confidence in downtown is going to make the North Valley a better place to have business and possibly also the South Valley. We can see that the city and the county—in the long run—are going to have to mesh together in one unit.[606]

Westfall went on to announce the formation of the eight-member Albuquerque Metropolitan Development Committee (AMDEC), headed by former City Commissioner Charles Lanier, to spearhead downtown development.[607] Like the earlier Albuquerque Growth Committee, this group, it was hoped, would serve to supplement the efforts of city government by bringing the expertise and influence of prominent business and civic leaders to bear on the problem at hand.

The powers of AMDEC, quite limited at the start, gradually grew. Its mandate was to sell and persuade, and it was vested with no legal authority and no funds. From the City Planning Department it got a number of studies on such subjects as population projections, traffic trends projected into the future, economic trends, and future business and commercial needs; these it disbursed to the some 350 downtown property owners upon request.[608] By June AMDEC had taken over responsibility for downtown development plans (which had to be fitted in with the City Planning Department's master plan for the whole metropolitan area). In working out a dispute over authority for downtown planning with the local chapter of the American Institute of Architects, it got the City Commission to appoint William E. Burk, Jr., chairman of the urban development committee of the Albuquerque branch of the organization of architects, to its ranks as a full member. But to ensure that its plans were drawn up with sufficient perspective and independence from local special interests, AMDEC decided to hire an architect-planner from outside the city to direct the program.[609] Twenty-four downtown property owners agreed to underwrite this post, and late in the year Ronald Ginn was given the assignment. Ginn was put in charge of an office, called Albuquerque-Downtown, located at the new city hall, and the planning department furnished him with technical and clerical assistance.[610] In a low-keyed fashion, AMDEC was developing muscle.

Whether it would be strong enough to overcome the obstacles in its path, primarily the pride and the long-cherished independence of many of the downtown businessmen, remained a nagging question, however. Developers sometimes tried for months to work out deals for tying together enough land for new high-rise buildings, often using binders and options and negotiating in secret, only to be stymied by a rugged individual who put an excessively high price on his parcel of land or refused to sell or lease under any conditions. Realtor C.K. Redd of Berger Briggs & Company was a frequent critic of such independence on the part of businessmen,[611] and he predicted that all attempts at voluntary redevelopment would fail because "It only takes one property owner to clobber a whole program." Redd favored federal urban renewal as the only possible way to develop the downtown. "Those boys have been at it for years and they know what they are doing. They have the authority to condemn property and this is what we need."[612] In December 1964, when approximately two hundred people gathered at the Alvarado Hotel and voiced their approval of the first phase of AMDEC's program, which called for about a year of detailed planning and preparation to implement the plans, they heard a warning from the guest speaker. Donald Knutson—contractor, developer and mortgage banker—described the success of urban renewal in his home city of Minneapolis and informed the downtown businessmen, "If you don't realize you're not competitive, you're going to die." They had better get moving and get moving cooperatively. Like Redd, Knutson assumed that federal urban renewal was the only answer because of its powers of condemnation.[613]

Throughout the following year the office of Albuquerque-Downtown worked on its grand scheme, and on January 21, 1966, a twenty-year plan for the core area was unveiled. A diamond-shaped design would be emphasized, with city, county and state buildings clustering at the northern vertex, where the city hall and the county courthouse were already located; federal buildings at the southern point, in the vicinity of the Bank of New Mexico Building and the Simms Building; a transportation center to the east at the intersection of Central and Broadway, to be called the Gateway Project; and Gateway West, consisting of an expansion of Robinson Park, around Eighth and Central. Vehicular traffic along downtown Central Avenue would be gradually cut off, transforming it into a pedestrian shopping mall, and an elevated north-south thoroughfare, Gateway Boulevard, would be constructed near the eastern edge. The plans also called for the construction of a second-story mall and designated the location of a proposed convention center, as well as pinpointing the sites for parking structures, hotels, apartment houses and an overpass across the Santa Fe Railroad tracks to connect the district with the new interstate highways. Albuquerque-Downtown suggested that assessment districts could be established to help private enterprise finance the development; no mention was made of possible federal assistance. The Downtown Association endorsed the program enthusiastically,[614] and a little later the City Commission voted to adopt it.[615] It seemed that the businessmen of the area, with a little prodding and aid from city hall, were ready to work together to implement this planners' vision.

Meanwhile, the City Commission was growing a little less cautious about urban renewal. Up to now, it had shied away from wholesale clearance projects in which the city would buy up all the land in a designated area, using the power of condemnation wherever individual owners refused to sell and tapping into federal resources to help finance the operation. Under such programs the federal government would pay two-thirds of the net cost and city government the other third, the net cost being defined as the difference between the total cost of the land, clearance, administration and site improvement and the amount received through sale to private developers.[616] Eyeing the South Broadway area, where the less ambitious program of low-cost, federally insured loans to homeowners had earlier been applied, the commissioners decided to make it a pilot project for full-scale urban renewal. A bond issue of $475,000 was drawn up to supply the city's one-third share. In the early months of 1966 the prospects for its approval looked hopeful. The opposition candidates for the City Commission—Domenici, Gurule and Kinney—endorsed the proposal.[617] But on election day the voters turned down this bond as well as one for a new city court-police station; apparently the citizens felt less enthusiastic about big government than their leaders.[618]

The new City Commission leaned more toward seeking federal aid than the previous one had done, and less toward depending on private enterprise, and during the early months of its administration the Albuquerque Metropolitan Development Committee and the Albuquerque Downtown plan languished in a state of limbo.[619] Even before the city election the plan had been in a vulnerable position. As early as 1965, when the Albuquerque Downtown office was releasing some of its preliminary designs, a local businessman had announced his intention to erect a small building on a spot earmarked for a grander use;[620] without firm backing from city hall the plan was sure to meet more formidable challenges. But the breath-taking changes offered in the plan would take enormous resources of cash, and the city commissioners pointed out that the money was just not in sight.[621]

In August they took the first step toward obtaining federal assistance by voting to set themselves up as the local urban renewal authority. Several citizens criticized them vehemently for going against the wishes of the people, who had defeated the urban renewal bond issue a few months earlier; some warned against the "perils" of "federal control"; and one man declared, "We've got to start fighting the Communists at home."[622] Undeterred by the criticism but having trouble finding time for the task, the commissioners appointed a new independent five-member Urban Renewal Board in January 1967. George Schreiber was installed as chairman, and H.L. Galles, who had served on the AMDEC, was named to the board in order to ensure continuity.[623] The following summer a director of the Urban Renewal Agency was hired, as well as a new city planning director. Plans for the prospective urban renewal project were beginning to shape up. The Albuquerque Public Schools indicated it was interested in acquiring a large parcel of land east of Broadway between Central and Lomas for a dazzling new educational complex, which would accommodate 10,000 to 12,000 students, 7500 from the immediate area and the rest attracted from all over the city. Special facilities and courses unavailable elsewhere would be offered, there would be no distinct grade levels, and adults would be encouraged to take evening classes.[624] In late September the City Commission approved the design of an overpass bringing Grand Avenue over the railroad tracks and then splitting it into a "Y" as it branched into Tijeras and Marquette in the downtown area. This scheme was different from the connecting link between the core district and the interstate highway system set forth in the Albuquerque Downtown plan, but it had the virtue of leaving unaltered the land coveted by the Albuquerque Public Schools.[625] And in November the city and APS jointly submitted a comprehensive urban renewal proposal covering the northeastern section of downtown and a number of acres to the east. In addition to the schools project and the Grand overpass, the plan called for a new police building, a new library, and several items specified in the Albuquerque Downtown plan, including parking structures and hotels. To help pay for the mammoth undertaking, some $31 million in federal money was requested.[626]

Over the following months the planning for the downtown district became more complicated as more people became involved in the decisions, but steady progress was made toward a resolution that would satisfy most of the interested parties. Less than a week after the announcement of the urban renewal proposal came the news that Albuquerque had been selected to receive Model Cities funds to help combat poverty.[627] Since the Model Cities area overlapped the urban renewal district, officials of this new program would have to be consulted. Even before Model Cities had entered the picture, responsibility for downtown development had been shared by the Urban Renewal Agency, the City Planning Department and the Metropolitan Transportation Department, not to mention the downtown businessmen and Max Flatow, who had been engaged as an architectural and planning consultant. In the confusion of competing bureaucracies and designs for the future, it was hardly surprising that a number of persons frequently got upset;[628] signs that the development plan was moving toward its goal, however, helped soothe

the frayed tempers. In early 1967 some private developers made preliminary arrangements for a convention center well to the east of the core district. The backers of downtown development wanted to put the facility somewhere in the city's center, as proposed in the Albuquerque Downtown plan.[629] In April 1968 the question was settled when City Commission Chairman Pete Domenici announced that the convention center had been incorporated into the downtown urban renewal program; with the likelihood of federal funds to help with the project, opposition to the central location dissolved.[630] And in August came the eagerly awaited word that the request for urban renewal funds had been approved. The $31 million had been reduced to around $25 million, as the educational complex had not been accepted as a noncash credit toward the local share of the total, but there remained the strong possibility that that money could be obtained at a later time through different channels. The city leaders were exultant. As Pete Domenici strode out of City Manager Robertson's office with the news, he kept repeating, "Holy Moses, this is great. Holy Moses, this is incredible."[631]

Great as the news was, it also led to further complications as federal guidelines and recently aroused citizens made the process of arriving at the final decisions regarding this urban renewal effort, now called the Tijeras Project, all the more involved. The only part of the project area where people had homes at this time was the section bounded by Broadway, Central, Interstate-25 and Lomas, and this was part of the Model Cities area. It was also the land earmarked for the large educational complex, but some of the residents, especially those in the southeastern corner, did not want to move. The previous June the U.S. Department of Housing and Urban Development, which administered the funds for urban renewal as well as for the Model Cities program, had issued a directive insisting on resident participation in all phases of urban renewal projects. In the fall of 1968 a group of dissatisfied residents, the Citizens Improvement Committee led by James Hontas, began petitioning for representation on the Urban Renewal Board. Giving encouragement and advice to the group were several poverty workers, including John Goldsmith, an organizer for Volunteers in Service to America (VISTA), one of the many programs sponsored by the Office of Economic Opportunity (which was run by the U.S. Department of Health, Education and Welfare).[632] Further complicating the picture was the news, which came around the end of the year, that the Department of HUD was converting some of its urban renewal funds to the Neighborhood Development Program (NDP), a new program which would concentrate exclusively on physical rehabilitation of Model Cities areas and which had the advantage (it was claimed) of providing grants after a delay of only three months.[633] So the Urban Renewal Board would have two types of urban renewal over which to pass judgment—one for the Tijeras Project and one for the Model Cities—and the two overlapped for the area designated for the educational complex. Meanwhile, the pressure for representation of the poor neighborhoods on the board kept building. In early February 1969 Domenici promised the Citizens Improvement Committee that a decision would be made in about ten days,[634] but several more weeks passed by without anything being done. Later that month the Model Cities Citizens Board approved an NDP plan for the first year,[635] and in March the Urban Renewal Board did likewise.[636] At last, in early April, the City Commission appointed Jack Candelaria, a community leader in the Model Cities area, to fill one of the positions on the Urban Renewal Board. Candelaria did not live in the district slated for the schools complex, but by this time the commissioners were considering cutting it out of the Tijeras Project in order to eliminate the confusion of having two different urban renewal projects for the same area.[637]

Over the next two years the planning, funding and actual construction for the Tijeras Project moved steadily along, but the branch of urban renewal which directly benefitted the poor people did not fare so well. By the beginning of 1970 work was underway on the police building, the bonds for which had been approved in the previous city election, and the Grand overpass.[638] In February HUD announced that phase one of the Tijeras Project, the defining of the area and the program, had been approved, and that approximately $19.5 million would be released to the city. Most of the reduction from the earlier figure of some $25 million was due to the schools complex project having been converted to the NDP: $1 million was granted to that project for the first year, and $3.2 million set aside for future work.[639] Soon afterwards the urban renewal agency began buying land in the fork of the "Y" of the Grand overpass for the convention center.[640] The Model Cities residents were not so lucky. In April of 1969 a formal request had been made for $8 million for various types of street repair, rehabilitation of houses, and buying homes in areas slated to be vacated. After a year of waiting, the Model Cities program was granted only $8,900 of NDP funds.[641] Caught between the shortfall of money and a commitment to move approximately fifty families away from the stench of a city sewage treatment plant, the Model Cities board had to dig into funds set aside for other purposes.[642]

With all the federally funded activity going on in the core area, the interested local groups continued to play an active part in the development. The Downtown Association persuaded the City Commission to close off four blocks of Central Avenue to make it a pedestrian mall during the month of heaviest Christmas shopping of 1967.[643] Two years later that group disbanded and reformed as Metro 70s for the purpose of spearheading development in the central business district, especially in the Tijeras Project area.[644] And in December 1970, businessmen and other citizens rallied behind the city's newest plan for the downtown. The plan retained some elements from the five-year-old Albuquerque Downtown plan—such as the four key corners of the diamond, the program to make part of Central a permanent shopping mall, and the proposals for more apartment houses, hotels and parking structures—and some new features as well—a new library and a civic plaza with underground parking. On the whole, the new design was less elaborate and expensive, more attuned to what the city could reasonably expect to achieve. Commenting on its evolution, City Planning Director Reuben Ramirez said, "It's not just a plan which comes out of the planning department. It is the result of interactions of several groups."[645] Through the tortuous and sometimes tortured interaction of the many forces that had come to bear, the plan and the planning process had been worked out. Private initiative was now working hand in hand with governmental bodies near and far, and the techniques and institutions for group planning and development were on a solid footing.

Cooperation in the Business World

The trend toward involving larger numbers of people in important decisions also affected areas where individualism had been more deeply entrenched than in politics, such as business. Businessmen became more aware of their common interests, and businessmen's associations grew larger and more powerful. The spheres of business and government, never completely distinct from one another, began to overlap conspicuously. Government bodies increased both their regulation of business and various forms of assistance to it, and cooperative undertakings involving both government and business became more common. And as the businessmen came to function more cooperatively with one another and with outsiders, the effective size of their businesses grew larger. Some businesses underwent dramatic expansion, diversifying their products and services and accumulating awesome financial resources. Even the small ones had access to more cooperative arrangements and government assistance than in years past. Taken together, these shifts toward group orientation carried the economy further away from a state of perfect competition and muted the sense of risk and adventure traditionally associated with the business world, but they made possible larger and more ambitious ventures than ever before.

In addition to the growth of group activities throughout the society, a factor that may have helped push the businessmen toward working together was the slackening of the post-World War II boom. During the 1950s the population within the city limits of Albuquerque increased 107.8 percent to 201,189 and that of Bernalillo County 80.0 percent to 262,199. In the 1960s, however, the growth rate slowed: the city included only 243,751 persons in 1970 and the county only 315,774 for percentage increases of 21.2 and 20.4 respectively.[646] The rate for the early seventies was slightly greater, with the city reaching 262,800 and the county 339,500 in 1972.[647] The growth of median family income in Bernalillo County adjusted for inflation tapered off in a similar fashion. After jumping 54.4 percent during the fifties, it rose a mere 10.2 percent during the sixties to an annual figure of $9031 in 1970 dollars.[648] Since the relative slowdown affected nearly all businesses, many of the owners and operators realized they had common problems and common goals.

An early instance of businessmen cooperating in an effort to strengthen the local economy was the formation of the Albuquerque Industrial Development Service. During the previous decade the defense industries associated with the military bases had helped stoke the Albuquerque boom and protect it from nationwide recessions, but there was always the danger that federal cutbacks could send the metropolitan area into a slump. In fact, this happened from time to time during the sixties, and by the early seventies the defense industries constituted a substantially smaller proportion of the economy than formerly. Aware of how vulnerable they were, a number of businessmen took steps to broaden the local industrial base. In April of 1960 the industrial development committee of the Chamber of Commerce put out an industrial recruiting brochure emphasizing Albuquerque's attractive features.[649] The next month real estate man Gene Hinkle, a member of the Heights Businessmen's Association, prodded the chamber to work more vigorously to bring in new industries.[650] In August a group of independent businessmen led by Hinkle met with a special Chamber of Commerce committee, and they agreed in principle to set up an independent association of future contributors to an industrial development fund.[651] The Albuquerque Industrial Development Association (later called AIDS) was established in September. The voting membership consisted of representatives that had made contributions to the fund, generally a thousand dollars each, and they elected a board of fifteen directors.[652] With all its financial muscle, the new organization could move effectively to recruit new industry.

Over the next few years business organizations continued to develop. In 1962 the Heights Businessmen's Association voted to rejoin the Chamber of Commerce, and the North Albuquerque Association came in as well.[653] AIDS gave birth to AID Corporation in 1963 in an effort to bring in still more money to help new businesses. A.F. Potenziani, who had led the drive for $100,000 for the city hall land, was named president. It immediately offered shares of stock to the public for $10 a share. According to the Small Business Investment Act of 1958, such a local development organization could provide 20 percent or more of a loan to a business, and the remainder, up to 80 percent, could then be obtained from the Small Business Administration.[654]

These efforts of the business community to consolidate its strength began to bear substantial fruit in 1966. In August came the announcement that, after more than ten months of negotiation with various industrial development groups, Levi Strauss & Company had been induced to begin operating a clothing manufacturing plant in Albuquerque. Instrumental in attracting the giant firm had been extensive surveys of available buildings and of the labor force and the commitment of AID Corporation to act as the leasing agent of a building that had been found suitable and to remodel it to fit the company's specifications.[655] Exhilarated with the success but mindful of the increasing need for more capital, AIDS launched a successful drive early the next year for $1 million to add to the industrial fund.[656]

Meanwhile, the political and business leaders were laboring to find a company to employ the workers who would be laid off when ACF Industries ceased its local operations around the end of 1967. ACF, with a city work force of twenty-one hundred, was one of the larger of the defense-oriented contractors, and some of the fears about the unpredictability of the federal defense bonanza were soon to be realized. In March 1967, however, came the word that business groups, with the help of New Mexico's congressional delegation, had persuaded General Electric to move into the government-owned plant which ACF was operating. Immediately after the departing company closed down, General Electric hired eight hundred of the workers for the manufacture of jet aircraft engines, and by the end of the decade it employed around twelve hundred.[657] The blow to the area's economy had been cushioned.

Less dramatic than the help which the state's congressmen and senators had given in landing General Electric for Albuquerque but more significant in the long run were the contributions made by several local institutions during these years, including the Albuquerque Technical-Vocational Institute and some of the banks. Backed by a bond issue and state and federal funds, TVI had begun operation in the fall of 1965 as a public training school for prospective workers in a wide variety of vocations.[658] In its efforts to ensure jobs for its graduates, as well as to cooperate with the business community at large, the school began to offer programs specifically geared to teach students the skills needed by industries which had committed themselves to coming to Albuquerque.[659] Around the same time, city banks started offering special inducements to companies and development groups seeking financial aid for new industrial plants.[660] These training and financing opportunities were incorporated into the overall packages which the development groups extended to prospective industries in the process of negotiation.

In 1968 still another type of aid was offered for the first time when Eidal International Corporation, which had originated locally but had recently become a division of Southwest Factories, Inc., headquartered in Oklahoma City, was considering moving into a new plant. The city government agreed to finance the construction of the plant through the use of industrial bonds,[661] a type of revenue bonds supported by the assets of the benefitting company. A city ordinance had provided for the use of industrial bonds as far back as 1959; from this point on they were frequently employed to help attract new industries. In late 1969, during the course of negotiations to persuade the Lenkurt Division of General Telephone & Electronics to set up operations in the city, the State Investment Council made the state permanent fund available for such bonds.[662] Thus vast resources of public money began to fill the growing need for capital.

Some of the actions by the federal government also had a favorable impact on local business conditions. Throughout the late sixties and early seventies the national War on Poverty was responsible for numerous programs in Albuquerque to improve the lot of the poor people, and some of these involved training out-of-work persons and placing them in jobs with city businesses. Operation Mainstream, one of the divisions of the Concentrated Employment Program, found positions for a number of previously unemployed; the first year the workers' wages were paid by the Concentrated Employment Program, the second year the employer paid half and the CEP half, and the following year and thereafter the private business footed the entire bill.[663] In the summer of 1969, following the decision of The Singer Company's Friden Division to begin manufacturing office machines in the city, the drive against poverty utilized a new mechanism to increase the labor force. The National Alliance of Businessmen worked out a contract with Friden whereby, for a grant of $179,000 from the U.S. Department of Labor, the company would train 150 unemployed persons over the next eighteen months and hire them as job openings occurred.[664]

The might of the federal government also lent assistance to fledgling enterprises. For years there had been the Small Business Administration, available to help out with loans and advice. In the wake of the War on Poverty came numerous other forms of aid. One of the beneficiaries was the Albuquerque Building Cooperative, a group of men from the north valley and the Model Cities area which organized in the fall of 1968. Working with the guidance of such agencies as the University of New Mexico's Center for Community Action Services, the Volunteers in Service to America (VISTA) and the Concentrated Employment Program, and securing grants and finding jobs through the help of these and other antipoverty programs, the cooperative branched out into construction work, boot making and shoe repair, and garbage collecting.[665] Numerous other small businesses whose proprietors and workers came from disadvantaged backgrounds were also offered federal assistance. In 1970 was established the National Economic Development Association to advise and help new Spanish-American entrepreneurs.[666] The businessmen who availed themselves of such programs might not be practicing free enterprise in the traditional sense of the expression, but they were making genuine contributions to the area's fluid economy.

Notwithstanding the help the various levels of government were giving much of the business community, many businessmen remained suspicious of big government and governmental intervention. In part this feeling was due to the old attitudes about individualism, self-reliance and free competition; in part it was because the growing complex of regulations actually restricted the ability of some businessmen to make money. At every hand new laws strictly spelled out what an entrepreneur could and could not do, and much of what had earlier been permitted was no longer allowed. There were the minimum wage laws, frequently amended to require higher wages and to cover more workers. There were tighter zoning ordinances and building codes. Some business practices were declared "unfair" and made illegal, and civil rights laws forbade discrimination on the basis of race, creed, color, national origin or sex. Working conditions were controlled by new legislation. A growing public movement led to stricter rules concerning pollution and the overall impact of industry on the environment. As a result of such regulations and many others besides, the long-cherished independence of the private businessman diminished. He was compelled to operate within the confines of a social and political system that was more interrelated and interdependent than ever before, and to abide by its restrictions while taking advantage of its benefits.

Even on the level of the individual business, large organization was becoming more important. Many small retail stores became unprofitable as giant chains, with their greater efficiencies and superior resources, spread throughout the metropolitan area selling their goods cheaply. A small business might succumb during an economic recession, but a large company could generally weather the storm. Of the retail businesses which continued to thrive, many were located in the large shopping centers which attracted customers seeking a variety of items and which hurt the stores in the nearby neighborhoods all the more.[667] The Park Plaza, a luxury apartment house which had been in financial difficulty for years and which was situated on the outskirts of the downtown district, was bought by a large eastern combine in 1970.[668] Three of the largest banks, which already had numerous branch offices in various parts of the city, became owned by statewide multi-bank holding companies. Many professional persons such as doctors and lawyers, long accustomed to acting independently, joined the swing to large offices located in centers of one kind or another.

In the course of this widespread consolidation of business ownership and management, some small enterprises were simply run out of business. In other cases, the proprietors grew tired of competing in the marketplace for small profits and found jobs with large companies or public institutions. From time to time, however, the consolidation worked in the small businessman's favor. In 1966 Custom Air Service Company, an Albuquerque firm which developed a commercial process for obtaining a high degree of cleanliness in air and rooms, merged with Becton Dickinson Company of New Jersey in order to acquire needed capital. Now a division of the larger company and renamed Envirco, Inc., the group exhibited its product at a trade fair in Germany and signed several lucrative contracts for it.[669] Over these years, a number of other locally based firms merged with national companies in their quest for growth and profits.

The number and variety of businesses in the Albuquerque area during the sixties and early seventies was far too great for any single firm to be representative. But exemplifying the trend toward growth and diversification more than most was a company with roots reaching back many years, Springer Transfer Company. In the fall of 1969 Emmanuel Schifani, its president, announced plans to build a $500,000 office building at 1625 University Blvd. NE, and at the same time he said that the company had entered the real estate and insurance businesses.[670] The following spring Schifani made public a dizzying package of further developments and future plans. Springer, at this time one of the biggest and fastest growing privately owned companies in the state, was about to go public and issue common stock in order to raise more capital. It had recently acquired Berger-Briggs Realty, a large old real estate firm in the city, and would soon build and own the new $4.5 million Hilton Inn at the intersection of University and Menaul. In the not-too-distant future it would develop a forty-five-acre research park in the southwest corner of the interchange of the two interstate highways.[671] For a business that had been on the verge of being partitioned off eighteen years earlier, Springer Transfer Company had come a long way.

Developing Patterns in the Urban Landscape

During the sixties and early seventies, the urban landscape reflected the general tendency of the city as a whole to become organized into large groups. The emerging clusters of residential housing and of businesses had been apparent earlier; now the overall pattern of nuclei arising throughout the metropolitan area connected by arterial roads became more highly developed and more striking. The people's tastes in residences also shifted in line with the increasing orientation toward groups. And the developers and builders themselves adjusted to the new conditions as best they could, often working more cooperatively with one another and with governmental bodies than in the past in much the same manner as the other Albuquerque businessmen.

Some of the successful builders from the fifties continued to use their old forceful approaches for the huge projects which were becoming more typical of the housing and real estate market, but changing circumstances led to a few spectacular failures. Early in 1959 Sam Hoffman, who had been responsible for Hoffmantown and other large subdivisions in the heights, returned to town to launch the most ambitious housing development in the city's history yet, Hoffman City. He and Victor Salazar, acting as his agent, engaged in a campaign to persuade the heirs of the old Atrisco Spanish land grant, located southwest of the city and on the west side of the Rio Grande, to sell much of their land for a new housing project. Ownership of large portions of the land on the west side of Albuquerque had been passed down from generation to generation for centuries, and the tradition of attachment to the land and the confusion of unclear property titles had been important reasons why that territory had not been developed so much as the east. But the campaign was spirited, and in April the Atrisco Board of Trustees voted to sell Hoffman 3,840 acres for a reported $1.2 million.[672]

In June Hoffman arrived in Albuquerque for the grand opening celebration for four model homes on the huge tract. Twenty-five thousand people attended the event.[673] The builder announced plans to construct 2,200 houses in the next year and a total of 12,000 over the next six years. He had taken up the project, he said, because it was a challenge. "I'll never turn down a challenge," declared Hoffman, "and if challenged I would try to build the first home on the moon."[674]

His aspirations, however, were doomed to be thwarted by a combination of unforeseen problems. On June 8 the State Contractors Licensing Board filed a complaint against Hoffman Homes, Inc. (the present name of Hoffman's company) for operating without a New Mexico contractor's license.[675] A month later the Atrisco board disclosed that hundreds of fraudulent deeds to the grant had been appearing and that extensive litigation would be needed to clear up the mess.[676] Still later it came to light that the grant had deeded mineral rights on the land to Roberto Herrera several years earlier, and these rights had to be gotten back before the Federal Housing Authority would approve the project. Hoffman bought the mineral rights from Herrera for $15 an acre for a total of $57,600. Then there was further negotiation with the FHA over such matters as house plans, streets, drainage and sewer and water systems.[677] None of these obstacles seemed insuperable, but they forced postponement of the start of construction, and this slowed sales. By early October about five hundred unbuilt homes had been sold, whereas Hoffman had expected to have sold over a thousand at this point. He told Salazar that the many delays in starting the project had created an almost unbearable tension. Within a few days the strain became too great for the man to cope with. In the early hours of October 13, 1959, Sam Hoffman and his wife exchanged angry words, and the developer drew a pistol, shot the woman and then turned the gun on himself. As Hoffman Homes, Inc. and the four model homes of Hoffman City closed for one day for the funeral of the man who had been the third largest home builder in the country five years earlier,[678] the other builders around the city wondered what this tragedy boded for the industry in the coming years.

Hoffman's disaster did not daunt Ed Snow, who arranged with the developer's heirs the following month to assume the commitments and liabilities regarding the mammoth project.[679] Shortly thereafter Hoffman City was renamed Snow Vista. But difficulties continued to plague the undertaking. Cutbacks in the defense industry forced some persons who had contracted to buy as-yet-unbuilt homes to move away, leaving Snow to struggle with the pyramid of financial obligations erected on the dream of future sales.[680] In 1960 five hundred units of Capehart housing were opened near the military bases for the use of military personnel, further eroding the private housing market.[681] And throughout most of the sixties, population and income in the Albuquerque area grew at a substantially slower rate than during the previous decade. In the early sixties the demand for new homes fell and so did prices—just when Snow needed a boom most desperately. The first of a series of lawsuits by creditors and others dependent on his success was filed in 1964. For the next several years he continued to build homes and to oversee his related operations, but his empire was sadly reduced from what it had been in the early years. In July 1968 he was working on the promotion of new kinds of real estate development when a heart attack struck him down at the age of forty-five.[682]

The third of the big developers of the fifties, Dale Bellamah, proceeded more cautiously than the other two, often allying himself with other large corporate interests for his biggest undertakings. He delayed the construction of his proposed $6 million regional shopping center for the southwest corner of Menaul and Louisiana, even though the city government had given its approval several years earlier and the giant $10 million Winrock Center was going up on the east side of Louisiana. In 1960 he changed his plans and sold the forty acres earmarked for his project to Homart Development Co., a subsidiary of Sears, Roebuck & Co., for around $750,000 on the understanding that it would build the shopping center.[683] In early 1961 Winrock opened and soon became the leading retail shopping area in Albuquerque. Two years later the Homart center, named Coronado and about two-thirds the size of Winrock, had its grand opening. Bellamah was now in a highly advantageous position, for he still owned about 120 acres to the south and west of Coronado Center—land which was rapidly appreciating in value—and he had sufficient financial resources to proceed with his various development plans.[684]

His development projects kept him busily occupied during the years following his land sale to Homart. Following the pattern established in the fifties but on a larger scale, he opened and expanded more housing developments and neighborhood shopping and business centers around the metropolitan area, particularly in the far eastern heights. One of his favorite long-term projects was the development of Jeannedale, his name for the expanse of land adjacent to Coronado. Shortly before the shopping center opened, Bellamah teamed up with C.C. Collie of Little Rock, Arkansas, and began construction of a $2 million ten-story apartment house near the intersection of San Pedro and Indian School.[685] His overall plans called for more construction in the area, eventually to total around $100 million, as demand warranted and available capital made possible. A different sort of venture drew much of his attention in the early seventies—the building of the two-hundred-room Four Seasons Motor Inn at the intersection of Interstate 40 and Carlisle. When it opened in late 1971, it included an indoor-outdoor patio with a convention-sized ballroom, and it was the largest luxury hotel in New Mexico.[686]

He took up residence in the top floor of the imposing structure but had little time remaining to enjoy his lofty surroundings. In April 1972 Dale Bellamah died of a heart attack at the age of fifty-seven, leaving behind a personal fortune estimated between thirty and fifty million dollars and consisting of the largest group of privately held corporations in the state. He had built and owned nine shopping centers in Albuquerque and Santa Fe, and the thousands of Bellamah homes scattered throughout New Mexico as well as his several hotels testified to his enormous impact.[687] The impact continued beyond his death, as his corporations continued to build and expand. In July the Dale J. Bellamah Corporation announced its intention to develop Loma del Norte, a 450-acre tract north of the city, into a planned community with houses, apartment dwellings, offices, shopping centers and a mobile home park.[688] And the following month the corporation unveiled plans to work jointly with American Cos. of Dallas in the construction of City Centre, an office complex consisting of twin six-story towers connected by a mall-like structure. This building would front on Uptown Boulevard, a new street cutting through the heart of Jeannedale.[689]

Bellamah's achievements notwithstanding, more and more of the development projects in the Greater Albuquerque area were being undertaken by large corporations with diversified ownership, often based out of the state. In 1968, for example, Western America Travel Center Inc. from Phoenix began work on a cluster of motels near the intersection of Interstate 40 and Eubank, with plans eventually to add restaurants, gas stations, a shopping center and a small convention center. Bellamah and a number of the residents of the nearby Princess Jeanne subdivision had fought the proposal for nearly two years in the channels of city government; they had succeeded only in having a medical complex removed from the plans.[690] The most spectacular of the new corporate building ventures, however, were on a far larger scale than anything ever attempted by the local developers and located far outside the city limits. On the vast expanses of the west mesa whole new communities were erected, almost small cities, and sophisticated nationwide advertising campaigns persuaded thousands of people from distant places to come there to live.

In April 1960 Horizon Land Corporation announced plans to develop the eighty-five-hundred-acre Black Ranch, which it had recently acquired for a reputed $1.6 million, into an integrated community to be named Paradise Hills. The development would have its own sewage and water systems, its own recreation and its own industry; in addition to the thousands of homes to be constructed there would also be apartment houses, a mobile home park, schools, community buildings, parks, a medical center, a golf course, a gun club and a riding academy. Paradise Hills was west of the Rio Grande and northwest of most of Albuquerque;[691] about a year and a half later came word of a much bigger project directly to the north of it. American Realty and Petroleum Company had bought the fifty-five-thousand-acre Koontz Ranch in neighboring Sandoval County from Ed Snow and was preparing to develop it into a huge community which it was naming Rio Rancho. The price of the land transaction was not disclosed, but Snow had bought it two years earlier from Victor Salazar and his associates for $5.2 million, and the deal was probably the costliest land transaction in the history of the state up to that time. The company planned to provide facilities somewhat similar to those scheduled for Paradise Hills, and, furthermore, twenty thousand acres would be set aside for industrial development.[692] Early in 1962 Horizon Land Corporation began advertising still another planned community, Rio Grande Estates, near Belen, a small town about thirty miles south of the city. And throughout the decade came announcements of other such transformations of large tracts of vacant land in various parts of New Mexico.

The company-made communities near Albuquerque thrived. Paradise Hills opened an industrial park its first year,[693] and in 1961 Curtiss-Wright Electronics moved there from smaller quarters in the city.[694] In 1967 the Rio Rancho Industrial Park began, and soon it had more firms than Paradise Hills.[695] Meanwhile the people kept pouring in, many of them retirees from the east seeking a pleasanter, less congested life than they had known before. And their dollars made it possible and profitable for the development companies to add more elaborate facilities than they had originally planned. In 1972, for example, luxury apartments opened in Paradise Hills, and the rental included automatic social membership in the Paradise Hills Country Club with tennis, dining and sauna. For another twenty dollars a month, the occupants could play golf.[696]

More powerful than the biggest corporations was the government, and the various levels of government were having an increasingly substantial impact on construction, especially housing. There was the growing body of regulations to which the developers had to adhere. Among the more significant of the new laws were a state subdivision law passed in 1963, affecting the practices of the development companies,[697] and county zoning, which from 1968 onward limited the number of dwellings per acre that would be erected on land outside the city.[698] More important than the new restrictions being enacted, however, was the increasing readiness of government to lend support, through tax advantages and through different kinds of subsidies, to housing for the poor and aged. In this area the federal government was most active.

The first large-scale instance of federal subsidies for low-income housing in Albuquerque occurred in 1964, when the New Mexico District Council of the Carpenters and Joiners Union built the Mountain View Apartments on Yale about a mile south of Central. There were income ceilings for the tenants—for example, a married couple with no children must earn no more than $4,850 a year in order to qualify—and the elderly were given first preference. Because of the restrictions and because the apartments were to be operated on a nonprofit basis, the Carpenters Union had been able to obtain an FHA-insured loan for the project at about 2 percent below the market rate with the federal government subsidizing the gap. With 21 buildings and 316 units, Mountain View was the largest apartment development in the state, and the low rents ensured full occupancy and a waiting list. The success of the venture led the union to add another 242 units in 1965 and 106 more in 1967. The latest addition was rented under a newly enacted FHA program through which if 25 percent of the tenant's income was not sufficient to cover the rent, the federal government would pay the difference. In order to obtain this benefit, the prospective tenants had to meet a number of new requirements, including a substantially lower income than the earlier rules specified. Remembering what the Capehart military housing had done to the local market and concerned about the possible impact of these additional apartment units, the Albuquerque Board of Realtors and the Home Builders Association tried to have them stopped but to no avail. Housing surveys showed that all over town the only apartments with high vacancy rates were in the luxury class, and Mountain View obviously offered them little competition.[699] Following the lead of the Carpenters Union, several other groups, including the League of United Latin American Citizens and an association of Black ministers, backed nonprofit apartment developments along similar lines in the late sixties and early seventies.[700]

At about the same time that the rent-subsidized apartment units were being added to Mountain View, city government began administering a housing program for the poor. Funds from the U.S. Department of Housing and Urban Development financed the securing of suitable homes and the paying of that portion of the rent which exceeded 25 percent of the tenants' incomes. Again local real estate and home building groups tried to quash the program, and again there was a long waiting list of prospective renters.[701] By mid-1968 215 families had been moved into sound housing scattered around the city.[702]

Other federally financed programs helped the poor repair their present homes. In 1965, during the early stages of the War on Poverty the Home Improvements Program was launched in South Barelas. Groups of young men were given instruction in building skills and then supervised as they made repairs on selected houses in the area. The homeowner provided some of the materials, and wages were paid by the federal government.[703] A few years later the Neighborhood Development Program renovated many of the homes in the Model Cities Area.[704] And in 1969 the Code Enforcement Program made available money for repairs in certain areas outside the boundaries of Model Cities, including Kirtland Addition, a predominately Black subdivision west of the military bases.[705]

Although big government was pushing into areas of the economy that had traditionally been mainly the province of private enterprise, conflict was kept to a minimum. In the first place, as we have seen, federally supported housing for the poor did little to hurt the construction and real estate industries, for the most lucrative sector of the market was in the middle- and upper-income range. And second, additional federally supported programs benefitted the private builders. Section 235 of the Housing and Urban Development Act of 1968 provided for interest subsidies on loans to buyers of homes which met FHA standards and yet were priced below a designated level provided that the buyers qualified on the basis of low income and assets.[706] In 1970 a new program was inaugurated, Turnkey Housing, whereby private contractors with private funding built groups of dwelling units, sold them to the Local Housing Authority of the City of Albuquerque, which was funded by the U.S. Department of HUD, and this authority then sold or rented them to poor people. The Albuquerque Home Builders Association not only endorsed the program but also formed a nonprofit corporation to participate in it. Said Howard W. Parsons, executive director of the group, "Our association for many years was opposed to public housing. But now the housing will be for sale and it will be so constructed that we will not create ghettos. The homes will be widely separated." Before the end of 1972 three of the Turnkey projects were completed and occupied by tenants who had been selected and trained by the Local Housing Authority to take good care of their new quarters.[707]

And thus, with the growing importance of large corporate structures and of government support, the suppliers of housing in Albuquerque underwent extensive changes. More important, however, to most of the residents, especially those with moderate and high incomes, were shifts in the kinds of housing being supplied. The level of expectations on the part of the typical home buyer and renter continued to rise along with their incomes, and dwellings became more commodious and well furnished. Between 1960 and 1970 the median number of rooms for occupied dwelling units in Bernalillo County rose from 4.8 to 5.0. In 1970 89.5 percent of the units had 1.00 or less persons per room; the figure had been 82.9 percent ten years earlier. The proportion with a private bath went up from 91.9 percent to 96.8 percent and with more than one bathroom from 29.2 percent to 40.1 percent.[708] Noting the changing tastes, Keith Burch, member of the Albuquerque Board of Realtors, commented in 1963, "There used to be a demand for three bedrooms. Now people want three or four bedrooms and a den." Spacious patios, built-in appliances, and many other conveniences and luxurious furnishings became commonplace.[709] The percentage of dwelling units equipped with air conditioning climbed from 12.1 in 1960 to 35.4 in 1970.[710]

Even more striking than the increasing space and luxury of the residences, which had been a more or less constant development for many years, was a shift in the living patterns. In spite of the rising income of most of the inhabitants of Albuquerque between 1960 and 1970, the proportion of dwelling units which were rented rose slightly for the first time since the end of World War II, from 33.8 percent to 34.7 percent, and the proportion of dwelling units which were not single detached structures went up from 11.8 percent to 22.3 percent. The percentage of structures consisting of five or more dwelling units climbed from 3.4 to 9.5.[711] It was in 1962 when the new trend toward living in apartments became significant. Of the new dwelling units for which city building permits were issued in 1961, 83.9 percent were single-unit structures; the corresponding figure for each of the previous few years had been about the same. In 1962 the percentage dropped to 63.2, and for most of the next ten years it was lower still, dipping to 38.6 in 1972.[712] Around the end of 1962 was completed the Continental Arms, the city's first group of condominium apartments and also its first luxury high-rise apartment building.[713] Numerous other impressive apartment structures went up over the following years. The developers were committing large sums of money to the proposition that apartment dwelling would grow increasingly popular.

Why did so many people come to live in apartments? By and large, renting is less expensive in the short run than buying a home, but considerations of cost cannot account for the shift. The average selling price of a home in Albuquerque had peaked in 1959 at $16,193 and then had slipped for several years. with its lowest point in 1962, the very year when apartment building had started to escalate. By the mid-sixties the average price had regained its earlier high, and it reached $25,537 in 1972. The new houses were going for considerably more.[714] Adding to the difficulty of buying was the rising interest rate on loans: the FHA rate went from 5 3/4 percent in 1959 to 7 percent thirteen years later.[715] The statistics we have already seen, however, indicate that changing preferences rather than cost underlay the change. The percentage of dwelling units in multiple structures rose faster than the percentage of rented units. Furthermore, the average material level of living for all types of dwelling units was on the rise; little demand remained for the simple five-room homes that had been the mainstay of the housing market immediately after the end of World War II. The people were not so eager as before to make sacrifices to get a home they could call their very own, and many gladly gave up some of their privacy and individualism for the convenience, the more elaborate accessories and the easy sociability to be found in apartment living. As Harry Gowins, manager of the Continental Arms, observed in 1963, "A lot of people are lonely and want companionship." He went on, "They can get it here," pointing to the central patio and pool.[716] Like the Continental Arms, many of the newer groups of apartments had inviting courtyards, swimming pools and other centers of group activity in their midst, and their inhabitants were drawn to these central foci in somewhat the same fashion that the Indians of the pueblos scattered across New Mexico had gathered in their plazas for centuries. In their choice of residences, as in so many other ways, the people of Albuquerque were showing their increasing tendency to come together in groups.

At the same time that many of the residents were coming to cluster together in apartment complexes and much of the new construction was being undertaken in cooperative ventures of one kind or another, the metropolitan area as a whole was taking on more of the appearance of a single, integrated entity. The function and the form of the downtown area continued to alter; no longer the tight focus for the most of the activities of the citizens, it became chiefly the headquarters of the most important institutions, the vital center from which authority extended. Other business and shopping centers around the city accommodated most of the people's day-to-day needs. And as various types and sizes of lesser foci emerged throughout Greater Albuquerque, they were tied together by an intricate network of large and small roads, giving an overall organic structure to what might look to a casual observer like undifferentiated sprawl.

Throughout these years the downtown was a source of anxious concern and a center of intense planning on the part of many civic and business leaders as they saw the district lose much of its earlier business. The opening of Winrock in 1961 and Coronado in 1963 further aggravated the plight of the downtown stores. In the early sixties, when numerous decrepit buildings in the area were being demolished, few new firms could be found to relocate in the empty spaces. The next few years saw the departure of the remaining department stores, including Montgomery-Ward, Kistler-Collister, Sears-Roebuck and Fedway.[717] At this time the Bureau of the Census defined the central business district as the area bounded by Lomas on the north, Broadway on the east, Coal on the south and Eighth on the west, consisting of approximately ninety square blocks; between 1967 and 1972 its retail sales declined 47.9 percent.[718] And equally distressing to many of the older citizens was the disappearance of several of the cherished landmarks. The Alvarado Hotel and the Franciscan Hotel, once favorite gathering places of local personages and illustrious visitors, and retaining their architectural splendor to the end, were razed in the early seventies.

These losses notwithstanding, much new construction and plans for more were bringing the downtowners hope. In 1960 the only tall structures in the city were the Sunshine Building on Central, the Hilton Hotel just off Central to the north, and the recently erected Simms Building one block south of the main street, at Fourth and Gold. But other new offices had gone up in the general vicinity of the Simms Building, and construction of the fourteen-story Bank of New Mexico Building was underway.[719] In the early sixties a $7.45 million federal office building and courthouse was built at 500 Gold SW, making the area south of Central Avenue for a while the busiest part of the downtown. Meanwhile, a cluster of local government buildings was taking shape a few blocks northward. The new city hall was located at 400 Marquette NW, the new police and municipal court building went up across the street, and the county courthouse one block to the south was remodeled extensively.[720] In 1966 an out-of-state development firm completed the National Building—eighteen stories high and the tallest in the city—at Fifth and Marquette, and a number of state agencies moved into the office space.[721] These two groups of office buildings—one in the southern sector of the central business district and one in the northern part—comprised two of the four points of the diamond which the downtown planners had been envisioning for the area, and realization of an overall harmonious design seemed within the people's grasp.

The Tijeras Urban Renewal Project, underway toward the end of the decade, provided the means for further development in the area. By late 1972 some of its features were ready for use, some were under construction, and still others were in the planning stage, exciting much public discussion. The new convention center in the "Y" of the Grand-Marquette-Tijeras overpass opened in October. To the west, Fourth Street was cut off between Marquette and Tijeras, and a city plaza covering most of two city blocks was being built with parking underground. On another newly consolidated superblock made possible by urban renewal, bounded by Lomas, Third, Roma and Second, the American Bank of Commerce, which had come to town just a few years earlier, was building a sleek, thirteen-story headquarters.[722] Slated to go up soon in the immediate vicinity were a new building for the First National Bank with an underground shopping mall, a new Albuquerque National Bank Building, and an office building in the style of an Aztec pyramid to be named Plaza Del Sol. The main branch of the public library, which had previously been located well east of the downtown, would also be moved to the area.[723] Stagnant for years and still on unsteady feet, the central business district was undergoing a remarkable physical transformation.

The changing appearance of the area was a manifestation of its altered function in the metropolitan area as a whole. The central business district in 1972 contained a far smaller portion of the city's commercial and professional activity than did the central business district of 1945, which had covered less than a third as much area. Comparison of the telephone directories of 1945 and 1972 reveals that the proportion of banks in the district had declined from 67 percent to 12 percent, of loan companies from 85 percent to 24 percent, of insurance agencies from 79 percent to 8 percent, of hotels from 76 percent to 18 percent, of movie theaters from 89 percent to 17 percent (none of which was flourishing), of jewelry stores from 60 percent to 16 percent, of furniture stores from 60 percent to 5 percent, and of department stores from 85 percent all the way to zero. In 1945 88 percent of the dentists and 77 percent of the physicians had offices in the district; only about 1 percent of each profession did so in 1972. On the other hand, the percentage of office buildings located in the area fell off only from 96 to 65, and of lawyers working there from 97 to 72.[724] Although the concentration of the city's activity in the downtown area dropped dramatically, corresponding, perhaps, to the diminished concentration of power and authority throughout society, it was still the most important center of power. Important institutions went to considerable expense to locate their headquarters there. And its sphere of influence extended over a much wider space and larger population than ever before.

Outside the central business district other nuclei of commercial activity and residences continued to develop. The two most important were Winrock Center and Coronado Center—by 1972 each had a higher volume of retail sales than the downtown—but several others, both planned and unplanned, did business on a scale approaching them.[725] New shopping centers sprang up at the intersections of busy throughways, as they had done during the fifties, and the improved system of roads and highways made them more accessible and convenient than earlier. As the shopping centers grew larger and more important in the lives of the citizens, they also became more elaborate and more highly integrated. Each developer planned carefully to bring in the best possible mix of firms that would increase the flow of business and enhance the vitality of the whole center. Some even included hotels, apartment houses and medical complexes. And outside the formal boundaries of the centers there was a tendency for other businesses to cluster, attracted by the already-established flow of consumers. Sometimes in conjunction with these centers, sometimes not, big office complexes were also erected near the important intersections; among the most notable were the First National Bank Building East at Central and San Mateo, seventeen stories high and for a brief time the tallest in the city,[726] and the Citizens State Bank Building, across Louisiana from Coronado and north of Winrock. As was the case with the shopping centers, the new office buildings were usually rented out to tenants whose business and professional activities complemented one another to a high degree. In such a manner, hundreds of business sub-communities arose around Albuquerque, each fairly integrated in itself but none really independent of the larger whole.

As the city grew and became more varied, more specialized types of centers developed. To accommodate the needs of industry, more industrial parks were created, always with easy access to the interstate highways or the railroad. Before 1960 there had been only two in the metropolitan area; the number grew to seventeen by 1972.[727] Medical centers grew at a prodigious rate. Splendid new hospital structures went up in the area west of the University of New Mexico, the university itself added a medical school in 1965,[728] and numerous smaller centers sprinkled the city at points where demand seemed to justify. In several instances retirement centers were built within easy walking distance of medical facilities. Still another variety of center catered primarily to tourists; within this broad category could be fitted both the Western America Travel Center and much of historic Old Town, with its elegant restaurants and its picturesque shops.

Residences also showed an increasing tendency toward clustering, although considerations of privacy often led to their being situated a little farther from the busiest intersections. Most likely to be located near the business centers were apartment buildings. In 1962 the luxury high-rise Alcade West was built on the outskirts of the downtown, and the Park Plaza, a similar structure not far away, followed a year later.[729] About the same time a large group of apartments, including the Continental Arms, was being constructed just north of the military bases.[730] Toward the end of the decade a much larger cluster emerged along the north side of Montgomery, from Carlisle several miles to the east. Prominent in this group was San Pedro Village, a six-hundred-unit, $7 million complex with three recreation areas and a neighborhood shopping center.[731] And throughout these years many other apartment structures went up around Greater Albuquerque, many of them in areas where previously there had been only single-unit homes.

Large numbers of individual homes were being built, too, usually but not exclusively in planned subdivisions. Typically, a subdivision would be developed near but not directly adjacent to an important thoroughfare. Less numerous than the houses in town but still significant were the ones going up outside, where the pace of life seemed slower, traditional cultures or natural beauty was closer at hand, and yet access to the city was only a matter of minutes by car. The neighboring small towns of Tijeras, Bernalillo, Corrales and Placitas began to regain population as the influence of the metropolis of Albuquerque spread further.[732] The company-made communities such as Paradise Hills and Rio Rancho with their imported inhabitants might have few cultural similarities to the older villages around the city, but they too were functioning as satellite communities. Wherever a citizen might choose to live, he could avail himself fairly easily of the variety and sociability and institutional benefits of the city, and his choice of residence was influenced by the manner in which he wished to relate to the city.

Running alongside the thousands of homes and businesses of Albuquerque and tying them together in a vast, intricate knot was the highly developed street system. As the city had expanded and the pattern of clusters had grown more pronounced, the size and shape of the roads had become more differentiated. When the 1949 traffic survey had been made, which Tingley had so vehemently opposed, most of the city's traffic had been concentrated along the lines of a cross, with Central and the nearby streets of Coal and Las Lomas (later renamed Lomas) handling the bulk of the east-west flow and the majority of the north- and southbound vehicles going along Fourth, Second and Broadway. A few more distant arteries—Rio Grande going north and south and Menaul and Gibson going east and west—were beginning to assume some importance.[733] By 1972, the traffic flow had become much more dispersed. The busiest roads by far were the extensions of Interstate 40 and Interstate 25 through town—the Coronado and Pan American Freeways—which had been constructed during the sixties. These highways, far larger than any in Albuquerque in past years, served as the main arteries of the city, providing ready access and abundant service to the most important centers. Lesser arteries—including the east-west thoroughfares Montgomery, Candelaria, Menaul, Lomas, Central, Lead, Coal and Gibson, and the north-south throughways Coors, Rio Grande, Fourth, Second, University, Carlisle, San Mateo, Louisiana, Wyoming, Eubank and Juan Tabo—coursed with vehicles traveling across the metropolitan area, and the traffic along these streets grew heavier as they approached the freeways.[734] To approximately the same extent that the business activity of Albuquerque no longer concentrated so heavily in the downtown area but dispersed among the greater and lesser centers of the city and along the larger and smaller streets, the vehicular traffic did likewise. Accommodating the flow in the less busy sections of the city were hundreds of smaller streets, some recent and some old. In the newer subdivisions many of the streets were laid out in a purposely irregular fashion to discourage through traffic, and a number of the new homes were built along tiny cul-de-sacs. In such a manner the traditional grid pattern of the streets was undermined, and a more organic design of small roads feeding bigger ones which fed yet bigger ones on up the scale came to emerge. To most residents of the city, traveling their accustomed paths with their eyes fixed on the nearby cars, street signs and buildings, the design would not be particularly evident; but if they were to fly into Albuquerque by night and look down on the vivid display of clusters and streaks of lights, they would see it almost as a whole. They would witness a visual projection of the developing structure of the metropolitan area.

The Drive for Liberal Reform

At the same time that large institutions were venturing boldly into new areas and aggressively expanding their reach, certain segments of the population were acting with increased vigor to spread their political and cultural influence. Such activist people—and most others as well—were turning more of their attention outward toward other people and new experiences, less of it toward their families and their own narrow concerns. The traditional religious practice of the 1950s was giving way to the secular liberal zeal of the 1960s. The energy charging the air and the excitement generated by dramatic changes taking place supported visions of a society unlike anything that had ever existed before. Providing much of the leadership for this surge of liberal reform were numerous well-educated, affluent and self-confident professional men, and sharing many of the same impulses and goals were members of groups which historically had had little power, including the young, the ethnic minorities and the women.

This outburst of political and cultural liberalism—the most substantial one since before World War II—began to assert itself in the early sixties. The election of John F. Kennedy to the Presidency of the United States in 1960 seemed to herald a new age of youthful vigor and idealism. The older liberals gained self-confidence, and the young people found new directions, goals and targets. The whole society was feeling, in varying degrees, ready to shuck off old restrictions, to try the untried, to aspire to new heights. At every hand the popular culture of the time demonstrated the expansiveness of the spirit: movies like *Never on Sunday* and *Zorba the Greek* delighted crowds with their exuberance and mild iconoclasm, musicians such as Bob Dylan delivered stirring songs protesting against prejudice and war, religious leaders exhorted their congregations with moral challenges, and political figures declaimed about new frontiers and making everyone truly free.

The most dramatic of the drives for reform during the early sixties, the civil rights movement, had only a limited direct impact on Albuquerque, where Blacks were few and overt racial discrimination was relatively muted, but the zeal it inspired had deep and lasting reverberations. News of racial incidents across the country, especially in the American South, mobilized local public opinion, and the reports of sit-ins and other demonstrations aroused active responses. One spring Saturday morning in 1960 a group of about twenty-five students from the University of New Mexico marched from Yale Park to the local Woolworth department store carrying placards with such slogans as "We are picketing Woolworth's because they segregate in their Southern stores" and "We protest discrimination based on color and creed." They pointed out that college students throughout the nation had been holding similar demonstrations protesting lunch counter segregation in the South.[735] As news about further developments in the civil rights movement reached the city, such as the Mississippi Freedom Riders in 1961 and the enrollment of James Meredith at the University of Mississippi in 1962, more local people became openly concerned and committed to the cause. In August 1963 there was a massive freedom march in Washington, D.C., and Joseph Gamble, president of the Albuquerque chapter of the National Association for the Advancement of Colored People, took part. When he returned he expressed his feelings. "It moved me very much to find so many people, not directly involved themselves, and yet concerned about me," he said. "The Anglo people there were equally concerned about getting complete freedom for us, their brothers, so that all Americans would be free Americans."[736]

The ensuing years brought further local support to the movement. A number of Albuquerque residents participated in civil rights activities in the South and told their friends back home of the obstacles they were encountering and the good they were doing. News of the march to Selma, Alabama, in early 1965 and the killing there of civil rights workers galvanized public indignation all the more. In 1964 Congress passed a public accommodations law requiring businesses which served the public to treat all citizens equally without regard to race, creed, color or national origin, and the following year it enacted a law providing measures to guarantee all citizens regardless of race the right to vote. These laws had little direct effect on Albuquerque, since a city ordinance passed back in 1952 had done locally more or less what the public accommodations law was designed to do and since discrimination at the polls had not been a problem for years; but indirectly, by helping to codify the evolving national conscience, they gave additional support and moral authority to civil rights activism. Best-selling books like *To Kill a Mockingbird* and popular movies such as *A Raisin in the Sun* and *Lilies of the Field*—both starring Sidney Poitier, a handsome Black actor who seemed to specialize in noble roles—contributed to the esteem with which the movement was widely regarded.

As the community became more sensitive to racial discrimination, pressure grew for action on the local front. Although Albuquerque probably contained less prejudice against Blacks than most other American cities of the time, members of that ethnic group were systematically restricted from renting and buying much of the housing in the area, and this type of discrimination particularly affected the aspiring Black middle class. The New Mexico Committee of the National Civil Rights Commission reported in 1960 that from 1950 to 1958 Blacks had bought 300 homes in Albuquerque, but all except 24 had been resales. Because of "the conspiracy of realtors and homebuilders groups who have adamantly refused to sell Negroes homes in the open market," the committee charged, Blacks who could find sellers had to pay higher prices than Anglos. The report told of substandard quarters rented at high rates, and it excoriated the builders and realtors for keeping public housing out of Albuquerque except for the Wherry Housing Development, which was located on military property near Kirtland and Sandia.[737] The following year the committee reported that all of the new homes sold to Blacks since 1950 had been built by a Black contractor in the South Broadway urban renewal area. Responding to these revelations, Walter Duke, president of the Albuquerque Board of Realtors, declared that the board had no official policy on discrimination. "But we have been cautious about placing any element in a neighborhood that might degrade it," he admitted.[738]

During these years most of the push for open housing came from groups with relatively small followings and from a growing number of dedicated individuals. Mrs. Mona Utter, for example, found accommodations for some fifty Black families from 1954 through 1962 by placing an ad in the paper, under the name of the Albuquerque Committee Against Discrimination in Housing, requesting the kind of housing sought by the family she was helping at the time.[739] In October 1962, however, came an incident which sharply dramatized the housing problems of the Blacks and rallied large numbers of citizens to the cause. Omer Ahmed, a Black honors student in government from Somalia, informed officials at the University of New Mexico that he was withdrawing from the university because he could not find a landlord in the area who would rent to him. Being a Moslem, Ahmed felt he needed to live in an apartment rather than a dormitory room in order to prepare his meals according to his prescribed diet. The previous year the university had found him a place, but when summer had come Ahmed had given it up to go to New York, and this year he had preferred to find accommodations on his own. He had applied at more than fifty apartments in the university area, sometimes receiving veiled excuses, once being told, "We don't rent to Negroes." Before leaving town, he commented scathingly to Dr. Sherman Smith, director of student affairs, "I've read about prejudice all my life but this is the first time I've actually experienced it."[740]

Reaction to the incident was immediate and heated. The local chapter of the NAACP drew up a proposed ordinance which would outlaw discrimination in the sale or rental of housing in Albuquerque, and the group submitted it to the City Commission.[741] The United Campus Christian Fellowship, a religious organization at the university, began circulating a petition calling on the housing office to list only apartments open to all students;[742] around the end of the year the Student Senate passed a resolution along similar lines; and Dr. Sherman Smith announced the university would change its policy accordingly.[743] Omer Ahmed decided to return to school, and several landlords volunteered to rent him an apartment,[744] but the momentum for a city ordinance on the matter continued to grow. The Albuquerque Committee of the New Mexico Council on Human Relations launched a drive to obtain five thousand signatures on cards which read, "I will accept with an open mind every individual who moves into my neighborhood regardless of his race or religion," and the support of religious leaders and people connected with the university was vigorously enlisted.[745] And coincidentally, the day after the drive was begun President Kennedy issued an executive order prohibiting racial and religious discrimination on housing built with federal grants, loans, mortgage insurance or guarantees—effective immediately.[746]

In the face of the rising public sentiment, the primary opposition to the ordinance under consideration remained the building industry. W. Howard Parsons, executive vice president of the Albuquerque Home Builders Association, contended, "Prejudices, unreasoning and unjustified as they may be, cannot be changed overnight by legislation and decree. They will not disappear by the adoption of a City of Albuquerque ordinance whether by issuance of an administrative order or any action of the home building industry alone."[747] Sentiments such as these, however, were voiced only by a dwindling minority, and on June 18, 1963, the City Commission unanimously gave emergency passage to an ordinance similar to the one the NAACP had earlier proposed.[748] A seven-member Fair Housing Advisory Committee was established to investigate complaints of violations; if a complaint was found valid and a satisfactory resolution could not be obtained, the committee would recommend that the city attorney prosecute.[749] A penalty of a three hundred dollars fine and a ninety-days prison sentence could be imposed.[750] Although the committee moved slowly and seldom pushed for prosecution, its impact and that of the ordinance behind it served to melt away most of the discriminatory housing practices in Albuquerque.

The university community, which had been in the forefront of the effort to pass the open housing ordinance, was making strides toward ending racial discrimination on a social level. The college fraternities and sororities were perceived by many of the other students as bastions of conservatism, and in 1961 the national charters of two of the fraternities still prohibited the admission of Blacks.[751] In 1963 the Inter-Fraternity Council turned down a bid for colonization status by Omega Psi Phi, a Black fraternity, and many student leaders vehemently denounced the refusal.[752] In 1964 the administration of the University of New Mexico asked the Board of Regents to declare that, as of June 30, 1965, the university would no longer recognize any group with a stated policy denying membership on the basis of race or religion.[753] The regents complied.[754] In April of 1964 the Inter-Fraternity Council invited Omega Psi Phi to start a colony at the university as a first step toward full fraternity status.[755]

In other fields besides civil rights, the university was a center of local liberal activity. As was happening on many other college campuses across the nation, many of the students and faculty, ignited by the idealism of the civil rights movement and encouraged by their successes in helping to end discriminatory practices, began to assert themselves vigorously against other types of restrictions. Throughout the early sixties members of the academic community took strong stands for "academic freedom," the freedom to explore and proclaim what they believed to be the truth without regard for community pressure. Their continued ability to do so was in large measure due to the forcefulness and political adroitness of Tom Popejoy, who had been president of the University of New Mexico since 1948.

In early 1961 seven faculty members signed a petition calling for the abolition of the House Un-American Activities Committee, and several indignant state legislators responded by proposing a bill to set up a committee to investigate the university. Two students—Mike Kyne and Mark Acuff, president of the junior class—began collecting signatures for a petition opposing the measure. Popejoy backed the petition gatherers: "The support the students are giving to a fundamentally important concept of freedom will, I believe, be appreciated by the entire university community." He went on, "We may agree or disagree with what the professors said, but we cherish their right to express themselves as citizens."[756] A few days later nearly a hundred university people converged on the Senate Finance Committee hearings in Santa Fe, among them Mark Acuff bearing the petition with 1927 signatures and President Popejoy eloquently defending the professors, and the committee voted to kill the bill.[757] In the spring of 1962, the faculty voted its opposition to a portion of the National Defense Education Act of 1958 which required students receiving federal aid to swear that they neither believed in, supported nor held membership in groups advocating illegal overthrow of the American government,[758] and another round of controversy with the outside community was launched. The American Legion called for an investigation of the university,[759] the New Mexico Civil Liberties Union asked for a public discussion of the test oath issue,[760] and Popejoy staunchly declared, "The university faculty and student body are thoroughly loyal to the U.S. government. It irritates me a good deal for anyone to question their patriotism."[761] Eventually the United States Congress repealed the test oath provision, and this particular issue melted away. But others, significant and trivial, kept rising to the surface, often fanned by the student newspaper the *Lobo*, which gave extensive coverage to national news. During the school year 1961-1962 Mark Acuff, now editor, found himself in a running battle with one of the regents.[762] John MacGregor, his successor, clashed openly with the head of the journalism department over editorial policy, and Popejoy again moved swiftly and effectively to quash the feud.[763] The president's efforts on behalf of academic freedom were enthusiastically received throughout most of the university community. In the fall of 1964 the Student Council passed a resolution expressing "its appreciation and gratitude for the sincere interest and unlimited trust that Tom L. Popejoy has always shown regarding students and their ability to handle themselves in a mature, responsible manner."[764]

If the University of New Mexico was the most important center for the lively expression of fresh ideas and the developing liberal consciousness in Albuquerque during the sixties, liberalism's strongest political arm was the Grass Roots Committee in the local Democratic Party. Many of its members came from the university community, and most lived in the heights on the eastern side of town. Formed in 1959, its first platform included some proposals much in the rational and efficient spirit also embodied by the Albuquerque Citizens Committee—utility regulation, more power to the City of Albuquerque to raise money, a merit system for all state employees below the policy-making level—and some proposals that were clearly liberal and designed to help the poor—a broader state minimum wage law and repeal of welfare deterrent laws.[765] Over the next several years the group retained its faith in an extended merit system, which the legislature soon passed into law, in part because of Grass Roots influence, but it became more aggressively liberal. Its platforms in the early sixties demanded a restructuring of the tax system, with more emphasis placed on income and inheritance taxes and less on sales tax, which it deemed regressive; raising the state minimum wage to the federal level and extending it to cover all types of employment; increasing welfare benefits; increasing the appropriation for the Fair Employment Practices Commission; and adding a penalty clause to the law prohibiting discrimination in public places. Being convinced that "fair trade" laws setting liquor prices discouraged competition and kept prices unreasonably high, the committee also advocated their repeal.[766]

As the reach of these reformers grew, so did their grasp. In 1960 five of the Bernalillo County Democrats it endorsed were among the nine later nominated by the party; in 1962 seven of the Democratic nominees from the county had received prior Grass Roots endorsement. That year one of their members, an energetic young lawyer named Henry Kiker, beat out John Flaska, an "old line party regular" who was supported by aides of U.S. Senators Dennis Chavez and Clinton P. Anderson, in the race for county chairman of the Democratic Party. The membership of the Grass Roots Committee had grown from its initial 60 persons to between 150 and 200 dues payers, and its influence was far out of proportion to its numbers.[767] Riding on the crest of the wave of public enthusiasm for reform, these predominantly middle-class activists were now one of the most potent political forces in the metropolitan area.

The growth of the liberals' influence went hand in hand with a broadening of their goals. No longer simply concerned with ending racial and religious discrimination and with passing laws more favorable to the poor people of the area, more and more of them became involved in a concerted effort to reshape society along what they considered more just, open and humanitarian lines. Their activities spread into numerous areas; three of the most significant in the Albuquerque area were improving the physical environment, protesting against the War in Viet Nam, and fighting poverty.

Back in the mid-fifties the city had enacted an air-pollution ordinance, but it was so weak as to be virtually ineffective. Compared to most other cities in America, Albuquerque still had remarkably clear air, and the people had been reluctant to take any measures that might discourage industry. As the years passed, however, increasing numbers of persons and automobiles began to make the thin air denser with particulate matter. Occasionally a haze would obscure the view of the Sandia Mountains. Gradually the citizens came to the conclusion that public action would have to be taken. Much of the problem was due to the dust from unpaved roads; an expanded program of street construction helped some. Another component of the pollution was ashes from trash burning. In 1962 the City Commission passed an ordinance forbidding the emission of "soot, cinders, dust, noxious gases or fumes," and it declared that any such emissions into the air "as to endanger or be detrimental to the health, comfort, safety or welfare of any person or of the public" may be declared a public nuisance. More specifically, it prohibited open fire burning of "any refuse, rubbish or garbage" except in cases where the fire department granted permission.[768]

As was the case with the fair housing ordinance, enforcement came slowly and by degrees. In late 1963, the prohibition against burning leaves and trash became effective—henceforth the unwanted debris would have to be hauled away by the garbage department.[769] For a while the city contented itself with giving verbal advice and warnings to such prime offenders as supermarkets burning their trash in smoky incinerators—this was called the education phase. In the latter half of 1965, though, citations began to be issued to accused violators.[770] By this time the city had a fledgling environmental health department with a budget of about $14,000, slightly less than half of which was provided by the U.S, Department of Health, Education and Welfare.[771]

As this city department expanded over the following years, so did the issue of protecting the environment in the public mind. Its most outspoken champions were the avowed liberals, especially those associated with the University of New Mexico, but business and political leaders also grew more sensitive to the matter. In 1969, when the company Parsons and Whittemore declared its intention to build a huge paper mill near Albuquerque in the Rio Grande Valley, the residents were torn between their enthusiasm for new jobs and industry and their fears concerning the impact of the plant on the natural environment. In early September the Executive Board of the Albuquerque Citizens Committee declared its opposition to locating the proposed mill in the vicinity of the city, and the Chamber of Commerce did likewise.[772] A few days later Parsons and Whittemore announced it had found no suitable site in the state where it was welcome, and it would build elsewhere.[773] Concern for the environment, once of interest to only a small minority, had become a powerful force to be reckoned with throughout the community.

Further removed from the influence of the people of Albuquerque but arousing more passionate feelings, especially among the young, was the War in Viet Nam. In the early sixties, when the nation had a fairly small number of military men committed to that remote part of the world, most Americans were not particularly enthusiastic about the venture, but their patriotism led them to give it their support. However, the years of escalation of the conflict, the recurring discoveries that American armed forces were more deeply involved than the public had been told, the apparently free hand with which the executive branch of the government had been conducting the war with little explicit approval by the Congress, and—most of all—the mounting frustration of never vanquishing the enemy gradually made the war increasingly unpopular. A 1964 editorial in the *Albuquerque Journal* opened, "The mess in South Viet Nam grows steadily messier." The writer acknowledged that the war was a "limited" one. "But 'limited,' too, is the patience of the American public which has been contributing heavily in lives and money to a struggle which daily seems to have less and less assurance of victory," he concluded.[774] In 1968, during the dedication ceremony for an enclosure for exotic animals at the Albuquerque Zoo, the father of a slain soldier in whose memory the structure had been built observed bitterly that his son had died in a purposeless battle.[775]

And to many of the young, who were being drafted to fight in a war for which they had probably less sympathy than any other sector of the population, the conflict in Viet Nam emerged as a symbol of what was arbitrary, oppressive and brutal in American society.

Active opposition to the war built as steadily and relentlessly as the war itself. For years there had been a small enclave of local pacifists, and they began to assert themselves more vigorously. In 1964, for example, while a civil defense training session in the use of bomb shelters was taking place in the basement of the University of New Mexico Geology Building, a group of about a dozen persons, mostly women and representing several religious faiths, stood outside bearing placards with such slogans as "The only shelter is peace." They passed out an information sheet asserting that "civil defense helps to make the idea of nuclear war tolerable."[776] As resentment of the war spread, many people who had been active in the civil rights movement came to embrace this new cause. Allen Cooper, a sometime university student who had campaigned in Albuquerque, in Washington, D.C., in Indianola, Mississippi, and elsewhere against racial discrimination and had been jailed several times for his zealous efforts,[777] was arrested in Mexico City in 1965 for demonstrating against American involvement in Viet Nam, and he was deported.[778] Not deterred in the slightest, the following year he notified the Internal Revenue Service that he would refuse to pay income tax because of his opposition to the way his money was being used.[779] In the university community opposition to the war was becoming an article of faith among the liberal majority. In 1967 the campus humor magazine *The UNM Juggler* ran some anti-war satire, provoking the easily aroused American Legion to label it a "communist" publication.[780] By late 1969 a coordinating committee, acting in conjunction with a nationwide organization, was organizing monthly protest rallies against the war. In the course of one of them, more than eight hundred persons led by six pallbearers with a black coffin marched from the university to the armed forces induction center downtown. Arriving at their destination. the crowd, sporting black armbands and black boutonnieres, listened to a Catholic priest read the names of New Mexicans killed in Viet Nam; meanwhile, a bell from the U.S.S. New Mexico rang at four-second intervals, once for every American casualty from the fighting.[781]

For all the passionate commitment it inspired, the anti-war movement in Albuquerque was necessarily too dependent on national and international developments to make much headway toward its goal. And for most of the decade, the environmental movement engaged the liberals' sympathies more than it did their energetic involvement. For the numerous ones who were ready and eager to deal directly with what they considered social injustice and to try to make important changes in their community, another large field of activity was opening up. The local War on Poverty could absorb all the idealism, energy and devotion the troops could muster.

When the United States Congress passed the Economic Opportunity Act of 1964, the first of a number of heavily financed and sweeping laws aimed at bettering the lot of the nation's poor, the War on Poverty, proclaimed dramatically by President Johnson and other prominent national leaders, was made an important part of the country's policy for the next several years. Exactly how poverty was to be eliminated was a little vague—many different kinds of programs were launched hopefully, and changes were made as new approaches came into favor—but most of the people associated with the antipoverty drive seemed to feel that an abundance of money, activity and good intentions could do wonders. They were also firmly convinced that a fresh start was needed, and to this end many of the traditional channels of political patronage were avoided so that the system which, in some people's eyes, had ensnared the poor in the first place would not be perpetuated. Sergeant Shriver, who was already in charge of the Peace Corps, was installed as head of the overall poverty program. The director of the program for each state was appointed by the governor, local program directors were appointed by local boards, and particular projects were subject to approval by regional branches of the Office of Economic Opportunity. Consultations with Congressmen were avoided; as a result of this side-stepping of established lines of political authority and the recurrent ineffectiveness in attaining its goals, the poverty program was frequently criticized by prominent leaders. But no one questioned its boldness and vision. Unlike previous welfare programs, this one would involve the poor in the decision making: the Economic Opportunity Act mandated "maximum participation of the poor."

On the local level the machinery of the poverty program underwent some shifts as the participants strove to arrive at an organizational structure that would follow the slowly emerging national pattern. In late 1964 articles of incorporation were drawn up for a board of fourteen members, including representatives of city and county government, the United Community Fund, and the Community Council, an influential organization of leading citizens.[782] The Economic Opportunity Board (EOB) was approved by the City and County Commissions, the positions on the Board of Directors were filled, and Ex-County Commissioner Harry Kinney was elected chairman. In February 1965 the group had a confusing session with Don Mathis, a representative from the Office of Economic Opportunity, during which a member's question, "Is this the kind of board you hope to work with?" was met by, "Guidelines are now being revised to emphasize points being slid over."[783] That spring, new guidelines were handed down requiring that one-third of the membership of each local board be public officials or their appointees, one-third agency members or their representatives, and one-third the poor themselves.[784] So about the same time that New Mexico's U.S. Senators Clinton P. Anderson and Joseph M. Montoya were beginning to complain about not being consulted on appointments to positions in the poverty program hierarchy, the Albuquerque EOB Board of Directors was reconstituted.[785] The dominating influence on the board shifted from the established community leaders—representing more or less the traditional elites—to persons with ties to the Grass Roots Committee. The new president was Art Blumenfeld, director of the Bureau of Business Research at the University of New Mexico and member for a time of the Grass Roots Executive Board, and the salaried position of executive director was filled by Clarence Gailard, who had just completed a two-year term as chairman of the Grass Roots Committee.[786]

Meanwhile, the poor people to be aided were also organizing along lines that largely ignored established political patterns in their communities. Beginning in November 1964, several of the poorer neighborhoods formed community improvement associations with the help of community development workers from the Peace Corps Training Center at the University of New Mexico. By around the middle of 1965, seven such groups had been organized—in South Barelas, an area about a dozen blocks south of Central, just south of Bridge Street, and east of the Rio Grande; in North Barelas, north of Bridge Street; in John Marshall, the only predominantly Black neighborhood involved at this time and located in the South Broadway area, east of the Santa Fe tracks; in East San Jose, situated south of John Marshall; in Santa Barbara-Martineztown, an old section north of Lomas Boulevard and east of Old Town; in Arenal, in the south valley just west of the river; and in the mid-north valley. The leaders of these associations were frequently young and inexperienced: Larry Barreras, president of the South Barelas group, and Rudy Baca, president of the organization in Santa Barbara-Martineztown, were both twenty-seven years old. The spirit of opposition to traditional politics was rife. One resident commented, "The poor people here in Barelas don't trust the politician. They think of community development as their problem, and they don't want anyone to take advantage of their desire to do something." The constitution for the North Barelas Community Development Association stated: "No district precinct chairman, chairwoman or justice of the peace shall be on the board of directors of the association, and no person shall use the association in any manner to further his political ambitions." For the time being, the established leaders and patrons of these neighborhoods were content to keep their hands off and see what developed.[787]

The push on the part of the poverty workers and their allies for a clean slate was also manifested in their strategies for making the people poor no more. One of the fundamental ideas was starkly simple: the people would be transformed into members of the middle class, like the majority of the Grass Roots Democrats and most of the professional social workers, and they would therefore acquire comfortable incomes. Poverty would be erased as from a blackboard. Speaking of the neighborhood residents being ushered into positions of responsibility in the poverty program, Clarence Gailard commented, "They themselves are not poor, and they will serve as an aspiration and model for the poor. They will know the necessary steps to be taken for action which responds to the needs of the poor. Ultimately, they will be able to press the case for the poor—to the city and the state—in terms of middle-class values." If the poor were to rise out of their impoverished condition, they would have to absorb such values as hard work and discipline. According to Art Blumenfeld, "To raise the income of the poor to a middle-class standard of living assumes, at the heart of the matter, the acceptance of middle-class values. And the changing of a value system takes time. . . ."[788]

This attitude was reflected in many of the proposed projects, especially during the early years. One of the most extreme examples was the plan submitted in July 1965 for "partnership parents," which was "designed to educate pre-school children from poor homes in the values of American middle class life." Children would be transported to suburban homes for three hours a day to observe such values in action, and the bulk of the money requested would go to professionals monitoring the program. After some consideration, this idea was discarded,[789] but the basic concept lived on in other forms. It underlay much of the urban renewal activity going on at this time—slum clearance, as it was sometimes called. One of the impulses for the city's leased housing program in 1968 was, as a journalist put it, "Take enough low-income families out of substandard ghetto dwellings, scatter them through the city in decent quarters and do this often enough and soon the ghettos will disappear."[790] And it was also largely responsible for the tremendous emphasis placed on education for the young. "To the extent that we can alleviate poverty," remarked Blumenfeld, "we must ignore those over twenty-five; we can only make them more comfortable."[791] The various prongs of the drive for education and vocational training included, among others, the Home Improvements Program, consisting of teams or workers learning the construction trade;[792] the South Barelas Training Center, where young people attended classes in such trades as landscape gardening and hotel service;[793] the Job Corps Center for Women, where young women from various parts of the country trained in basic skills at an annual cost averaging $5500 per enrollee;[794] Head Start, a preschool program designed to give poor children enough background to compete with their future middle-class classmates;[795] the Tutor Corps, an association of high school student volunteers who gave special help to elementary and junior high school students from poor neighborhoods;[796] Upward Bound, an intensive summer school administered by the University of Albuquerque for high school students who were poor but were thought to have the potential for higher education;[797] and the New Careers Project, for aspiring students attempting to combine a limited course of academic study at the University of New Mexico with training and work at a social agency.[798] On the shoulders of such young people who underwent these training programs rode most of the hopes of the poverty workers.

Not all of the aspects of the local poverty program, however, were geared toward remodeling the people into solid middle-class folk. Although the poverty workers had a tendency to feel they knew what was best for the poor, the residents of the target neighborhoods also had a voice, and almost everyone involved in the antipoverty effort recognized the value of these people's taking an active part in the decision making. Years earlier two community centers had been established in the area—the Barelas Community Center in North Barelas and the East San Jose Community Center—and they had been popular successes. Run by the City Parks Department, their purpose was primarily recreational, but several welfare agencies operated on their premises on a limited basis.[799] The newly formed community associations soon began to campaign for similar centers in their own neighborhoods. In the summer of 1965 the South Barelas Community Improvement Association asked for $194,000 for a community service center and a job training center. The Board of Directors for the Albuquerque-Bernalillo County EOB ratified the plan, but the hitch was that, according to Title II of the Economic Opportunity Act, locally approved community development projects had to be funded on a matching basis with the community providing 10 percent of the money. By October about $10,000 remained to be raised, and Clarence Gailard made a special plea at a meeting of the Grass Roots Committee. "Unless we get the $10,000, I will feel that the poverty program has failed in this county," he declared. "The war on poverty, unless it gets a good deal of community support, isn't going to get off the ground." The Grass Roots Democrats responded by pledging to help raise the funds,[800] the money was found, and Grass Roots members were in the vanguard of numerous subsequent efforts on behalf of the poverty program.

These two new centers began functioning in February 1966, and shortly thereafter applications were made, approved and funded to open four more community centers—one in Martineztown; one serving the South Broadway, Kirtland, John Marshall and East San Jose neighborhoods; one for the poor in the north valley; and one for the impoverished areas of the south valley. These facilities came to house such services as family consultation clinics, prenatal and postnatal clinics, vocational rehabilitation agencies, child day-care operations and offices for the Legal Aid Society. In addition, a recreational center was established in South San Jose.[801] The middle-class poverty workers continued to regard these centers and their services as less primary than the more direct approaches to raise the people out of poverty, but they were quite able to rationalize their existence. Said Dr. Lester M. Libo, Associate Professor of Psychiatry at the University of New Mexico Medical Center, "Most people from deprived areas feel helpless and hopeless; perhaps we can improve their strength to make them not feel that way."[802] EOB Board President Art Blumenfeld took a broader view: "They [the centers] must be a focal point for the community; a place where people go to vocalize their frustrations; a place where people can identify their problems and participate in action to alleviate them. If this is successful I don't care what else happens."[803]

In subsequent years the poor people did come to vocalize their frustrations to a greater extent, lashing out at the conditions and institutions which angered them. Often their targets included the professional poverty workers themselves, with whose goals and methods they were not in complete accord. The purity of the liberals' vision of the War on Poverty was further undermined by the increasing influence of local politics as various individuals and factions contended for the juicy plums being offered by the federal government. And although a number of the aspiring poor people were able to utilize the machinery of the antipoverty program to achieve a higher standard of living, poverty retained its stubborn presence in the city—most of the needy could simply not be transmuted into typical middle-class citizens by the techniques which were being attempted, perhaps not by any techniques. Nevertheless, the liberals' drive against poverty was succeeding in making life materially better for many of the downtrodden of society, and, equally important, it was helping them gain greater measures of power and respect.

The significance of the liberal consciousness in Albuquerque during the sixties and early seventies, however, was not only a matter of what it was able to accomplish. In a broad historical view this version of liberalism was the most important political focus of the people's efforts to cope with and adjust to the ongoing changes in the organization of society. As the various institutions had grown larger, communication among levels of the hierarchies had become more difficult, and many of the persons involved had come to feel that their voices were not being heard. They sensed they were acting the parts of lifeless cogs in huge, impersonal machines which were grinding away toward soulless ends. Yet these years of institutional growth were also the years when, in many ways, society was also becoming more permissive. Restraints on most personal expression were being relaxed to a degree unprecedented in America's history. The tension between these two sweeping trends—growth of large groups and waxing permissiveness—resulted in numerous conflicts, and in most obvious respects the liberals cast their lot on the side of greater freedom for the individual. As a group they campaigned against such traditional restrictions as sexual taboos and racial distinctions, and they also fought against the impersonality of large institutions, including the military bureaucracies of the U.S. government. They favored the creation of new vistas for the individual—in the arts, in education, in work and in social behavior. Some of their biggest contributions lay in the innumerable things they did to make the big institutions more responsive to the people whose lives they touched and more amenable to human variation and expressiveness.

Their emphasis on individual freedom notwithstanding, the members of the liberal community were not averse to group behavior. If they had been, they would have made scant headway against the powerful forces and ingrained attitudes with which they vied. They were loosely united by a more or less shared vision of the way they felt society ought to be; if some elements of that vision were naive or impracticable, it was nonetheless a driving, inspiring force. Many of the liberally inclined were active on several fronts of their crusade. The Action Committee on Human Rights, for example, worked against sexual censorship, racial discrimination and poverty during the mid-sixties.[804] Permissive though it was in many respects, the liberal vision contained a number of definite points that many members of the Albuquerque community were reluctant to accept, and the liberals did not hesitate to press for legislation to enforce certain new prohibitions which they felt were for the general welfare, such as rules against discrimination and pollution. Despite their hostility to much institutional behavior, they were eager to erect new bureaucracies to deal with what they considered pressing concerns, including poverty and health care. In the final analysis, this group of free spirits was not quite as free as most of its members thought; like the people of any other group, they adhered roughly to a set of "do's" and "don'ts." But in their devotion to their cause, in their battles for "the people" and against "the establishment," they found, for a time, a dignified and lofty sense of purpose in a world that was bewildering to many. And although the coming years brought a toll of disappointments, frustrations, and shifting allegiances, it was partly through their efforts that the personal dimension in society retained color and glow.

The Growth of the Youth Culture

The young people of Albuquerque, especially the students and in particular the most vocal and influential ones among their number, constituted one of the most important sources of support for the liberals. With the natural energy of their years and their idealism, they felt ready to take on the task of helping to reshape society, and they were eager to champion the causes of the groups without much power, of which they felt they were one. Indeed, one of the main causes of the discontent was the growing disparity which they perceived between their political influence, which was mostly indirect because a citizen had to be twenty-one years of age in order to vote, and their numbers and economic importance. The enrollment at the University of New Mexico shot up from the 1959-60 figure of 7284 to 19,814 in 1971-72,[805] and current fund expenditures per student rose from $1123.70 to $2116.70 for an increase of 34.4 percent adjusted for inflation.[806] During these same years the student population of the primary and secondary schools in the county increased only from 64,660 to 91,093, but the public expenditures per student jumped from $219.75 to $706.68 for a 129.4 percent increase corrected for inflation.[807] In the meantime the population and median family income of the metropolitan area as a whole were growing at a respectable but considerably less spectacular rate.

The cultural impact of the young people and of what various observers referred to as the "youth movement" and the "student movement" was also increasing rapidly. The whole society seemed preoccupied with the glamour of youth. Interest in sports boomed: the athletic budgets for the public schools skyrocketed,[808] and the Albuquerque Dukes, the local professional baseball team, went up from Class D status in 1960 all the way to Triple A by the start of the 1972 season.[809] Young fashions such as miniskirts and blue jeans became the rage. Rock music gained in artistry and prestige. Youthful slang crept into conversation at nearly all levels. With their growing numbers and their increasing share of the limelight, the young people took themselves extremely seriously, and many of them came to move beyond the more temperate positions and claims of their liberal elders.

The early stages of this wave of youthful assertiveness seemed mildly adventurous but innocuous. Toward the end of the fifties some of the more venturesome of the young dipped into such traces of bohemian life as could be found in Albuquerque. In early 1959 the owner of a bookstore opened up a coffee house downtown and encouraged "free expression" on the premises. There patrons who might be college students, sophisticates or actual "beatniks" engaged in discussions of the evils of censorship, poetry, politics, the police and whatever else came to mind while volunteer musicians performed on the guitar, violin or flute.[810] Within two years four more coffee houses were added to the Albuquerque night scene, as numbers of the young flocked to witness the beatniks, with their informal attire and their air of studied indifference to American striving.[811] "Many people have said that the Beat rebellion is without a cause, but this isn't exactly true," explained one avowed beatnik.

"It's more of a rebellion against America's false values. Americans seem to have lost the ability to wonder. All they think about is getting ahead of the Joneses and watching television."[812] Their preference for artistic pursuits over more typical middle-class activities had an undeniable appeal to the restless young, but these eccentric dropouts seemed hardly the pied pipers who might lead masses of the young people seriously astray.

In the rising excitement of the early sixties the beatniks fell out of the public eye; the students who were seeking channels to express their frustrations and assert themselves turned more toward political activism. As we have seen, young people at the University of New Mexico took a leading role in the local civil rights movement, and many were eager to combat what they considered social injustice wherever they found it. In their denunciations of racial discrimination and other restrictions of freedom, campus leaders did not hesitate to claim they knew better than their more conservative elders. While he was editor of the *Lobo*, Mark Acuff asserted that most American newspapers had "horribly declined" and were motivated by considerations of advertising and economics rather than by a desire to create "radical criticism, new ideas and expression of intelligent imagination." In contrast, college newspapers were the last stronghold of a truly free press, since they were not run for the sake of earning a profit "and their editors are generally young and unfrightened." Students were better able to bring about necessary changes in society than their parents, he contended, because they lacked older people's "inherent bigotry."[813]

It soon became apparent that students at the University of New Mexico and elsewhere in the country were not confining their activism to the usual liberal causes, that their rebelliousness and their demand for more voice were surfacing in unanticipated ways. In early 1965 American newspapers were emblazoned with news of the Free Speech Movement at the University of California at Berkeley. This sequence of protests and strikes seemed to have a more amorphous target than earlier student movements: it attacked administrative rules governing student behavior, traditional conventions concerning acceptable language, and the bureaucratic structure of the university itself. In Albuquerque the reports aroused activists and provoked anxiety among administrators. When asked about the pervasive unrest, campus spokesman John Salazar said, "Students want respect."[814] The following October the regents at the University of New Mexico adopted a broad policy defining the rights and responsibilities of the regents, the administration, the faculty and the students. Although the regents had the ultimate authority and responsibility for the running of the university, it stated, they would not interfere with the decisions of the administration, faculty or student government "except as these may have been arrived at in a capricious, unfair or arbitrary manner." More specifically, the regents "recognize and approve the right of free speech and honest expression of opinion on any subject by any member of the university community, whether the subject relates to on-campus or off-campus issues. . . . Off-campus speakers speaking on campus, if approved in accordance with university regulations, should be allowed free expression of their views. Students with diverse points of view should permit such speakers to be heard without harassment. . . . No student has a right to interfere with others in their pursuit of an education. It is assumed that a student who so disregards the rights of others will be disciplined appropriately."[815] With the basic rules so expressly codified, it was hoped that the university could avoid the turmoil rocking many other institutions of higher learning.

Potentially explosive issues, however, were already arising at the university, severely testing President Tom Popejoy's influence and skill to keep the peace while retaining the support of the faculty and students. In the fall of 1964 James Allen Kennedy, a transfer student from Loyola University in Chicago, announced that he was chairman of the newly formed Albuquerque chapter of the W.E.B. Dubois Clubs of America.[816] FBI head J. Edgar Hoover had recently denounced the organization as a Communist front, and on this basis Popejoy stated that the university would refuse to grant affiliation with the chapter.[817] Kennedy insisted that the club had no Communist ties, and Dr. Edwin Hoyt, chairman of the department of government, came out in favor of granting the club a charter, but the president stood firm.[818] In November of 1965 the U.S. Supreme Court struck down the law requiring Communists to register, and Kennedy openly declared, "I am and have been a member of the Communist Party USA since June of this year."[819] During the ensuing furor Popejoy insisted that the university would uphold the civil liberties of all students, including Communists, so long as they obeyed the laws.[820] The appeal of Communism on the university campus was limited, the controversy soon faded away, but a new militant group, the Students for a Democratic Society (SDS) became active and obtained a charter. Originating in the protests of the civil rights movement, SDS was currently involved in student activism nationwide, and although it had no ties with foreign governments, many respectable people regarded it as subversive. At the University of New Mexico its efforts were mainly confined to making evaluations of courses and professors, declaring its sympathies with militant ethnic groups, and encouraging radical criticism of American government and society.[821] The next large-scale campus controversy, however, was not set off by a militant organization but by a branch of student government. The Student Speakers Committee invited Stokely Carmichael, an advocate of Black power who had allegedly spoken out in favor of draft evasion and urban guerilla warfare, to address the university community in early 1968, and a storm of criticism erupted from the United Veterans Council, a state legislator and citizens from conservative parts of the state. Popejoy steadfastly insisted on the right of the students to invite whomever they pleased. Toward the end of January Carmichael cancelled his engagement, and the angry voices on each side quieted down.[822]

In July 1968, after twenty years at the helm of the largest university of the state, Tom Popejoy retired, and Ferrel Heady, a relatively inexperienced recent arrival to Albuquerque, became the next president.[823] Throughout the academic community and across New Mexico people watched to see how the institution would fare under the new leadership. The first challenge was fairly minor. The summer edition of the *New Mexico Quarterly*, published by the university, was devoted exclusively to Senator Eugene McCarthy's campaign for the Democratic nomination for President; appearing just before the national Democratic convention and clearly favoring the liberal candidate it was covering, the publication was widely read and vehemently criticized by citizens who felt the university should stay out of politics. Heady responded by asking the faculty publications committee to "conduct a review of the matter."[824] A thornier issue arose in October, when about a hundred students opposed to the War in Viet Nam gathered to watch an NROTC drill being conducted on Zimmerman Field and then moved onto the field, interfering with the procedure. The protesters were ordered to disperse, some did not, and campus authorities recognized among those remaining three students who had previously been active in campus protests—Manny Wright, Larry Russell and Allen Cooper. Noting that the 1965 statement on rights and responsibilities had declared that "No student has the right to interfere with others in their pursuit of an education," Vice President of Student Affairs Harold Lavender immediately suspended the trio. A groundswell of support for Wright, Russell and Cooper swept the campus: Radical Rush, a coalition of New Left groups, distributed leaflets and called for an open meeting of the student body at the Student Union Building, and the Executive Committee of the New Mexico chapter of the American Association of University Professors issued a statement calling for the administration to observe due process and hold a hearing.[825] Bowing to the pressure, Heady lifted the suspension pending an appeal to the Student Standards Committee. That body reaffirmed the suspension,[826] whereupon the three students directed a further appeal to President Heady. In a special meeting the faculty passed a resolution asking the president "to exercise clemency" in the case and another resolution declaring that "questioning" of university programs should be done within established procedures and "based upon rational and free discourse with full respect for the rights of others."[827] In late December Ferrel Heady lifted the suspension "conditional upon the future conduct of the students," bringing the episode to a close.[828] Whether such wavering in the face of public pressure would be to the long-term benefit of the university, however, remained unanswered.

Reading and hearing about the rising tempo of activism at the University of New Mexico, many older residents wondered what, other than expressing their displeasure with war and with authority in general, the students were accomplishing. To a degree that was probably not obvious to a distant observer, the students were slowly carving out a world for themselves, increasing their group solidarity and extending the boundaries of their freedom and influence. In their attire, in their casual conversation, in their political activity and even in the classrooms, they were demonstrating increased unanimity of behavior and thought. When the university curriculum did not offer classes they wanted, students moved more aggressively than in the past to petition for new courses. A "free university" was established and ran sporadically in the second half of the sixties and on into the seventies; there professors, students and volunteers from the community at large taught informal classes with titles like "Psychedelic Drugs," "Non-Violence—An Alternative to Traditional Conflict Resolution," and "The Social Implications of Clinical Behaviorism."[829] Meanwhile, the traditional policy of *in loco parentis*, whereby the university assumed a sort of parental responsibility for the students in attendance, particularly in such matters as where they were allowed to live, was steadily receding, and in 1970 the faculty voted to eliminate it altogether.[830] Two years later four of the dormitories were opened to both sexes,[831] but more and more of the students were electing to reside in off-campus apartments, which were totally free of university supervision. The young people were also gaining representation on many previously all-faculty committees:[832] as the university came to exert less control over their lives, they were getting a little more influence on the governance of that institution. And they were also getting more tangible public support. Free health services at the University of New Mexico were increasing, and a growing number of the students were receiving financial assistance in the form of scholarships, government loans or federally backed work-study employment.[833]

In the lower age groups—the high school and junior high school students—activism and assertiveness against the authority of older people was slower to take hold. In 1967, for example, when a group of about twenty-five antiwar college students began passing out leaflets at Albuquerque High School explaining techniques of avoiding the draft, they were set upon and beaten by a large crowd of high schoolers.[834] But gradually, like expanding ripples from the splash of a large stone thrown into a pond, the militant spirit spread wider and wider.

Even before the onset of activism in the pre-college grades, the Albuquerque Public Schools and the city government had made some efforts to go out of their way to cater to the students' interests. Back in 1955 the school system had established the Albuquerque Youth Council, consisting of delegates from each of the city's high schools and junior high schools, a board of eight commissioners elected by the delegates, a chairman, and adult advisors. Although the primary function of the council was to act as a public relations link between the students and the adults of the community—its most publicized activity was to organize Youth Day, the one day a year when young people took over the offices of city government—by the mid-sixties it became involved in such weightier undertakings as an advisory board to the juvenile probation office, a parent guidance workshop and a sex education workshop.[835]

Public officials were having less success with providing entertainment for the young people, however. In April 1964 city government sponsored a teenage dance at the civic auditorium for the first time since the monthly dances had been canceled in 1959, a gang fight broke out, and the officials decided not to risk a repetition.[836] Toward the end of the following year, after much discussion between city officials, teenagers and other interested citizens, an ordinance was passed permitting the establishment of privately owned dance halls for young people from fifteen through eighteen years of age. Many of the teenagers resented the dress regulations and the prohibitions against drinking and smoking that were written into the ordinance, but they now had more access to nighttime entertainment than in the past.[837]

Such measures to meet their needs notwithstanding, the teenagers seemed beset with a superabundance of problems. Their complaints were aired in numerous newspaper articles, conferences and formal and informal protests, and such topics as drinking, drugs, the generation gap between the youngsters and the adults, and parental authority were recurrent. At a 1961 meeting with parents sponsored by the guidance department of Highland High School, a panel of four teenagers said that parents should be willing to delegate more responsibility to their children as they grew older, and, most important, families should discuss their problems.[838] In August 1965 at the first annual Governor's Conference for Children and Youth, entitled "Who Am I in This Mad Mad World?" many of the participants complained vehemently. According to Arnold Padilla, age seventeen, subsequently chairman of the Albuquerque Youth Council, "The problem is that adults are always setting down rules, setting down patterns. They should give a child something to follow, but they should teach him to think for himself. I think parents should be guides and advisers instead of leaders who are always telling you exactly what to do."[839]

The restiveness of the students was also reflected in a growing number of protest demonstrations, suspensions from school and rebellious clashes with authority. One of the most conspicuous emblems of the spirit of assertiveness against traditional middle-class restraints was long hair and facial whiskers; in the second half of the sixties there were several instances of students being suspended because their hair length did not conform to the principal's mandates.[840] (In contrast, in the only notable incident involving hair styles at the University of New Mexico, when the football coach excluded the shaggier players from attending the 1968 awards banquet, the Committee on Academic Freedom and Tenure scored the move as "a violation of those students' rights."[841]) Rebelliousness became a common pattern of behavior, often surfacing on slight provocations. In 1967, when the State Legislature refused to appropriate anywhere near as much funding as the school district had requested, a number of the teachers at West Mesa High School called in sick, and much of the student body likewise evaporated.[842] Earlier that year, at John Adams Junior High School, a pilot project in which sixth graders attended classes at the same location as seventh and eighth graders, the sixth graders held a march to protest being excluded from the school dances. "We don't want a sissy picnic," the youngsters declared defiantly. "We just want to dance."[843]

By the spring of 1969 the most active of the high school and junior high school students had reached a broad consensus on the changes they wanted made, and they were making a concerted effort to publicize their views and have them implemented. Students Open Forum, a loose coalition of high school students across the city, drew up a statement of "Civil and Human Rights for Students," which asserted, "Academic freedom should be a civil right guaranteed to every student in our nation. . . . This freedom should include the right to inquire into, learn and impart any knowledge in every field of interest without school interference." Among the more specific planks of the Students Open Forum platform were ending racial discrimination in the schools, eliminating regulations on dress and hair styles, gaining a voice in the selection of administrators and course material, and winning the freedoms to organize activities inside and outside of school and to distribute leaflets and other publications.[844] Some of the students were publishing "underground" newspapers, which, according to the current restrictions, had to be distributed off-campus. An issue of one of them, *The Joint Effort*, included excerpts from a widely read essay "The Student as Nigger," which read in part: "The main thing that's taught us in schools is how to be good niggers, how to obey the rules, dress in our uniforms and play the game, and DON'T BE UPPITY."[845]

If that was what the schools were attempting to instill in their charges, clearly they were not succeeding. Responding to the pressure from the various student groups, Daryl Harrell, executive assistant to the superintendent, met with the Students Open Forum in March to hear the complaints. Superintendent Chisholm commented, "I think it is very necessary to spend some time and effort to see if we are communicating with students. . . . We have got to work with students and faculties to find acceptable ways to do these things."[846] The Albuquerque Public Schools Citizens Exchange Group, an informal assembly of teachers, parents, students and other local citizens, held a number of meetings to discuss the issues.[847] And slowly, such exchanges of opinions led the way to a relaxation of some of the rules. By late 1970 most of the responsibility for dress and hair style codes had been placed in the hands of the student governments, and restrictions on hair length had been eliminated at all but one city high school.[848] As the students gained more freedom and influence, the intensity of their dissatisfaction began to abate.

Having seen the results of a little easing of restrictions, people in positions of responsibility in the school system began to consider more sweeping changes. In the summer of 1971 school board member Dan McKinnon began meeting with youth groups to get firsthand information on what kind of new rights the students wanted the most. That fall a tentative policy on student rights and responsibilities was drawn up,[849] and it was debated and revised on into the next year. In its later versions it provided guarantees meeting most of the demands made earlier by such organizations as the Students Open Forum: the right to wear political buttons, armbands and other badges of expression; the right to distribute leaflets and publications at specified campus locations, so long as the material was not obscene or libelous; the right to form political and social organizations provided that any student was allowed to join; the right of the students to dress and wear their hair as they pleased provided that no one's health was endangered; student government input into decisions on the curriculum; an appeals procedure for the more severe types of suspension; and other, less publicized rights. It codified in broad outline and considerable detail what a student could and could not do, and it substantially reduced the discretion of the individual principals to mete out punishment according to their own standards.[850] On May 22, 1972, the Albuquerque Public Schools Board of Education formally adopted the new policy;[851] in doing so it went a long way toward defusing the social and political unrest that had been seething in the schools for the previous decade.

During these same years when the young people had been busily pushing for more rights in the schools, they had also been gaining more institutional benefits in the society at large. As has been seen, much of the efforts of the War on Poverty had gone toward helping the youth of the poorer neighborhoods. Such agencies as the Youth Employment Service and Dial-a-Teen also reached out into the other parts of the city to find young people jobs.[852] Throughout the metropolitan area churches and civic groups were offering special programs for the youth. In 1970 a Youth Services Center was established to provide job service, information on such subjects as the draft, and various kinds of entertainment to all interested young persons.[853] And in 1971, after many years of struggle in that direction, a constitutional amendment was passed to lower the national voting age to eighteen.[854] No longer could young men be shipped off against their will to fight in a war chosen by persons beyond the reach of their votes.

Underlying the militant activism of the junior high school, high school and college students of the sixties and early seventies was the emergence of a youth subculture that was sometimes so different from and antagonistic to the dominant American modes of behavior that it was called the "counterculture." The relatively quiet beatniks of the late fifties and early sixties were joined by hordes of additional dropouts from middle-class society, mostly young and long haired, generally highly critical of competitive striving, and preferring marijuana and the "mind expanding" hallucinogens such as mescaline and LSD (lysergic acid diethylamide) to alcoholic beverages. Their aggressive non-conformity, their opposition to the War in Viet Nam and their use of illegal drugs brought them into frequent conflict with the authorities of the "straight" world, especially the police, often referred to as the "pigs." A new vocabulary of drug language arose; among the more common terms were "pot" and "grass" for marijuana, "acid" for LSD, "stash" for one's supply, "narc" for informer, and "bust" for arrest. In the area around the University of New Mexico, where most of these Albuquerque "hippies" resided, "head" shops catered to their trade, offering such items as underground comic books and drug paraphernalia. In the time left over from their jobs or their studies these "hippies" were often involved in such pursuits as arts and crafts, astrology, and meditation, and their social lives were frequently highlighted by gatherings where people who might not even know each other's last names passed around marijuana cigarettes or "joints" in darkened rooms. The almost religious communal feeling might be heightened by "psychedelic" music on the stereo set, bizarre posters looking down from the walls, strobe lights flashing and incense burning.

The world of the hippies and less extreme currents of youthful non-conformity and experimentation exhilarated the young people of the city. Rock music bands such as the Beatles, the Rolling Stones and the Jefferson Airplane filled the radio waves with songs of love, drugs, hard times, politics and numerous other topics of passing and eternal concern. Young vendors sold their crafts outside the Student Union Building at the University of New Mexico while traveling groups of actors gave performances a few feet away. People passing on the street paused to engage in excited conversations about new trends in education, new songs, new prospects for the environment, new anything. In the rich, manic intensity of the atmosphere, few gave much thought to yesterday or tomorrow; serious discussions of social and cosmic problems alternated with blithe, childlike fantasies. Movies like *Getting Straight*, depicting a graduate student who comically confronts the absurdities of established higher learning; *Z*, a taut drama about persecution of political leftists; and *Yellow Submarine*, an imaginatively concocted animated cartoon starring the Beatles, drew enormous crowds and inspired lively debates. And providing the background, sometimes, it seemed, the framework, was the music. Record sales soared, bands played in parking lots and concert halls, lines from the lyrics were adopted as slogans, and young people traveled great distances to attend rock festivals, where famous groups performed for days, avid audiences mingled and passed drugs among themselves, and inhibitions were forgotten. The spirit spread far across the society and into unexpected places. It was not unusual to find bearded carpenters hammering away at a relaxed pace with a radio blaring out rock music, and some professional people began to use music and marijuana as aids to their socializing. But the heart of the youth culture and the consciousness which it engendered were the areas around the schools and universities, particularly the University of New Mexico. A student could be walking back to his apartment some evening, be attracted by the faint sound of a rock band pulsating in the distance, wander over to investigate, and suddenly come upon a party in full swing in the middle of a blocked-off street, couples dancing with abandon and the sweet smell of marijuana hanging in the air. At such moments the intoxication of youth was so overpowering that the cosmos seemed to open up and everything appeared possible.

The Rise of the Ethnic Minorities

With the increasing attention being paid to improving the lot of society's downtrodden and with the growing activism of the reformers, other groups which had previously had little power began to assert themselves. Among the most visible were the ethnic groups—the Spanish Americans, the Blacks and the American Indians. The members of the ethnic minorities wanted the goals for which the civil rights movement had striven—free entry into the larger society, full and unrestricted participation in it, and the abolition of racial discrimination—and they also wanted more. Growing numbers of them were becoming skeptical of the value of plunging into the melting pot of mainstream American society, improving their material welfare at the cost of their traditional sense of identity and solidarity with their own kind. So, on a variety of fronts, the ethnic activists began to push for incorporating their interest groups and their specialized demands into the institutions of society. As important segments of the larger society, they wanted society to accommodate their felt needs; they were convinced that their individual members could best cope with the pressures of modern life if they had the support of sympathetic groups and institutions; they did not worry that such special treatment seemed to undermine the traditional liberal position that everyone should be treated exactly the same, for they were convinced that the Anglo majority already had more than adequate sources of support. And to look after their own interests, they struggled vigorously for more power.

In their campaigns for more power, rights and privileges, the ethnic minorities were aided by the fact that their numbers were growing faster than the population of the Albuquerque metropolitan area as a whole. As we have seen, this had not been the case during the previous decade, when vast numbers of Anglos had poured into the city and county, making the demographic composition more typical of the country at large. In 1960, of the 262,199 persons in Bernalillo County, 26.6 percent were Spanish-surnamed, 1.8 percent were Black, and 1.3 percent were Indian, with the remainder, which was overwhelmingly Anglo, amounting to 70.9 percent. Over the next ten years the Anglo dominance diminished: of the 1970 county population of 315,774, 39.2 percent were Spanish-surnamed, 2.1 percent Black, 1.8 percent Indian, and 56.8 percent other. The overall reason for such a dramatic shift during the sixties was that although the ethnic minorities continued to migrate into the metropolitan area at roughly the same rate they had during the previous decade, the Anglos did not. From 1950 to 1960 their number had risen 89.8 percent; it actually fell 3.6 percent over the course of the sixties.[855] A prolonged agricultural depression in the northern part of New Mexico continued to send impoverished Spanish-Americans to Albuquerque to seek jobs, the post-World War II migration of many Blacks to the cities of the West kept up, the declining hold of their traditional culture contributed to the influx of Indians, but the defense industries in Albuquerque, which had attracted vast numbers of Anglos during the fifties, underwent a relative decline.

The ethnic minorities also improved their social and economic position vis-à-vis the Anglos. Statistical information is not available for all the groups, but the Spanish-Americans can probably be taken as representative. Median family income adjusted for inflation of the general population in Bernalillo County, which had gone up 54.4 percent between 1950 and 1960, rose only 10.2 percent between 1960 and 1970; during the latter decade the increase for Spanish-surnamed families was 16.8 percent.[856] In 1960 the median number of school years completed by persons twenty-five years of age or older in the general population was 12.2 as opposed to 8.7 for the Spanish-surnamed; by 1970 the gap narrowed to 12.5 for the general population versus 11.1 for the Spanish-surnamed.[857] And when one notes that the majority of the new Spanish-American residents had moved from poverty-stricken rural areas, one realizes that these figures probably understate the scale of their material and educational betterment.

As the population and economic base of the ethnic groups increased, so did their demands. Overt discrimination had not been a large problem for the Spanish-Americans and Indians for years, and the civil rights movement had eliminated most of the obvious barriers for the Blacks; but to many of the ethnics, especially those who were having trouble penetrating into the middle class, the social and economic system seemed unduly to favor the Anglo majority. Leading the edge of discontent were a number of articulate reformers and radicals, and their followings were swelled with hundreds of less educated but no less dissatisfied persons clamoring to grasp the better life that seemed almost within their reach. Many of the more conservative members of the ethnic groups did not favor the militant leaders and actively mistrusted them; nevertheless, the surging activism of the new organizations which were getting underway helped bring the society to treat all the ethnic minorities with more attention and respect.

Of all the emerging minority leaders in the Albuquerque area, none was more charismatic and controversial than Reies Lopez Tijerina, a former Assembly of God minister from Texas. In 1955 the itinerant preacher had bought 160 acres in Arizona and set up a small community of his followers, with a church, a school and a grocery store. Partly as a result of harassment by neighbors, the effort eventually collapsed, and Tijerina resumed his travels. In California, separated from his family, he had an experience which was to fuel his visionary drive for years to come. "I had left my warm bed into the cold weather because I felt the urge to pray in the open," he recounted. "But I went to sleep, and in the morning the sun woke me and dew had covered me all over. That night, I asked God to show me the future of my life. It shaped me all my life. From there, I turned to New Mexico, I saw frozen horses. They started melting and coming to life in a very old kingdom, old walls. Then I saw three angels of law and they asked me to help them. They said they had come from a long way. Those tall pines I saw meant New Mexico. When I started doing research into the land grants I found they were not dead. They were just frozen. They are living political bodies."[858] The land grants to which he was referring had been made by Spain as far back as 1715, consisting of millions of acres of land now included in seven western states, and their legitimacy had been recognized in an official protocol explaining the Treaty of Guadalupe Hidalgo, which had ended the War with Mexico in 1848. Some three hundred of the land grants were located in New Mexico; a number were still intact and owned by the heirs of the original beneficiaries. Tijerina and his allies charged, however, that the federal government had ignored the rights of many of the heirs when it had designated much of the land as public domain and "let rich men take possession" of other portions. He determined to lead a campaign to restore the land to the poor Spanish-Americans who, he was convinced, were the rightful owners.[859] "Nothing can squash justice," he declared. "Justice will win."[860]

To win back the land grants he founded the Alianza Federal de Mercedes (Federal Alliance of Land Grants) and set up headquarters in Albuquerque. In July 1966 about a hundred members marched sixty-two miles to Santa Fe to present their demands to the governor. Unsuccessful at winning concessions, they did bring their grievances about the land to the public's attention, and they also complained about job discrimination in the government and nonenforcement of an article in the state constitution requiring public school teachers to be able to speak Spanish.[861] The following September, at an Alianza Convention held at the Albuquerque civic auditorium, Reies Tijerina told the more than nine hundred persons attending from various parts of New Mexico and adjoining states his program for action. Starting with the towns "which are all Spanish and all heirs," and eventually moving on to Albuquerque and Santa Fe, the organization would hold elections in which the "heirs will be the only voters." Any opposition would be arrested by the Alianza's constable for disorderly conduct and attempting to incite a riot. Bypassing the state court system, which he felt he could not trust, he would apply for federal injunctions to keep the National Guard and the United States marshals from interfering in the process.[862]

Such a bold scheme had a tremendous appeal to many of the poor Spanish-Americans of the area, who had grown accustomed to feeling that the law was on the side of the status quo and the well-to-do. Through an almost mystical transformation, it appeared that the law would switch sides and enable them to dispossess the dispossessors. Not surprisingly, the plan aroused vehement opposition among the people of the state with much to lose, and they were determined to fight what they considered the irresponsible forces of disruption at every step.

After the convention Tijerina and his men began a sequence of moves in northern New Mexico which were as bizarre as they were dramatic. On October 22, 1966, about a hundred members of the Alianza converged on the Echo Amphitheatre at Carson National Forest near Abiquiu, hoisted a blue flag, and proclaimed the Pueblo Republica de San Joaquin del Rio de Chama. The next day four times that many returned, declared a citizen's arrest of two forest rangers, tried and convicted them for trespassing, sentenced each fifty dollars fine and eleven months and twenty-one days in jail, and then suspended the sentences.[863] Several months later the U.S. District Court ordered the Alianza to turn over its membership records, whereupon Tijerina refused, contending that the Alianza Federal de Mercedes had been dissolved. A new organization with the same headquarters, Alianza Federal de Pueblos Libres (Federal Alliance of Free City States), was formed. The Alianza made plans for a "Showdown Day" in the early summer of 1967, when the organization would try to take over some 600,000 acres around Coyote, a small town in the north. Law enforcement officials got wind of the plan, and on the eve of the projected takeover, June 3, they stopped two cars in the area and arrested eight persons, one of whom was Cristobal Tijerina, Reies's brother, on charges of unlawful assembly and extortion stemming from the gathering at Carson National Forest and a later one at Tierra Amarilla. They also found in the cars some weapons and the long-sought membership records. The leader was still at large, however.[864] Two days later, when the arrested members were at the Tierra Amarilla courthouse to be arraigned, Reies Tijerina suddenly appeared leading a raiding party of about twenty armed men. Over the next hour and a half, when Tijerina and his men were occupying the courthouse, the eight members under arrest were freed, a policeman and a jailer were wounded, and the officers of the court were helpless. Then the band vanished into the wilderness, taking two hostages, and a combined force of National Guardsmen, forest rangers and state police fanned out for the manhunt. A number of days later Tijerina arranged for his surrender.[865]

Now deeply in trouble with the law but exciting the passions of many of the poor Spanish-Americans and their sympathizers more than ever before, Tijerina continued to declaim for his cause. Out on bond, he appeared at rallies to raise money for his defense; at one of them he declared, "No one can explain why we are fighting in Viet Nam. There, they are bombing in violation of law. And they tell us not to use violence."[866] In October the Alianza held another convention; among those in attendance were representatives of militant Spanish-American organizations from other states, Black Power advocates from Los Angeles, and James Kennedy, representing the Students for a Democratic Society.[867] Several months later the SDS at the University of New Mexico issued a statement in support of the Alianza.[868] In December Tijerina went to trial for assaulting the two forest rangers at Carson National Forest and was found guilty,[869] but he appealed. The following month Eulogio Salazar, the jailer who had been wounded during the courthouse raid, was beaten to death by persons unknown, and the state was deprived of one of its chief witnesses against the Alianza leader.[870] In the spring of 1968 he gained national prominence when Ralph Abernathy, head of the Southern Christian Leadership Conference, named him to lead the southwestern segment of the Poor People's March on Washington to be held to dramatize the drive against poverty. Around a thousand persons marched through the streets of Albuquerque on May 18, singing "We Shall Overcome" and "He's Got the Whole World in His Hands" and converging on the Old Town plaza for an enormous rally to hear Tijerina, Abernathy and Roman Catholic Archbishop James Peter Davis deliver speeches. Immediately afterwards Reies Tijerina and a contingent of New Mexicans went to Washington to participate in the main march.[871] Two months later he announced he was entering the race for the governorship of New Mexico "to give the poor people a voice in politics,"[872] but the State Supreme Court ruled him off the ballot in October because of his felony conviction.[873] Toward the end of the year he went to trial for three charges stemming from the raid on the Rio Arriba courthouse. Tijerina himself gave a sixty-minute summation speech which was a striking mixture of oratorical brilliance and incoherence. He argued that he had tried to prevent the violence, and, pointing at the team of prosecutors, he shouted his conclusion: "I feel the state is guilty at this time, and these men should be behind bars. I'm not suggesting a citizen's arrest, but

I think they should be punished by the law." The jury was evidently impressed, and it acquitted the fiery defendant.[874]

From that high point, however, Tijerina's fortunes went rapidly downhill. In February 1969 the U.S. Circuit Court of Appeals sustained his earlier conviction for assault on the two forest rangers.[875] In June his wife burned two forest service signs, and he attempted a citizen's arrest of a forest ranger who tried to interfere; the U.S. District Court found him guilty of charges connected with the incident the following September.[876] Two months later Tijerina was tried in State District Court on four charges stemming from the courthouse raid and found guilty on two of them—false imprisonment of Deputy Sheriff Pete Jaramillo and assault with intent to kill or maim the late jailor Eulogio Salazar.[877] Imprisonment by the state would have to wait, however, for the sentence to the federal penitentiary had precedence. With their leader finally silenced and out of touch with the membership, the Alianza languished and split into factions.[878] But other Spanish-American activists continued to make waves.

One of the sources of activism on behalf of the ethnic minorities in the area was the War on Poverty, for some of the workers associated with the various programs became aggressive advocates for the poor people with whom they were involved. This partisanship did not sit well with many of the local politicians, who regarded it as outside agitation and interference. Following the courthouse raid in 1967, eight Democratic legislators from Bernalillo County issued a statement asserting that "there is a very close connection between OEO [Office of Economic Opportunity] employees and the uprising at Tierra Amarilla,"[879] and in subsequent months a number of poverty workers openly sympathized with the Alianza. A few days after the raid about thirty-five members of the Los Duranes Community Improvement Association, one of the community organizations represented in the local Economic Opportunity Board, marched into a meeting of the Albuquerque Board of Education and made a number of demands concerning Duranes Elementary School, among which was a call for the ouster of Principal John Gedders, who had held his position for twenty-one years. The leaders of the demonstration were Charles Cansino, the president of the association and a welfare department caseworker with three clients in Los Duranes, and Gilberto Ballejos, "spokesman" and EOB representative for the group. Commenting on their opposition to Gedders, Ballejos said, "We simply want someone who can communicate with those who don't speak English. We feel a principal who speaks Spanish can communicate with the parents better." Many of the older residents liked the present principal and bitterly opposed Cansino, who had come from San Antonio, Texas, and Ballejos, who had been born in Mountainair, New Mexico, taught Spanish for five years in Washington, D.C., and currently resided in a different part of the city. The following month the two were voted out of office; nevertheless, a year later the school system transferred John Gedders to another school.[880] After losing his position in the association, Gilberto Ballejos became a teacher of adult classes for the EOB. Having participated in the 1966 march to Santa Fe, he already had ties with Tijerina; in April of 1968 he and Charles Cansino helped lead a strike of about a dozen students at Washington Junior High School, including two of the Alianza leader's children. Their demands included getting a Mexican-American principal, hiring the same percentage of Mexican-American teachers as students, putting Mexican-American food in cafeteria, and eliminating the "racist IQ tests." The striking students were suspended, but the action brought more pressure on the school administrators to be sensitive to the minorities.[881]

A shake-up in the management of the EOB led Ballejos to resign from his teaching position that spring, but the next August he resurfaced in still another capacity—as spokesman for the Brown Berets, a new organization of militant young Spanish-Americans with loose ties to the Alianza. He declared, "We formed to protect ourselves, our interests, our lives if necessary. We're trying to do something about things—like the injustices in the schools." Following the killing of a Spanish-American by an Albuquerque policeman, he led a group of the members into a meeting of the City Commission and demanded that the officer be suspended and a civilian police review board be established.[882] A few days later the commission ordered the police department to inaugurate a community relations division consisting of a Black, a Spanish-American and an Anglo.[883] Again the powers in the Albuquerque community had not acceded to the militant demands as presented, but again they had bent somewhat to the pressure.

During the late sixties the more moderate members of the Spanish-American community were also pressing for concessions, and they, too, were meeting with some success. In March 1966 the Equal Employment Opportunity Commission held a conference in Albuquerque on racial discrimination, but most of the Spanish-American delegates walked out, charging that the EEOC itself was guilty of discrimination and indifferent to their problems.[884] Five months later the Civil Service Commission announced that it was beginning a drive to improve employment opportunities for Spanish-Americans in federal agencies operating in Albuquerque. Allen Howerton, head of the commission in New Mexico, noted that although approximately 30 percent of the federal workers in the city were Spanish-American, they were concentrated in low-paying jobs. Some agencies, he emphasized, would have to make a greater effort to train their employees and promote through the ranks rather than fill the choicest positions with already-qualified outsiders.[885] Toward the end of the decade the League of United Latin American Citizens, a predominantly middle-class organization which had not been particularly active since the end of World War II, began to push on a variety of fronts, including Spanish-American culture at the state fair, bilingual education and low-income housing.[886]

Meanwhile, the other ethnic minorities in the metropolitan area were also making strides. The gains of the Blacks, riding the crest of the civil rights movement, were well publicized, but the Indians, less numerous and less aggressive, were improving their lot as well. As early as 1952 the Indian students at the University of New Mexico had formed the Kiva Club, a social organization which they used from time to time as a political forum.[887] Six years later the government-supported Bordertown program had been instituted whereby high school students from nearby reservations could reside in the dormitories at Albuquerque Indian School and commute to public schools across the city, where they could get the same education as their Anglo contemporaries.[888] In the sixties Indian penetration of the larger society and Indian self-consciousness accelerated. An Indian village was incorporated into the state fair in 1964, with dwellings, exhibits, dancers and artisans making such specialties as blankets, Indian bread, Kachina dolls and sand paintings.[889] In 1967 was formed the Albuquerque Pow Wow Club for socializing and participating in traditional native dances. Observed Ralph Zotigh, one of the leaders. "Today the Indian must make a major transition from the reservation environment into the Great Society. The major industrial centers have replaced the circular camps." A primary purpose of the club, he explained, was to help the Indian keep his identity in this "new world of uncertainty."[890] Other aids to the Indians venturing out of their traditional existence came quickly. At the time there were no Indian lawyers practicing in the state, but later that same year scholarships specifically for Indians were offered at the University of New Mexico Law School covering an eight-week summer pre-law program as well as the regular academic year.[891] And in 1969 a significant new effort was begun to help bridge the gap between the reservations and the outside world in regard to health care. The Indian Health Service inaugurated the Community Health Representative Program, under which representatives from the various tribal groups across the state took training courses organized by the health service and the respective tribes working in conjunction, and then the representatives went out to the reservations, conducted educational campaigns, led sanitation drives and performed paramedical services.[892] With the educated Indians who so chose acting as intermediaries, the world of the reservation was gradually being brought closer to the greater society and, to a rudimentary degree, being integrated into it.

At the University of New Mexico all three ethnic minorities were growing in influence. According to one survey, the proportion of the freshman class which was Spanish-American rose from 10.5 percent in 1963 to 25.2 percent in 1968.[893] Blacks and Indians were similarly increasing their numbers. At a forum sponsored by the local chapter of the American Association of University Professors in February 1969, two student representatives of each of the three groups voiced their dissatisfaction with the way the university was accommodating them. Joe Abeyta complained about the built-in discrimination of giving tests in English instead of Spanish. Veronica Velarde contended that the Indian student was regarded more as a "museum piece" than as a human being, and Leslie Chapman commented, "The faculty as a whole can be accused of gross ignorance of Indians as they are today." The Blacks were particularly vehement. Complained one, "Nobody looks at me as Ron Sanford the Black, but Ron Sanford the athlete. If I wear bell bottoms, or go without a shirt, or don't shave for a couple of days, people get unhappy. I have to be spit and polished all the time. I'm tired of making people happy." Barbara Brown said the university needed a Black studies curriculum. All the representatives present emphasized the need to have faculty members of their own backgrounds to turn to for advice and moral support.[894]

On the last day of the month, some Black and Anglo students conducted a silent demonstration before the beginning of a basketball game with Brigham Young University, and they raised their right hands in clenched fists to give the Black Power salute during the playing of the national anthem. They were angered that the Mormon Church, which ran Brigham Young, excluded Blacks from full membership.[895] Brigham Young's victory that night added to their frustration, and several weeks later the Black Student Union requested the Student Senate to cut athletic ties with that university. Star player Greg Howard read a statement declaring, "The humiliation and anxiety suffered by the Black athletes who have to participate in events against BYU go beyond the realm of academic tolerance." The senate voted as requested, but the action had no direct effect on the athletic program.[896]

In May the United Mexican American Students charged the university with discriminating against the Spanish-American workers at the physical plant, who held low-paying, nonsupervisory positions. President Ferrel Heady said he could find no evidence of such discrimination, and the faculty voted to refer the complaint to the University Grievance Committee.[897] Dissatisfied, the student group sent their charges and supporting documents to the U.S. Department of Health, Education and Welfare, and an investigating team was dispatched. As had been the case with the Civil Service Commission three years earlier, the investigators reported that there was no clear discrimination, but an "overall pattern of inequities" did exist in regard to salaries and advancement. They advised stronger efforts to promote persons to supervisory positions through the ranks. Gilberto Ballejos, who had been elected spokesman for the disgruntled physical plant workers and also head of the Albuquerque Citizens Grievance Committee, recently formed over the issue, felt the report was too soft. "If you've found discrimination, call it discrimination," he declared.[898] President Heady said that the HEW proposals would be integrated into the university's Affirmative Action Program to help minority groups.[899] Over the next several months a specially constituted committee of three faculty members, one vice president and one student investigated the matter further and came up with a report similar report to the earlier one. They found "no pattern of intentional discrimination" but suggested that the presence of Spanish-Americans among the supervisors and on the staff of the director of personnel would improve the situation.[900] This report, too, was scored as a "whitewash"—by the United Mexican American Students, Ballejos and Rudy Ortiz, chairman of the Bernalillo County Democrats [901]—nevertheless, it contributed to the growing pressure to force the important institutions to integrate the ethnic minorities into their structures.

Momentum was also continuing to build for ethnic studies curricula. In the spring of 1969 the English department offered a course in Black literature and the sociology department one in race relations.[902] A year later a workshop course was set up in which the students and the teacher would plan a Chicano studies program. (The term "Chicano" was becoming more popular than "Spanish-American" and "Mexican-American" as a designation for that ethnic group, in part because its connotations of peasantry seemed more forceful.) Dr. Louis Bransford, director of the emerging program, gave the rationale for such a course of study:

> It is our hope that through this program we can educate men and women who will not only be competent in certain academic or professional areas, but who will also be able to maintain ties and enhance their identity with their people. We hope to send doctors, and lawyers, and teachers, and recreation specialists, or other professionals, back into their communities equipped with the skills and broad-based understanding that will help them to truly serve the needs of their people. [903]

The 1970-71 academic year saw the creation of programs in Black studies and Native American (Indian) studies and the establishment of centers on campus for each of the three ethnic minorities.

On the campus of the University of New Mexico and, to a lesser extent, in the community at large, society was becoming more culturally pluralistic and less tightly focused around the dominant Anglo patterns. The annual spring fiesta at the university, once a celebration in cowboy dress, was now centered around Spanish-American activities. "Soul" music, highly expressive and sung by Blacks, became widely popular. Ethnic fashions of attire were common sights, and the language adopted greater numbers of phrases of ethnic origin. By 1972 the state fair had added a Black cultural exhibit and a Spanish Village.[904] In the entire history of the city, ethnic pride and self-awareness had probably never been higher.

The ongoing tendency in the society toward group orientation gave added strength to the positions of the ethnic minorities. Since the members pressed their demands in terms of the ethnic groups to which they belonged, they had greater power and influence than they would have had as individuals. Generally more attuned to individualistic striving, some of the Anglos looked on resentfully as they saw their own competitive positions being undermined by the programs offering special treatment to the aggressive interest groups. In the workaday world the ethnic groups were also helped by the trend toward large groups. The percentages of private wage and salary workers among the Spanish-speaking and the Blacks in Bernalillo County in 1970 was not appreciably different from that of the population as a whole, but a greater proportion was employed by government (24.7 percent of the Spanish-speaking workers and 27.8 percent of the Black workers as opposed to 23.9 percent of all workers), and a lesser proportion was self-employed (4.3 percent of the Spanish-speaking and 2.9 percent of the Blacks versus 6.0 percent of all those working).[905] As large groupings came to predominate all the more, it seemed that the ethnic minorities would be in good position to reap still greater benefits.

Women Take on a Larger Role

Moving in the wake of the ethnic minorities and pressing its demands along similar lines was an important group which was neither ethnic nor a minority—the women. Like the members of the ethnic cultures, the women were somewhat more attuned to group action and less to striving on an individual basis than the dominant members of society, and they, too, benefitted from the increasing trend toward large groups. In Bernalillo County in 1970 3.9 percent of the female workers were self-employed and 25.8 percent worked for some branch of the government, whereas 7.3 percent of the employed males worked for themselves and 22.7 percent for the government.[906] But the women had a much more pervasive presence throughout the society than any of the ethnic minorities, and changes in their role and status had a greater potential for restructuring human activity. Ultimately, changes in the women would have to be accompanied by compensating changes in the men; virtually all human relations would be affected.

Ever since World War II increasing numbers of women had been opting to enter the job market instead of staying at home and keeping house. In 1940 23.3 percent of the women in the county fourteen years of age or older were in the labor force, in 1950 the figure was 26.6 percent, and it climbed to 35.0 percent by 1960. Meanwhile, the proportion for men stayed in the neighborhood of eighty percent, as it would continue to do.[907] For the most part, the women who began to work outside the home during the fifties entered occupations that already included a substantial number of their sex, such as professional and technical work, sales jobs, private household work and other service positions. The percentage of all the employed women who held managerial positions or did blue-collar labor other than in households declined, and the divergence between the occupations held by the female workers and those held by the males increased.[908] Although more women were earning money in the marketplace than earlier, most of them seemed content at this time to stay fairly close to their traditional roles.

As it did in so many other areas, the decade of the sixties ushered in extensive changes for the working women. Their number continued to grow—by 1970 40.9 percent of the women in Bernalillo County sixteen years old or older were in the labor force[909]—and increasingly they were entering occupations that traditionally had been the province of men. The proportion of all the working women in blue-collar jobs and in positions of responsibility over other workers grew.[910] Although still a tiny minority, the number of women employed by Sandia Corporation rose 46 percent—from 90 to 132, while its entire work force remained around 7,100.[911] Even the least reputable occupations gained female representation: while male arrests for major crimes went up 25.7 percent between 1960 and 1970 nationwide, female arrests jumped 74.4 percent, and much the same thing happened in the Albuquerque area.[912]

Over the twenty-year span from 1950 to 1970, the distributions of men and women in the county in most of the U.S. Bureau of the Census occupational groups came to resemble each other more, the only exceptions being in farmers and farm managers, operatives and kindred workers, and managers and administrators,[913] and the gap in the last category, which was narrowed during the sixties, can be at least partially accounted for by the fact that many of the female employees had not yet had time to work their way into high positions. The distributions of the sexes in most of the industry groups also became more similar during this period.[914]

The development of the new, more influential role of women in society, however, was not just a matter of more and better jobs; it had repercussions throughout the body politic and the mores. Like the ethnic minorities, women were aided in their struggle to assert themselves by legislation and court decisions. The national Civil Rights Act of 1964, which forbade employers to discriminate on the basis of race, creed or national origin, also outlawed sexual discrimination, and this prohibition had a much wider impact than the framers of the bill had foreseen. In 1965 the Equal Employment Opportunity Commission ruled that classified advertisements for jobs "may not indicate a preference based on sex unless a bona fide occupational qualification makes it lawful to specify male or female."[915] Subsequently it was decided in the courts that "bona fide occupational qualifications" had to be on the basis of physical strain.[916] The following year the Albuquerque Police Department held its first class for policewomen, and the enrollees were given the same training and pay as their male counterparts.[917] The New Mexico Legislature passed a law, effective June 1969, which gave women easier access to legal abortions than earlier. One of the conditions under which abortion was permitted was the danger of "grave impairment of the mental health of the woman," and the testimony of two physicians was required to verify this danger. Mostly on this basis, in the first twelve months over seven hundred legal abortions were performed in the state as opposed to seventy the year before the law went into effect.[918]

In other areas women were gaining more freedom. The introduction of oral contraceptives in 1964 brought to many almost foolproof security from unwanted pregnancy and therefore the same possibilities for sexual freedom as men.[919] As fashions in clothing shifted and became less restrictive, more women began to wear blue jeans, slacks and pants suits. The young women were the first to go in for such "male" attire in a big way. During the late sixties the dress codes of most Albuquerque high schools prohibited the girls from wearing slacks except under certain circumstances such as very cold weather,[920] but pressure was building to change the rules. In December 1969 Diane Brew was suspended from West Mesa High School for refusing to adhere to the code, which she called "unfair"; she was the fourth girl suspended that year at the school for the same reason. Her mother stood firmly behind her. "The matter of pants may seem like a very unimportant matter to some people, but the matter of human dignity is not," commented Mrs. Brew. "Isn't that really what education is all about?"[921] Over the next year, when dress codes were extensively liberalized in high schools across the city, girls gained the right to wear slacks whenever they chose.[922] At about the same time, nurses at Bernalillo County Medical Center began to wear pants uniforms.[923] Especially among the young but to a large extent throughout the society, women were donning pants every time the fancy struck them, and there was little that any men who might have wanted to could do to stop it.

Although much of the shifting of the sex roles was taking place spontaneously and through the individual actions of thousands of women who were coming more to assert themselves, activist groups provided a leading edge for their protests. Late in the decade the Albuquerque chapter of the National Organization of Women (NOW) began to push for the repeal of laws restricting abortion, the establishment of child day care centers, the ratification of a constitutional amendment guaranteeing women the same rights as men, and other changes to benefit their sex. The group set up an employment bank to help qualified women find jobs that had previously been closed to them, one task force to study the role of western religion in reinforcing women's secondary status, and another to encourage young women to get as much education as possible. Observed Therese Conant, the leader, "Too many women are just appendages to their husbands—they depend on men for shelter and an identity." They called themselves "feminists"; according to Merrillee Dolan, "A feminist is a woman who truly wants to be regarded as a human being." She elaborated, "Women are tired of living in a world whose rules were made by men and for men. We don't want to become like men, but we want a total restructuring of the status of women in our society."[924]

Some of the women involved in the Albuquerque chapter of NOW felt that the group was a little too conservative, and they formed the Women's Liberation Front, which met once a week to discuss the problems they were having and their roles in society. Lucia Montague commented, "We find that a lot of our problems are not personal problems but social problems all women face in their relationships with men, their kids, their jobs and their housework." As their awareness of and their dissatisfaction with their positions intensified, they saw much to criticize in the way society functioned, including the commercials which depicted "women as dumb servants in the home who are not capable of having any interests except cleaning the house." Most of the members were connected with the University of New Mexico, and they voiced their concern with the dormitory regulations there, the availability of birth control information, and what they perceived as discrimination in the graduate school.[925]

In their efforts to make the general public more conscious of their grievances, the women's groups took to the streets. In the spring of 1969, on Mother's Day, members of the local chapter of NOW staged a protest against the "hypocrisy" of the institution. They marched in several shopping centers with signs declaring "Rights Now, Not Roses," "Support the Equal Rights Amendment," and "Separate Church and State—Repeal Abortion Laws," and they handed out leaflets to the passersby.[926] To commemorate the fiftieth anniversary of the passage of the constitutional amendment for women's suffrage, on August 26, 1970, approximately thirty-five members of NOW, the Women's Liberation Front and the Southwestern Female Rights Union gathered at city hall and burned symbols of the oppression of women—facsimiles of marriage licenses, voter registration receipts, hair curlers and nude pictures from men's magazines. When Assistant City Attorney Frank Mims appeared on the scene and made a derogatory remark, someone squirted him with liquid detergent, and a scuffle ensued. Elsewhere in the city, several discussion sessions were held on the subject of women's rights, including a "teach-in" at Roosevelt Park. More sedately, the League of Women Voters had a reception for its members and the press.[927]

The heart and core of the women's movement in Albuquerque was at the University of New Mexico, and here it made its greatest strides. Between 1960 and 1970 the proportion of the student body which was female rose from 30.7 percent to 39.8 percent.[928] As late as 1967 only 4 percent of the law students were women; their share shot up to 12.5 percent in 1972.[929] With their increasing numbers and their growing share of the limelight, the women were able to get the university to accommodate some of their most fervent demands. In 1970 a new noncredit course was established, "The Second Sex: Explorations in the Revolution of Women." Taught by five women activists, it had for its texts a number of feminist publications, including *The Feminine Mystique* by Betty Friedan, national president of NOW.[930] Early in the spring semester of 1972 the faculty voted to inaugurate a women's studies program and a women's center. Among the backers of the proposal was Dr. Marcia Tillotson of the English department, who had argued persuasively that "women's experiences have been overlooked and are of considerable academic value to male as well as to female scholars in many fields."[931] Many of the female students gave the new project their enthusiastic support; the Women's Law Student Association, which earlier had persuaded the law school to hire a female professor, began to give legal counseling at the women's center.[932] And the women also secured more nonacademic support at the university. In the fall of 1970 the undergraduate and graduate student governments began to subsidize a day care center on campus for students' children.[933]

One of the most crucial areas affected by the shifting role of women in Albuquerque and elsewhere was the family. Throughout most of the years since the end of the Second World War the divorce rate had risen, as the society at large had assumed more of the responsibilities once held more exclusively by the family, such as education, recreation and welfare, as the shifting of values had made persons who once had much in common no longer compatible, and as increased freedom and opportunity had made the married women less dependent on their mates.[934] The rate climbed higher during the turbulent sixties and early seventies. Toward the end of the period under scrutiny, an increasingly noticeable minority of the married women were choosing not to assume their husbands' last names, a larger group of both married and unmarried women were insisting that their names be prefixed by "Ms." rather than "Miss" or "Mrs." in order that they be no more labeled by their marital status or lack of it than the men, and perhaps a majority of the wives were asserting themselves more and submitting less to the authority of their husbands. Many of the women were uncertain how to act in their emerging roles and how to relate to men; the men, unaccustomed to being so challenged, were frequently uneasy and defensive. As members of both sexes tried to work out appropriate responses to the changing situation, sometimes even groping for their basic identities, many sexual relationships failed. Many survived, however, and many new ones were born. The evolution of a less nuclear and less authoritarian type of family structure was underway.

Most of the women of the Albuquerque area who were participating in the changes, though, were less interested in pondering the historical implications than in enthusiastically venturing into new areas. At every hand time-honored barriers were collapsing. In 1967 a three-week pilot project was tried at Garfield Junior High School in which boys studied home economics and girls shop;[935] by 1971 high schools all over the city had courses with such titles as "Survival for Bachelors," "Bachelor Know-How" and "Family Living," and these had large male enrollments.[936] In the early seventies high school and junior high school girls tried out for and, on at least one occasion, won positions on heretofore male athletic teams.[937] By late 1972 most of the physical education classes at the University of New Mexico were coeducational.[938] More of the job stereotypes broke down as young women began to work as filling station attendants[939] and young men as telephone operators.[940] In 1971, for the first time in more than a decade, Albuquerque Public Schools got a woman for a high school principal.[941] That same year Corrales, a small community to the north of the city, incorporated in order to be better able to control its growth; and the residents elected Barbara Christianson for their first mayor,[942] the highest elective office held by a local woman since Dorothy Cline had presided over the County Commission at the end of the fifties. The remainder of the decade promised to be a time when women would bask in expanding glory.

The Local War on Poverty

Other interest groups in the metropolitan area also pressed for more power and privileges. Among the more visible were the government employees and the old people, but the overall tendency spread to smaller minorities and to more vague and generalized groups as well. Stirred by the local liberals and militants and bolstered by the expanding machinery of the antipoverty programs, even the poor, who traditionally played a mostly passive role in the economic system and who had not previously acted very cohesively, slowly became a force to be contended with. As their self-awareness and assertiveness grew, they came to push steadily for what they perceived to be in their best interests.

From the early stages of the War on Poverty, the professional social workers and their political allies were committed to the principle of "maximum feasible participation of the poor" and to getting them to assert themselves aggressively. Earl Raab, a consultant with the California State Welfare Department, wrote, "Participation as a principle of the anti-poverty program has emerged, not only or even primarily as a means of motivating people to upgrade themselves occupationally and educationally, but as a value in itself. And the value is power, political power."[943] If the poor people seized their share of the power, it was felt, they would gain proportionate social and economic benefits, and the most serious of their problems would melt away.

But how to get the reins of power into the hands of the downtrodden? The poverty workers hoped that through group participation in the programs, the poor would obtain more self-confidence and effectiveness than when they had acted as individuals. In describing the Community Action Program, which was the name given the assemblage of community-related projects under the auspices of the EOB, Board President Art Blumenfeld emphasized the group nature of the plan: "This is a group approach to the problems of poverty—not an individual approach. In this way the program is unique. Group participation is everything; the more people participating in the CAP [Community Action Program] project, the more leadership we get."[944] Acting in accordance with the guidelines from the Office of Economic Opportunity and sometimes taking their own initiative, the poverty workers energetically promoted organizations of the poor people in the target areas to act as power blocs, and they were also instrumental in getting representatives of the poor on boards and committees that exercised influence in the poverty-stricken neighborhoods. Shortly after the formation of several of the early community improvement associations, Bryant Stuart, a caseworker for the State Department of Welfare, began to help organize Life with Pride Clubs for women on welfare, and before the end of 1965 more than three hundred women had joined fifteen such clubs in the area.[945] In addition to requiring representation of the poor on the EOB Board of Directors, the Office of Economic Opportunity mandated that poor people be on other bodies overseeing antipoverty projects; as a result, an agreement was worked out in 1966 with the Albuquerque Bar Association whereby the Board of Directors of the Legal Aid Society, which operated with EOB funding in several community centers, would consist of nine members nominated by the bar association, nine by the Legal Aid Society and nine by representatives of the poor.[946] The addition of a Model Cities resident to the Urban Renewal Board in 1969 further extended the potential power of the poor.

Whenever cutbacks in government funding were threatened, the poverty workers and the poor residents rallied to apply political pressure. In the fall of 1967 rumors began to circulate of a cut in state welfare checks, and Dr. Jerome H. Noskin, chairman of the board for the Health and Social Services Department (HSSD), advised members of Life with Pride to let their legislators know how they felt. The group began passing around handbills,[947] and no cuts were made. Early the next year, Charles Cansino, who was then connected with the Los Duranes Community Improvement Association, declared at a press conference called by representatives of the poor that welfare recipients should get checks covering 100 percent of their needs instead of the legally required 95 percent so that they could "bring their children up in dignity."[948] The State Legislature, however, lacked the money or the desire to meet the demand. In January 1969, faced with a shortfall of funds caused by a large increase in the number of welfare applicants, Health and Social Services

Department Director John Jasper announced a 10 percent reduction in benefits, and a vehement groundswell of protest erupted. Leon Hawn, a supervisor for HSSD, labeled the proposed slash "a catastrophe" and led a protest meeting in Martineztown. Hawn's group merged with a larger organization formed over the issue, Citizens for Welfare Rights, which fired off telegrams and appeals to high state officials and called for a massive protest meeting at the South Broadway Community Center.[949] Governor David Cargo then quashed the scheduled cut. At the meeting John Jasper told the protesters that he had frozen the salaries of the department workers in order to make the available money go further, that he, too, wanted the benefits to cover 100 percent of the recipients' needs, and that he hoped the legislature would make the necessary appropriations.[950] Around the end of the month the President's Commission on Income Maintenance Programs held two days of hearings in Albuquerque, and the poor residents and the welfare workers criticized the present system for being inadequate and excessively rigid.[951] But as the critics were soon to learn, there were limits to what they could achieve with their kind of pressure. In the fall of 1969 the State Board of HSSD learned that welfare grants had passed the point beyond which the federal government would contribute. Again a reduction of benefits was announced, and this time it stuck.[952]

Meanwhile, on the national level, administrators and Congressmen, concerned because the early stages of the War on Poverty did not seem to be making the progress they had hoped for, were developing and enacting new programs designed to be more responsive to the needs of the communities. One of the most ambitious was the Model Cities program, through which certain selected "model cities" could get money from the U.S. Department of Housing and Urban Development (HUD) in order to launch a coordinated attack on all the problems of a designated poverty-stricken area, including matters of housing, streets, sanitation, health, education and employment. Other federal programs would be brought in to reinforce the attack. More than was the case with earlier federal antipoverty efforts, the administrative responsibility would be decentralized, with the local governments of cities involved running their own programs. The individual projects, however, were subject to HUD approval. The national legislation authorized the overall program to last six years—one year of planning and five of action.[953]

Albuquerque's request for Model City funding was drawn up by the community aid coordinator in the city manager's office, John Cordova, an intense and highly committed young man who had been involved in the early urban renewal activities of the city and had labored strenuously to find new housing for displaced poor persons.[954] The part of town he included in the application consisted of two adjoining sections—an area about four miles deep and a mile to a mile and three-quarters wide, bounded on the north by Interstate 40, on the east by Interstate 25, on the south by Woodward Avenue, and on the west by the tracks of the Santa Fe Railroad; and a smaller area bordering on Bridge Boulevard on the north, the tracks on the east, the South Second Sewage Plant on the south, and the Rio Grande on the west.[955] The larger part included the neighborhoods of Santa Barbara-Martineztown, John Marshall, South Broadway and San Jose; the other made up South Barelas. The entire Model Neighborhood Area, as the two parts came to be called, included about six square miles of land and fifteen thousand residents.[956] The area, which was close to the central business district, was home to many poor Spanish-Americans and Blacks, and it suffered from dilapidated housing, a high rate of unemployment, large numbers on the welfare rolls, low average education, ill health, scant public improvements and a high rate of crime, especially among the young. It was manifestly the largest concentration of poverty in Albuquerque.[957] When the word came from Washington in November 1967 that a Model Cities grant had been approved for the area, the residents and the public officials began to prepare for the most intense antipoverty work yet to hit the city.

The administrative machinery of the new program was designed to minimize conflict among the different levels of government while giving the people from the target neighborhoods more representation and power than they had in the already-existing structures, such as the EOB. John Cordova was made director of Model Cities, with the rank of city department head,[958] but he and his staff also had to work with the community associations of the Model Neighborhood Area, the Model Cities Citizens Board and the Joint Policy Board. The Citizens Board consisted of three representatives of each of the community associations in the area—Santa Barbara-Martineztown, South San Jose, South Barelas, John Marshall and South Broadway—and one representative from each of the following organizations: Southwest Valley United Community Associations, Coordinated Action for Senior Adults,

League of Latin American Citizens, Sociedad de Oportunidad, Life with Pride, American G.I. Forum, East San Jose Community Recreation Association, Ministerial Alliance, National Association for the Advancement of Colored People and Federation of Community Associations. Recommendations made by the Citizens Board were then considered by the Joint Policy Board, which included eight members of the Citizens Board and one representative from each of eight community agencies, including the EOB, the City Commission, the County Commission, the Chamber of Commerce, the Community Council, the Albuquerque Public Schools, the University of New Mexico and the University of Albuquerque. That body passed its recommendations along to the City Commission, which acted on them and submitted the final versions to the appropriate office in HUD. During the period devoted to planning (originally scheduled to last a year, it spread over nineteen months) there were still other sources of citizen participation in the decisions, as the Model Cities staff conducted hundreds of interviews with the residents, set up numerous planning committees, and collected several volumes of information about the neighborhoods.[959] As a result of these tiers of decision making, it was felt, the poor people would not be intimidated, and the more influential members of the community would also have a say.

In practice, however, the major influence in the new structure did not follow precisely along these lines, partly because of the methods of funding. The Model Cities turned out to be a bonanza source of federal funds, and everybody wanted the money for Albuquerque or for his own selfish or un-selfish interests. The general formula was that for every dollar the city put up, within limits, four dollars would come down from HUD, and the city's share did not have to be in the form of cash. For the planning stage, half of the local contribution could consist of staff time. The Model Cities money could then be supplemented by other federal programs already underway in the area.[960] Sometimes this meant even more federal matching funds. Once the money came to the Model Cities program, it was considered, for the purposes of applying for new grants, "community" money, and it could be used to bring in more funds through the EOB Community Action Program, for which the formula was nine dollars from the Office of Economic Opportunity for every dollar from the community. Thus for certain types of projects, one dollar voted by the City Commission could be transformed into thirty-six, thanks to the largess of the United States government and its departments of Housing and Urban Development and Health, Education and Welfare. For the second action year, $80,000 in city money, all of it going into administering the program, was matched by $2,826,000 by the federal government, and much of this was used to attract still more federal money, bringing the total up to $5,500,000.[961] If one counted the funding for all the federal programs that were active in the Model Neighborhood Area, the total would be several times higher.[962] Small wonder, then, that poverty workers and residents began to refer to the federal government as "Uncle Sugar." The Joint Policy Board and the City Commission were reluctant to make any cuts in the requests submitted, whatever doubts they may have harbored, for they felt the funds would be substantial boosts to the local economy. The members of the Citizens Board, for their part, relied heavily on the guidance of the Model Cities staff and other professional poverty workers. So although not represented on any of the policy-making and decision-making boards, the professionals had a large hand in running the program.

Acting with the help of the poverty workers and sometimes coming up with new ideas on their own, the residents of the Model Neighborhood Area sponsored a wide range of projects, many of which were more tangible and less visionary than their predecessors. The representatives voted the largest share of the funds at their disposal to the Model Cities Alcoholism Treatment Center, which was affiliated with the Bernalillo County Medical Center; governments of the city, county and state; and the National Institute of Mental Health.[963] In conjunction with the EOB, they helped support Quebrar, an organization for the treatment of heroin addiction, and Comprehensive Child Care and Development, a preschool day care and education project, as well as a number of other programs.[964] One of the most popular projects was the Model Cities Cultural Center, which was at first resisted by the City Commission on the grounds that it was a frill but which eventually became so successful that a second branch was opened.[965] The Citizens Board established a newsletter to inform the residents of developments in the Model Neighborhood Area and to contribute further to the gradually increasing sense of community. And the board gave its support to many other projects large and small, providing assistance to such diverse groups as old people, persons who had run afoul of the law, struggling entrepreneurs, young couples, aspiring students, and residents seeking new housing.[966] To a greater extent than was true of the initial projects of the War on Poverty, the undertakings of Model Cities represented what the poor wanted for themselves.

If the establishment of Model Cities was a step toward more active participation of the poor and of the community leaders in the antipoverty drive, it also marked a decline in the influence of the middle-class liberal reformers, who had spearheaded the effort from the beginning. As a matter of fact, the liberals had begun to lose their dominance several months before Albuquerque's application for Model Cities funds was first approved, and their crusading spirit suffered further setbacks as the machinery of the War on Poverty became all the more integrated into the local political system. It was with mixed feelings that they watched the institutionalization of the programs into the impure and patronage-ridden structure of Albuquerque society.

One of the opening rounds in the struggle by community leaders to gain more power in the poverty programs got underway in April 1967, when Mrs. J.R. Modrall, the representative of the City Commission on the EOB Board of Directors, recommended that five new members be added to the board, to represent the business and industrial interests. Dr. David Hamilton, an economics professor at the University of New Mexico who was active in the Grass Roots Committee, argued that the business and industrial community "had never expressed interest or concern in solving the problems of the poor," and the measure was overwhelmingly rejected. Mrs. Modrall then resigned.[967] To take her place, the City Commission appointed Charles Davis, a long-time power in valley politics, a leader of the opposition to the Grass Roots Committee in the local Democratic Party, and a supporter of the successful City Commission candidates in the last election,[968] and the stage was set for a more serious confrontation.

In August EOB Director Clarence Gailard, who had formerly been chairman of the Grass Roots Committee, fired an employee of one of the community centers. The community association headquartered there felt it should have jurisdiction over such matters, and it complained loudly. New Mexico Governor David Cargo, a Republican who owed his election to the support of large numbers of crossover Democrats, issued a directive that the Albuquerque-Bernalillo County Economic Opportunity Board could expect no more funds until it gave the neighborhood community centers more of a voice in running their own affairs. In response, the board changed the firing of the worker to a one-week suspension and told Gailard to consult with the neighborhood boards before taking such action in the future. During the ongoing controversy the larger political implications became more apparent, as Cargo recommended "more concern on the part of the EOB on nonpartisan employment of personnel," Gailard charged that some valley political figures were regarding the directorship of the EOB as "a very nice patronage plum for politicians of both parties," and Davis called for Gailard's resignation.[969] The animosity continued to fester and the leaders to maneuver until a board meeting the following February, when Mrs. Robert Reineke, president of the League of Women Voters and the County Commission's representative to the EOB, made a motion to fire the director. It carried nineteen to eight by secret ballot, Clarence Gailard was out of a job,[970] and the Grass Roots liberals suffered their biggest setback thus far.

The repercussions were widespread and lasting. A number of other poverty workers resigned from their positions, including Gilberto Ballejos.[971] Protesting against the way the meeting and the voting had been conducted, Dr. Hamilton resigned from the board.[972] And over the next several years the EOB went through a succession of directors, as the competition among the various factions and the conflicts between Office of Economic Opportunity guidelines and the wishes of the community associations led to mounting frustrations. The transition of the poverty program from an idealistic quest to a political and bureaucratic institution was not smooth, but it proceeded along relentlessly. In May 1970 John Cordova, who had been having trouble getting along with some of the other officials in city government, was ousted by the city manager,[973] and Model Cities, too, became less of a crusade and more a matter of practical politics and administration.

On the community level a backlash was setting in against some of the more zealous of the poverty workers, in particular against the Volunteers in Service to America (VISTA), a group sponsored by the local EOB but not under its direct control. In the spring of 1970 Arnold Levy, an EOB representative from Mid-North Valley, declared, "They're nothing but troublemakers. Ship the entire pack back home. All they can do is make the situation worse than it already is." City Commission Chairman Charles Barnhart echoed these sentiments: "I sincerely believe that all that money that's been spent on VISTAs in the Model Neighborhood Area is a waste. It is also offensive for VISTA to bring in a man from Florida [National VISTA Area Supervisor John Goldsmith] who is not informed on our government programs and our goals, and permit him to deliberately breed distrust among the people." Goldsmith, who had helped organize a successful push by residents of the Model Neighborhood Area for representation on the Urban Renewal Board the year before, denied that VISTAs were troublemakers, but he admitted that they were now having to walk with a "light foot" in order not to arouse further opposition.[974]

As the role of the reformers receded, the various community associations began to act with greater independence, sometimes going against the wishes and plans of the poverty workers. Although this development was often frustrating to the officials in the antipoverty program and city government, it was an indication that the long-sought dream of more power to the poor people was beginning to bear fruit. In the overall process of deciding the future directions for the local War on Poverty, the communities which were already the most cohesive and had the strongest established leadership were frequently the most resistant to the plans of the antipoverty bureaucracy. Even these communities, however, underwent significant changes, as the leaders found it necessary to cooperate to some degree with the administrative structures and to involve greater numbers of the residents in the decision making.

The compositions and personalities of the different neighborhoods involved in the Model Cities program had a bearing on the politics. The poorest and the most demoralized, as well as the most receptive to the various aspects of the War on Poverty, was South Barelas, a predominantly Spanish-American community at the southern border of which a city sewage treatment plant emitted foul odors into the air. The young and aggressive South Barelas Community Improvement Association obtained, as we have seen, some of the earliest and biggest funds from the Office of Economic Opportunity. The two predominantly Black neighborhoods, South Broadway and John Marshall, had the lowest average length of residence, and these areas were also fairly eager to embrace the new federal programs. The proportion of participants in the various aspects of the Model Cities program who were Black was significantly higher than the Black proportion of the Model Neighborhood population. The other two neighborhoods, San Jose and Santa Barbara-Martineztown, were Spanish-American, and, for the most part, their residents had stronger community ties than characterized the Model Neighborhood Area as a whole.[975] San Jose was represented by two very different organizations. The East San Jose Community Association—founded in 1952 and connected with the East San Jose Community Center, which had been established by the City Parks

Department in 1955—was the oldest and largest of all the community associations in the area, and the group was so proud of its record of never taking handouts that it steadfastly kept its neighborhood out of the federal antipoverty program, including Model Cities.[976] South San Jose, on the other hand, did not have such a tradition and was quite active in many aspects of the program. Santa Barbara-Martineztown was the largest of the participating neighborhoods and had well-developed lines of political influence. Contributing to its political and social solidarity were such institutions as the Martineztown House of Neighborly Service, sponsored by the United Community Fund and the Presbyterian Church, and the presence of such long-established leaders as Mel Archuleta; Licho Martinez, who claimed to be descended from the man for whom Martineztown was named; and Manuel Sanchez, who had earlier served as chairman of the Democratic Party in Bernalillo County. All three ran grocery stores which served as foci in the community, and each owned other land as well.

During the course of the planning period for Model Cities, Albuquerque architect Max Flatow worked in conjunction with the Model Cities staff and many of the residents to develop a land-use plan that outlined a number of physical improvements and specified zoning for the various parts of the area. South Barelas would be zoned industrial, and the residents would be relocated elsewhere in the city. Most of the remainder of the Model Neighborhood Area was slated for residential zoning in order to prevent further deterioration because of industrial encroachment and to enable the residents to qualify for federal assistance to improve their homes. The cost of implementing the plan was projected at $8.9 million, to come in the form of Neighborhood Development Program funds.[977] Most people were enthusiastic; the city confidently moved on to the next step of seeking ratification by the neighborhoods involved.

The first elections went as the administrators and planners had expected. In December 1968 South San Jose voted to approve residential zoning as called for by the plan. Later that month the people of South Barelas went along, voting for industrial zoning and relocation.[978] But over in Santa Barbara-Martineztown, resistance was building up to the proposed shift from industrial to predominantly residential zoning, for several of the community leaders recognized that the plan would prevent them from expanding their businesses and would force them to spend money to bring rental property they owned up to code. Santa Barbara-Martineztown Community Improvement Association, which the more established leaders in the neighborhood had thus far avoided, favored the change,[979] and over the next several months the contending parties vied to outmaneuver each other. On the night of January 8, 1969, the board of the community association voted to schedule the zoning election for two days later. The next day Licho Martinez and Mel Archuleta fired off telegrams to U.S. Senators Clinton Anderson and Joseph Montoya making charges of a "Model Cities land grab"; that afternoon a Montoya aide met with Model Cities Director John Cordova to find out, as specifically as possible, what the land-use plan would entail; a few hours later, without notification of the press, residents of the area met and voted by a show of hands not to hold the scheduled secret-ballot election.[980] Some people charged intimidation, however, believing that the residents hesitated to oppose the will of their patrons in a face-to-face encounter, so the property owners of Santa Barbara-Martineztown circulated a petition calling for another vote. On January 16 they voted by secret ballot ninety to forty-seven not to hold the zoning election, and the issue seemed settled.[981] In February the Model Cities Citizens Board approved the Neighborhood Development Program (NDP) plan;[982] it looked as though funds for improvement would go to the rest of the Model Neighborhood Area. Licho Martinez, now an elected representative on the Citizens Board from Santa Barbara-Martineztown, asked the City Commission on March 7 to set aside NDP funds for the area while the community worked out an acceptable zoning plan.[983] Five days later the Urban Renewal Board approved the NDP first-year plan exclusive of Santa Barbara-Martineztown.[984] Pressure was growing to hold the long-avoided election on zoning for the recalcitrant community, and it was rescheduled for March 22. That night the property owners voted by secret ballot eighty-four to eighty-one in favor of keeping the area zoned industrial.[985] Resident participation had overruled the planners.

The City Commission, the Model Cities staff and much of the news media and the public at large were upset by the turn of events. Commented City Commission Chairman Pete Domenici, "The sad thing about the vote is that the plan drawn up for Martineztown is one of the best I've seen. . . . As long as we're participating in the program, even though we'd like to see it carried out, we have to go along with the federal guidelines and what the residents say." A Model Cities staff member was at a loss to account for the vote: "We've explained the issue so many times I can't see how they could misunderstand."[986] A number of months later this disappointment was overshadowed by an even more serious one when the federal government awarded Albuquerque only about one-ninth of the original request and the Model Cities Citizens Board and the Urban Renewal Board were forced to cut back drastically on the NDP plan.

The early 1970s brought another confrontation between the residents of Santa Barbara-Martineztown and the planners for the Neighborhood Development Program. The ambitious educational complex which Albuquerque Public Schools had pushed for inclusion in the downtown urban renewal project and which had later been transferred to the Neighborhood Development Program was subsequently scaled down to a replacement for Albuquerque High School, the oldest public secondary school in the city and recently condemned. It would take up less area than originally planned, but some space occupied by homeowners would have to be condemned. In the early stages, little resistance to the proposal surfaced, and the Citizens Board voted its approval. In early 1971, however, some of the residents of the section of Martineztown scheduled to be occupied by the new school formed the Citizens Information Committee and began voicing protests. At a February meeting with members of the Urban Renewal Board and the school board, they presented a survey indicating that 78 percent of the people affected did not want to move. Later that month the Urban Renewal Board decided to cease acquiring the land until the matter was resolved. In April the City Commission and the school board voted their approval of carrying out the plans for the school site, and the Urban Renewal Board followed suit. Meanwhile, the opposition was growing stronger. Near the end of the month Licho Martinez was elected the new president of the Model Cities Citizens Board, and that body withdrew its approval of the proposed location.[987] In the face of mounting citizen resistance, other boards and commissions involved reluctantly changed their positions, and Albuquerque Public Schools started looking elsewhere.[988] Again the intractable residents of Martineztown had prevailed.

Over the next year and a half, Model cities politics continued to seethe as the residents of the component neighborhoods became increasingly adept in strategic maneuvering. Although Licho Martinez had ascended rapidly through the ranks to the most powerful position on the Citizens Board, his long-established political power was not sufficient to protect him from attacks by those who felt he was bestowing too much favor on his friends. Angered by his stance on the distribution of housing funds, a coalition of Blacks and young Spanish-Americans led by Joe Green voted him out of office in July 1972. Martinez led a walkout of six board members, and during the next several weeks positions shifted with dazzling rapidity. Green was elected the new president, but an assistant city attorney ruled that since the vote was held after the walkout, the post would go to the duly elected vice president, Mauro San Martin, an ally of Martinez's.[989] Then the board removed San Martin as well as the previously elected secretary, and it elected Green again.[990] However, his sponsoring organization, Sociedad de Oportunidad, removed him as its representative and replaced him with its president, San Martin, who had previously resigned as the representative from South San Jose.[991] That neighborhood, one of the centers of opposition to Martinez, immediately chose Green for its new representative,[992] but since he had been off the board for a few days he was no longer president. In late August the issue was resolved, for a while at least, when Joe Green nominated Rudy Baca, representing the American G.I. Forum, Licho Martinez led another walkout, and Baca was elected president by those remaining by acclamation.[993] Although the developments might have seemed chaotic to those distant from the antipoverty programs, they exemplified a spirited sort of democracy in action. The level of participation by the residents of the Model Neighborhood Area and the degree of skill which they exercised had probably never been higher.

By late 1972, efforts were finally underway to develop Martineztown along lines which its residents wanted. The U.S. Department of HUD earmarked $4.5 million to go for preparing the neighborhood for residential renovation; the money would cover the cost of professional planning, acquisition and clearance of land, relocation of housing, pavement of streets and a program of public works. The residents and the planners were holding numerous meetings to work out the details.[994] By standing fast and insisting on their rights, the people of the neighborhood had managed to bring the planners and administrators of the poverty program around to their view and to get the benefit of substantial government funding as well.

The increased power of the poor people of Albuquerque during this period was also reflected in many other developments within the anti-poverty apparatus—some significant, some trivial. As they were often more interested in what they saw as direct benefits and less in long-term uplift than many of the professional poverty workers, they came to insist that poor people from the target neighborhoods be hired in the poverty programs whenever possible.

They were most successful in Model Cities, where their power was the most concentrated.[995] Whether the individual programs turned out successfully or not, the people working in them got bigger incomes than before the onset of the War on Poverty. Another issue which sometimes found the poor residents and the professionals on opposite sides, and in regard to which the residents usually got their way, was the matter of services. According to Clarence Gailard, the poverty program was designed to bring services to the poor not as an end in itself but in order to involve the neighborhoods and to get them to function as "effective power blocs."[996] James Jaramillo, a later EOB director, expressed himself along similar lines and added, "I think we may have fallen into a trap of becoming too service oriented."[997] But the poor liked the services; they used them extensively and made them part of their lives. An EOB board member from John Marshall, Paul Stein, expressed a common sentiment when he declared that the EOB should keep on providing them "because we've become dependent on the services and want them continued."[998]

In the long run, the increased participation and influence of the poor in city politics and in the various programs of the war on Poverty did not herald an end to poverty. Some of the poor used the programs as ladders to ascend to higher economic levels, more took advantage of the available services to alleviate their impoverished conditions, but the overall state of dependency in the target neighborhoods remained high and may have actually risen. Nevertheless, the growing political power of the poor people and the growing assumption of responsibility for them by the branches of government and the society at large were highly significant developments. Another minority group—and in a society that confers high status on economic wealth, an intrinsically weak minority—was gaining a more important position in the society as a whole. And as this happened, power and authority were being dispersed farther and farther in such a manner that even the weakest members had more access to it than before.

City Life Loosens Up

At the same time that various groups which traditionally had had relatively little influence were growing more powerful, authority and control were being dispersed in many other ways as well, some of them affecting the deepest fibers of the society. The complexes of ideas, beliefs and attitudes that bound the people together and provided the fundamental ground rules for behavior—religion and the system of justice—became less restrictive and imposing. The educational system, which served to impart to the young not only techniques for achieving success but also basic social values, grew less authoritarian. Self-control relaxed as well, and people came to express and indulge themselves all the more spontaneously. And as authority loosened in countless other ways and areas, command and outright coercion were frequently replaced by persuasion and social pressure.

Although religion was much less in the public eye than it had been during the fifties, it was undergoing a greater amount of ferment. Old forms were changing; old sources of authority were becoming less absolute. The significance of some of these shifts was more profound than the people of such a restlessly secular period could easily appreciate.

The most clear-cut changes occurred in the most formally structured religious institutions, such as the Catholic Church. Concerned that the church might be out of step with modern times and losing touch with vast numbers of the flock, the Pope and other leaders convoked the Council of Vatican II, out of which came several significant breaks with the past. The most visible was changing the words of the mass from Latin to the native languages of the Catholics throughout the world, thereby making the ceremony more understandable and accessible. The first Catholic mass in English held in Albuquerque took place on October 12, 1964, at the Albuquerque Civic Auditorium, and about thirty-five hundred people attended. At the end of the following month all Catholic Churches across the country shifted to English liturgies.[999] Soon came other changes to make the church less formal and to give the communicants more sense of participation. The altar was moved from the extreme end of the church building to a position between the priest and the congregation, and the priest began to conduct the service facing the people instead of with his back toward them. In this manner the Spirit of God was made to seem in the midst of the people instead of remote and on high. The growing informality spread to many other aspects of Catholic religious observance as well. Ever since the 1880s, the catechism had consisted of standard answers to standard questions: "Who made me?" "God made me," and the like. Now, learning proper attitudes was superseding memorizing what had traditionally been considered factual information. Explained Father A.A. Schneider, Superintendent of Schools for the Archdiocese of Santa Fe, "A child still has to know God exists before he knows God loves him. But more emphasis is put on God loving him than on anything else."[1000] Loosening its structure in such fashions, the Catholic Church was following the path of most other institutions in the western world.

On the college campuses the old forms of Catholicism were stretched even further. In October 1966 the Newman Center at the University of New Mexico began holding some evening masses with the congregation singing such popular songs as "Michael Row Your Boat Ashore" and "Blowing in the Wind" to the accompaniment of guitar music.[1001] The following year the Newman Forum invited as a guest speaker Rev. Malcolm Boyd, the Episcopal priest whose book of unconventional devotions *Are You Running with Me, Jesus?* had appeared earlier, and a small controversy was aroused in the outside community.[1002] Across town at the University of Albuquerque, which had been established in the early 1950s as the College of St. Joseph on the Rio Grande, the theater presented that May a *Liturgical Happening*, a pastiche of skits including, among others, a nun's fashion show, a beatnik's informal prayer, an LSD party broken up by three matrons from the Ladies' Aid, a bingo party ending in a catfight between two gossips, a Viet Nam battle in which the opposing fighters prayed for guidance and then were killed, and a funeral for God.[1003]

The adventurous mood of the times was also affecting most of the Protestant churches. Especially during the early and middle sixties a number of the clergy asserted their influence on the side of social activism and breaking down old barriers. Some fought against sexual censorship; more committed themselves to the cause of civil rights. On learning of the death of a Northern minister at the hands of whites during the 1965 march on Selma, Alabama, the Albuquerque Ministerial Alliance, the Albuquerque Council of Churches and the United Church Women jointly declared a "day of concern" with special services at two designated churches. At this time Rev. Franklin Heglund spoke of "the debunking of the dignity of man in our nation."[1004] Old practices and prejudices were out of favor; instead, people were being exhorted to open their hearts to the Spirit of God and become truly free.

In spite of the ongoing changes in the churches, fewer persons were participating in organized religion during the sixties. Many of the areas where the churches had traditionally made significant contributions, such as education and welfare, were increasingly being taken over by government bodies. Catholic education was particularly hurt. A number of parochial schools ceased functioning, including St. Mary's High School, which closed its doors in 1967 after forty-six years of continuous service; and the University of Albuquerque had to drop its intercollegiate athletic program because of financial difficulties. By 1971 there were thirty-six Catholic schools in the Archdiocese of Santa Fe as opposed to sixty-four only ten years earlier; over the same period the enrollment had fallen from 17,000 to 9,234.[1005] The elaborate and heavily financed programs of the War on Poverty made many of the religious charities less needed. And as the extended activities of the churches came to appear less relevant to modern society, their authority also waned. People turned less readily to their priests and ministers for guidance in their personal lives, relying instead on their own judgment and that of their peers. Thousands of young Catholics went their own way on the issue of birth control, on which their church took a steadfastly traditional stand. As a result of the declining influence of religion in the lives of many of the people and also of the resentment with which large numbers of the more conservative viewed the shifts in their churches, attendance at religious services dropped.

Probably no society, however, remains very secular for very long, and during the latter part of the sixties signs began to crop up of a vague sort of revival. Disoriented by the onslaught of tumultuous social change, many people, especially among the young, began to dabble in a wide range of somewhat religiously oriented activities. The ecology movement and the interest in natural foods demonstrated an almost worshipful attitude toward the natural environment. Enthusiasm for astrology became a fad, revealing a hunger for mysticism and certainty. More directly religious was the impact of such popular cults from the Orient as Transcendental Meditation and the Hare Krishna movement. At about the same time a new and home-grown type of Christian fervor began to appear, the Jesus movement. Most of the devotees were young, and many had recently turned away from drugs to "find Christ" as their savior. In 1967 a number of local "Jesus freaks" formed the Young Life Club, and the loosely knit organization developed branches in several of the high schools and held huge meetings, sometimes attracting more than a thousand people.[1006] Their enthusiastic singing and their evangelical ways branded them as unconventional to most of their fellow citizens, but these faithful were convinced they were ushering in a new religious awakening.

Meanwhile, the justice system was undergoing an extensive transformation. A sequence of court rulings, legislative decisions and other moves in the public arena were making the rules more uniform and less subject to the

271

vagaries of the individual police officers and judges. The accused, in particular the poor persons arrested, were given fuller protection and support than in the past. And although the body of laws continued to grow larger and more complicated, mirroring the increasing size of the public institutions, punishments for breaking the laws became, for the most part, less harsh.

In the second half of the sixties court decisions tightened the rules for admissible evidence in criminal trials, making it harder for the prosecution to use duress or heavy-handed persuasion to obtain convictions. The most important of these was the verdict in Miranda vs. Arizona, 1966, in which the United States Supreme Court ruled that confessions were inadmissible unless the suspect had first been advised of his rights to remain silent and to have an attorney present during questioning, and the suspect had indicated that he understood these rights.[1007] A year later, while police agencies across the country were still reeling from the effects of the decision and adjusting to the new procedures, the U.S. Supreme Court moved to give juveniles most of the same legal protections as adults, including the rights to get notice of charges, to be represented by an attorney, to remain silent, to confront and cross-examine complainants and witnesses, to obtain a transcript of the proceedings, and to appeal the decision to a higher court.[1008] Shortly thereafter the New Mexico Supreme Court ruled that juveniles had the right to trial by jury, and it removed them from the jurisdiction of county court and made juvenile court a part of the state district court system.[1009] In a few quick strokes, the process of meting out justice was thus made less overwhelming to the accused and less paternalistic.

The local courts were also adding restrictions to the power of the police. Leading the charge was Municipal Judge Harry Robins, whose political experience and outspoken views made him a formidable force to be reckoned with. Born in Odessa, Russia, in 1901, he had come to the United States with his parents three years later, grown up in Ohio, studied and practiced law, contracted tuberculosis, and in 1942, like many other tuberculosis patients who later achieved prominence, moved to Albuquerque. Robins straightaway began establishing himself as an influential leader in local political circles, serving as assistant district attorney from 1943 to 1947, as chairman of the Bernalillo County Republican Party from 1948 to 1952, and then as state chairman for the Republicans for a term beginning in 1952. While in this post he spearheaded a successful drive at the 1952 national convention to get state chairmen recognized as members of the national committee.[1010] During these years his political positions were fairly conservative and fairly typical of the Republican Party; commenting on his visit to the committee hearings in Washington held by Senator Joe McCarthy, he declared in 1953, "It is a revelation to watch some of these witnesses appear before the committee and stand behind their constitutional rights. I would tear them to pieces much more than does McCarthy."[1011] In later years, however, Robins's political ambitions subsided, his ties with the Republican Party loosened, and his sympathies became more liberal and libertarian. After another term as assistant district attorney, from 1959 to 1960, and several years of private practice with his son, he campaigned for the elected position of municipal judge in 1962 and won, professing his concern for the "little man."[1012] Throughout his terms in that office, he often sided with the accused, but he retained his capacity to tear the opposition to pieces.

Late in 1969 the judge staked out a lenient position in regard to drug offenses. On October 9 he openly disagreed with District Attorney Alexander Sceresse, who favored imprisoning addicts who refused to divulge their sources of supply. Robins indicated he would suspend the sentences of those convicted of misdemeanor narcotics offenses if they enrolled in the federally funded Narcotics Addiction Rehabilitation Act program administered at Bernalillo County Health Center.[1013] A little over a month later he declared unconstitutional the section of the drunk driving law which prohibited a habitual user of narcotics from operating a motor vehicle, for he opined that the law would apply to persons taking methadone in conjunction with the rehabilitation program. "Shall we punish a human being because he has an illness?" he asked. "Whenever I have an opportunity, I would rather put him on a program which will get him away from the habit."[1014]

In the late sixties and early seventies the unconventional behavior around the University of New Mexico often brought confrontations between the students and other young people and the police, and many of the resulting disputes over law-breaking and harassment ended up in Robins's court. In April 1970, for example, Officer Robert W. Moody brought in three long-haired youths for violating the city ordinance prohibiting hitchhiking from the sidewalk. Robins threw out the case, declared the ordinance void because it went "beyond the bounds" of the state statute on hitchhiking, and lectured Moody, who admitted he did not "personally like" the long-hairs residing in the university area. "When you destroy the rights of these kids because of their looks and their long hair, it's not right," the judge said. "You know doggone well why you're arresting them and handcuffing them. You hope you'll find that one of them is a criminal, and you'll have a feather in your cap."[1015]

Over the next several months the antagonism between the judge and the Albuquerque Police Department heightened, but Harry Robins held his ground. On December 3, 1970, Officers Robert Moody and James Webb, angered and frustrated by Robins's treatment of them and their arrests, requested that he be disqualified from presiding over their cases in the future. Acting Police Chief John Duffy supported their request, but Robins declared, "If they try to disqualify me, I'll just tell them to go to blazes."[1016] A few days later he made an offhand remark that he would resign if enough policemen signed a petition asking him to do so, but when the overwhelming majority of the police force put their names on such a petition, he chastised them for "diversionary tactics."[1017] The Albuquerque chapter of the National Association for the Advancement of Colored People, the Student Senate at the University of New Mexico, and the Grass Roots Committee of the Bernalillo County Democratic Party immediately announced their support for Robins.[1018] Community feeling about police behavior and the courts grew more vehement and polarized. On December 14 angry young Chicanos and Blacks presented the City Commission with demands to fire several policemen and to put an end to arrests for hitchhiking and vagrancy.[1019] The tension finally eased, for a while at any rate, on December 17, when the city manager announced the suspension of enforcement of the ordinances against hitchhiking, vagrancy and loitering—the three laws which Judge Robins and a number of other persons had accused the police of using for harassment.[1020] The same day New Mexico Attorney General James Maloney, himself a former Albuquerque municipal judge, delivered an opinion backing Robins in the disqualification dispute.[1021] The embattled judge and his views had emerged victorious.

Over the same years that the local, state and federal courts were adding to the restrictions on police activity, free or inexpensive legal assistance was being made more available to the needy. The Legal Aid Society, funded first by the Community Chest and later by the United Fund, had served the indigent in Albuquerque on a limited scale since 1950; in mid-1966 it was expanded through a $110,000 grant from the Office of Economic Opportunity, and it began to open up branch offices in the community centers of the poor neighborhoods.[1022] Like many of the other agencies associated with the War on Poverty, the Legal Aid Society came to take on an anti-establishment tone, aggressively seeking out new clients and informing them of rights of which some had been previously unaware. The caseload also shifted: in 1965, the last year the society had received all its financial support from private donations, 67 percent of the cases involved domestic relations or divorces; in contrast, during the first three months of 1967, only 37 percent fit into this general category, and most of the remainder were bankruptcy cases. The poor were using legal assistance more frequently than in the past, and increasingly they were using it to stymie their wealthier creditors.[1023] Upset by this trend, by the resorting to advertising, which the legal profession had traditionally regarded as unethical, and by the federal guidelines in general, the Albuquerque Bar Association moved in 1970 to dissociate itself from the Legal Aid Society and to offer an alternative plan of legal help to those who could not afford to pay.[1024] But the society, now dominated by liberals thoroughly committed to the antipoverty program, continued to flourish. Its chief counsel, William C. Fitzpatrick, proclaimed of the type of legal aid provided, "It's not charity, it's a matter of rights."[1025]

Poor persons accused of criminal offenses had access to other sources of legal assistance, and during these years these sources also increased. The traditional system had been for the court to appoint an attorney to serve an indigent client free of charge; such appointments were spread out among the local lawyers so that no one had an unfairly heavy burden. A problem with this practice, however, was that many lawyers spent more time and energy on their paying clients and tended to slight their non-income cases.[1026] In 1968 the New Mexico Legislature passed the Indigent Defense Act, which provided funds for the defense of poor clients.[1027] Two years later the U.S. Supreme Court ruled that states must provide the poor with counsel at preliminary hearings for criminal prosecutions.[1028] The gap between what the poor and the rich could get in the way of legal help was narrowing, but it was still present, for lawyers could still earn larger fees defending the wealthy. The establishment of the public defender's office for U.S. District Court in 1971 further shrunk the gap.[1029]

Another development that helped promote equal justice for all was the streamlining of the court system. For years the lowest level of judges in the state consisted of the justices of the peace, who earned five dollars for each case they tried and who might or might not be members of the bar. Their system of remuneration, their lack of strict qualifications and their large number—there were fifty-one in Bernalillo County alone—led to a wide diversity in the quality of the justice they meted out, and some were notorious for their heavy fines. In late 1966 the state constitution was amended to replace the justices of the peace with a much smaller number of magistrates, to be paid a flat salary of $14,000 a year. These new judges were required to be members of the bar, and they also had to meet stricter requirements concerning conflict of interest. In order that the relatively few magistrates could handle the volume of work coming their way, provision was made for most traffic fines to be paid by mail instead of in court.[1030] The magistrate system worked well, and other changes followed to make the functioning of the courts still smoother. The State Supreme Court ruled that, as of July 1, 1971, all district court crimes had to be tried within six months of the indictment.[1031] A few months after that date, the City of Albuquerque worked out a new procedure for dealing with such minor offenses as shoplifting and violations of zoning, health and animal control ordinances: the apprehending officer was given the option of simply having the accused sign an agreement to appear in court instead of arresting him and booking him.[1032] Such rulings and procedural innovations not only made the justice system more equitable and efficient, they also tended to ease the tribulations of the defendant.

As the community became more sensitive to the rights of the accused and less inclined to assume automatically that the police were doing their proper job, more checks on police behavior developed. Responding to the growing complaints of police brutality, in 1967 City Manager G.B. Robertson named a three-member committee of city officials to investigate such charges.[1033] In 1969 the Albuquerque Police Department established an internal affairs unit to look into possible violations by members of the force.[1034] Some of the citizenry, however, were not content to have the city government keep itself in line, and more controversies ensued. In June 1972 the recently formed Black Coalition, of which John Goldsmith was a prominent member, charged that Patrolman John Johnson had beaten two Black boys at the Albuquerque Sports Stadium.[1035] Frustrated because the City Personnel Board had overruled disciplinary measures against policemen, they also demanded that a Black be appointed to the board. Several days later Johnson was arrested for assault and battery,[1036] and on July 31 it was announced that the five-member Personnel Board would be expanded to seven, with one of the new members to be recommended by the Black Coalition.[1037] Another dispute arose in November, when Blacks complained about excessive force being used in the arrest of an armed robbery suspect at the YMCA.[1038] The city manager appointed a citizens committee to investigate the matter, and although some fault was found with the arrest procedure, no disciplinary action was taken.[1039] During this same general period the county jail was also under public scrutiny. In late 1971 a grand jury inspected the conditions twice and indicted two deputy sheriffs for beating drunken prisoners.[1040] Midway through the next year the inmates created a series of disturbances and complained loudly about poor conditions; the County Commission agreed that drastic improvements were needed, and it took control of the facility in August.[1041] The results of such overseeing of the police and jail by members of the public were not always quite what the protesters wanted, but the agents of law enforcement were put on notice that the people were holding them accountable for their actions. Legal justice was becoming a little less a high authority over the community, a little more a matter of community consensus.

Throughout most of these years the increasing attention being paid to the rights of the accused was accompanied by growing leniency toward the offenders. More people came to question whether imprisonment made wrongdoers reform, and the judicial use of probation, suspending sentences and taking cases under advisement became more common. Such alternatives to incarceration allowed many offenders who were not considered dangerous to society to go free while keeping them under the threat of punishment should they again go astray.[1042] In 1972 the harshest punishment for any crime was eliminated when the U.S. Supreme Court declared that the death penalty as currently on the books across the country was illegal because it was not being applied uniformly.[1043] Many conservatives were beginning to wonder if authority was relaxing to such an extent that criminals were laughing at society.

Of all the aspects and areas of society affected by the relaxation of authority, probably the most radical shifts in this direction took place where there was the most growth and experimentation. In the sixties and early seventies many of the citizens of Albuquerque had prodigious faith in the power of education, and, as we have seen, the educational system expanded dramatically as measured by the number of students and the size of the expenditures. Education, so the more idealistic hoped, would be the primary means of developing a better, more utopian society. Some of the most dedicated teachers and administrators believed that it could best carry out its function if they accentuated the positive, de-emphasized compulsion, and nurtured a free and supportive atmosphere which would allow the students to develop their natural curiosity and creativity. Many others less committed to improving society simply felt that the old techniques were not working particularly well, and they were searching about for better ways. The new educational processes which evolved were substantially looser and more spontaneous than their predecessors.

The traditional model of classroom teaching consisted of a teacher, whose authority was nearly absolute, imparting information, making assignments and giving tests to students who passively absorbed the material and demonstrated their knowledge upon demand. The natural assertiveness of the students was channeled into competing with one another for grades. In practice, of course, the teacher had never been in total control of the educational process, and the students had not docilely done everything that was expected of them; nevertheless, authority had been highly concentrated in the teacher. For a number of years, the model had become gradually less rigid as educators had begun to encourage more active participation on the part of the students. During the 1950s, for example, science teachers put more emphasis on students learning by conducting laboratory experiments and less on memorizing lists and formulas.[1044] But it was not until the onset of the next decade that traditional practice was extensively challenged.

As more money poured into the educational system and new ideas excited the atmosphere, student participation became a more prominent feature. The more widespread use of workbooks, teaching machines, television instruction, sophisticated laboratory equipment and other such impersonal learning aids enabled the students to get more actively involved and, in a number of instances, to set their own paces. By 1965 Albuquerque Public Schools had in-class television instruction in science, Spanish and music,[1045] and the use of phonographs and tape recorders was becoming common. Many teachers were employing other methods to draw the students out and to get them to think more on their own. Some used variations of the Socratic method to lead the students on to discover for themselves basic principles of the subjects under study.[1046] Research projects were given more encouragement—sometimes with the students working individually, sometimes in groups. To make the learners even more a part of the process, teachers occasionally resorted to dramatic reenactments of the material. Junior humanities classes at West Mesa Junior High School in 1970, for example, studied the events leading up to the Civil War by dividing into political factions, making speeches, forming alliances, and holding mock elections for the Presidency of the United States, the outcomes of which did not always correspond to what could be found in the history books.[1047]

The growing focus on the students was especially evident in certain influential programs outside the mainstream. In 1967 the Westinghouse Learning Corporation established the Educational Advancement Center for students who needed remedial work and whose parents were willing and able to pay the hundred dollars for tuition. Elaborate testing was used to determine the strengths and deficiencies of the student before he entered the program, and plans were made for his progress over a period of about fifty sessions each lasting approximately two hours. Upon arriving at the center for a session, the child would sign a contract to complete the assignment for that day, which was broken down into a series of "microtasks" so as not to present him with too great a challenge. Using self-instructional material such as textbooks, workbooks and audio-visual equipment, he would then work at his own speed. When he satisfactorily completed his task, he would be rewarded by being given a block of time in the "reinforcement area," where he could play games, read comic books or talk with the staff, whichever he desired.[1048] The approach worked so well that it was adapted, with a few changes such as use of ethnic materials and more personal instruction, for a program funded by Model Cities at Lincoln Junior High School in the fall of 1972.[1049] Some "free" schools—private, unaccredited schools run for children whose parents were opposed to what they regarded as the repressive nature of public schools and modern society—went still further in the direction of fostering individual development. At Celeste School, opened in the fall of 1968, in Corrales, a small community to the north of Albuquerque, children of various ages indulged in more or less spontaneous learning and play under the mild supervision of four adults, two of whom were certified teachers. Occasionally a teacher would ask the students if they wanted lessons; if the answer was affirmative, lessons would be given. In a given two-week period, the children dabbled in, among other things, mathematics, reading, making pottery, fixing a motor, building a tree fort, making woodcut prints, working with a computer and spending an afternoon on a sandbar on the Rio Grande.[1050]

The more conventional classroom activities in the city did not go so far in new directions as these somewhat experimental programs, yet even there the increased attention being paid to the individual students was accompanied by a general diffusing of authority. The ratio of teachers to students increased,[1051] but the function of the teachers underwent a subtle change. As impersonal teaching devices, independent study and group projects were used more frequently, the instructors came to act less as the central sources of information and more as leaders who advised, encouraged and supported the students. The use of outside speakers, volunteer tutors, teaching aides and team teaching further diluted the traditionally tight central focus of the classroom.

The general loosening of the structure of education also affected the subject matter. Less emphasis was placed on rigorous and traditionally prestigious subjects such as the sciences, which had received abundant attention during the fifties, and students turned more to relatively nonacademic areas. The boundary between school studies and the outside world was blurred; more people were coming around to the view expressed by a teacher at Celeste School—"You can't separate learning from living."[1052] Even summer vacations could be occasions for recognized educational experiences. In June of 1972 the principal at Highland High School announced that students from all over the city could sign up for courses ranging from a week-long study trip to Mazatlan, Mexico, to learning political science by working for a candidate or party, to backpacking in the Pecos Wilderness, to more conventional subject areas such as photography and poetry, and receive high school credit.[1053] At the university level, in addition to the regular courses, the special classes created as a result of student petitions and the offerings of the free university, there was the University of New Mexico Community College, where one could take noncredit courses in such areas as auto maintenance and the story of Albuquerque. Of all the burgeoning fields of nonacademic study during these years, the largest was vocational training. The Albuquerque Technical-Vocational Institute (later renamed Central New Mexico Community College), which opened its doors in the fall of 1965,[1054] expanded rapidly over the next seven years to an enrollment of approximately 1800 full-time and 4500 part-time students, and it was also training 250 unemployed or underemployed persons at a separate location, the Albuquerque Skills Center.[1055] And under the auspices of various antipoverty programs, thousands of other people underwent vocational training, often combining their learning with work for which they were paid.

With the increasing attention being paid to nonacademic studies and the growing public interest in fighting poverty, schools in poor neighborhoods began to get more funding. The National Defense Education Act was expanded to cover a broader range of subject areas; the Economic Opportunity Act of 1964 added new money and programs for education of the poor; and the Elementary and Secondary Education Act of 1965 provided for still more federal money, the amount for each school district depending on the number of children from families either earning less than $2,000 annually or on welfare, to be used to alleviate "educational deprivation."[1056] The proportion of state and local educational funds being directed to the poor areas also rose. By 1971, according to a report filed with the federal government, schools in low-income sections of the city had at least as good resources, by and large, as those in the rest of Albuquerque, and the statistics enumerated in this report did not count federal money provided to support Indian education or by the Elementary and Secondary Education Act.[1057] And the low-income-area schools, which historically had had the least success in educating their students, were among the most ready to try new techniques to arouse the young people's interest. In the fall of 1970 Albuquerque Public Schools established two new projects, the School Without Walls and the School on Wheels, for students from poor backgrounds who were having trouble coping with conventional education; both ventures combined formal education and vocational training, and both expanded over the following years.[1058]

All across the city, the many-sided changes in the educational process were affecting the nature of what was being learned. As learning by doing became more important and memorizing facts less so, and as the students were exposed to a growing variety of sources of information and other stimuli, they became more oriented toward picking up an assemblage of techniques and habits and getting a feel for their subjects. The emphasis on individual development and on group interaction meant that much of what they were being taught consisted of what kind of persons they should be; social values were becoming more central to education. Many educators were enthusiastic about the new broad approach to learning, they were glad to see the decline of the old narrow focus on clearly defined subjects comprised of bodies of more or less objective information, and they welcomed the trend toward training the whole student, not just his mental faculties, but these shifts brought about losses as well as gains. The students' testable knowledge, at least according to traditional criteria, was measurably less than that of their predecessors.

Meanwhile, other aspects of the educational system continued to grow looser. Behavior and dress in the classroom became more informal. On the university level it became more common for teachers to address their students by their first names, and it was not unusual for younger instructors and teaching assistants to be on a mutual first-name basis with the students both inside and outside of class. Desks and chairs began to be shuffled around in new arrangements according to the nature and mood of the course. Several of the high schools experimented with "modular" scheduling, an involved yet flexible type of system whereby the students had different schedules of classes lasting for varying periods of time on the different days of the week.[1059] College education, which had traditionally consisted of four years of study interrupted only by summer vacations, became more subject to other interruptions and dispersals. In 1970 the University of New Mexico established the Cooperative Education Program in Engineering, allowing engineering students to alternate taking classes and holding jobs semester by semester, thus gaining valuable experience and defraying some or all of their expenses.[1060] On a less formal basis many other students came to spread their college studies over a number of years, working part-time and taking light course loads or simply dropping out for a while to save money and decide what they wanted to do next. The partial breakdown of the distinction between grade levels proceeded in a different manner in the elementary schools. In 1963 distinct levels for the first three grades were abolished at the Heights Catholic School, and the children were encouraged to forge ahead in each subject area at their own particular speeds. Albuquerque Public Schools was reluctant to try this sort of innovation, but over the following years more Catholic schools in the area experimented with eliminating grade levels.[1061] As far as the general public was concerned, probably the most radical steps being taken by the educational system were in the area of awarding grades for students' achievements. A number of educators were convinced that competition for grades interfered with learning, and some went so far as to declare that such labeling of students was threatening, unjustified and repressive. Grades other than "satisfactory" or "unsatisfactory," "pass" or "fail," or other similar designations were actually abolished in many of the vocational training programs, and university students gained the option of taking a limited number of courses on a "credit-no credit" basis. In the courses for which grades were still being issued—and these constituted the overwhelming majority—the growing leniency of the teachers was shown by the general tendency of the grades to improve year by year while scores on standardized tests dropped.

As the various aspects of the educational process became less tightly controlled, educational administration also grew less authoritarian. In the early sixties the superintendent of Albuquerque Public Schools was Dr. Charles Spain, who had occupied the position since 1956 and who held the reins of power with almost as tight a grip as his predecessor, John Milne, but elsewhere in the state there were signs that superintendents and other administrators were losing much of their stature. In 1963 at a workshop conducted by the New Mexico School Boards Association for new members, Allan MacGillivray, president of the organization, observed that school boards had operated for generations much like private empires. "But in the last twenty years," he went on, "the population explosion buried boards under an avalanche of pupils and problems, and the boards and their egos, the superintendents, realized that they need help from a public so long ignored." Consequently, he noted, the boards opened up their meetings, invited the press, asked for the assistance of citizen committees, and became more responsive to the public.[1062] The growing militancy of the teachers and a change in the funding process to a system whereby each school district had to get money directly from the State Legislature further diminished the independence of the superintendents, and their average tenure became shorter.[1063] By the latter part of the decade, the pressures exerted by teachers, students and parents for changes in the schools were severely restricting the abilities of the principals to implement the mandates of their superiors or to act on their own; their positions also were growing less comfortable and stable.[1064] Throughout the administrative structure, persons who had been accustomed to dealing forcefully with those under them were having to adjust to using a lighter touch or get out of the system.

In May 1965 Dr. Spain died of a heart attack,[1065] and the Albuquerque system was exposed to the sorts of pressure that had been building elsewhere. His replacement was named a little over three months later—Dr. Robert L.

Chisholm, who had been superintendent of schools for Richland, Washington.[1066] Over the next several years the Albuquerque Classroom Teachers Association (ACTA), a union to which the majority of the local teachers belonged and which was associated with the National Education Association, flexed its muscles. In April 1966 it adopted a ten-point program in regard to such matters as salaries, class size and definitions of duties, and it proclaimed, "A quality education program calls for good communication and mutual respect between teachers and administrators, between the professional staff and the lay board of education, between the profession and the community."[1067] Chisholm was able to deal with the ACTA, but matters over which he had no control and little influence were looming up on the horizon. Money was a perpetual problem, and examiners indicated that unless the educational resources of the city high schools were substantially improved by the fall of 1969, they would lose accreditation. As of February 1968 the legislature had not allocated the money needed to raise the standards to the required level. Toward the end of the month the New Mexico Educational Association issued a demand for Governor David Cargo to call a special legislative session to consider school finances, but he balked. At that point the membership of the ACTA voted overwhelmingly to strike, the Albuquerque Federation of Teachers, a smaller union, did likewise, and the Albuquerque schools shut down.[1068] Bowing to the pressure, the governor announced he would appoint a task force to come up with new recommendations for school finances. Six days after the strike vote had been taken, the teachers, having demonstrated their power and having permanently altered the machinery of educational politics, agreed to return to work.[1069] Thirteen months later Chisholm resigned from his post, declared that the financial outlook for Albuquerque Public Schools was "dismal," and took a higher paying job as superintendent of schools in Arlington, Virginia.[1070]

In June 1969 the school board asked an Albuquerque man to be the next superintendent, Dr. Tom Wiley, who had extensive experience in state and local educational politics. Wiley had come to Albuquerque in 1907 at the age of one, had been educated in the city, and had taught in Bernalillo County schools before going into administrative work. In the forties he had been superintendent of county schools; following the consolidation of city and county schools in 1949, he had served as John Milne's administrative assistant for two years and then as state superintendent from 1951 to 1954; more recently he had been teaching educational administration at the

University of New Mexico. Although he had not applied for the position of superintendent of Albuquerque Public Schools, he agreed to take it for two years,[1071] and immediately he set about the task of reorganizing the system to make it operate more efficiently and more responsively. Wiley announced a plan of decentralization calling for three area superintendents who would be under his authority yet could function with a certain amount of autonomy. Such specialized educational services as music, art, speech and guidance were also partially decentralized. In words that must have cheered the ACTA, he described what he felt was the proper relationship between the administration and the teaching staff.

> The most important relationship within the entire system is between teachers and pupils. Administration is merely a means to the end of facilitating good teaching. The board has no other reason for creating an administrative establishment. Therefore, every effort will be made to keep communication lines more open between the administration and the teaching staff, based upon the premise that good teaching is dependent upon high teacher morale and high morale is largely built upon good salaries, wholesome working conditions, assistance with problems, and recognition of achievement in the classroom. The overtone at all administrative levels will be upon services to the classroom, control will be the undertone.[1072]

Having crowned his long career in education with his reorganization of Albuquerque Public Schools, Tom Wiley retired in mid-1971, to be replaced by Ernest Stapleton, who had risen through the ranks of the school system.[1073]

The loosening of control which was being manifested in such fundamental aspects of society as the educational process, the justice system and religion was also apparent throughout the social structure. Traditional centers of authority of all kinds—including political leaders, employers and parents—became weaker. Self-discipline also declined, to be replaced by the power of group pressure. This broad trend or group of associated trends could be examined in any number of areas, but the findings would be much the same. Much earlier we looked at changes in the level of sexual activity as an indication of a general relaxation of control; during the decade of the 1960s changes of this nature came so rapidly that they were called the "sexual revolution."

The people's increasingly open interest in sex was reflected in the movies that came to Albuquerque. Some were about young people tormentedly struggling with love and sex; in 1961, for example, *Splendor in the Grass* depicted two teenagers in love who, partly as a result of parental pressure, never engaged in sexual relations with each other and whose love was blighted by time and circumstance. In 1963 appeared *David and Lisa*, about two troubled young patients at a mental hospital whose awakening feelings for one another helped them toward recovery. Many of the advertisements for the films began to emphasize the sexual content: the public was informed that in *The L-Shaped Room* "Sex is not a forbidden word!" and that *What's Up Tiger Lily* was "all about life, love . . . fun and all that (sigh) thing we all crave but can't mention in motion picture advertising." As the stories grew more turbulent and rambunctious, male leads became more and more prominent, displacing the female stars who had done so well only a few years earlier. In 1964 came *Tom Jones* with Albert Finney, and the movie focused more heavily on the sexual romps than had the eighteenth-century novel. Two years later *Alfie*, starring Michael Caine, depicted the episodic sexual adventures of an irrepressible and irresponsible London cockney. Sexual interest also had a bearing on the boom of the "art film" in the decade of the sixties. These movies, whose quality might or might not match their pretensions but which almost invariably contained an intense mood, a somewhat puzzling plot and a depiction of sexual intercourse, were especially popular at the theaters in the university area, including Don Pancho's, the Lobo and the Hiland. Fitting into this loose category were such European-made imports as most of the films directed by Bergman, Fellini and Antonioni, as well as a few Hollywood products like 1962's *Phaedra*. The most sexually explicit of all the locally shown movies, however, usually had little artistic quality to recommend them. In the early 1960s such establishments as the Roxy and the Esquire began regular showings of soft-core pornography. Toward the end of the decade more small theaters specializing in sex films were in business, and the fare was harder-core pornography. Meanwhile, the big suburban theaters were sometimes presenting the sort of subject matter that earlier would have been left to their sleazier competition. In late 1968 and early 1969 *Candy*, based on a racy best seller, was drawing crowds to the Fox-Winrock.

Sexually explicit magazines and books were also proliferating. Civil authorities tried as best they could to stem the tide through legal means, but the current of the time seemed against them. In February 1961 city police raided three newsstands, confiscated hundreds of allegedly obscene publications, and arrested four persons for violating the section of the municipal ordinance on disorderly conduct which forbade selling obscene material.[1074] Three of those charged were found guilty,[1075] yet they won on appeal because the ordinance had failed to define the term "obscene."[1076] In March of the following year the City Commission replaced the ordinance with a new one defining "obscene" as anything that "offends the contemporary conscience";[1077] obtaining a conviction, however, proved as difficult as before. Several months later the assistant district attorney issued an opinion that the *Playboy* magazine calendar for 1963 was obscene, the publishing company which handled the item sued the city attorneys and the chief of police, and District Judge Robert Reidy ruled that the calendar was legally permissible.[1078] Subsequently the city officials determined to narrow their focus to materials about which there appeared to be little doubt. In December 1967 police arrested Phillip R. Mayne, owner of the Yale Street Grasshopper Book Store, located near the University of New Mexico, for selling obscene books. Of the five seized as evidence, the most patently obscene seemed to be *My Secret Life*, a classic of Victorian pornography. Municipal Judge Harry Robins found Mayne guilty on that one count the next March,[1079] but the bookseller appealed. When the case came up in district court in November 1969, the assistant city attorney decided abruptly to move to have it dismissed.[1080] The city officials were evidently further limiting their criteria for what they considered obscene.

Of greater interest to most of the local citizens was what they could see without opening a book or standing in line for a movie. Manner of dress evinced the new openness—this was particularly noticeable for the women, whose lives were conspicuously less restricted than formerly. Throughout the sixties skirts became shorter and shorter, exposing more of the female leg to the onlookers than most had ever before seen in public on the well-dressed woman. That fashion ebbed, but by the early 1970s halter tops became the rage among many young women, and they were frequently worn to high school and college classes. A number of nightclubs began to feature waitresses and dancers who were "topless," that is, who had their breasts exposed. The enormous increase in erotic stimulation lent support to the widespread impression that sexual activity was growing more abundant.

The relaxation of control in this dimension and others ushered in basic alterations in relations among people. Since authority was less concentrated and imposing than before, persons in positions of authority had to rely more on persuasion and subtle pressure in order to get their way; and more frequently than in the past, they had to give in to the will of their subordinates. One of the most striking illustrations of this shift was the course of developments in an area where the city fathers had once used heavy-handed tactics—annexation of adjoining land.

In the early years of the decade the city government embarked on its most aggressive campaign to bring in new territory since the late 1940s, when it had annexed some thirty-seven square miles while riding roughshod over the protests of many of the new residents. The first thrust came in the spring of 1960, when the City Commission announced its intention to annex about ten square miles of the south valley west of the Rio Grande and south of the city limits. The people of this booming residential area, however, proved ready to give battle. More than a thousand concerned citizens showed up at a meeting at Rio Grande High School on April 6 to discuss the matter, and only three indicated they were in favor of annexation. Several people said the city wanted them in only to increase its revenues and pay off its bonded indebtedness. Commented one, "If we wanted to live in the city we'd move there."[1081] Less than two weeks later the Southside Boosters Club met and assumed leadership of the drive to block the city's plan. The members favored incorporating into a separate town.[1082] The next day a confrontation shaped up as the filing of a petition for incorporation was followed in a few hours by a City Commission resolution initiating the establishment of an arbitration board of seven members to decide about annexation.[1083] With the prospect of a heated and protracted legal fight looming up to determine which action had precedence, the warring parties then called a truce, agreeing to desist from efforts to annex or incorporate for a year.[1084]

Although this attempt at expansion had been blocked, the developments of the next three years seemed to favor city hall. Ed Snow, who was developing the Hoffman City subdivision project on 2,800 acres of the old Atrisco land grant southwest of Albuquerque, requested annexation of the development, and in September 1960 the city took it in despite the land grant heirs' protests that only 640 acres had been paid for.[1085] A year later, the truce between the city and the south valley residents having expired, the people of the communities of Atrisco, Arenal, Five Points and Armijo voted on a proposal to form an independent town, and the measure was defeated, 1,903 to 443.[1086] The threat of such communities using this means to avoid annexation in the future was eliminated in 1963, when the State Legislature passed statutes prohibiting any village from incorporating if it was located within a five-mile "urbanized area" surrounding an already incorporated municipality unless that municipality approved the incorporation.[1087] That legislature also established a new method of annexation: an incorporated municipality could take in by simple resolution any unincorporated area which had been completely encircled by the municipality for five years.[1088] A further problem for the south valley was pressure from the State Health Department for an adequate sewer system in the area. The city could provide sewers; most of the valley residents had only septic tanks, which sometimes posed health hazards. About the only bright piece of news from state government as far as most of them were concerned was the following opinion issued by the attorney general: "Where a village is annexed to a town, the property within the village at that time would not be subject to ad valorem taxes to retire the present general obligation bonded indebtedness of the town."[1089] As a result, the immediate tax disadvantage to the residents whose land was annexed would not be great.

Not everyone in the valley area opposed joining Albuquerque, and in 1963 and 1964 the city annexed a number of small and large tracts whose owners were eager for municipal services. Often the tracts were not, strictly speaking, contiguous to the city limits, so they were added by a "shoestring" method, with the city also annexing narrow strands of nontaxable property, such as schools and county roads and rights-of-way, leading out to them.[1090] The long sewer lines which resulted could hardly be paid for by the meager increments of taxable property, but the purpose of the city seemed to be to make whatever inroads it could into the valley and to make uneconomical the independent water and sewer districts which were getting underway by denying them rights-of-way over direct paths. One of the most spectacular of these additions took in 127 acres of the south valley, including the new subdivision Paradise Acres and land connecting it with the city limits near the southeast corner of Hoffman City, now renamed Snow Vista, consisting of the right-of-way along several roads and a narrow 1,000-foot-long strip through property belonging to the Atrisco land grant. This annexation, which occurred in January 1964, extended the city limits almost two miles to the south.[1091]

Its appetite whetted by its recent successes, five months later the City Commission voted to implement its most ambitious plan of annexation yet, a proposal to take in some 11,800 acres of county land, including a 649-acre strip 50 to 100 feet wide which extended along the perimeter of Bernalillo County. Were this attempt to succeed, Albuquerque could in five years swallow up the rest of the county according to state law. The city had the power to annex the encirclement strip, contended the commissioners, because more than half the land being brought in was done so by petition of the owners—the city itself, the University of New Mexico, and D.W. Falls, Inc., which had the deed to and planned to develop Volcano Cliffs, a large and picturesque expanse on the west mesa. The City Planning Department had drawn lines on a map of the county in such a way that the rest of the land was "contiguous" to that owned by these three parties. This time, though, the city had overreached itself. Two of the other landowners affected, Rex Mattingly of Corrales and the Schwartzman Packing Company, filed a suit to stop the move, and District Judge D.A. MacPherson issued a permanent injunction blocking the annexation. He expressed concern about two nontax paying bodies, the university and the City of Albuquerque, uniting to force taxpayers into the city against their will. A still greater objection was that it was "unreasonable." He referred to an authority on municipal corporations which stated: "The extension is not unreasonable if the territory embraced is nearly all improved and necessary for municipal purposes. But if the territory is sparsely settled, situated remotely from the thickly settled portion of the municipality, would receive no advantage or benefits from annexation but would be burdened with additional tax, and the residents of the territory prefer to remain without the municipality, it should not be annexed." Therefore, it was not to be annexed.[1092]

This court decision, which corresponded closely to the sentiment of most of the metropolitan area, set the tone for next skirmish. Over the objections of Commissioners Ralph Trigg and Emmanuel Schifani, the City Commission voted in September 1964 to annex some 8,200 acres—Volcano Cliffs, still applying for admission and still basically vacant; a substantial acreage of improved land in the north valley owned by persons opposed to joining the city; and a connecting strip consisting of about ten miles of roadway. Before the vote was held, Trigg commented, "It seems to me the public feeling is about fifty to one against this. In fact, I have had only one phone call from a person favoring the annexation."[1093] Judicial feeling was no more enthusiastic: the following month Judge MacPherson ruled against the proposal, declaring it "arbitrary and capricious" and therefore "unreasonable."[1094] Still determined to push the boundary of Albuquerque further into the north valley, the City Commission then turned to the arbitration board method. Around the end of the year it designated an area to be annexed and appointed three members to the board in accordance with state law. In January 1965 came the election in which property owners from the area voted on their three representatives; it was won by the slate opposed to annexation, led by former County Commission Chairman Gerald Cornelius.[1095] The six members of the board elected a seventh to be chairman, and they deliberated into February before deciding, four to three, in favor of the valley residents. Justifying the decision, Cornelius pointed out property along Rio Grande Blvd. NW that had gone without water and sewer lines for eleven years after having been annexed.[1096]

Later that month came the climax of the resistance to annexation. Spurred by a chorus of indignant constituents, the State Legislature enacted a two-year moratorium on any further additions of territory to the City of Albuquerque except in cases where 100 percent of the property owners affected wanted to come in.[1097]

During this period of restricted annexation the city continued to absorb small shoestrings of land in the north and south valleys. Most of its new territory, however, was added on the east side of town,[1098] where throughout the decade large numbers of residents were requesting to have their land annexed. Overall, the most significant developments over these two years in regard to annexation were a general cooling off of tempers and a growing realization by city officials of the dangers of flouting public opinion.

The end of the moratorium brought no dramatic change, for the leaders in the City Commission at this time were opposed to bringing people into the city against their will. Ralph Trigg, the commission chairman, had earlier declared there would be no forced annexations.[1099] After the next city election, in October 1967, Pete Domenici became chairman, and he proposed orderly extension of city services into county areas before moving to take them in. "By utilizing planned annexation," he announced, "we will do away with the friction and ill will which in many cases in the past has earmarked annexation."[1100] And as a result of city government's treading lightly in this matter and paying heed to the wishes of the residents, the controversies surrounding annexation died down. In this sensitive area and in others, the public officials were learning to be less forceful in imposing their will, to be more flexible and conciliatory.

Political and Civil Unrest

Toward the close of the sixties and on into the beginning of the seventies the tumultuous changes that were shaking Albuquerque society reached a peak of intensity, and the rising tension seemed to threaten the foundations of the social structure. The liberal reformers' hopeful idealism of earlier years, beset with mounting frustrations as many of their plans turned out differently from the ways they had expected, lost much of its luster, and their voices grew more strident. As the young people, the members of the ethnic minorities, the women, the poor and other groups which previously had had little power became more assertive, conflicts with the authorities and with persons who wished to preserve the status quo—and also conflicts among the newly emerging groups themselves—heightened. The shifting status of such groups and the deep-seated changes in the nature of social authority led to greater uncertainty about who was in control and to what extent control should be exerted; many of the people involved attempted to resolve these questions by asserting whatever influence they could muster and fighting among themselves. And the rising energies that fueled the excitement and aggressiveness of the people pushing into new areas and trying new kinds of endeavors extended into other sorts of aggressive and unconventional behavior as well. Crime and other varieties of strife not directly related to the ongoing social changes were growing rapidly.

Throughout the 1960s the public interest in and fascination with conflict and violence had become increasingly apparent in the movies. In 1963 *Dr. No*, introducing Sean Connery as British secret agent number 007 James Bond, showed in Albuquerque; according to the advertisements, "the double '0' means he has a license to kill when he chooses . . . where he chooses . . . whom he chooses!" Subsequent James Bond films, including *From Russia with Love*, *Goldfinger* and *Thunderball*, with their slick combinations of glamour, adventure, gadgetry and mayhem, drew in throngs of ticket-buyers, inspiring a host of imitators. Bond's deceptions, violence and forbidden pleasures were all right, so the feeling went, because he was fighting for democracy, but his style of living was obviously a greater source of appeal than his being on the right side. A more dubious hero, the Man with No Name played by Clint Eastwood, made his entrance in 1966's *A Fistful of Dollars*, an inexpensively made western filmed in Italy in which the taciturn leading character killed numerous unsavory types. This movie and its equally bloody sequels propelled Eastwood to stardom. The role he played was more nihilistic than Connery's James Bond, and later films seemed to treat social order and authority more ambivalently still. In 1967 appeared two critically acclaimed films—*Bonnie and Clyde*, which depicted its violent, bank-robbing protagonists in a somewhat sympathetic light, and *Cool Hand Luke*, in which a rebellious ne'er-do-well is imprisoned for a minor offense, becomes an existential hero and achieves martyrdom. If violence was titillating, rebelliousness was fashionable. Perhaps the goriest, and one of the best-made, movies along these lines was *The Wild Bunch*, made in 1969. A story about the destructiveness and destruction of a collection of over-the-hill western gunfighters, it attracted an enthusiastic following especially among the young. And hundreds of other movies, increasingly violent and iconoclastic, attracted crowds over these years.

The lawless streak in popular culture was paralleled by growing violence in the society at large. The nation's crime rate was steadily rising. Americans across the country were stunned by the assassination of President John Kennedy in 1963, and other slayings of prominent leaders, including both Martin Luther King, the most illustrious of the civil rights activists, and Robert Kennedy, the dead President's brother, in 1968, followed disturbingly. Even more unsettling, because they involved large numbers of otherwise more or less law-abiding citizens, was a series of urban riots beginning in the mid-sixties. In August of 1965 young Blacks residing in the Watts section of Los Angeles went on a rampage of destruction and looting, and each of the following years through 1969 saw several major riots in large American cities. In most cases the disorders erupted in inner city areas with predominantly Black populations, and overtones of racial hostility were apparent. The aftermath of King's assassination saw destructive riots break out in a number of metropolitan centers, including Washington, D.C., Baltimore and Chicago. Young Whites were the primary participants in some cases, however, as in the violence that took place during the 1968 Democratic national convention in Chicago and in the 1969 riots in Berkeley, California. Moreover, the nation's college campuses, sparking with dissatisfaction over such issues as the War in Viet Nam and the growth of huge and impersonal bureaucracies, were also volatile during these years and frequently ignited with violent demonstrations, mass rallies and destruction of property.

The riots, which were becoming endemic with the advent of spring and summer, deeply troubled many thoughtful citizens because they appeared to be symptoms of profound social unrest and might even be precursors of revolutionary activity. Sifting through their voluminous data, some social scientists and historians found parallels with earlier periods of turmoil and rioting—the Luddite destruction of machines during the industrial revolution in England, for example, or the European outbreaks of 1848, or the Paris Commune of 1870, or the industrial violence of nineteenth- and early twentieth-century America, or the American race riots of the 1920s. But significant differences were also discovered. Most of the examples of collective violence over the last hundred years or so up until the 1960s involved fairly definable groups struggling with one another and not against the sociopolitical system itself. The recent outbreaks, on the other hand, manifested a relatively low level of attacks on persons; the primary targets were property, institutions and symbols of authority. In the "ghetto" riots of American cities Black-owned businesses were often firebombed along with establishments belonging to Whites, and most of the personal violence was directed against policemen rather than Whites in general. And when White students went on the rampage, they voiced their anger at the "system" and frequently expressed their solidarity with the Blacks and other ethnic minorities they regarded as oppressed. The riots themselves showed little evidence of advance planning—they generally seemed to ignite spontaneously when large groups of dissatisfied people, sweltering in the heat with time on their hands, were angered by something as fortuitous as a news event, a police arrest of one of their number or even the cancellation of a rock concert, and the rage spread like wildfire. That so many people were so frustrated and so susceptible to the lure of mob violence, however, seemed to bode ill for future social stability.[1101]

No such outbreaks had occurred in Albuquerque, but in recent years the local crime rate had risen even more precipitously than in the nation as a whole. In 1945 Albuquerque's rate for major crimes per 100,000 residents (covering murder, aggravated assault, robbery, burglary, auto theft and larceny over fifty dollars—rape is omitted from these figures because the Federal Bureau of Investigation's Uniform Crime Reports did not tabulate that crime in Albuquerque until 1958) was 680.4, well below the national average for cities of its size. In the early fifties the rate for crimes against property (burglary, auto theft and larceny over fifty dollars) began to rise steadily; the rate for crimes of violence (murder, aggravated assault and robbery) started ascending at a more or less similar pace toward the end of that decade. Around the middle of the sixties Albuquerque's rate for major crimes passed the national average for cities in its population category, with crimes against property leading the way, and in 1969 the overall figure reached 5,433.9 per 100,000.[1102]

Equally alarming to the general public was the dramatic increase of criminal behavior among the young. In the 1950s cases involving the use of marijuana and other narcotics had been rare, but the following decade had seen an enormous growth in the popularity of marijuana smoking, a lesser yet quite serious rise in the use of hallucinogenic drugs, and the emergence of a drug culture that seemed to be centered in the vicinity of the University of New Mexico. Among younger students and student-aged residents vandalism was increasing rapidly; the favorite targets were schools, cars, traffic signs and public works in general. City parks were popular gathering spots for the restless young, and a number of these places were inflicted with wanton damage and acquired dangerous reputations. In the fall of 1963 a young man was injured by gunfire in Rio Grande Park.[1103] Two years later a delegation of residents from the neighborhood around Roosevelt Park appeared before the City Commission with a petition requesting lighting for the park and a curfew; Patrick Lynch, their spokesmen, complained of threats to their children during the daytime and nightly noises "ranging from shouts to screaming and calls for help."[1104]

The tense and aggressive mood of the city, of which these signs of social disorganization were disturbing symptoms, continued to wax in 1969. People controlled themselves less tightly, tempers flared more readily, and the community showed a greater tendency to polarize into opposing camps.

On February 27, during a demonstration held by a group of activists protesting recruiting on the campus of the University of New Mexico by Dow Chemical Company, one of the suppliers of napalm for the War in Viet Nam, a group of opposing students, some of them athletes, challenged the demonstrators. A slight scuffle ensued, and one of the demonstrators pushed was John Walker, who was currently serving as executive secretary of the New Mexico Civil Liberties Union. Walker, weighing about 150 pounds, thought he was about to be attacked by several hefty football players, and he whipped out a tear gas gun and yelled to one of them, "I'll kill you." Charges were filed against the civil libertarian, and in May he was found guilty of assault. Walker's fifty-dollar fine and thirty-day sentence were taken under advisement.[1105]

Less than a month later the University of New Mexico became embroiled in its biggest controversy thus far since the end of World War II. Lionel Williams, a Black teaching assistant and doctoral candidate in the English department, had distributed to his freshman classes copies of several poems by Lenore Kandel, a San Francisco writer, and he had held class discussions on the material. Although some of the pieces were quite graphic and a few of the students were at first shocked by the language, none raised any objections, and Williams's classes proceeded in an orderly fashion for a couple of weeks. Toward the end of March, however, the father of one of the female students read the handout, reacted angrily, and demanded that the legislature do something about the outrage. Over the next few months one of the works passed out, "Love-Lust Poem," became the focus of an acrimonious dispute which involved cultural mores and the nature of language and which pitted members of the university community against much of the rest of the state and generation against generation. Persons who had not thought about poetry for years became avid readers and instant critics. The text of the poem is as follows:

Love-Lust Poem

I want to fuck you
I want to fuck you all the parts and places
I want you all of me

all of me

my mouth is a wet pink cave
your tongue slides serpent in
stirring the inhabited depths
and then your body turns and
then your cock slides in my open mouth
velvety head against my soft pink lips
velvety head against my soft wet-velvet tongue

your cock/hard and strong/grows stronger, throbs in my mouth
rubs against the wet slick walls, my fingers hold you
caress through the sweat damp hair
hold and caress your cock that slides in my mouth
I suck it in, all in, the sweet meat cock in my mouth and
your tongue slips wet and pointed and hot in my cunt
and my legs spread wide and wrap your head down into me

I am not sure where I leave off, where you begin
is there a difference, here in these soft permeable membranes?

you rise and lean over me
and plunge that spit-slick cock into my depth
your mouth is on mine
and the taste on your mouth is of me
and the taste on my mouth is of you

and moaning mouth into mouth

and moaning mouth into mouth

I want you to fuck me
I want you to fuck me all the parts and all the places
I want you all of me

all of me

I want this, I want our bodies sleek with sweat
whispering, biting, sucking
I want the goodness of it, the way it wraps around us
and pulls us incredibly together
I want you to come and come and come
with your arms holding me tight against you
I want you to explode that hot spurt of pleasure inside me
and I want to lie there with you
smelling the good smell of fuck that's all over us
and you kiss me with that aching sweetness
and there is no end to love[1106]

The first public intimation of the breaking scandal came when University President Ferrel Heady and Vice President Sherman Smith were summoned to a meeting of the Senate Finance Committee in Santa Fe on Friday night, March 22. The legislators pointed to copies of the poem and vented their rage. Senator Robert Ferguson, Democrat-Eddy County: "In my opinion, it's the most disgraceful thing I've ever seen since I've lived in New Mexico." Senator Frances D. Hargrove, Republican-San Juan County: "That's the most filthy stuff I've ever read. If I had my way about it, I would cut your budget down until you couldn't operate until you cleaned that place up." The committee members were particularly incensed that Lionel Williams was still teaching. Heady and Smith admitted that the material was obscene, but they insisted that, according to university regulations, Williams was entitled to a hearing. The committee was not mollified; Chairman Harold Runnels, Democrat-Lea County, declared, "If I'd had my daughter there, I'd have licked the living hell out of him before night."[1107] The body made plans to delete $50,000 from the budget appropriation for the university and use the money to fund an investigating committee.[1108]

Over the next few days the anger on both sides of the issue spread throughout the university and across the state. The English teaching assistants and graduate assistants met Sunday night, and a majority decided to teach "Love-Lust Poem" in their classes to show their support for Williams. The next day Kenneth Pollack, another teaching assistant, appeared in Williams's classes as a guest lecturer and described homosexual acts to the freshmen. Other students began circulating a petition which read: "We the undersigned support Lionel Williams' right of academic freedom and his right to due process. We furthermore think that if UNM is to be a free university, the state legislature should not control material taught by teachers." Outside the university the combatants were no less energetic. The American Civil Liberties Union sent Governor Cargo a telegram urging him to veto the shifting of the $50,000 from the university budget, and the New Democratic Coalition of New Mexico stated, "If there is any institution in New Mexico which badly needs to be investigated, it is not the university, but the Legislature." On the opposing side was the Albuquerque Chamber of Commerce, which formed its own committee to investigate the matter. And sharing the center of the storm with Williams was President Heady, who followed guidelines recommended by the American Association of University Professors and appointed a Special

Advisory Committee—consisting of Dr. Hubert Alexander, chairman of the Faculty Policy Committee; Vice President of the Graduate School George Springer; Professor John Green, chairman of the Committee on Academic Freedom and Tenure;[1109] and, a few days later on the request of these three, Richard Elliot, president of the Graduate Student Council—to conduct hearings on the matter.[1110]

On Wednesday, March 26, President Heady suspended Lionel Williams and Kenneth Pollack from their teaching assignments pending the outcome of the Special Advisory Committee's deliberations. He indicated he was acting on the basis of new information that had come to light, but many in the university community suspected he had yielded to legislative pressure, and campus protests escalated.[1111] Dr. Joseph Frank, chairman of the English department, and Dr. Roy Pickett, head of freshman English, refused to appoint replacements for the two teaching assistants; on Thursday Heady suspended them from their administrative duties and named Dean of Arts and Sciences Hoyt Trowbridge acting chairman of the department. Four hours later an *ad hoc* faculty meeting was held, and those in attendance voted 224 to 48 in favor of immediate reinstatement of the teaching assistants. A controversy raged over whether Heady had acted within American Association of University Professors guidelines in suspending Williams and Pollack while their case was being heard. That afternoon English Professor Gene Frumkin read "Love-Lust Poem" to a cheering crowd of about seven hundred gathered on the mall outside the Student Union Building, and he declared he did not believe it was obscene.[1112] The fevered atmosphere heightened on Friday. A throng about twice the size of the one the previous day swarmed onto the mall and heard Frumkin read the poem again; listened to Black Mountain poet Robert Creeley read selections from his own works as well as from Walt Whitman, Allen Ginsberg, D.H. Lawrence and others; and took in a number of other speeches, including one by Governor David Cargo and one by Barbara Brown of the Black Students Union, who claimed that Williams had been fired because he was Black. Electrified by the uninhibited rhetoric of the rally, that night about a thousand students embarked on an all-night "teach-in" in the Student Union Building, examining such topics as "What Is Pornography?" and "Theology of Sex."[1113] In the early morning hours they regrouped, elected four chairmen—Brian Gratton, John McGuffin, Barbara Brown and Arturo Sandoval—and drew up a list of nonnegotiable demands, which included the reinstatement of the teaching assistants and the acknowledgment that "there is no pornography in a free academic community." If the demands were not met, they declared, they would call for a partial boycott the following Tuesday, with the regularly scheduled classes to be conducted informally and to deal with the poetry issue instead of course material.[1114] The suspensions were not rescinded, and many of the students and faculty went along with the one-day boycott. Tuesday afternoon saw another rally on the mall, which concluded with a march across campus to President Heady's office. By now the militant students' demands had grown more extensive; about twenty representatives of ethnic minorities on campus met with Heady and told him they wanted an end to racial discrimination and the start of ethnic studies programs. They also demanded his resignation.[1115]

The people who opposed the teaching of the poem tended to be older and less concentrated around the university community, but they were no less indignant. Many held positions of authority in Albuquerque and throughout New Mexico, and they could wield power effectively. On March 28 city police raided the Yale Street Grasshopper Bookstore, seized sixteen copies of *Word Alchemy*, the book of poetry in which "Love-Lust Poem" was published, and arrested the owner, Phillip Mayne, and a salesman for selling pornography. A similar charge against Mayne, for selling *My Secret Life*, was awaiting appeal at district court.[1116] Two days later the University of New Mexico Board of Regents announced its support for Ferrel Heady's course of action.[1117] And for hundreds of miles around, citizens were meeting and putting pressure on their legislators to bring an end to indecency at the university.

On April 9 the Special Advisory Committee at the University of New Mexico finally made its report. Noting that the students in the suspended teaching assistants' classes, in particular the younger ones, had not found the controversial material objectionable, it found that "the conflict centering on the teaching of Williams and Pollack is largely a manifestation of the generation gap." The two were praised for their teaching abilities, but it was questioned whether a freshman class was the proper place to conduct experiments "to lift gutter language to the level of poetic language." The committee recommended that better procedures be established for supervising teaching assistants and that Williams and Pollack be returned to teaching immediately.[1118] President Heady went along with much of the report, but he criticized former English Chairman Frank and Dean of Arts and Sciences Trowbridge for being insufficiently responsive to complaints, and he scored Williams and Pollack for exercising poor judgment. He refused to reinstate the two teaching assistants until the English department had instituted adequate control procedures.[1119] Heady's stand pleased few of the university people who were angry about legislative interference; the next night about three hundred protesters gathered on the lawn of his home, six of whom were arrested for refusing to leave the premises.[1120] Two days later, on April 12, President Heady announced that he was satisfied with recent changes in the English department's regulations and that the suspended assistants could return to teaching.[1121] The mood on campus began to cool a little. On the fifteenth classes were suspended for a day of self-examination, and students, faculty, administrators and townspeople gathered in groups to try to sort out what lessons had been learned from the extended confrontation.[1122]

Over the next several months the poetry episode remained a controversial topic in the community, continually resurfacing in conversations and public speeches and exerting a constant influence on university affairs. Authorities at the University of New Mexico became hypersensitive to public relations: later that spring the Student Speakers Committee was persuaded not to invite Lenore Kandel to come for a lecture the following year, in August the regents voted to halt distribution of the current issue of the literary magazine the *New Mexico Quarterly* because of language that might be deemed offensive, and use of controversial material in the classrooms was discouraged.[1123] Court decisions, on the other hand, seemed to favor the protesters. The six students arrested on Heady's lawn were freed because the law they had violated was found unconstitutional,[1124] and the pornography charge against the owner and a salesman of the Yale Street Grasshopper for selling *Word Alchemy* was dismissed because, according to Municipal Judge Frederick Mowrer, the possible obscenity of one poem does not render an entire book obscene.[1125] And throughout this period politicians and faculty members declaimed vigorously over the vices and virtues of the newly formed and funded legislative committee to study the university.

Although the dispute concerning teaching of "Love-Lust Poem" at the University of New Mexico was the most spectacular controversy in Albuquerque during 1969, it had been accompanied by no actual violence. Elsewhere in the city clashes of various sorts were becoming more common, and some of these were violent indeed. On March 26, just four days after President Heady's fateful meeting with the Senate Finance Committee, occurred the first killing of a local law enforcement officer in the line of duty since the slaying of Policeman Frank Sjolander in 1954. Sheriff's Sgt. Julian Narvaez stopped a car he suspected had been stolen, guns were fired, and he died. The assailant, twenty-eight-year-old Pete Garcia, was wounded, and his friends took him to a hospital, where he recuperated and awaited murder charges.[1126] The public outcry was considerably more mixed than after the 1954 killing, for the details were murkier and Garcia, an ex-convict and a heroin addict currently undergoing methadone treatment, was a leader in Quebrar, an organization which was devoted to drug rehabilitation and which was funded by the local Economic Opportunity Board. A trial held in September resulted in a hung jury.[1127] Out on bail, Garcia worked actively in such antipoverty projects as the building of a park for poor people.[1128] A second trial followed in December, and the jury found him guilty of the reduced charge of voluntary manslaughter; he promptly appealed the decision and posted bond. Meanwhile, the political ramifications of the case were growing more complex. That same month Quebrar signed a Model Cities contract with the city to operate an expanded narcotics addict rehabilitation program, it was subsequently discovered that Garcia was one of the applicants for the $6,000-a-year job as coordinator, and City Commission Chairman Pete Domenici declared Quebrar would be using "poor judgment" if it hired the man.[1129] Under the resulting pressure Pete Garcia eventually withdrew his application.

All this time the nighttime disorder in the city parks was growing more deadly. On June 22 of the same year nineteen-year-old Gilbert Sanchez was shot and killed in Roosevelt Park, located about a mile west of the university and a mile east of the central business district.[1130]

The following fall arguments about the administering of justice aggravated the already-uneasy relations between the police and the poorer communities of the city. On October 10, the day after Judge Harry Robins announced his split with District Attorney Alexander Sceresse on the question of jailing addicts, Chief Counsel for the Legal Aid Society William Fitzpatrick testified before the Metropolitan Crime Commission and called Sceresse a "political hack" whose "disenchantment" with the Narcotics Addict Rehabilitation Act program began with his "enchantment" with running for governor. Fitzpatrick was questioned about a bulletin being passed out to persons enrolled in the NARA program which read, "The police are there to protect you. Do they? Or are they picking you up? Or trying to scare you or embarrass you publicly?

Or roughing you up for no good reason? If so, the Legal Aid Society or the New Mexico Civil Liberties Union may be able to help you. They are anxious to try. . . ." The legal aid counsel replied, "We didn't publish it, we didn't pass it out, but I don't disagree with a single thing it says."[1131] A public dispute over the bulletin raged for the next month. The Fraternal Order of Police called for Fitzpatrick's resignation, but hordes of liberals rushed to join the Legal Aid Society and the expanded membership voted overwhelmingly to retain him.[1132] The heated denunciations on both sides had succeeded in dislodging no one from his position; the opposing segments of the community, however, were more antagonistic than ever before.

For the remainder of the year and on into the next, flaring tempers and clashes with authority continued to break out across the metropolitan area. In the spring of 1970 the center of the turbulence shifted back to the University of New Mexico. Despite the efforts of the university authorities to keep a lid on the growing disorder and to avoid offending the State Legislature, the students were becoming increasingly sensitive to what they regarded as social injustice and increasingly ready to take matters into their own hands.

On the last day of February the Brigham Young University basketball team came to town to play the University of New Mexico Lobos. Remembering the silent protest held by Black students and sympathizers before the game the previous year, many in the crowd who came to watch expected some sort of disturbance, but most were shocked with what ensued. During the pre-game playing of the national anthem a group of students pelted the playing floor with debris, including eggs, kernels of corn and balloons filled with kerosene. The game was delayed about forty minutes while the trash was being cleaned up, the BYU players were cheered when they came on the floor, but no arrests were made at that time.[1133]

Four days later U.S. Senator Strom Thurmond came to Popejoy Hall to deliver a speech on invitation of the Student Speakers Committee. Much of the university community had been angered by the news that a busload of Black school children had been overturned by a White mob in Lamar, South Carolina—Thurmond's home state—the previous day, and the stage was ripe for another confrontation. When the senator began to address the audience, several students interrupted him with pointed questions about his views on the bussing of Black children for the purpose of school integration. The format established by the Student Speakers Committee called for a question-and-answer session at the conclusion of the speech, and Thurmond tried to continue with his prepared text. The questions and heckling from the audience, however, proved too disruptive, and the talk was cancelled—the first time in the history of the university that unruly opposition had prevented an invited speaker from expressing his views.[1134]

Campus police identified two of the disrupters—Allen Cooper and William Orzen, a twenty-seven-year-old graduate student in sociology—and the next day charges were filed against the pair for violating the section of the 1965 statement on rights and responsibilities which declared that "students with diverse points of view should permit" speakers from off-campus "to be heard without harassment."[1135] That evening a symposium of thirty people from the university and the outside community gave talks on "How to Save the University."[1136] Over the next month, while the campus waited for the Student Standards Committee to conduct hearings on Cooper and Orzen, the tension continued to rise. On March 9 workers found a crude bomb under the floor of the ROTC building at the university; campus police deactivated it just fifteen minutes before it was set to explode.[1137] The following day the County Sheriff's Department arrested Orzen and Cooper for throwing debris at the BYU basketball game.[1138]

With the pleasant April weather came gatherings and demonstrations on a variety of issues. On the fifteenth a rally protesting the use of tax money for the War in Viet Nam was held at Robinson Park on the western side of the downtown area. Among the participants were Dr. Edwin Hoyt of the political science department at the university, Rev. Homer Pacely of the National Association for the Advancement of Colored People, the Brown Berets, an acid rock band named Judas, and the Youth for Radical Progress, which displayed a Viet Cong flag during the proceedings. After the speeches, one of which attacked the "killing and maiming of the bodies, the minds, and the spirit of our young men—an obscenity that defies description," the group moved to the Federal Building and conducted a sit-in at the offices of the Internal Revenue Service.[1139] One week later "Earth Day" was celebrated all over the city to show concern for the pollution of the natural environment. Bus fares were reduced to a penny for that day as a means of encouraging people to leave their cars at home. Teach-ins and panel discussions were held at the universities, schools and elsewhere. Chicanos rallied in Tingley Park in the southwest part of town and then marched through Barelas, led by a mariachi band and a rider on horseback and kept in line by marshals from the United Mexican American Students. But for all the festivities and spirit of cooperation, a somber atmosphere was provided by the anxious rhetoric and the surgical masks which many of the students wore to emphasize their fears about air pollution.[1140]

While the Earth Day ceremonies were going on, the Student Standards Committee was deliberating in the Student Union Building at the University of New Mexico. During a stretch when Allen Cooper was waiting outside the hearing room, Steve Stillman, a senior who resided in the Pi Kappa Alpha fraternity house, walked up and punched him in the jaw, knocking him down. Several other fights broke out. Order was restored,[1141] however, and the hearing continued for several more days. On April 28 a decision was announced: both Cooper and Orzen were found guilty of violating university policy by disrupting Senator Thurmond's speech, and both were placed on probation. By and large, the resolution pleased the student body more than the administration; Vice President of Student Affairs Harold Lavender considered the penalty excessively lenient and announced he would appeal it to President Heady.[1142]

A few days later outside influences roiled the atmosphere further. The Poetry Series Committee, which included faculty as well as students and which at this time exercised more independence than the Student Speakers Committee, invited Lenore Kandel to read from her works at Popejoy Hall. Many of the citizens of Albuquerque were irate, and several aspirants to public office were quick to pounce on the issue. County Commission Chairman Ed Balcomb, who was running for governor, called on angry parents to arrive early with Bibles and barricade the building. District Attorney Alexander Sceresse, also a gubernatorial candidate, declared he would prosecute the poet if proper complaints were made.[1143] The chairman of the Poetry Series Committee and the presidents of the undergraduate and the graduate student governments then issued a joint statement branding Balcomb's and Sceresse's tactics "even more disturbing than the recent activities of Messrs. Orzen and Cooper."[1144] At this point, on April 30, came the sudden news that President Nixon had sent American troops into Cambodia.[1145] This apparent expansion of the War in Viet Nam, coming at a time when students across the country had been hoping and believing that their efforts had been instrumental in winding the war down, outraged and frustrated the young people intensely, overshadowing recent local developments. Seething with defiance, an overflow crowd poured into Popejoy Hall the next evening to hear Miss Kandel. Having been warned of Commissioner Balcomb's threatened barricade, she opened with a selection from the Bible, the thirteenth chapter of First Corinthians—"Though I speak with the tongues of men and of angels, and have not charity, I am become as sounding brass, or a tinkling cymbal. . . ." She went on to read a number of her own works, including some antiwar poetry and "Love-Lust Poem." At the conclusion the audience gave her a standing ovation.[1146]

The following Monday, May 4, came news that ignited the volatile situation at the university. At Kent State University in Ohio an unruly crowd of students protesting against the recent invasion of Cambodia was fired upon by National Guardsmen, and four were killed.[1147] All afternoon angry students and faculty talked excitedly with one another; classes were held, but few could concentrate on the subject matters. That evening movie actress Jane Fonda, who had been publicizing her antiwar views widely, addressed a crowd of about six hundred at the anthropology lecture hall and condemned the recent developments. Afterwards she led the group to the lawn of President Ferrel Heady's home for an impromptu rally. A strike committee was organized, and it chose the slogan "They shoot students, don't they?" after one of Miss Fonda's recent films, *They Shoot Horses, Don't They?*[1148]

On Tuesday aggressive action by both the authorities and the protesters led to more drastic confrontations. Governor Cargo activated a portion of the New Mexico National Guard "for the duration of disturbances" at the University of New Mexico.[1149] President Heady made the penalties for the disrupters of Thurmond's speech more severe: William Orzen was put on probation for the rest of the year and would be suspended the next, and Allen Cooper, who had been placed on probation earlier for his part in interfering with an ROTC drill during the fall of 1968, was immediately dismissed from school.[1150] The presidents of undergraduate and graduate student government endorsed a strike being planned for next day. That night a large rally was held on the mall; after it broke up about a hundred students marched to the Air Force ROTC building on campus and occupied it, and another group took over the Student Union Building.

Throughout Wednesday minor hostilities flickered across the campus. At six in the morning the students who had spent the night in the Air Force ROTC building were told they would be arrested if they stayed, and they departed. Strikers erected a barricade at one of the main entrances to the university. President Heady called a moratorium for noon, and members of the university community, many wearing black arm bands, expressed their sorrow over the killing of the Kent State students. At around two in the afternoon a scuffle broke out at the flagpole between students, mostly Black and White athletes, arguing over whether the flag should be at half mast. Several were injured, three with stab wounds. At that point university officials decided to close the campus until Monday. Academic Vice President Chester Travelstead addressed the students on the mall and asked them to go home "for the safety of us all." With the crowds dwindling and the opportunities for further confrontation apparently diminishing, the militant organizers of the strike searched about for something to catch the public eye. A group including Allen Cooper returned to the Student Union Building and made it their headquarters for the duration.

As the university officials had hoped, the campus was fairly quiet on Thursday. At the strike center in the Student Union Building activists discussed the War in Viet Nam, the Kent State incident, the recent developments at the University of New Mexico, the low wages that the physical plant workers were receiving, the ROTC and the role of the university in the military-industrial complex. Their sessions were interrupted by a bomb scare which caused the evacuation of the building, but they were allowed to reenter. That night the authorities worked out plans to seek a court injunction against the students occupying the building.

For most of Friday preparations were being made to force the evacuation of the Student Union Building through legal means. At seven that morning Vice President Lavender read to the protesters an order from the regents that they leave by eight-thirty. Meanwhile, attorneys were seeking an injunction to force the vacation; because Allen Cooper, one of those named, requested a hearing, it was not signed until around three-thirty that afternoon. At nine that morning State Police Chief Martin Vigil requested and received permission from Governor Cargo to use the National Guard in the evacuation. During the afternoon President Heady; Eric Nelson, president of the undergraduate student government; and the strikers participated in negotiations to end the occupation peacefully, but nothing was resolved—partly, perhaps, because all the regents could not be reached before their scheduled meeting at 5 P.M. During the meeting President Heady and Chief Vigil engaged in three telephone conversations, but the hectic pace of new developments impaired their communication. Heady was unaware that the National Guard would be used until a few minutes before their arrival, and the two officials missed meeting with each other as they had planned until after the arrests were underway.

At approximately six o'clock 130 city and 56 state police officers in full riot gear arrived at the occupied building. The court order was read to the students inside, and all who wished to leave before the arrests began were given the opportunity to do so. Eric Nelson asked Chief Martin Vigil to explain what constituted "resisting arrest" so that the occupiers would know what not to do; Vigil complied. The arrests of those remaining then proceeded in an orderly fashion. But at about six-twenty, while the students were being loaded on a bus to be taken away and booked, two batteries of National Guardsmen arrived on campus and began a sweep of the area around the Student Union Building.

The contingent of the National Guard, numbering close to two hundred men, had been ordered to the scene because Vigil felt that a show of force might be necessary and because he had heard rumors of plans by militants to resist arrest and to cause widespread destruction of property. The area outside the building, fairly quiet just an hour and a half earlier, was now crowded with hundreds of students and townspeople who had flocked in to witness the evacuation. To these civilians, the guardsmen, wearing gas masks, grasping their rifles with unsheathed bayonets, and advancing around the building in both directions, looked like faceless automatons and called up images of the Kent State killings. From the point of view of the soldiers, the civilians seemed scarcely less threatening, screaming insults as they did and taking countless photographs. Through a mix-up in communications between the guard and the state police, no order to leave was read to the crowd, and they did not know the exact purpose of the advancing batteries. In the resulting confusion and panic, not everyone got out of the way in time, and at least ten persons received bayonet wounds, some sufficiently serious to require hospitalization. A volunteer medical unit, named MASH after a popular antiwar movie with that title, administered first aid; Visual Coalition, a group of students formed to get photographic records of the events of the strike, was equally active. After the two batteries of the National Guard had completed their sweep, the order to disperse was finally read to the crowd, and no more violence erupted. Around eleven-fifty that night the guard left the campus. For months thereafter, however, dried blood from the wounded, shellacked over to prevent its removal, gave mute evidence of the violence on the mall that evening of May 8, 1970, and citizens angrily debated the wisdom of bringing in the troops with their bayonets bare.[1151]

That summer the spirit of confrontation spread to the city employees. The most rebellious were the city maintenance workers, including the garbage collectors, who held a week-long strike in July over such matters as time-and-a-half pay for overtime and the right to collective bargaining. The first day of the strike they padlocked the entrance to the city yards; when Deputy Chief of City Police Albert Swallows, who was wearing plain clothes and had not identified himself, burned off the lock with an acetylene torch and tried to push a worker out of the way, the striker knocked him down with a left hook. The maintenance workers won their demands,[1152] but meanwhile the police department was also having its problems. Angry because they felt they were not sufficiently paid for their increasingly hazardous work, the policemen had formed a union the month before and threatened a slowdown; a settlement was reached around the same time as the maintenance workers' strike.[1153] In August came the news that Albuquerque had had the second highest metropolitan crime rate in the country during 1969,[1154] and in the following month was made public a study of police departments in four southwestern cities, noting problems of motivation and morale within the Albuquerque force.[1155] On October 22 Chief Paul Shaver announced his retirement after twenty-two years of command; a few days later the new internal affairs unit made its report on an investigation of Montessa Park Detention Center, resulting in the dismissal of its director and a jailer and the demotion of two deputy chiefs. The assistant chief was recuperating from a heart attack, so the reins of power fell temporarily into the inexperienced hands of Legal Adviser John Duffy, age thirty-two.[1156]

That fall there were a few scattered incidents of protest by the university students. For example, when President Nixon gave a speech at Highland High School in October, police and secret service kept out a number of long-haired persons, and two students were arrested for causing a disturbance.[1157] But the most publicized instance of unconventional behavior by collegiates around that time was the election of a male for homecoming queen[1158]—a development which distressed many of the alumni at the University of New Mexico but which hardly posed a threat to the established political system.

Elsewhere in the city, however, many persons, especially members of ethnic minorities, were becoming more militant. The deteriorating relations between the Albuquerque Police Department and some of the neighborhoods was a major source of friction. At the December 14 meeting of the City Commission at which a number of people presented demands about the firing of certain policemen and the suspension of unpopular city ordinances, two fairly new organizations, the New Breed and the Black Berets, emerged as aggressive spokesmen for their ethnic groups. The New Breed, under the leadership of VISTA Supervisor John Goldsmith, was a smoothly run organization of young Blacks which conducted a number of projects, some of them funded by the Economic Opportunity Board, and which was always ready to spearhead complaints of police brutality.[1159] More recently formed, less sophisticated, but by no means less assertive was the Black Berets, a Chicano group led by Richard Moore, himself a former VISTA supervisor.[1160] The next day Harry Kinney, vice-chairman of the City Commission, met again with the two groups. In the course of the angry tirades of criticism, one Black Beret called Kinney a "white, bald-headed punk," whereupon the commissioner announced, "I personally have had enough of this tonight," and departed.[1161]

The subsequent suspension of the city ordinances against hitchhiking, vagrancy and loitering seemed to do little to alleviate the discontent. On March 27, 1971, the Black Berets led a "March for Justice" of about four hundred persons from Robinson Park to the city hall. The marchers carried signs hearing such slogans as "Chicano Power," "Justica O Muerte" (Justice or Death), "No pigs in our community," and "Down with the pigs!" and they were escorted by expressionless motorcycle policemen. Upon their arrival at the steps of city hall, a list of demands was read; immediately afterwards Minister of Justice for the Black Berets Richard Moore called for the release of all minority group members from jail because they had been imprisoned by "racist courts and juries not made up of their peers."[1162]

During these months attacks took place on policemen and their equipment, as well as on persons and property connected with the Black Berets and the Alianza Federal de Pueblos Libres, Tijerina's group. Although the assailants frequently got away, each side blamed the other or its sympathizers. The intense hostility verged on paranoia. Around the end of 1970 the Black Berets formed a "community patrol" to follow police cars in the south valley area and keep a check on harassment of Chicanos. Following an incident in

March in which a group of Black Berets demanded to see a policeman's badge number while he was investigating a suspected crime, Judge Robins found one of the members guilty of interfering with an officer. "I understand your situation and have followed it closely," he explained, "but I cannot condone a vigilante committee."[1163]

That same month the city appointed a new chief of police—Donald Byrd, who had been assistant chief of the Dallas police force.[1164] The announcement was met with mixed emotions, as dislike of Texans had been a strong undercurrent in much of New Mexican culture for more than a century, especially among Spanish-Americans. On the seventeenth, a few days before Byrd's arrival in the city, minority representatives voiced their opposition at a meeting with three of the city commissioners at the Old Town Boys Club. Asserted Joe Garner, "This thing is going to blow up in your faces. There is still too much discrimination going on here. It's subtle, but it's here." Max Carmona asked City Manager Richard Wilson, who was also from Texas, if he felt it was wise "to have a Texan to keep the peasants in line."[1165] Following his installation in his new position on April 1,[1166] Chief Byrd began making friendly overtures to minority group organizations,[1167] but the momentum of the antagonism between the police and many of the people continued to roll on.

As 1971 moved into the hot months, a few hopeful indications could be found that the festering mood of the city might cool. The recent changes in law enforcement seemed likely to improve policy-community relations in the long run. In mid-April a threatened strike by city employees was averted by the establishment of a five-day work week.[1168] The atmosphere of the country as a whole seemed to be growing a little friendlier: urban riots had become less frequent and less savage, and college students were turning their attention to the ecology movement. At the University of New Mexico many were losing interest in politics altogether. Nevertheless, many Albuquerqueans, especially those among the poor and the young, were patently dissatisfied. Student unrest, less common at the university level than earlier, was growing more intense in the high schools. The losses to vandalism by the Albuquerque Public Schools climbed to $75,962 for the 1970-71 school year.[1169] The annual number of narcotics arrests in the city, which had exceeded a hundred in 1968 for the first time, reached 952 in 1970.[1170] And in June of 1971, the unemployment rate in Bernalillo County hit 6.8 percent, the highest for a month in more than ten years.[1171]

On Thursday evening, June 10, police arrested two persons for drinking in public and a third for disorderly conduct at Yale Park. Shortly thereafter a group of people in the park began throwing rocks at an unmarked police car and other vehicles, and seventeen more persons were arrested for destruction of public property.[1172]

The following night during a musical event at the Civic Auditorium, an announcement was made that a free rock concert would be held Sunday afternoon at Roosevelt Park.

That Sunday, the thirteenth of June, the weather was warm and beautiful. Several hundred people came to Roosevelt Park in the afternoon—some because of the promised music, which never transpired, but most simply to enjoy themselves in the pleasant surroundings. The majority of the people were young, and some were drinking beer and smoking marijuana. Municipal ordinances were being violated, but such petty violations were fairly commonplace in that park and others around the city.

Around five-thirty three plainclothes policemen, members of a recently inaugurated park patrol, noticed some people drinking beer, and they radioed for assistance. Two police cars arrived; uniformed officers arrested six young Chicanos for drinking in public; the protesting suspects were handcuffed and put in the cars. A group of about thirty people gathered and began complaining loudly. An unidentified object—perhaps a frisbee, perhaps a beer bottle—hit one of the cars, and the police rushed over and arrested a young man they were convinced had thrown it. More objects began to fly through the air, and the police radioed for more help.

When reinforcements came, the melee grew wilder. Attempting to clear the park, police charged the crowd with nightsticks; some witnesses and television footage indicated that, on several occasions, excessive violence was used in making arrests. On the other hand, the crowd was becoming steadily angrier. A number of fights broke out, and rocks and bottles pelted the police. One officer arrested a bottle-throwing youth, discovered he had lost his car keys, and had to be rescued by another police car. The mob attacked the abandoned car, freed the prisoner, turned the vehicle over, and did the same with another police car. A wrecker arrived and righted the overturned automobiles, but suddenly the crowd began running in all directions. The police fired tear gas until they exhausted their supply, then used firearms while retreating to the adjoining area around the Albuquerque Public Schools offices. Two police cars left behind were overturned and set on fire. Having gained a victory of sorts over the police, most of the rioters then went downtown to see about the fate of their arrested friends.

By shortly after eight that night about fifty young people were sitting on the city hall steps, yelling. Across the street in the police headquarters, Chief Donald Byrd was meeting with a group of Chicano activists, including Richard Moore of the Black Berets. After listening to vehement complaints about police brutality, Byrd asked the group if they could disperse the crowd. They assured him they could, and Byrd announced he would request to have the arrested persons released on their own recognizance.

Neither the release of the prisoners nor the efforts of the Chicano leaders, however, impressed the mob outside, which was composed of roughly equal numbers of Chicanos and Anglos. They broke windows in the police building and the county building and set fire to a car belonging to a New Mexico Ranger parked beside city hall. Around ten-thirty the rioters turned their attention from government targets and began to surge south on Fourth Street, smashing and looting local businesses.

About this time, as police were arresting vandals and looters downtown, Roosevelt Park began to fill again. Three rioters attempted to break into the Cee Vee Liquor Store nearby and were shot by security guards; news of the incident angered the throng. Word spread that the building would be burned with the guards inside, so the police picked them up around midnight, leaving the structure unprotected. The mob helped itself to the liquor and set fire to the building. It lit the skies like a gigantic bonfire while the rioters drank its wares. Across the street, radio reporter Pat O'Hearn commented into his tape recorder, "The atmosphere has changed from that of a riot into kind of a gigantic beer bust." But some of the crowd were bent on further destruction. A few minutes before one the Audio Visual Building in the Albuquerque Public Schools office complex was set on fire. The fire department refused to answer the call until firemen could be assured of police protection; by the time they arrived, around four-fifteen in the morning, the building was a total loss. By then the rampage had subsided. The rioters were too tired and too drunk to continue, and police enforcement of a curfew discouraged further activity.[1173]

The next day, while the ashes of the Audio Visual Building were still smoldering and the damaged downtown businesses were being boarded up and the morning sun was lighting up the debris in Roosevelt Park, concerned citizens were anxiously wondering whether a rally scheduled for two in the afternoon at the park should be held. At a meeting among government officials, Chicano representatives and some antipoverty workers, it was decided to go forward with the rally to avoid antagonizing the young people. So the rally opened at the park, a few minutes behind schedule but on a peaceful note. Police had been withdrawn from the area and were planning strategy. Juan Garcia, a community field worker with Model Cities, made the first speech, asking the people to work together and help eliminate police brutality and harassment. He was followed by Fr. Luis Jaramillo of the Black Berets, New Mexico Attorney General David Norvell, Lieutenant Governor Roberto Mondragon, Richard Moore of the Black Berets, and an assortment of others who wanted their turn at the microphone. Most of the leaders' words were conciliatory, but from time to time they were interrupted by enthusiastic shouts from the crowd, cries of "Chicano power" and "people power." A brief fight broke out between advocates of "Chicano power" and long-haired Anglos preferring "people power." Beer and hard liquor were passed out in bottles with burnt labels. As the rally died out, people began milling around aimlessly yet with a reckless sense of self-confidence. A photographer commented that the group "was feeling pretty powerful . . . saying how they'd made the pigs run and everything."

Someone yelled, "Let's go sit on Central," and the crowd began to move in that direction. No police were in sight; they had expected the rally to continue longer. Reaching the main street of the city, the crowd turned right, toward Yale Park and the university area. For a while there was no violence; then a few rocks were thrown at Galles Oldsmobile and Cadillac Co. Members of the mob, which was now two or three hundred strong, began to pick up the smooth, round rocks that filled the median on Central Avenue and hurl them at the small businesses across from Yale Park. Looters made forays into Butterfield Jewelry Store, scooping up handfuls of watches and baubles. Another group began smashing windshields of the big cars on display at Galles, and three were overturned. An American flag was captured from somewhere and burned.

About an hour and forty-five minutes after the first window had been broken, twenty-three state police suddenly drove up from South Yale Street. They cleared Yale Park. Immediately afterwards two busloads of city police appeared, followed by more patrol cars and the National Guard. Quiet having been rapidly restored to the area, law enforcement officers moved to Roosevelt Park in anticipation of curfew violations. A curfew had been set for seven o'clock—only an hour and a half away.

A crowd of about three hundred gathered and shouted at the National Guard, which was quietly occupying one end of the park. Some of the mob grew bolder and began to throw rocks and Molotov cocktails at the guardsmen, but not much of a response was provoked. Around six-thirty the guard started to put on gas masks and place shields on their helmets and gather in formation. A loudspeaker ordered the people to disperse or be arrested for violation of the curfew. At seven the guard began to march across the park, driving what remained of the mob into the waiting hands of the city police, who had been inconspicuously positioned at the far end. This effectively snuffed out the violence and destruction which had shaken Albuquerque over the past twenty-six hours.[1174]

The Tension Subsides

For a number of weeks shock waves from the two days of rioting reverberated throughout the metropolitan area and beyond. On the evening of June 16, 1971, two days after the final day of disorder, six off-duty city policemen left a party given by a fellow officer and threw a tear gas grenade into Roach Ranch West on 120 Yale SE, a small store specializing in counter-cultural items and described by the police as a "hippie hangout." Witnesses reported the vandalism; Police Chief Byrd suspended the offenders for ten days without pay.[1175] Governor Bruce King appointed a special commission to investigate the riots, but many people felt that some of the members were too much identified with the political establishment or too much involved themselves in the developments leading up to the violence to be fair and objective.[1176] The Black Berets held a sit-in at the governor's office at Santa Fe to protest the commission, and eight of them, including Richard Moore and Fr. Luis Jaramillo, were arrested.[1177] Meanwhile, hundreds of other citizens were raising their voices vigorously to attack or defend the agents of law enforcement. In a move to quiet the tumult, Governor King dissolved his special commission a few days later and asked for a grand jury probe of the recent disorders.[1178]

The public outcry over the riots overshadowed significant developments in city government. On the twenty-eighth of the month G.P. Reyes resigned from his seat on the City Commission in order to accept a transfer in the Homart Development Company to Mexico City. By law his position would have to be left vacant until the October election.[1179] A special election to amend the city charter was held the following day. Former City Commission Chairman Pete Domenici had chaired a committee to recommend charter revisions; the most sweeping of the amendments they had proposed would replace the five-man unpaid City Commission with a mayor-council structure, with the mayor to be elected by the city as a whole, each of the six councilors to be elected by district, and all to receive a salary. This form of government, it was hoped, would help provide leadership with the central authority, time and support throughout the community to deal effectively with the difficult problems now surfacing. Other amendments included clauses on human rights, environmental protection and home rule. In a light turnout, the voters passed all the propositions except for the ones implementing the mayor-council system; analysts concluded that, upset as the citizens were with city government, they were not eager to have their leaders paid.[1180]

Adding to Albuquerque's problems were new demands being made by the police, the firemen and the city blue collar workers for higher salaries and improved fringe benefits. The majority of the police were threatening to resign if their demands were not met, and the prospect of another strike by maintenance workers was looming up.[1181] In early July, however, settlements were negotiated and ratified by the unions involved.[1182] City government had gained time to brace itself for future crises.

All summer long the city parks continued to be trouble spots. On the night of July 17 Ronald Gallegos, a serviceman home on leave, was stabbed to death in Roosevelt Park by an unknown assailant.[1183] A few days later the City Commission began to implement a plan which had been under consideration for several months calling for a "crash pad" where transients could spend the night in an undeveloped park near the Rio Grande north of Central Avenue.[1184] Many people favored the establishment of such a facility so that wandering young people would be drawn away from Roosevelt Park and Yale Park and away from the densely populated sections of the city, but few wanted it in their own neighborhood. Angry residents of Old Town and Duranes, which were near the proposed crash pad, protested angrily; reluctantly, the city commissioners withdrew their approval.[1185] Citizens who preferred cracking down on the unruly young people rather than appeasing them gained more influence as

316

the summer wore on. In August eleven persons, mostly East Central business-men, filed a suit against the city claiming that it "created and is performing and maintaining a public nuisance" at Yale Park; as a result, district court issued a temporary restraining order closing the park.[1186] On September 27 the City Commission gave final passage to a curfew for all city parks from midnight to six in the morning. Yale Park was reopened for the same hours as the other parks.[1187]

The political turmoil of this period notwithstanding, minor indications of renewed harmony in city life could be found. Here and there, persons distressed by the widespread crime, drug use and aimless violence were banding together to help combat the disorder, to cool the heated tempers, to bring the rebellious spirits into the fold. Although their efforts met with only limited success, the momentum was gradually building.

A few hopeful signs had already begun to appear well before the riots. One of the earliest manifestations of this new spirit in Albuquerque was the Jesus movement, underway since the late sixties. Small groups of "Jesus freaks" offered their residences as havens where people could wander in and hear Christ's message. One such home was His House, a large log cabin on top of a hill rented in December 1969 by Richard and Terry Emerson. A person walking in would see a. huge cross made of two logs, sketches and paintings of Jesus, and a variety of multicolored posters with such slogans as "Invite Some-one to Peace thru Christ" and "Religion Is a Drag but Knowing Jesus Isn't." Long-haired youths would sit around strumming guitars, eager to talk with newcomers. One of them volunteered, "When I came here for the first time I was ripped on acid, but that was the last time. Now I'm stoned on Jesus."[1188] After about a year of operation His House closed down, but other such centers took its place.

During roughly the same time, other citizens were forming secular groups to help society's lost and lonely. The Albuquerque Suicide Prevention and Crisis Center was established in 1968; from an office supported by private donations, volunteer workers took telephone calls from distraught persons.[1189] In the fall of 1970 student government at the University of New Mexico funded AGORA, where people with problems could walk in, talk with student volunteers and then be referred to professional agencies if their circumstances warranted.[1190] The following February eleven students at Manzano High School, themselves former drug users, organized Student Activists Against Drug

Abuse,[1191] and within two months the membership swelled to over a hundred persons actively involved in counseling, delivering speeches and meeting with civic and governmental groups.[1192] And sprinkled across the city were dozens of similar budding efforts.

In the months immediately preceding the June riots, a group of political activists began pushing to stop the construction of a road near the Sandia Crest.[1193] Their activities involved a certain amount of confrontation with governmental agencies and their ongoing programs, but the larger issue in question—protection of the scenic open spaces outside the residential areas of the city against encroachment by developers—became somewhat of a unifying theme in local politics. Petitions were circulated, and a small "plant-in" of trees in the path of the road site was held.[1194] As public opinion shifted in favor of the environmentalists, political developments did likewise. Freezing of federal funds halted the road construction,[1195] and by late May the City of Albuquerque and the Rio Grande Council of Governments were maneuvering to acquire land in the foothills of the Sandias as a buffer against future development.[1196] That summer the activists turned their attention to the five dead volcanoes that jutted dramatically into the sky on the western side of Albuquerque. Worried Mrs. George Eisenberg, leader of the Save the Volcanoes Committee, "I'm so deathly afraid someone is going to plop an ugly restaurant on top of them or put up an industrial park or load them up with towers and lights." Responding to the pressure, the city leaders proposed a general obligation bond issue for $500,000 for purchasing land for open space.[1197]

On July 26 came a development which had a bigger impact on the public mood than the open spaces debate—the return of Reies Lopez Tijerina. After serving more than two years in federal prison on two counts of assault in Carson National Forest, the Spanish-American leader was placed on three years' parole on the condition that he hold no office with the Alianza. He still faced state terms for kidnapping and assault in connection with the court-house raid at Tierra Amarilla, but for the time being he was free on appeal bond and home with his people. A jubilant crowd of supporters met him at the Albuquerque airport with mariachi music.

It was immediately apparent that the imprisonment had made a profound impression on Tijerina. He told the people present, "I won't exchange those 775 days I spent in prison for anything although I suffered and was separated from loved ones. What I discovered in prison you cannot learn in college or anyplace else. And I give you my heart-felt thanks for everything." It seemed to be a new, nonmilitant Tijerina speaking, but his words soared with the same visionary spirit his old speeches had carried. "I can see the day when man will realize every man is his brother. I feel that way now—as if everyone is my brother. My responsibility will be to make that possible."[1198] Civic authorities were not sure quite what to make of this transformation, but they welcomed the conciliatory tone.

Not all minority spokesmen were faring so well. In September two of the three area VISTA supervisors, including John Goldsmith, were terminated from their positions because of charges from the Dallas regional office of the Office of Economic Opportunity that they had failed to supervise in an "adequate manner." In vain the two claimed that politics were behind their ouster.[1199]

It seemed that the people of Albuquerque were coming to avoid the extremism that had recently characterized local politics and social life. The campaign leading up to the fall municipal election was lively but less strident than many earlier ones. The seventeen-year-old Albuquerque Citizens Committee was dissolved, and most of its membership regrouped with elements of the Peoples Committee for Better Government, which had been its chief rival, to back the Albuquerque Unity slate. On election day, October 5, the winners of the four-year terms on the City Commission were Ray Baca and Robert Poole, both of Albuquerque Unity; the unexpired term vacated by G.P. Reyes was won by Mrs. Nancy Koch, a moderate candidate running as an independent.[1200] The record number of voters also approved the bond issue for the purchase of open space.[1201] Holdover Commissioner Louis Saavedra became the new chairman. As the new commission prepared itself for the predictable onslaught of city problems and complaints, it found itself operating in an atmosphere of unusual tranquility. The gripe sessions held to listen to resident's problems were scantily attended.[1202]

The conciliatory spirit was being felt in the courts as well. When the persons arrested in connection with the June riots appeared in municipal court, Judge Robins dismissed most of the cases. A grand jury criticized him for his leniency, but he contended he had really had no choice, for the arresting officers frequently could not recognize the defendants and many persons had been brought in for violating a curfew which was subsequently declared illegal.[1203] In September a civil suit filed by six persons against members of the New Mexico National Guard for the bayonet stabbings at the University of New Mexico in May of 1970 was brought to trial; the jury decided in favor of the National Guard.[1204] The following month charges were dropped against all the persons arrested for occupying the Student Union Building during that episode.[1205]

Over this period the Albuquerque Police Department was moving under the leadership of Chief Donald Byrd to improve relations with the community. In July a "storefront" office was set up in the Model Cities area as a pilot project to perform minor neighborhood services and to enhance public relations.[1206] Forty policemen participated in an "Officer Bill" program with film presentations and coloring books in many of the elementary schools that fall.[1207] Early in 1972 a course for policemen in racial and cultural relations, with guest speakers from various city neighborhoods, was set up at the University of Albuquerque.[1208] Shortly afterwards, the department launched "Operation Identification," a drive to persuade residents to borrow police engravers and put their social security numbers on any belongings that might be stolen; over a thousand residents took advantage of the opportunity.[1209] Little by little, public hostility to the police was being chipped away.

At the same time, some of the most militant activists were turning more violent and being discredited. On November 8, 1971, State Policeman Robert Rosenbloom stopped a car containing three members of a Black militant group from California, and gunfire from the vehicle killed him. For the next several weeks authorities conducted a widespread manhunt for the three. Suddenly they emerged from hiding, boarded a jet at the Albuquerque airport, and hijacked it to Cuba.[1210] Two persons, including the mother of one of the suspects, were arrested for harboring the fugitives. Although the Black Coalition raised funds for their defense, most of the community expressed vehement indignation over the crimes committed.[1211]

Another slayer of a law enforcer, Pete Garcia, made the news in early 1972. His manslaughter conviction had been set aside the previous summer by the New Mexico Court of Appeals,[1212] he had been retried in December and again found guilty,[1213] and he had once more begun an appeal. Free on bond, he walked into a downtown cafe on January 6 and got into an argument over a pay phone. In a burst of fury he pulled out a pistol and shot three men. Garcia vanished from sight, but police went to his home and arrested his wife for possession of five ounces of cocaine.[1214]

On the twenty-ninth of the month occurred a more controversial shootout. Acting on an anonymous tip, three city detectives and three state policemen held a stakeout at a highway construction site south of Albuquerque. Two men slipped in that night and attempted to break into a storage shed containing dynamite; challenged by the police, one of them, perhaps both, drew a gun. In the ensuing gunfire the two were killed. When morning came police discovered that the dead men were Rito Canales and James Cordova,[1215] two Black Berets who were scheduled to appear on local television and make charges of brutality in the state penitentiary.

When the other Black Berets learned the news, a public outcry erupted. Black Beret leader Richard Moore charged that Canales and Cordova had been killed elsewhere and their bodies moved to the construction site, and that they had been assassinated to prevent their testimony about the penitentiary from being made public. Seventy-five persons conducted a candlelight vigil in their honor at the police station,[1216] and ten times that number attended a special memorial service.[1217] Over the next week numerous organizations pushed for a special investigation of the matter.[1218] In an effort to cool the anger and to bring about better communication among the concerned parties, Reies Tijerina, who had recently been declaiming for racial unity, hosted "The First Dinner of Harmony and Brotherhood for Justice" at Alianza headquarters; and seventeen civic leaders, law enforcement officials and minority leaders attended.[1219] The following weeks saw a gradual reduction of the tension. In early March a grand jury reported its findings: the killings did take place in the manner indicated by the police and were justifiable homicides. Several other persons connected with the Black Berets were indicted for unlawful possession of explosives taken in previous thefts.[1220] In the long run, the effect of the episode at the dynamite shed was to undermine the influence of the Black Berets in the larger community.

Tijerina continued to channel his energies and abilities toward civic and racial harmony. His following was not so numerous or fervent as formerly, but city leaders cooperated enthusiastically. He spearheaded a "Brotherhood Awareness" conference in early April with elaborate entertainment and speeches by citizens ranging from prominent businessmen to an ex-convict. Typical of the sentiments expressed were the words of Dr. Solomon Brown, a Black physician: "The question isn't whether all men are brothers. God settled that. The question is whether we have the strength and the will to make human brotherhood the guiding theme in our lives."[1221]

For the most part, the spring of 1972 was quieter than that season had been for the several years preceding. The disruptions in the public schools lessened.[1222] Minority group anger and the War in Viet Nam, however, continued to be a source of friction. As the weather grew warmer, the authorities wondered whether another outbreak of destruction might be in the offing.

A spark was provided the first weekend in May when President Nixon ordered the resumption of the bombing of North Viet Nam and the mining of that country's ports. On Monday the eighth students at various colleges across the country began a wave of demonstrations; the next day the spirit reached the University of New Mexico. After a noon rally on the mall, about three hundred students began marching along Central toward the downtown. When they reached the intersection with I-25, they decided to block the freeway, and this they did with barricades of trash cans, pieces of guard railing and a bus stop waiting bench. Chief Byrd arrived on the scene around two in the afternoon and tried repeatedly to talk the crowd into letting him lead them in a march back to the campus. One of the leaders reassured him, "This isn't a rock-throwing kind of thing," but a number of the people began to chant, "Stay, stay, stay . . . ," and refused to follow police instructions. An order to disperse was delivered over a microphone, tear gas was fired, the barricades were cleared, and the crowd retreated to the university area, to make plans for another march the following day. As the students walked back, a few confrontations with the police ensued; some arrests were made and two persons were wounded by birdshot.[1223]

Meanwhile, the undergraduate Student Senate and the Graduate Student Association Council passed a joint resolution condemning President Nixon's actions but opposing a proposed strike. The statement concluded:

> Most of all we wish that we maintain our cool, that no violence occur, that no property damage be senselessly inflicted and that all university forces, including legal help, medical help, community services and even the highest echelons of university administration aid in conveying our opinion and theirs where it will mean the most. Should something go wrong, we will need all the services the university has to offer, and we ask them to be prepared.[1224]

At ten the next morning about a thousand protesters gathered on the campus mall for a rally. Half an hour later a few hundred of them began marching to Kirtland Air Force Base, where they were joined by more and conducted a sit-in at the entrance, chanting, "What do we want? Peace. When do we want it? Now." The police arrested thirty-five persons for blocking the intersection and used tear gas to move the crowd, which then turned back toward the university. "One, two, three, four, we don't want your fucking war," the crowd shouted on their way back down Central. On two instances vehicles attempted to run over the marchers; one was repelled by rocks and the driver of the other was arrested. The protesters blocked the intersection of Central and University Boulevard for awhile before being driven back into Yale Park, bordering on the campus. Throughout the afternoon, rowdy and high-spirited students would gather in groups only to be dispersed by canisters of tear gas thrown by the police. Around four-thirty, during a lull in the skirmishes, a dozen demonstrators walked up to the officers and passed out carnations. An hour later the park was finally cleared, but another massive protest rally was held on the mall that night.[1225]

On Thursday, while tear gas was blowing across the campus burning the eyes of the studious and the rebellious alike, a band of several hundred protesters roamed around looking for more support. Whenever they attempted to move off university grounds, they were blocked by the police with their canisters. Such confrontations were seldom very heated; the mood of the crowd was as frolicsome as it was angry.

At nine that night a delegation of five students led by Jerry Buckner, vice-president of the undergraduate student government, went to city hall and asked permission to conduct a candlelight march. After considering the proposal, four city commissioners and the city manager traveled to the University of New Mexico campus and offered to sanction such a demonstration the following night "as long as it is in a peaceful manner."[1226] The details were worked out, and Friday evening over fifteen hundred marchers bearing candles, signs and peace banners walked from the university to Ridgecrest Park in the Southeast Heights, where they held a twenty-minute vigil, and back to the mall for the largest rally of the week. As they marched they raised their voices in such songs as "We Shall Overcome"; obscenities were seldom heard. Commented Acting City Manager Herb Smith, "I think this is the beginning of restoring the communication between [the protesters] and the community, which was what we were trying tonight."[1227]

Over the next few days other city-sanctioned rallies and forums were held on the subject of the War in Viet Nam. At one of them, near a World War II artillery piece in Bataan Park, a reporter spotted Judge Harry Robins, who said he lived in the neighborhood and had come to "listen to these young people." "And I don't like the war either," he went on; "What the hell, you'll find me anywhere."[1228] On May 17 the case of the demonstrators who had been arrested for blocking the entrance to Kirtland came up in Judge Robins's court. After complimenting the police for showing restraint, he found the offenders guilty but put their sentences under a year's advisement.[1229]

Throughout the summer and fall minor incidents rippled through the city's political surface, but there were no large-scale disturbances. Judge Robins clashed with policemen testifying in municipal court on a number of occasions, once fining an officer ten dollars for contempt for storming off the witness stand.[1230] In September a group of citizens who felt the judge was too controversial mounted a drive to have him recalled from office; they collected more than 8,500 signatures by late November.[1231] Representatives of minority groups continued to express dissatisfaction over what they considered unfair treatment by branches of city government, but the disputes were settled peaceably. In the national election held that fall, former City Commissioner Pete Domenici won the senate seat being vacated by the retirement of Clinton P. Anderson.[1232]

The return to a more settled mode of behavior was reflected by the popular culture of this period. The mass entertainment media still showed violent tendencies, but more and more, the sympathies were on the side of law and order. Such movies as *The French Connection* and *Straw Dogs* showed criminals being vanquished. Even Clint Eastwood modified his persona of the destructive loner to become a policeman, although an unusually violent one, in such works as 1971's *Dirty Harry*. In the more domesticated medium of television police shows were growing more popular, yet one of the most widely watched of all the new programs was *The Waltons*, a nostalgic view of a fictional American family during the Great Depression.

On the local front numerous signs were cropping up of a partial return to traditional values. Two of the movie theaters specializing in pornographic fare began showing old films instead. Church attendance was on the upswing, and in February 1972 the rock opera *Jesus Christ Superstar* drew a throng of nine thousand to the University Arena.[1233] The theme of the latest homecoming celebration at the University of New Mexico was Nostalgia '72.[1234] All across the metropolitan area people were giving renewed attention to their jobs and their families. And as their behavior grew less adventurous and unconventional and their concerns gradually turned inward, it was becoming apparent that the whole society was entering a period of relative quiet and adjustment to the changes that had shaken Albuquerque and the world outside so tumultuously for the previous ten or so years.

5

ALBUQUERQUE IN 1972

To a visitor who had last seen the city in 1945, Albuquerque in 1972 would present a startling contrast. One of the first changes he would notice would be the enormous growth of the metropolitan area. Over the twenty-seven years while he was gone the population of Bernalillo County had jumped from about 90,000 to 339,500, and that of the city itself from around 50,000 to 262,800.[1235] These figures he could only guess at, but as he drove around the Albuquerque area he would probably be stunned by the physical transformation which had taken place. The massive old downtown buildings no longer seethed with their former activity, and many had been razed. Traffic on Central Avenue in the area was down, retail business was moribund, but slightly to the north and the south clusters of sleek government and commercial office buildings were giving Albuquerque an impressive skyline. If he left the city's center and drove east on the freeway I-40, itself a bigger thoroughfare than existed anywhere in the country in 1945, he would be struck by the substantial business and shopping centers at the main intersections, and he would eventually discover that these were just a few of the dozens of nuclei of activity dispersed around the metropolitan area. Leaving the interstate highway and going along the lesser arteries and side streets; he would be impressed by the miles of suburban developments more opulent than most residents of an earlier era might have dreamed possible. Having seen firsthand the evidence of so much urban growth, he would probably not be surprised to learn that the area of the city had expanded from about twelve square miles to eighty-six.[1236] With residential development stretching from the foothills of the Sandia Mountains on the east to the volcanoes on the west, Albuquerque seemed less like a rugged community thriving in the midst of natural splendor and more like a gigantic living organism expanding and adjusting its structure according to some dimly perceived natural process.

If our visitor stayed on in the city for several weeks or months, he would find that the people also had changed vastly, even more than those living in most other parts of the country. Visits to the well-furnished homes, the bustling shopping centers, the spacious offices and the elegant restaurants would heighten his impression of increased wealth, for median family income adjusted for inflation had approximately doubled. Taxes, to be sure, took a larger proportion of the money than before, but the wide array of government services contributed substantially to the overall high level of living. In most respects, the majority of the residents of Albuquerque seemed to have very nearly attained the affluence for which earlier generations had striven so vigorously.

Closer acquaintance with the people would reveal that far more than their material circumstances had altered. The new wealth had contributed to a substantial relaxation of many of the social controls: institutions and relationships among the people were generally less authoritarian than previously, and spontaneity and expressiveness were less inhibited. The changing economic climate had bought about other important shifts as well. As large businesses and other organizations had gained competitive advantages over smaller ones, as the people had come more to enjoy their gains and to relax their strivings, and as the penalties of headlong growth had become more apparent, the overall economic system had moved further from the traditional framework of individualistic competition and had become more of a loose structure of groups of various sizes and on various levels, some of these groups overlapping one another, all more or less working together. The changes in the economic system toward more emphasis on large groups had led to parallel shifts in governmental structures, in other institutions of society, and in the behavior and attitudes of the people—practically everyone had become more group oriented. These two interrelated broad social changes—the relaxation of authority and the increased orientation toward groups—had made profound impacts on the motivations and the character of the people. So our friend would find that large numbers of persons were less competitive than their forbears had been, and they were more likely to extol the virtues of cooperation. More important decisions were made by committees after consultation with outsiders who might be affected by the outcomes; less of a premium was placed on individual decisiveness and steadfastness. The ethic of every man for himself provided that basic rules of fair play were adhered to had given way, to a substantial degree, to a belief in looking after the group, and civic and governmental bodies assumed more responsibility for the poor and weak. As the individuals had been left less to their own devices to succeed or fail, society had become less dynamic and dramatic, yet it retained its color in other ways—in the increased variety of experience possible in large groups and in a big city, in the more exuberant expressiveness allowed by the loosening of the bonds of convention, in the warm feelings of solidarity with one's cohorts.

With so many more people in the metropolitan area than in 1945, the city needed a larger governmental structure just to keep order. The increasing interest in large organizations and the expanding public appetite for services further encouraged the growth of government; by 1972 it loomed larger in the lives of the residents than ever before. The number of government workers in Bernalillo County, just 8,059 in 1950, had reached 26,320 twenty years later.[1237] Total expenditures for city government had skyrocketed from $613,000 for fiscal year 1945 to $55,254,388 for 1972,[1238] an increase of 588.9 percent in real buying power.[1239] The contribution of more distant governments had grown even faster. As a result of the War on Poverty, urban renewal and hundreds of other relatively new programs, the total outlay of federal funds in the county had shot up to $675,540,052 for fiscal year 1972.[1240]

As the various levels of government had become bigger and more complicated, their outreach had extended into areas of city life previously left alone. We have seen how local and national government assumed greater responsibility for flood control, for improving transportation and education, for bolstering industry and lowering unemployment, and for aiding poor people and ethnic minorities; we have seen the heated political fights that took place over these issues. There were numerous less controversial new areas of government assistance as well. Federal and state funds contributed to the arts,[1241] the city-supported Hospitality House provided a wide range of activities and services for residents over the age of fifty,[1242] and the City Parks Department offered inexpensive swimming and tennis lessons to anyone interested.[1243] Along with the expanded government involvement in society had come more extensive government regulation, for legislative bodies and public agencies had seen need to keep close tabs on the funds they were dispersing, and they had also assumed greater responsibility for ensuring that individuals and groups did not affect one another adversely. In addition to laws dealing with racial discrimination, air pollution and development of subdivisions, there were a city ordinance on size and placement of commercial signs,[1244] a county noise-control ordinance,[1245] a state law requiring daily inspections of meat processors,[1246] and thousands of other government-established rules touching on an expanding variety of human activity.

The growth of government activity had led to overlapping of city, county, state and federal functions, and these layers of government had become progressively more intertwined. In 1945 5.9 percent of the revenue of the City of Albuquerque had come from other governments, mostly from the State of New Mexico;[1247] by 1972 that portion of the revenue had risen to 17.5 percent, mainly from federal grants.[1248] Such programs as the Economic Opportunity Board, which involved the matching of local and federal funds, and Model Cities, which also got its monies through the matching of local and federal funds but was in the position of declaring all its resources local for the purpose of matching again, through the Economic Opportunity Board and other agencies, and drawing in still more money from the U.S. Government, had made the picture all the more complicated. For some strands of state and federal assistance, it would have taken an accountant trained in public finance weeks to unravel the sources of all the funds, and even then he might not be sure of his conclusions. In order to reduce duplication of efforts and to make the administration of the programs more efficient, the different levels of government had begun to operate many of their programs jointly. The city and county school systems had merged back in 1948; twenty-four years later cooperative ventures of the city and county also included, among others, the Environmental Health Department,[1249] the Alcohol Traffic Safety Program[1250] and the Manpower Office, which coordinated the federally assisted projects to train unemployed persons and place them in jobs.[1251] The Bernalillo County Health Department was run by the state with the cooperation of the county and city, and the federal government provided much of the monetary support.[1252] Many of the antipoverty projects were partially supervised by city government, and almost all of them involved some degree of consultation and control by local people. When Quebrar, the EOB-sponsored drug addiction treatment organization, became particularly controversial in early 1972, it was renamed La Llave and put under the jurisdiction of a joint City-County Treatment Center Board, which also oversaw the Alcoholism Treatment Program.[1253] The spirit of cooperation among governmental bodies also reached into areas where conflict had long been rife. Late in the year the City Commission worked out plans with residents of the north and south valleys outside the city limits for the installation of water systems there, the cost of which would be defrayed by federal grants.[1254]

With the involvement of more than one branch of government, as well as numerous interest groups and individual citizens, in many of the programs and decisions affecting the public, governmental action was sometimes slow and cumbersome. Federal and state guidelines were followed deliberately, boards pondered over alternative courses, public hearings were held, and the issues were aired in the mass media and debated in numerous formal and informal meetings; at any step of the way unanticipated snags or shifts in public opinion could block a project that had been carefully nurtured for months or years. Nevertheless, much did get accomplished, sometimes on a very large scale. The adoption of merit systems for city, county, state and federal employees below the level of policy making had contributed to smoother operation of government, and even the political parties were organized along relatively evenhanded and impersonal lines.[1255] The growing use of specific job descriptions, of rationalized administrative structures, and of standardized bureaucratic procedures helped expedite the process of decision making and reduce the power of persons along the way to use their influence in arbitrary fashions. And the marshalling of large numbers of persons, each with his own clearly defined area of responsibility, made possible the completion of highly complicated and drawn-out tasks. In 1972, after years of studies, hearings, land acquisition and relocation of residents, work was underway on the widening of San Mateo Boulevard, one of the most important north-south arteries of the city.[1256]

In spite of the increased numbers of people involved in and affected by government, in one major respect it had less impact on Albuquerque than earlier—the influence of individual city leaders. The city commissioners and other high officials of 1945 had provided a dramatic focus for public life. Their words and actions had given Albuquerque much of its color, and they had contributed substantially to setting the tone of the society. Over the years, however, the spreading of the powers of decision making into the lower echelons of government and throughout hundreds of committees and informal groups of citizens had limited the ability of the top leaders to stamp their imprint on what went on around them. The bold gesture and the quick decision had largely given way to patient organizing.

The members of the City Commission represented a broader cross section of the population than ever before, but their personalities were generally less imposing than those of their predecessors. Harry Kinney, the chairman, was an engineer for Sandia Corporation with years of experience in city and county politics. An able planner and organizer, he got along well with most of his fellow citizens and was sometimes referred to as "Harmonious Harry." The position of vice-chairman was occupied by former Albuquerque policeman Ray Baca, the leading vote-getter in the October 1971 election. Baca was the first locally born Spanish-American to be elected city commissioner,[1257] and he made particular efforts to have the city hire more members of ethnic minorities.[1258] The other three commissioners were Louis Saavedra, head of Albuquerque Technical-Vocational Institute; Robert Poole, a lawyer who had previously served as board member of the Economic Opportunity Board, chairman of the Fair Housing Board, and president of the Legal Aid Society;[1259] and Nancy Koch, a past president of the local Junior League and the first woman ever to win a seat on the commission.[1260] With their experience and their ties to the various segments of the community, they were in good position to channel citywide feelings into workable policies. Flamboyantly autocratic Clyde Tingleys they were not.

Since most of the city commissioners depended on other jobs for their incomes and since city government was much bigger than in earlier years, more of the responsibility for the day-to-day operations fell into the hands of the city manager. Many people around the city had found fault with City Manager Richard Wilson for his part in the handling of the June 1971 riots, and several candidates in the subsequent city election, including Baca and Poole, had called for his ouster.[1261] After dangling in uncertainty for a few more months, in March 1972 Wilson requested a vote of confidence and a salary raise; failing to get them, he resigned.[1262] The commissioners named as acting city manager Herb Smith, who had been director of the Planning Department for a little over a year after previously heading a private planning firm in New Jersey.[1263] Smith's decisiveness and his willingness to take the initiative in such touchy matters as the sponsoring of a candlelight antiwar march in May impressed the City Commission. In July he was installed as permanent city manager.[1264] So in many ways the most influential voice in local government was a newcomer with no proven support among the electorate. Herb Smith's intelligence, nerve and self-confidence were serving him and the city well, but his power base was hardly substantial.

Lower down in the political spectrum were hundreds of other persons of influence—some of them experts at getting along and looking after their own people and interests, some dedicated and hard-working bureaucrats, and more than a few forceful administrators with reputations for ramming through difficult decisions. Most, though, were cautious about overextending themselves and causing resentment by appearing to be too greedy for the lime-light. They were wary of raising their heads so prominently that they might get chopped off. Fiery idealists might inspire their followers for awhile, but sudden shifts of the political winds were likely to blow them out of office. To find such magnetic and powerful personalities as were fairly commonplace around the time of World War II and earlier, one would have to seek out the likes of Reies Lopez Tijerina, whose following among the mainstream was marginal at best.

The old spirit of aggressive risk taking was more prominent in the private sector, but there also systems and organizations had become more important, individuals less so. A Dale Bellamah or an Emmanuel Schifani might put together business deals on a scale dwarfing anything Albert Simms or his compatriots could have mustered during the forties, yet most of the major business activity was centered around large conglomerates which even the top people had limited freedom to maneuver. And small businessmen, who earlier had been the backbone of the economy, now had less of the market. Ownership of places of business by chains had grown to such an extent that they controlled 31 of the 49 department stores (as opposed to 4 out of 15 in 1945), 25 of the 82 pharmacies (3 out of 28 in the earlier year), 127 of the 213 grocery stores (5 out of 151 before), 152 of the 439 restaurants (none before), and 16 of the 109 hotels and motels (none before). The number of banks had only risen from 3, each operating in a single location, to 6, but their operations were now conducted at 55 separate locations.[1265] The traditional notion of businesses vying energetically with one another in a state of nearly perfect competition had become outmoded.

Much of the shift toward large business organizations had come about because of the changing appetites and needs of the metropolitan area over the years. These are reflected in the changing distributions of employment by the U.S. Bureau of the Census classifications of industry and occupation. By and large, basic industries traditionally requiring large amounts of physical labor had come to use a smaller proportion of the work force—from 1950 to 1970 the percentage of employed workers in Bernalillo County involved in agriculture, forestry and fishing had dropped from 3.24 to 1.08; in manufacturing from 7.95 to 7.60, and in construction from 16.56 to 7.04. On the other hand, industries involving the complex interactions of large numbers of people had increased their share: the percentage of employees in communications had risen from 1.02 to 1.97; in finance, insurance and real estate from 4.07 to 5.91; and in the service industries as a whole from 22.89 to 38.20.[1266] Occupational statistics had shifted along similar lines. Farmers and farm managers had gone down from 1.71 percent to 0.15 percent; craftsmen, foremen and kindred from 17.88 percent to 12.24 percent; and operatives and kindred from 11.16 percent to 8.82 percent. Among the occupations which had risen proportionately were professional, technical and kindred—12.44 percent to 22.39 percent; clerical and kindred—14.47 percent to 19.86 percent; and service workers—10.57 percent to 13.88 percent.[1267] As the society had become more oriented toward human services, businesses with the capacity to organize the efforts and the judgments of large numbers of persons had prospered. Vital lines of authority, of expertise, of communication had become more prominent, giving the business community a highly developed structure and system of flow.

The impetus toward bigness had affected far more than just the size of specific business organizations; it had altered the ways in which the businesses functioned. More small businessmen had opted for loose associations with larger organizations in order to reduce their risks and improve their competitive positions. Variations of franchising, through which an individual would arrange to operate his own establishment while using the name, the lines of supply and the basic guidelines of a large chain, had become more common. Another popular type of arrangement was for many independent businesses to buy from the same large wholesaler, thereby gaining some of the cost efficiencies available to large organizations; in 1972 most of the independent grocery stores in Albuquerque were supplied by Associated Grocers of Colorado. The loose linkages with other groups also extended beyond the confines of the business community. We have witnessed how business and government became more interdependent and interrelated over the twenty-seven years since World War II, how government came to regulate business activity more extensively and at the same time to offer more assistance through providing advice, training workers, supporting new construction, recruiting new industries and undertaking numerous other helpful programs. Action in the public sector had gone far toward tying the individual businesses into the diffuse yet increasingly integrated network of the larger community. Changes in the landscape and the street system had a somewhat similar effect: increasingly, businesses had to make adjustments to fit into the emerging physical configuration of the metropolitan area and to take what advantage of it they could. The developers and other businessmen who recognized and exploited the trend toward shopping and business centers had been among the most successful during the recent years of headlong growth. The construction of the interstate highways through the city had helped advantageously located places of business enormously. A new trend in transportation of goods was for a huge truck trailer full of wares to be shipped to Albuquerque by rail, for a driver with a truck cab to hook it up at the station yards and to drive it along an interstate highway or other main artery to an industrial center, and for the wholesalers and retailers to then take over the distribution. The tracks of the Santa Fe Railroad, the interstate highways, the lesser arteries and the side streets were thereby functioning as physical lines of flow, paralleling and interacting with the organizational flow charts which were becoming all the more prominent in government and business.

In spite of this overall stiffening of the business world in Albuquerque and beyond into interlocking systems, however, there continued to be a place for small enterprises and competition. As always, some businesses failed and others rose to take their places. Furthermore, the big organizations tended to be slow moving; small groups were sometimes in better positions to avail themselves of newly opening opportunities. Often the big and the little groups developed symbiotic relationships: a highly specialized organization or a single consultant could provide services to a large corporation or a government agency which that body could not easily handle itself. And far removed from the centers of business power there were always parts of the economy which were informal and fluid. Vendors sold everything from telephone pole glass insulators to turquoise jewelry to military uniforms at the weekend flea markets around the city[1268] and at the mall of the University of New Mexico campus. Suburban housewives held garage sales to get rid of accumulated clutter. Drug dealers known only by their first names made furtive transactions in city parks. With the growing informality and spontaneity suffusing the people's lives, there seemed little chance that big business or government would ever make significant inroads into this sort of activity.

Although the private and public sectors of the economy of Albuquerque in 1972 were much more intricately organized and structured than in 1945, and the persons at the tops of the hierarchies were more widely separated, by layers of intermediate management, from those at the bottom, the metropolitan area had come to have less of a social elite. As the society had opened up more and allowed persons with less conventional life styles and more widely varying backgrounds to advance, the persons in the highest positions had come to have less in common with one another. Many of them had attained their levels through their abilities to get along with and to organize their coworkers, and they frequently found it more important to maintain good relations with the other members of their organizations than to cultivate close associations with leaders of different groups. Less common than in years past—and less prominent in the public eye—were the card games among members of the establishment, the parleys in the big downtown hotels, the elaborate socializing, even the consciousness of belonging to a superior class of people.

The decline of the influence of the upper class had been accompanied by shifts in the ways culture was transmitted and civic responsibilities were handled. In earlier years many of the powerful had been acutely conscious of their role as cultural leaders. Albert Simms had funded musical festivals, Clinton P. Anderson had been active in the governance of the Albuquerque Little Theatre, and Will Keleher had written books. These people and many of their friends had not only enjoyed cultural pursuits, they had regarded such activities as important trappings and privileges of persons in their social positions. But over the years the arts had become more democratized. Less formal varieties had sprung up in profusion, and greater numbers of ordinary people had come to be interested. The world of art and culture had expanded to such an extent that it could no longer be dominated by a class of cultivated amateurs; what cultural leadership as existed in 1972 was dispersed among government councils, university departments and professionals who were willing to devote most of their energies to their art.

The handling of such civic responsibilities as attending to the needs of the poor and troubled had undergone a somewhat similar shift. In 1945 and earlier, many of the eminent personages of Albuquerque had regarded charitable work as a duty, and they had done what they could, often on an individual basis, to relieve suffering and to provide others with the opportunity to rise to success. Some donations by wealthy benefactors had been on such a scale as to determine the success of a particular institution for the coming year. Women with leisure time had volunteered for long hours of meetings, fund drives and direct assistance to the poor and sick. The sense of obligation borne by the elite had been shared to a lesser extent by those with less time and money; almost everyone had striven hard to care for his friends, neighbors and families. But with the changing nature and declining prominence of the upper class and with the overall relaxation of the sense of individual duty, the picture had decidedly changed. Although some people continued to go out of their way to do good works for no compensation, their impact on the community was far less significant than before.

Yet the city in 1972 was in most respects a more hospitable place for the downtrodden. Government programs and private nonprofit agencies provided an abundance of services and supports, and they were less likely to exhort the persons being helped to improve themselves by their own efforts. As individuals had withdrawn from some of their traditional community responsibilities, groups and institutions had readily stepped in. And they did more in the way caring for the weak than individual citizens had ever done; the growing group consciousness was making the community act more like an integrated unit which attended to the needs of all of its parts.

Foremost among the organizations which were contributing to the succor of the people were the various levels of government. The fronts of the federally financed War on Poverty often dominated the headlines, but hundreds of less spectacular government programs to provide assistance were also underway. The U.S. Department of Agriculture issued food stamps for persons with low incomes; in fiscal year 1972 $8,852,176 was spent on that program in Bernalillo County.[1269] Direct welfare payments channeled through the New Mexico Health and Social Services Department were higher than they had ever been before.[1270] A number of different programs to provide the poor with housing were in operation, and the Federal Housing Authority, which was responsible for two of them, also offered counseling to families having trouble finding suitable accommodations.[1271] Whenever floods swept through the poor neighborhoods and destroyed property, the Economic Opportunity Board, the Small Business Administration and city government were ready to lend assistance.[1272] And numerous other government-backed forms of help, some highly specialized, were available to people in need, ranging from DESEO—an organization formed to aid convicts, ex-convicts and their families[1273]—to

Dial-a-Ride, a program offering free taxi service to New Year's Eve partiers who felt they were too drunk to drive home safely.[1274]

The University of New Mexico was also active in various forms of community service. It operated the Institute for Social Research and Development (ISRAD), a collection of programs utilizing academic expertise to provide assistance to the city, the state and the federal government. Among its divisions were the Technology Application Center, funded by the National Aeronautics and Space Administration; the Bureau of Business Research and the Bureau of Government Research, funded by the state; and the College Enrichment Program, New Careers, and the Home Improvement Project, backed by federal antipoverty grants. Some of its ventures into social programs sparked controversy, but the days of strict separation of the academic world from outside involvement were long past; in the fiscal year 1972 ISRAD spent $2,363,206.[1275] Another type of university service was the clinical law program, whereby law students earned credits toward their degrees by performing basic legal services under the guidance of their professors for people associated with the university and for persons with low incomes.[1276] There were other types as well—medical students and their professors working at the Bernalillo County Medical Center, architects and architecture students interviewing residents and planning projects at the Community Design Center, and scores of programs in which a few persons participated for short times. As was the case with members of the other professions, educators had become increasingly involved in group programs, and many of these consisted of one kind or another of public assistance.

Numerous smaller organizations around the metropolitan area were contributing to the growing system of help and support. There was a variety of nonprofit groups, such as Family Consultation Service, which addressed itself to problems in marriages and home life,[1277] and Parents Without Partners, an organization for divorced and widowed parents.[1278] From 1950 to 1970 the percentage of the work force employed by nonprofit membership organizations had risen from 1.16 to 2.23.[1279] And some private businesses had moved further away from narrow concerns with their own profit margins. A number of them jointly financed the Consumer Credit Counseling Service of Albuquerque, an agency which helped debt-ridden persons develop plans to pay off their obligations.[1280] In October 1972 the Albuquerque Industrial Development Service and the Industrial Foundation of Albuquerque, the leading forces in the local drive to bring in new industry, issued a joint policy statement declaring they would work to create "new wealth for Albuquerque and New Mexico by developing an ever-increasing number of diverse, desirable export manufacturing, export service and export warehousing jobs for the area's unemployed, underemployed, returning servicemen and up-coming youth." These new jobs, however, should "not conflict with the local and state environmental goals" and they should be "preferably non-defense oriented."[1281] It seemed that much of the private sector was coming around to the belief that what was good for society would ultimately prove good for business.

Private donations and volunteer work, which had traditionally been the backbone of community service, continued to play a significant role, but even this area was now characterized by extensive organization. Most of the charity groups were associated with the United Community Fund, which conducted annual drives and which sought funds from state and federal governments and from private foundations as well as from individuals. Much of the fund raising was done by aspiring young executives who were lent to UCF by the firms which employed them; they underwent elaborate training and then worked full time for several months running campaigns in the areas assigned to them.[1282] On a lesser scale, a recently established organization named the Volunteer Action Center acted as a clearinghouse to direct volunteer workers to the local agencies that needed their services.[1283]

As the overall society had come to place more emphasis on looking after each of its members and less of a premium on individual risk taking, the individual citizens and families had also grown more conscious of security. Workers in hazardous occupations had pushed successfully for more safety regulations. Voters had furnished much of the impetus for the growth of government assistance programs. Persons in all levels of society had availed themselves increasingly of various kinds of private insurance plans—between 1948 and 1972 the proportion of persons in the county working for private firms who were in the insurance business had risen from 1.31 percent to 2.25 percent.[1284] Many business firms were keenly aware of how important personal security had become to their employees, and more and more were offering them group insurance and pension plans.

Probably the single most telling sign of the growing interest in personal safety and security was the dramatic surge in the health care industry. In 1945 the city government had spent $3,000—0.34 percent of its total expenditures—on health and hospitals; the figure for 1972 was $602,656—1.09 percent of the budget.[1285] At the University of New Mexico the percentage of the yearly budget spent on student health had gone up from 0.46 (amounting to $5,314.80) to 1.12 ($470,320) over these years.[1286] Albuquerque Public Schools had made no particular provisions for handicapped students in the 1944-45 school year, but twenty-seven years later it had special classes—in some cases a special school—for 1,304 youngsters in this category.[1287] And in the county as a whole, the proportion of the work force employed in hospitals or other health services had risen from 3.72 percent in 1950 to 6.24 percent in 1970.[1288]

Although practically everyone was more concerned with health care than formerly, it was in the public sector that the biggest strides had been taken. The federal government's Medicare program provided health insurance for retired persons, and the state and federal governments both contributed to Medicaid, a similar program for people on welfare.[1289] As might be expected, the several branches of government shouldered particular responsibility for the health of the poor people, who were in the worst position to cope with the skyrocketing medical costs, but many of the benefits of public health were available to anyone who wanted them. The Public Health Service, administered in Bernalillo County by the State of New Mexico and funded by the state and federal governments, offered a multitude of services, including a daily clinic for venereal diseases, clinics for preschool children, immunization shots for children, heart and lung programs, birth control programs, physical examinations for city and county employees, and public health nurses who visited county homes.[1290] Branches of the Public Health Service operated in most of the EOB-sponsored neighborhood centers;[1291] in addition, two federally funded family health centers operated in impoverished areas of the city.[1292] The medical school of the University of New Mexico, which had taken over the operation of the Bernalillo County Medical Center, administered the federally subsidized Maternity and Infant Care Project, which sent teams consisting of one or more doctors, nurses, social workers, nutritionists, laboratory assistants and clerks to staff four intensive care stations and three portable stations dispersed around the metropolitan area.[1293]

As health care had proliferated, it had extended further into fields distantly related to traditional medical practice. A program of occupational therapy was underway at the Veterans Hospital.[1294] That hospital and other local institutions were also heavily involved in alcoholism treatment.[1295] At the recently established Bernalillo County Mental Health Center patients with emotional problems who could not afford private psychiatrists but who were not so severely debilitated as to be committed to the state mental hospital in Las Vegas received treatment. Specialized programs there dealt with chronic unemployment and drug abuse.[1296] An extension of the mental health center, New Directions, operated out of the Public Health Service and provided counseling and treatment for disturbed young people, and the teenagers were also referred to other organizations and agencies in the community.[1297] To a much greater extent than in the past, the nurturing of good health was being regarded as a social responsibility, not just a matter of curing isolated pathological conditions.

With the abundance of health care and other supports available to the people of Albuquerque and with their overall high material level of living, they no longer felt such an intense need to strive for a better life. Over the years the gradual relaxation of their efforts in this direction had led to a widespread relaxation and dispersal of authority throughout the society. The turbulence of the sixties and the beginning of the seventies had accelerated this trend, and it was still underway. In 1971 city police were allowed for the first time a voice in the selection of their uniforms—they picked lighter, less elaborate and less expensive outfits.[1298] In 1972 the presidents of undergraduate and graduate student government at the University of New Mexico were named as advisers to the Board of Regents.[1299] Almost every aspect of city life—including politics, the system of justice, religion, education and employer-employee relations—was considerably less authoritarian and more open to individual differences. The shift had affected the powerful and the weak alike: the elite classes had lost some of their prestige, and young children were treated more permissively and were less under the absolute control of their parents. When persons came together, the dominant ones were less likely to issue orders than in the past; persuasion and indirect pressure were more the rule. In both style and substance, command and subservience had largely given way to more nearly evenhanded interactions.

This fundamental transformation of the nature of authority was demonstrated by myriads of smaller shifts. Employment statistics reflect the altered relationship between the buyer and the seller. Although the proportion of workers in the service sector of the economy had risen from 22.89 percent in

1950 to 38.20 percent in 1970, the proportion engaged in personal services had fallen from 7.32 percent to 5.37 percent.[1300] Persons no longer served other persons as much as before; various kinds of self-service and labor-saving devices were more common. The proportion of persons employed in laundries and cleaners had dropped from 2.07 percent in 1948 to 0.83 percent in 1972, in barber and beauty shops over those years from 0.82 percent to 0.73 percent, and in photographic studios from 0.15 percent to 0.05 percent[1301]—this in spite of the growing interest in photography. Fewer restaurants regaled their patrons with elaborate service, and the number of taxicab drivers was probably fewer than it had been when the population was much smaller. In many cases, establishments which continued to feature customer service were losing out to smoothly organized mass operations such as fast food chains and discount houses, which had comparatively smaller labor costs and could offer lower prices.

Even the most conservative institutions were affected by the loosening of authority. At the military bases the enlisted men were no longer required to do KP duty, and most had private rooms which they could decorate any way they chose within the bounds of neatness and safety.[1302] The fraternities and sororities at the University of New Mexico had dispensed with most of their rules governing behavior, and only a few continued to have housemothers. Mrs. Edna Rich, one of the remaining ones, commented, "I never check on the boys anymore. I feel they are old enough to care for themselves."[1303]

A highly visible byproduct of the general relaxation of restraints was the informality that had suffused the society. Men were less likely to don coats and ties, women were less often seen in dresses, and blue jeans were popular casual wear for both sexes. Colorful clothing had become more common; black suits and white shirts were much rarer than formerly. Although most homes were furnished more sumptuously, the furniture, dinner ware and decorations had a simpler, less ornate appearance. Most social conventions and rituals were looser and less rigorously observed. Speeches and introductions were less stylized, acquaintances were more likely to address one another by their first names, language which had once been stigmatized as vulgar was relatively commonplace, and more persons ate with their elbows on the table. Old forms were stretched and sometimes totally ignored as people comported themselves in a more casual, open and spontaneous manner, giving freer expression to their emotions and impulses. They no longer felt so constrained to strive after high culture and high society. The most popular single gathering spot during the New Year's Eve celebrations ushering in 1972 was not a big downtown hotel featuring lavish parties as in some earlier years. It was the civic auditorium, where a country music concert was being held.[1304]

The people's increased appetite for openness and diversity was matched by the variety of experiences which the city offered. The proportion of Spanish-Americans in the local population was not much different from what it had been in 1945, but their culture was more visible and influential. Nineteen of the public schools had inaugurated programs of bilingual education,[1305] and one of the best-selling novels of the year was Rudolfo Anaya's *Bless Me Ultima*, a story about a Spanish-American boy growing up in a small New Mexican town.[1306] Another important source of contact with life outside the mainstream of traditional American experience was the University of New Mexico, where one could find God's plenty of offbeat characters, political groups and cultural offerings alongside multitudes of more conventional types. And there were many other opportunities for interesting encounters and pastimes all across the metropolitan area. Like a number of other special interest groups, older citizens had gained more prominence in the public eye; a hobby show was held for them at the civic auditorium.[1307] Responding to the burgeoning interest in growing plants, the Council of Albuquerque Garden Clubs and the Cooperative Extension Service of New Mexico State University at Las Cruces jointly presented a garden clinic free to the public.[1308] As was the case with the people as individuals, the city as a whole had become less tightly focused around striving for material betterment.

One of the most vivid indications of the increased attention being paid to activities which were enjoyable in themselves rather than means to achieve distant goals was the rise in sports and recreation. In 1945 city government had allocated $32,000, 3.58 percent of its budget, for recreation; the corresponding figures for 1972 were $2,393,991 and 4.33 percent.[1309] During the intervening years the sports fever had steadily grown locally and nationwide, and athletics had become a major industry. The most successful of the professional athletes—such persons as Bobby and Al Unser, nationally prominent automobile racers from Albuquerque—earned prodigious amounts of money; but the vast majority of the sports enthusiasts were spectators and amateur participants who gained only entertainment, sometimes physical well-being and a fleeting sensation of the high drama of absolute victory or defeat that had become comparatively rare in the organized and secure workaday world. Newspapers gave abundant coverage of the major sports events across the country, and in many a home persons spent much of their weekends avidly watching games on television. On the local level the Albuquerque Dukes, the city's professional baseball team, had been raised from Class D status in 1960 all the way to Triple A by the start of the 1972 season.[1310] The major athletic teams at the University of New Mexico were at least as big an attraction; toward the end of the decade of the sixties attendance at the basketball games was the highest in the nation for college teams. To meet the soaring demand for sports, the schools had poured in more and more money: the athletic budget at the University of New Mexico had nearly tripled during the 1960s, the high school football budget had jumped from $5,000 to $145,000 over those years, and the sports budget for the junior high schools had leapt from $2,500 to $25,000.[1311] As these figures also demonstrate, the less glamorous sports had been growing in recent years at an even faster rate than the big name ones. More people with only ordinary ability had become active participants. Many had turned to golf: in the 1960s the one public golf course had been joined by four more, and the estimated 1,200 players had risen to about 7,000. Growing appreciation for bowling during those years had led to the addition of three new bowling alleys, bringing the total to eight.[1312] In the early seventies tennis had become widely popular. The enthusiasm was also spreading to activities which in the past had hardly been considered sports at all, including cycling, hiking and jogging. In 1972 physical fitness was more popular and widespread than it had been since the years when large numbers of the people had had to earn their income through physical labor. Now it had little direct effect on their jobs, but it enhanced their enjoyment of what went on around them.

A somewhat similar phenomenon was the booming popularity of the arts. Long-established artistic groups and rank newcomers were thriving alike, drawing in unprecedented numbers of participants and spectators. The Albuquerque Little Theatre derived most of its support from some ten thousand season ticket holders; commented Director Bernie Thomas, "We go out and reach for the average guy. Once we've got him in, he'll be back." Several smaller theater groups—in Old Town, in Corrales and elsewhere—were also flourishing. The Albuquerque Symphony Orchestra did not attract so many paying customers—like a growing number of other cultural groups, it used federal grants to supplement its revenue—but it too performed before a wider audience than ever before.[1313] Members of the orchestra gave demonstrations and ensemble concerts at the public schools in order to cultivate more widespread appreciation for their form of music.[1314] In May they held a free concert at the Albuquerque Zoo. About three thousand people lolled in the grass while taking in a program ranging from such popular favorites as "When Johnny Comes Marching Home" and "Colonel Bogey March" to such classical standbys as Schubert's "Rosamunde Overture" and Borodin's "Polovtsian Dance."[1315] Popejoy Hall at the University of New Mexico was the setting for a broad array of concerts, plays and other types of performances. Museums and art galleries exhibited lively displays of visual art. For persons who preferred less formal varieties of culture—and these were burgeoning more rapidly than the traditional ones—there was an abundance to choose from. Record stores were doing a heavy business supplying the young people with their favorite kinds of music, and in June approximately fifteen thousand young fans packed into University Arena to hear a concert by the Rolling Stones, a rock group from England.[1316] Wall posters enlivened thousands of homes and apartments; cameras clicked all over the city as more people had become fascinated with making pictures themselves; more buildings were bedecked with outside murals. Macramé, weaving, metal work, woodcarving and scores of other relatively unpretentious arts and crafts had gained acceptance at local fairs and in numerous commercial and domestic settings. More than at any previous time since the establishment of New Town in the 1880s, the arts at all levels were an integral part of the life of Albuquerque.

In the face of the almost all-embracing set of fundamental changes that had taken place in the metropolitan area and in the world outside between 1945 and 1972, perhaps one should be cautious about overstating the extent of the transformation. Many of the same people populated the city throughout the period. Such preoccupations as making money, looking forward to the weekend, improving one's lot, worrying about taxes and electing better politicians to public office were commonplace during both times, although their form and intensity shifted perceptibly. The huge blue sky, the sharp peaks of the Sandia Mountains and the broad shallow ribbon of the Rio Grande continued to enchant the residents. Nevertheless, there was no denying that the overall pattern of human existence had been significantly altered—slightly for some people, dramatically for others, irreversibly for all. On Saturday morning, April 8, 1972, an event took place that few would have conceived of in earlier years. Hot air balloons from all across the country were gathered together at Coronado Center for a balloon festival sponsored by Radio and Television Station KOB.[1317] Approximately twenty thousand persons, many times more than were attending the Brotherhood Awareness conference being held the same weekend, were on hand to watch the launchings.[1318] As the gas heaters fired noisily, the big, brightly colored and expensive balloons soared aloft, their lucky passengers waving to the crowds below. And later that morning, people all over Albuquerque gazed up to see the sky gaily decorated with the distant globular objects drifting through the light breeze like weightless Japanese lanterns.

6

THE TRANSFORMATION IN THE MIND

The flourishing of the arts, the sports boom, the growing variety of activities around the metropolitan area to appeal to almost every taste and whim—these were only the most obvious manifestations of the sweeping changes that had been taking place in the thought, psychology and culture of the people. The profound shifts which took place in the economic and social realms in Albuquerque between 1945 and 1972 brought about a transformation of the mental set of the society on a similar scale. By the early 1970s many of the people's concerns were quite different from what they had been at the close of World War II, and even matters which had changed little were often perceived differently.

Most of the changes in thought and perception were due to three broad phenomena highlighted in this historical account. The first is the displacement of individualistic competition by cooperation and orientation toward large groups. We have seen how this shift, which originated in the economic sphere, affected the overall structure of human relationships and of social organizations and how it even made a substantial impact on the physical appearance of the landscape. It was also responsible for the growing tendency for persons to relate to life around them in terms of groups and large systems rather than in terms of isolated individuals and concerns. It had a substantial bearing on the way they were coming to regard themselves—not so much as personalities important in their own right, more as significant components of larger social organisms.

Second, the general relaxation and dispersal of authority throughout the society—caused chiefly by the rising level of affluence and the declining motivation to strive onward toward even higher levels of material living—had a widespread influence. At the same time that the leaders were being forced to share more of their power with their subordinates and that behavior was growing less formal and more spontaneous, the mental set shared by most of the population was shifting in a similar direction. People's opinions were growing less susceptible to influence by high authorities; high culture was becoming less exalted. And there was an increasing tendency for thought to be more concerned with the tangible, the here and now, the earthly, rather than to dwell in the realm of the ideal and transcendent.

The third important phenomenon affecting the people's minds and attitudes was the twenty-to-twenty-two-year cycle moving from a period of turbulence and adventurousness to one of relative calm and consolidation and then back again. The underlying cause of this recurring cycle lies outside the scope of this book; nevertheless, because it seems to influence many of the same aspects of human life as the other two broad shifts, it is important to recognize its presence. During the turbulent phases—roughly the 1940s and the 1960s on into around the middle of 1971—the people were particularly eager to challenge established authority and to venture down untried paths; these were the times when the limits of permissiveness expanded the most and when the most visible and dramatic changes took place. In contrast, the quieter phases—the 1950s and the 1970s after the first year or so—were characterized by more harmony and respect for tradition. It was during these years that the people exhibited the most concern for security; many undramatic yet significant strides toward looking after the needs of the people were then taken. The mental activity of the society was similarly influenced by these periodic fluctuations. The 1940s and 1960s were times of high drama. Particularly in the latter period intellectual and artistic experimentation was rife; new breakthroughs, real or apparent, were common. The quieter periods, on the other hand, were less sensational and more hospitable to traditional forms. These were the times, by and large, when the previous bold experiments were picked through and either absorbed into the cultural mainstream or pushed underground. But regardless of which part of the historical cycle the people might happen to be in at a particular time, the broad one-directional transformation of society and culture continued to take place. The speed of the changes might vary, certain fashions might rise and fall and then rise again, persons might assume the roles of revolutionaries one year and a few years later become staunch pillars of the community, yet important fundamental changes in the behavior and the thought of the society would be only superficially affected.

The overall effects of these three phenomena on the people's minds frequently overlapped, and it is not always easy to determine which general cause underlay which specific change. The superimposition of the cyclical fluctuations on the one-directional shifts was largely responsible for the dramatic explosion of artistic and intellectual adventurousness of the 1960s and the beginning of the 1970s. Before and after this period, the changes were relatively muted, and in a few ways they seemed to move in a counter direction. Only through comparison with the surrounding years can one roughly estimate how much of the mental shifts of these years was due to the cyclical effects and how much to the other two phenomena—the displacement of individualistic competition by group orientation and the relaxation of authority. These two, as indicated in the first chapter, were somewhat interrelated from the start. Both had been ultimately caused by the ongoing quest for material betterment: large groups had been formed partly because they could better deliver goods, and the eventual attainment of a fairly high level of living had led to the easing of authority and discipline. And the fact that the large groups could provide their members with increased security had further allowed these members to relax their striving. Consequently, it should not be surprising that some of the impacts of these two phenomena should blend together.

The most obvious of the changes in the mental set were in the area of values. During the years around 1955 and earlier, most of the people put a premium on assertiveness, competitiveness, ruggedness and pride. Examination of the classified section of the 1945 Albuquerque telephone directory reveals that approximately 50 percent of the businesses listed were named after persons; the proportion in the 1972 directory was about 40 percent. As we have seen, persons who were determined to stamp their imprints on their environment and to leave their name wherever they could—such individuals as Clyde Tingley, Chester T. French, Sam Hoffman, Ed Snow and Dale Bellamah—were more common early in the period under study than later. Representative advertisements from the years during and immediately after World War II illustrate this flavor of assertive pride: "Finest of the Famous Silver Streaks" (1945 Pontiac);[1319] "First in Fudge" (Welch's candy bar of that year);[1320] "The Latest Greatest Scripto Pencil!" (a mechanical pencil of the time);[1321] "Nothing So Satisfies Your Desire for Superb Style and Pride of Ownership . . . As Pieces in . . . Quaint French Provincial" (furniture);[1322] and, five years later, "Today we will dedicate to God our $600,000 church plant, complete in every respect, the largest in the Southwest" (First Baptist Church at Central and Broadway).[1323] The movies of these years and the way they were merchandised exhibited this same spirit: "Most Tempestuous and Forbidden of the World's Great Love Stories" (*David and Bathsheba*, 1951);[1324] "The Mightiest Adventure of Them All" (*African Queen*, 1952);[1325] "The giant adventure of all time!" (*The Big Sky*, 1952);[1326] "The story of a man who was too proud to run!" (*High Noon*, 1952).[1327]

In contrast, the tone characteristic of popular culture in the late sixties and early seventies, though frequently flamboyant in its own way, was relatively unforceful and unassertive. The advertisements used fewer capital letters, fewer exclamation marks and fewer contrasting styles of lettering, and their claims were much more low-keyed. Consumer goods were presented in attractive lights rather than aggressively pushed: "A little powder sure does a lot for an underarm spray" (Arrid Extra Dry deodorant);[1328] "Introducing the Toyota Carina... It might be new to you but we've been living with it for a long time" (automobile);[1329] "Ed Wait bought York central air conditioning because we told him it was quiet. You can call him and find out if it really is."[1330]—all from 1972. Many of the movies concerned subjects similar to those common earlier, but they were promoted in a different vein. In 1971 *McCabe & Mrs. Miller* was advertised as "The story of a gambling man and a hustling lady and the empire they fashioned from the wilderness";[1331] *Ryan's Daughter* was billed simply as "A story of love . . . ."[1332] Two of the most successful films of 1972, *The Godfather* and *The Last Picture Show*, were advertised without any claims about their subjects whatsoever.

A similar shift took place in the personal worlds which the individual members of the society were building around themselves. Aggressively acquisitive, the people of the 1940s and 1950s sought out possessions which reinforced their self-images. In their minds, large size and impressive appearance were closely associated with quality. The typical new car and new house were almost always bigger and showier than last year's models. But sometime in the early sixties the trend began to shift. Numerous persons who could afford to do otherwise opted to buy small, utilitarian foreign cars such as Volkswagens, Datsuns and Toyotas. This tendency was especially pronounced among members of the university communities, who in many other respects comprised the leading edge of the transformation taking place. And more and more people were choosing to live in apartments—this in spite of the widespread high level of affluence. By the early seventies the phrase "Small is beautiful" was frequently heard.

Throughout the years, when the people looked beyond the worlds of their personal possessions and families and friends on outward to the larger political communities, their values influenced what they saw and how they reacted to their perceptions. The residents of Albuquerque, by and large, thought highly of their city, and they continually tried to improve upon it, but their attitudes and efforts underwent significant changes. Early in the period, they were eager to demonstrate their immense pride for the city; sometimes it seemed that they regarded it as the most outstanding municipality in the number-one country in creation. In 1948 newspaper advertisements heralded the world premiere of the motion picture *Albuquerque*: "Blazing Guns Made History Each Day . . . And Warm Lips Made Memories at Night in Albuquerque . . . The Glory Town of Nature's Spectacular Southwest."[1333] Stars Randolph Scott and Catherine Craig were on hand for the festivities, and the Kimo and Sunshine Theaters drew huge crowds.[1334] In 1951 the Chamber of Commerce sponsored a contest for the best slogan for the city; the winning entry was "Albuquerque—Land of Mañana—Wonderland of Today."[1335] The *Albuquerque Journal* featured story after story about Janet Latsha, who came to town in 1949 at the age of six apparently dying of asthma and then recovered under the influence of the salubrious climate. Declared her mother, also an asthma sufferer, "Albuquerque will be our home from now on. This must be what heaven is like."[1336]

The migration of outsiders like the Latshas to the metropolitan area was a prime source of the residents' pride, for this movement not only certified Albuquerque's attractiveness but also made it bigger. A number of *Journal* editorials during the forties and fifties congratulated the city for its headlong growth. Sometimes they compared Albuquerque favorably with other rapidly growing areas, as in a 1948 item "In Pace with El Paso."[1337] (In a similar vein of urban rivalry, an editorial in 1953, "Will We Be Outdone?" chastised the city for falling behind Santa Fe in the race to build a civic auditorium.[1338]) There was a general feeling of disappointment when the 1950 census figures revealed that the population within the city limits had not reached 100,000. Most of the time, however, the population figures brought forth exultation. A 1958 editorial marveled, "We who have been here for some time have difficulty in keeping on top of our capabilities and our potential. The outsiders see the picture and come swarming into our midst. We live in a miracle city with many of us not realizing the magnitude of the miracle."[1339] And when the 1960 census figures showed that the population exceeded 200,000, there was more rejoicing.[1340]

But shortly thereafter the tenor of public opinion began to alter. A newspaper article written in 1962 by City Manager Edmund Engel was titled "Doubling of Population, Physical Growth of City Brought Many Problems."[1341] A 1968 editorial, "Frightening Picture," worried about a recent study predicting that in the year 2000 Bernalillo County would contain nearly 1,000,000 people and 700,000 passenger cars.[1342] The growing concern over congestion, crime, pollution and damage to the environment was making many citizens question their traditional assumptions about the advantages of growth. Regulation of urban growth was an important issue in the 1971 City Commission campaign; none of the front-running candidates favored headlong expansion. After a relative lull during the sixties, the population again rapidly increased in the early seventies, but more residents seemed to worry about the growth than to brag about it.[1343]

As the preoccupation with assertiveness, competition, growth, bigness and related values became muted on every level, other values gained prominence. Out of the struggles of businessmen to pull together to save the downtown, of politicians and citizens to help the poor and protect the environment, of ethnic minorities and young people to relate to the larger society, and of myriads of other groups locally and nationally to cope with problems in their increasingly interrelated worlds came greater emphasis on cooperation, succor and concern for the group. In 1969 an editorial in the *Albuquerque Journal* exhorted the citizens to help their neighbors to the north support the Santa Fe Opera.[1344] One of the most popular songs of 1972 was Bill Withers' "Lean on Me," asking the listener to "Lean on me when you're not strong, / And I'll be your friend, / I'll help you carry on, / For it won't be long / Till I'm gonna need / Somebody to lean on."[1345] The runaway best-selling novel of the year was *Jonathan Livingston Seagull* by Richard Bach, about a gull which struck out on its own to learn to fly better than any of its kind had done before and then returned to its home flock to lead its fellow gulls to the heights it had attained.[1346]

The broad shift from individual assertiveness to concern for the group involved not only the behavior and values of the people but their basic perceptions as well. In politics, in business, in virtually all spheres of human endeavor, the leaders came to be seen less as powerful individuals who could bend circumstances through the force of their will and more as persons who, like their slightly less impressive fellow human beings, were often dependent upon influences beyond their control. Fewer people turned to the words of the famous for guidance in their everyday lives; more followed the advice and example of their peers. News stories celebrating the colorful eccentricities of such personages as Clyde Tingley gave way to discussions of the backgrounds of issues and surveys of public sentiment. In the movies and on the stage, the acting styles became more subdued and understated. The star system underwent a decline. Critics wrote about and sometimes despaired over the death of the hero. The lessening prominence of the hero and the standout personality in general, however, was due as much to changes in the way the people around him perceived his relationship to other people and events as it was to changes in the big man himself.

On a still more fundamental level, the changes in the way the individual came to be viewed affected not just the most outstanding members of society and the leading fictional characters but practically everyone. In the days when the economic system was largely geared to individualistic competition, the social and cultural focus was on the individual—on his uniqueness, his strength, his colorfulness, his intrinsic worth. If he was to strive vigorously on a lonely and often frightening course, he needed all the support he could get; society furnished much of this support by glorifying his life and his endeavors. If he was to concentrate his attention on his goals, with perhaps the comradeship of single special lifelong mate, he needed compensation for all the spontaneous emotional and sensual gratification he was having to forego along the way. This compensation was available in the form of the heavy romanticism in which love and solitary adventure and enterprise were often bathed. In the perceptions and the fantasies of the people, their strenuous efforts comprised dramatic undertakings in which they, ordinary figures though they might be, played leading roles. But as the economic and social system came to depend more on group cooperation, the emphasis shifted. The old ways of looking at life began to seem overblown and melodramatic. Novels which had once been popular favorites became virtually unreadable to a growing segment of the public. Popular culture came to celebrate persons who were less preoccupied with their own unique personalities. The emotional color of the culture was no longer concentrated in the traditional type of romanticism but was dispersed among the wide variety of possibilities for artistic, social and sensual delight readily at hand.

The shift from the romantic glorification of the individual is readily apparent from a brief look at the popular culture. The national best-selling novel and the most popular book at the Albuquerque Public Library in 1945 was Kathleen Winsor's *Forever Amber*, about a beautiful woman in Restoration England who led a strenuously passionate life as she went through a succession of lovers including the king himself.[1347] Although she manifestly preferred the company of her first lover, who rejected her because of her lowborn status, many readers found her morals wicked and irresponsible, but her courage and her self-reliance, as well as the suffering which her escapades and the vicissitudes of fortune inflicted upon her, won her a sympathetic place in the hearts of the reading public. More in the mainstream of the attitudes of the times were words from the popular song "The More I See You": "There is nothing that I wouldn't do / For the rare delight of the sight of you . . . . / I know the only one for me can only be you."[1348] The exaltation of love and adventure and the tension between the pure ideal and the temptations to stray are apparent in many of the movies of the years following the Second World War, some of which resemble moral exempla about the conflict between good and evil. Cinema advertisements usually emphasized their passionate content—"Mean . . . Moody. . .Magnificent" (*The Outlaw*, 1947);[1349] "Raw Adventuromance of . . . Passionate Love . . . Burning Vengeance!" (*Angel and the Badman*, 1947);[1350] "Love That Was Like an Explosive Weapon . . . and Then the Gun in Her Hand Went Off!" (*The Possessed*, 1947);[1351] "Everytime He Touched Me . . . My Heart Stood Still!" (*My Foolish Heart*, 1950);[1352]—yet almost nothing in the way of explicit sex was presented on the screen. As the people gradually came to channel their energies and impulses less forcefully and as the sexual revolution got more underway, however, the focus on individual adventure, heroism and romance grew less intense. Love became less idealized and more simply a matter of two people finding a measure of happiness and satisfaction in one another's company. The rampant energy of the sixties brought forth few highly charged dramas about individuals but numerous iconoclastic works that mocked old attitudes and old forms alike. And when the mood of the society turned inward again in the early seventies, it did so in a way that would have seemed alien to the people of twenty or thirty years earlier. The popular 1970 movie *Love Story* was touted as a return to romance, but the presentation of sex and the language were much earthier and more graphic than anything in *Forever Amber*. The highly acclaimed and unconventional *Sunday Bloody Sunday*, which played in Albuquerque theaters in 1972, was billed simply as "The emotional ups and downs of two people trapped in the throes of a love affair."[1353]

The ways the people perceived the day-to-day events going on around them underwent a similar alteration. Early in the period the newspapers devoted abundant coverage to lively and dramatic human interest stories—about the antics of the politicians, the successes of the businessmen, the pranks of the young and a multitude of other varieties of striking incidents involving particular persons in particular circumstances. Vivid details and memorable quotations were highlighted, whether the subject was a high official like Clyde Tingley or a young girl like Janet Latsha. In 1947, for example, the *Albuquerque Journal* recounted on page one the episode of a sixteen-year-old girl who disappeared a few hours before her scheduled wedding and resurfaced the next day in the custody of the Dallas police, records now showing that she was already married to a man in a nearby county.[1354] When a cab driver was apprehended for the murder of the wife of a soldier stationed at Sandia Base in 1950, the *Journal* reported his words, "I shot her because I loved her," a line that might have come from a popular story of the time.[1355] Such stories in the papers, over the radio and on the lips of the citizens were all part of the rich, person-centered cultural fabric of the time. But as groups became more important and individuals less so and as impersonal forces and considerations came to loom larger, interest in anecdotal detail waned. People wanted to get the big picture and an overall feel for what was happening without being distracted by random vignettes, and so they became no longer so attuned to individual drama.

Related to the decline in the romantic glorification of the individual and his striving and also connected to the overall loosening of authority was another broad shift—the changing of the nature of aspiration and its effects on the culture. During the time before the transformation was very much underway, the abstract notion of perfection was important to the people; it was an ideal toward which to aspire. An advertisement in 1945 went, "Here's How to Put Your Clothing Dollar on a Sure Thing! Sure—Because You Get • Perfect Tailoring • Latest Styling."[1356] In his inaugural address of the same year, President Franklin D. Roosevelt declared, "We shall strive for perfection.

We shall not achieve it immediately—but we shall still strive." Two paragraphs later he noted, "Our Constitution of 1787 was not a perfect instrument; it is not perfect yet."[1357] Although all realized that perfection was not actually attainable, they felt it was a worthwhile target to aim at, like trying to make civilization a utopia or love pure and spiritual.

The esteem in which lofty notions were held permeated the culture. As we have seen, the visual art, music and theater which were most admired were high and not of the masses. Language was frequently vivid and colorful, but the best speakers tended to eschew vulgar terms and to cultivate elegance. The popular songs which expressed serious feeling generally used images which were meant to inspire the listener rather than make him feel their tangible presence. Typical are lines from 1945's "Till the End of Time": "Long as roses bloom in May / My love for you will grow deeper with every passing day. / Till the wells run dry / And each mountain disappears, / I'll be there for you, to care for you through laughter and through tears. . . ."[1358] If the people were bothered by the gap between their noble aspirations and the reality of their daily lives, they simply strived all the harder.

Over the passing years, however, cultural expression became less lofty and idealized. In 1970 Victor Emert, a former heroin addict, decorated the chapel at the University of Albuquerque with such humble materials as a horseshoe for the omega in "AΩ," the iron tip of a plow for part of "Swords into Plowshares," and a calf's muzzle fashioned into a crown of thorns. He explained, "The idea of redemption, as Christ came to save the worthless of the Earth and showed that by putting things to the right purpose they become beautiful, has a very special meaning for me. You see, I, too, came back from the wilderness and was saved by divine guidance."[1359] At about the same time William Reinicke, a policeman, was fashioning a four-foot-tall replica of former Police Chief Paul Shaver's badge to be displayed in the new departmental headquarters.[1360] Probably more noticeable to most of the people than such changes in visual art was the fact that language was becoming more down to earth. The controversy surrounding Lenore Kandel's "Love-Lust Poem" may have been the most spectacular local manifestation of this shift, but there were thousands of less dramatic indications. One of the most popular songs of 1972, "The First Time Ever I Saw Your Face" sung by Roberta Flack, contains the lines "The first time ever I lay with you / I felt your heart so close to mine / And I knew our joy would fill the earth . . . ."[1361] Most listeners were much more moved by the emotional content than they were shocked by the mention of sexual relations. The use of fairly explicit language, in fact, better enabled them to be caught up in the mood of the piece. Most songs employed more abundant and more concrete imagery than in the past—"Don't fly, Mr. Bluebird, I'm just walking down the road, / Early morning sunshine tells me all I need to know" from "Blue Sky" by the Allman Brothers Band[1362]—for the aim was more to intensify the everyday feelings of the audience than to inspire it to great heights. The whole society had shifted its sights toward the portion of life that was tangible, immediate and accessible.

Aspiration and transcendence did not disappear from the culture, but they became more muted and diffuse. By the early seventies striving for perfection was almost unheard of, and few thought anymore in terms of loving someone "till the wells run dry and each mountain disappears." Nevertheless, such matters as love, comradeship and religion were still sources of inspiration. The transcendent peaks were not so rarefied and tightly focused as before; they were more likely to incorporate feeling and sensation. Persons cultivated heightened awareness of the world around them and their place in it. Education and religion put more emphasis on one's experience of an immediate situation and less on abstract principles and goals. Jonathan Livingston Seagull led his winged companions soaring not toward the good but in quest of a state of being that wedded physical sensation, grace and achievement.

Meanwhile, in their day to day lives, people were relating to more and more institutions, organizations and other groups, some of which overlapped one another. As a result, the old boundary lines became less rigid and distinct. Traditional compartmentalizations of spheres of human knowledge, life, and experience also began to break down. We have seen how education opened up, with more outsiders becoming involved in the teaching and learning process, with vocational training making the schools and the work places more interdependent, with the schools becoming heavily involved in aspects of the War on Poverty, and with the increased emphasis on combining abstract knowledge and personal experience. In a similar fashion, health care professionals came to work more hand in hand with social welfare workers. Persons with vastly different experiences and expertises worked together to implement huge projects that might take years to complete. In the political arena expert knowledge, strongly held values, passionate opinions and special interests came together to hammer out compromise solutions. All aspects of the society were becoming more interrelated, organized and integrated.

At the same time that the movement from one type of knowledge, experience, state of mind or place to another was becoming less abrupt and more fluid, the physical appearance of Albuquerque was changing. As seen in the second chapter, the residents of Albuquerque in the years around 1945 showed a marked preference for rectilinear forms. Most of the streets, especially in the older sections, intersected in a grid pattern, and the majority of the big downtown buildings approximated sturdy rectangular solids. This proclivity for boxes, right angles and straight lines permeated the words and behavior of the people. Chester T. French demonstrated it in the opening lines of his creed: "Four major thoughts I would leave with you, to help you build a rich, full and rewarding life. Four sides you should have in your building to make it stand firm and four square." The terms "square" and "straight" were often used to indicate honesty and forthrightness. Persons were expected to stand erect with square shoulders; a square jaw was a mark of character.

Over the ensuing decades, however, the sturdy rectangular shapes were displaced more and more by diagonals, curved lines and free forms. As organizations and structures grew larger, right angles and boxes grew more cumbersome; the need grew for a smoother, more organic flow to and from the central focus. Hence arose such shapes as the interstate highways with their curved ramps and buildings in which relatively subordinate spaces radiated out from the center. To get onto one of the big interstate highways, a driver did not wait at a stop sign or traffic light for the opportunity to go forward; rather he turned into a curved ramp on which he could pick up speed at just the right rate in order to merge into the traffic. Some pedestrian traffic began to function in a related fashion. New sidewalks for the campus of the University of New Mexico, which in 1972 had been designed but not yet constructed, were gradually curved and grew wider or narrower in order to accommodate the organic flow of persons hurrying to class or strolling casually about. Furthermore, as society grew more relaxed and permissive, the discipline of straight lines and right angles gave more way to the spontaneity that could be expressed in deviations from the traditional norm. New streets and structures, especially those constructed in the least formal sections of the metropolitan area, went up in freer and more varied shapes. And among the young people of the sixties and early seventies, rebelling against the restrictions imposed by their elders, "straight" and "square" were epithets of derision.

As the components of society and of life itself became less isolatable, persons directed their attention more to whole systems. Statistical methods, which were used to survey systematically large bodies of data, became more widely used in almost all fields of knowledge. Politicians relied less heavily on dazzling rhetoric and paid greater attention to polls of their constituents' views on personalities, images and issues. Other types of systems approaches also grew in popularity. To cope with the complexities of large organizations and massive projects, managers and consultants devised elaborate flow charts designating how the multitude of requisite tasks was to be performed. Even areas which had once been largely the province of individual imagination, such as architecture and movie making, became pervaded by systematic thinking. Specific details were not so important as they once had been; instead, the emphasis was on the big picture, the overall shape, the gestalt.

Even though life as it was experienced and perceived was becoming a little more fluid and continuous, a bit less characterized by abrupt changes, hard edges and rigid rectilinearity, in some respects the increasing organization of society led to more standardization and regimentation. In order for large numbers of people to interact smoothly with one another, they had to conform to a greater degree than previously to certain standardized roles and expectations, at least in their public life; no longer could they rely so much on the force of their personalities to get them what they wanted. Large bureaucracies required their employees to function according to specific job descriptions so that tasks would be accomplished in systematic and predictable fashions. The high degree of interdependence among the members of society made communication all the more important; the need to facilitate the easy flow of unambiguous information led to language becoming more conventionalized and data being coded according to standard forms. To cite just one example out of many, in 1963 the United States Post Office instituted the use of ZIP codes to designate specific geographical areas for addresses on letters.[1363] Such regimentation bothered many of the citizens, for not only did these trends run counter to traditional notions of individual freedom, they also seemed to conflict with the spontaneity and permissiveness which were becoming more widespread. In practice, however, the conflicts could usually be at least partially resolved. The actual functioning of the large bureaucracies was generally more fluid and the lines of authority less rigid than the official flow charts seemed to imply. A data processor might wear informal attire and function with a high degree of independence so long as he got his job done. An architect might utilize standardized prefabricated materials and modular design units, but he could still make each apartment or office unit a little different and his overall design unique.

The single tool that helped the people the most to implement the standardization necessary for the smooth and efficient functioning of large systems was the digital computer, and over the years since World War II this instrument was rapidly developed and its applications widely expanded. Simple in concept, its entire operation was generally based on the binary system of numbers; depending on which digit came up, the answer for each step of an operation was either yes or no. Yet a large computer could handle extremely complex operations consisting of hundreds or thousands of steps. It could be programmed to make adjustments for feedback; that is, it could perform different operations on the data according to whether intermediate answers met certain pre-established criteria. As a result of extensive improvements in computer technology, by the late sixties and early seventies instruments with dazzling speed, enormous storage capacity and the capability to carry out a wide array of operations were becoming commonplace. Unaffected by such human characteristics as feeling, imagination, aversion to tedium and susceptibility to frustration, the computers ground out answers to the most intricate quantifiable problems with the clarity and precision of a baseball umpire shouting "Safe" or "Out."

Based on mathematical logic as they were, computers were speedily accepted as powerful tools at such centers of scientific research as Sandia Corporation, but it was not long before they were utilized in operations more directly affecting large numbers of people. In 1958 a computer system was installed to regulate the water system for the City of Albuquerque;[1364] the next year many of the traffic lights were put under computer control.[1365] In subsequent years the devices were adapted to handle still more complicated matters. The City Data Processing Department began utilizing a computer in 1969 to determine which traffic intersections were the most likely to be the scenes of accidents; these trouble spots were given heavier police patrol.[1366] It was in the area of data processing and information storage that some of the greatest strides were made in computer technology. Each letter of a word could be punched into a memory bank where it was stored as a number, each word therefore became a unique sequence of digits, and any report so stored containing a given word or group of words could be retrieved electronically much faster and more efficiently than by any other method. Police, doctors, scientists, librarians and many other persons who might need access to a wide range of information began to avail themselves of computerized data. Data banks covering almost every imaginable subject abounded, and the fledgling information industry grew like wildfire. In 1971 Bernalillo County committed itself to buying a computer system large enough to handle the data processing needs of every county in the state.[1367] By the end of the next year the computer terminals at the Technology Application Center, one of the divisions of the University of New Mexico's Institute for Social Research and Development, had the capacity to retrieve more than two million documents including photographs transmitted digitally from satellites orbiting the earth.[1368]

As a result of the increased importance of communication and transmission of information, one might expect language to become more highly developed. Indeed, the addition of thousands of specialized terms swelled the vocabulary of the society taken as a whole. Numerous dictionaries and glossaries of words necessary to particular disciplines and areas were compiled, and unabridged general purpose dictionaries became longer. Nevertheless, the working vocabularies of most of the individuals shrank. The growing interdependence of the members of society had led to greater specialization of function, and single persons no longer had to be concerned with as wide a range of activity, verbal or otherwise, as before. Furthermore, since one of the main uses of words is to exert influence over other people in order to get one's way, the reduced impetus toward striving had tended to make people less verbal. A related consideration is the fact that words are a highly conventionalized, very deliberate and conscious medium of expression. A person learns to talk and write through years of training; like striving after a distant goal, elaborate verbal communication requires tight focusing of one's attention; careful speech and composition are not especially spontaneous. As the people grew more relaxed and more ready to give vent to their impulses, they came to disperse their expressiveness more widely—in physical gestures, in music, in visual art, in mixed art forms and in an expanding range of other behavior and media.

Signs of the declining orientation toward words can be found throughout the culture. The first edition of the best-selling novel of 1945, *Forever Amber*, was 972 pages long; *Jonathan Livingston Seagull*, its 1972 counterpart, contained only 93 pages, nearly half of them consisting of photographs. Paragraphs were shorter. The Sunday magazine section of the *Albuquerque Journal* included several short stories each week of 1945. Over the years this feature was dropped. The movies of the forties sparkled with bright, snappy dialog, but verbal wit in the cinema declined notably with time. In one of the most outstanding films of 1968, *2001: A Space Odyssey*, the dazzling visual effects contrasted sharply with the meager words of the characters. The speech of the young people, once a lively spawning ground for imaginative new additions to the language, became vaguer and less varied, more dependent on nonverbal signals. Writing in 1963, a local journalist noted, "Many . . . nuances are indicated only by the inflection of voice, or by a shrug of the shoulders, which accompany the slang expression itself. It is therefore difficult, even for the teenagers, to supply adequate definitions for the slang they speak."[1369] Even the advertisements changed in this same general direction, with grammatically complete sentences being displaced more by clusters of words and with more of the space being taken up by pictures and visual design. Libraries continued to be popular public institutions, but their holdings diversified to include a greater proportion of phonograph records, prints, slides and other types of nonverbal media. Between 1950 and 1970 the proportion of the work force in Bernalillo County employed in printing, publishing and allied industries dropped slightly, from 1.02 percent to 0.93 percent; over the same period the percentage working in radio broadcasting and television rose from 0.18 to 0.31.[1370] It seemed that the enthusiasm for language which had enlivened Western culture since the onset of the Renaissance was being dampened.

Of as great a significance as the declining interest in words and in their elaborate manipulation were shifts in the ways they were used. During the years up through the Second World War, the typical vocabularies of the people, especially the educated ones, included an abundance of words which were approximate synonyms but which could be employed to differentiate fine shadings of meaning. "Russet," for example, did not exactly mean "brown," nor "pusillanimous" "cowardly," nor "in fine fettle" "in good condition." Each term and phrase had its own precise definition, connotation and degree of decorum, and one could learn the distinctions only through careful attention and experience. Similarly, such grammatical niceties as the difference between the subjunctive mood and the indicative were fairly widely observed, and public speakers were well equipped with arsenals of rhetorical devices and flourishes to give their messages more impact. Even the relatively uneducated members of society had impressive verbal facility; often they could make up with the vividness of their language what they lacked in elegance. The elaborate and sometimes idiosyncratic vocabulary and syntax of the times well suited the people's needs. They could dexterously use the language to create individual and personal worlds around themselves, and if they were sufficiently skilled and forceful, they could impose their visions on others. Through the medium of words, they could imbue their actions and dreams with color and high excitement.

As individualism grew less pronounced in the society, as emotions came more to be expressed nonverbally, and as the rising degree of organization led to the need for easy and unambiguous flow of information, however, language centered around fine distinctions of personal perception lost much of its function. For the vast majority of the people, verbal communication became less colorful and less highly developed, yet it did take on certain new capabilities.

Reflecting the increasing organization of society, language became more standardized. The number of root words commonly used shrunk, and those remaining became the core of a large proportion of the communication. Prefixes and suffixes with more or less fixed meanings were frequently appended to the root words; in this manner a given term could be transformed in systematic fashions with a minimum of confusion. In a number of cases, a word which had traditionally been assigned one part of speech would be used as another. Thus "contact" and later "parent," both originally nouns, became verbs as well. As a result of these kinds of simplification and standardization of the vocabulary, speech and writing became less varied and less vivid, yet fairly complicated and precise structures of communication could be erected. Business executives, bureaucrats and information managers could keep abreast of what was going on in their organizations and in the world outside, and they could exert a measure of control over the formal structures of society.

In ordinary discourse, where verbal precision was not particularly necessary, people tended to shy away from complex linguistic transformations involving strings of prefixes and suffixes, but the same general tendency toward uniformity of usage was underway. The meanings of many words, especially slang terms, became stretched to such an extent that they could be used in a wide variety of vaguely similar circumstances. As the people grew less concerned with precision, the connotations, the associations and the general feel of a word became more important. Talking and writing like one's comrades made a person feel more like a member of a group and less isolated. This tendency toward uniformity of language within a group was particularly pronounced among the ethnic minorities, the young people, and other segments of the population with a self-conscious identity, but it was also increasingly characteristic of society at large.

Paralleling the development of the formal lines of information flow and bureaucratic control made possible by the rise of a standardized impersonal vocabulary was the emergence of a variety of loose and informal verbal structures, ones which were felt rather than objectively perceived. One could say that as the skeletal structure of communication grew, so did the heart and the flesh. Political speeches, for example, became looser. Orators no longer tried to impress their audiences with their verbal power, and they knew better than to bore the crowds with technical explications of their programs, which were likely to be more complicated than in the past. Instead, they were more likely to hit on a number of loosely related subjects important to the people, weaving themes, images and popular phrases into a presentation which might say little that was definite and specific but which would convey a general impression of the speaker's leanings, his personality and his vision of the world. Many other types of verbal constructs came to manifest this tendency toward evocativeness and loose association of images and of feelings. Advertisers concentrated more on creating moods for their products rather than making high claims. Magazine writers composed flowing pieces which seemed relatively unstructured but which presented assemblages of quotations, vignettes and other tidbits of information molded together to produce a more or less unified point of view. Adapting techniques developed by such innovative poets of years past as T.S. Eliot and Dylan Thomas, many writers of popular songs began to string together images which were as stirring as they were cryptic. Most of the young listeners did not try to analyze the surrealistic rush of images in the often crude but generally forceful and imaginative songs of Bob Dylan; but many of their generation adopted these pieces as their rallying cries. In 1972 one of the most popular of all songs was Don McLean's "American Pie," a lament for the lost innocence of young people and their music. Obscure references to a plane wreck in the 1950s in which three singers died, to other singing stars and musical events, and to a wide range of news items, feelings and experiences familiar to young people of the past decade and a half were run together. The refrain was a telescoping of such references, images and emotions into a tight, almost trite ditty: "So bye-bye, Miss American Pie / Drove my Chevy to the levee but the levee was dry. / Them good ole boys were drinkin' whiskey and rye / Singin' this'll be the day that I die, / This'll be the day that I die."[1371] Because the words could draw on such a broad expanse of shared associations in the memories of the listening audience, because their impact was due as much to the emotions they aroused as to their denotative meaning, and because they were fused together in a unified mood, this song and others like it won an enthusiastic response.

Such free-flowing verbal structures reflected slight yet fundamental shifts in the patterns of human activity. Instead of focusing so exclusively as in the past on whatever tasks they had on hand, people tended to be more easily diverted; their attention became more diffuse. Music filled the air at the grocery store, at the dentist's office, at many workplaces. Visual art came to enliven many a previously barren space and distract the passersby. Conversation became a little less purposeful and premeditated, a little more random and playful. Orientation to specific facts gave partial way to a general feel for the atmosphere. In the perceptions of many of the people, reality lost some of its precise boundaries and hard edges and became more continuous.

It was natural, then, that the looseness of form that was coming to characterize popular songs, magazine articles, advertisements, and speeches affected more substantial works of artistic creativity as well. Because art was no longer quite so separated from the rest of life and because virtually all areas of human endeavor were more interrelated than before, individual works did not have to stand so sturdily on their own. Artists and writers were able to express themselves more spontaneously, drawing on associations and techniques outside their disciplines to broaden their range.

Literary works showed less evidence of tight, deliberate construction. They were less likely than previously to have clear-cut beginnings, middles and ends. Instead of having a straightforward exposition of the background set before him, a reader might be thrust into the midst of the action and have to piece together from clues what was going on. The conclusion of a novel might be open ended, implying that what had taken place was just a preliminary to much more that might happen later. In between, the reader was likely to be treated to a meandering plot or combination of plots involving numerous characters of interest, some of whose predicaments were never resolved. And as less attention was focused on the central character or characters, character itself tended to become a less significant ingredient of the story. Setting, mood and uncontrollable circumstance grew in importance. To draw their audiences closer to feeling and experiencing the unfolding of the stories, authors relied less on traditional conventions and more on ungrammatical clusters of words, pictures and other nonliterary techniques which could elicit immediate and powerful responses.

Still more telling evidence of the increasing spontaneity of art was the remarkable growth of nonliterary expression. Music and the visual arts flourished, appealing more directly to the senses than printed books ever could. During the sixties and early seventies the citizens of Albuquerque embraced a wider variety of such culture, high and low, than ever before. In 1962 the first New Mexico Arts and Crafts Fair was held in Old Town;[1372] seven years later it was moved to considerably larger facilities at the state fairgrounds.[1373] Meanwhile, other crafts fairs were established, and the art section at the state fair boomed. In 1966 Popejoy Hall opened at the University of New Mexico,[1374] and it immediately became the most important outlet in the city for the performing arts. One year later Albuquerque got its first city museum.[1375] The residents flocked to take advantage of these and similar new facilities, and they showed their burgeoning appreciation for art and culture in many other ways as well. In the early sixties the enrollment in the College of Fine Arts at the University of New Mexico began rapidly rising; between 1966 and 1971 the number of art majors jumped 95 percent while the size of the student body as a whole went up only 50 percent.[1376] One of the most outstanding centers for lithography and print making in the country, the Tamarind Institute, came to the university in 1970.[1377] Students in the Albuquerque Public Schools also became more actively involved in art: special programs in art education were inaugurated and expanded,[1378] and some high school students embarked on film making projects.[1379] More persons availed themselves of opportunities outside of the usual educational channels to broaden their cultural horizons. In 1972 adults had twenty-one different noncredit courses in arts and crafts to choose among at the College of Continuing Education at the University of New Mexico,[1380] and children of various age groups could take Spanish dancing classes at the Model Cities Field Office.[1381] And outside the public institutions and away from the headlines the fascination with art and music surged vibrantly, with tens of thousands of people attending rock and classical concerts, with many more listening to music on their radios and phonographic equipment, with brilliant displays of graphic art adorning the shopping centers and murals bedecking the sides of many a building, with homes and apartments and offices being enlivened by more art objects, and with greater numbers of persons enthusiastically savoring the esthetic delights of everything from elegant jewelry to barbed wire.

As these varieties of art proliferated, their forms grew looser and freer. Illustrative art—including painting, print making, photography and commercial art—grew much more widespread. Museums and art galleries became more abundant; newspapers and magazines devoted increasing proportions of their space to pictures; commercial advertisements were more dominated by graphic art and photographs. And in each of these types of illustrations the composition became less tightly focused. In the 1940s and earlier the center of attention was prominently highlighted, usually in the foreground and near the middle of the piece. Bold verticals, horizontals, and occasionally diagonals for added dynamism were employed for dramatic emphasis. The boundaries were usually clearly defined; in the case of advertisements and magazine covers the borders often received special treatment. With the passage of time, however, much of the central focus and the stark drama dispersed. Composition became more expressive and adventurous and less obviously contrived. Greater use of color and other visual effects to delight the eye such as abstract design and varying photographic focus dazzled and diverted the onlookers. Line drawing declined,[1382] perhaps because interest in precise definition and delineation of subject matter was on the wane. On the other hand, photographs, which were less susceptible to complete control by the artist than other types of illustrations, grew more popular, and greater numbers of residents took up photography for pleasure. The involvement of more ordinary citizens in the production of visual art further contributed to the declining separation of art from the rest of life and to its relaxation of form.

Even abstract art, long the special province of the avant-garde, became more widespread in the metropolitan area. Dillard's, a lavish department store built in Winrock Center in 1972,[1383] had an abundance of gaily colored abstract and semi-abstract designs in some of its sections, and in 1971 the City of Albuquerque constructed in the Model Neighborhood Area Dennis Chavez Park,[1384] which included an amphitheater with free-form adobe shapes and upright wooden posts arranged in an irregular pattern in its midst. All art, including its least representational forms, was no longer set off so much from the rest of life but was being made part of the everyday experience of the mass of the population.

Parallel shifts were taking place in the world of music. Popular music of the 1940s adhered closely to traditional forms, staying with major or minor keys and generally emphasizing main melodic lines. With the exception of jazz, most pieces were tightly structured. But over the years music became more widely popular and formally looser. As serious composers had begun to do in the early years of the century, popular musicians experimented with new kinds of scales and with polyphonic techniques. More songs were written with irregular musical phrasing to accommodate verbal phrases that would not fit into uniform structures; in this way music became less predictable and more like spontaneous speech. And a greater variety of instruments and other producers of sound effects were employed to broaden the range and expressiveness of music and to stretch its form all the more.

The art forms in which large groups of people collaborated underwent similar changes. Particularly during the sixties and early seventies moving pictures and, to a less dramatic extent, television became looser and more adventurous. Like novels, movies came to be characterized by less tightly structured plots and less attention to the major characters. Often a viewer would have to spend the first several minutes trying to make sense of what was unfolding before him and to get immersed in the film. And like paintings and single photographs, movies were presenting more dazzling visual effects. Color was more widely used; the compositions of the individual frames tended to have less of a central focus; differential photographic focus and other techniques were used to induce the audiences to feel what was going on rather than perceive it from a detached point of view. More use was made of the moving camera, and the images were made to flow more smoothly from one to another. As plot and character became more diffuse, special effects became more highly developed and more important. And background did too: some directors, like Robert Altman in 1971's *McCabe & Mrs. Miller*, seemed to go out of their way to introduce indistinct fragmentary conversations and other peripheral elements to enrich the texture of their works.

Such remarkable cinematic innovations notwithstanding, most people were going to the movies less often than during the 1940s. Fewer films were being made, and those produced generally stayed longer at individual theaters.

For their entertainment, people were turning more and more to television, a less demanding medium. Turning on a television set was a far easier and less deliberate decision than travelling to a movie house; a television program did not rivet the attention of all the people in the room to the same extent as a movie on a big screen. Conversation, housecleaning, even school work could be underway while the set rumbled along in the background, and the frequent commercial interruptions seemed to encourage people's attentions to wander all the more. So even though television became the most communal of all cultural media, with millions of households across the country tuned simultaneously to the same shows, it also grew into one of the most diffuse, featuring loose sequences of vivid images, vignettes and fragments of information, opinion and feeling, and seldom building up to high drama or intellectually intricate constructs.

Even the most durable and slowest to change of the arts—architecture—manifested this diffusion of focus. The distinction between indoors and outdoors became less marked, as buildings were designed to blend in more harmoniously with other buildings and the landscape, as they were given more windows and skylights to let in more light and views of the outside, and as their occupants brought in more living plants. Similarly, the internal spaces were less likely to be discrete rooms set off by doors; instead, the floor plans became more open, and transitions were more often suggested by slight changes of levels, by half walls and screens, by shifts in color and decor.

Virtually all kinds of new structures had less of a formal central focus than their predecessors. Instead of highlighting a living room, where families used to spend a large portion of their time and to entertain most visitors, more homes came to give at least equal emphasis to a less formal family room, and kitchens were more closely integrated into the flow of traffic. Fewer public buildings were centered around elaborate entrances and impressive central spaces; more, like the Administration Building at the Southwestern Indian Polytechnic Institute, were constructed around hallways which gave almost equal access and importance to all parts. The typical design elements also became less formal and more spread out. Ornate decoration became rare, just as rhetorical flourishes had receded from writing and speech. No longer so concerned with making their materials look lofty and elaborate, architects turned more of their attention toward incorporating ordinary objects and surfaces into their overall design. Rough textures on walls and ceilings provided visual interest; mechanical service areas and equipment were often featured prominently instead of hidden; modular elements were employed to give a general sense of unity to a structure or group of structures. And as the focal unity of most new buildings became less concentrated, people gradually came to perceive them not so much as prominent edifices on the landscape, more as sequences of spatial experiences.

At the same time that the recognized art forms were growing more diffuse, more of the world outside seemed to be opening up to esthetic and sensual and even mystical delight. Although Albuquerque and most other metropolitan areas around the country were increasing in size, more people were becoming interested in nature and in making it an important part of their lives. In 1964 the Albuquerque Board of Realtors began holding annual landscaping contests.[1385] That same year the local Chamber of Commerce formed a Civic Beautification Committee, which worked actively to revive public interest in Arbor Week.[1386] More than fifteen hundred trees were planted during Arbor Week activities in 1966;[1387] in October of that year the Chamber of Commerce inaugurated a series of annual bus trips into the Sandia Mountains to look at the aspens in their brilliant autumn yellow.[1388] A few days later Modesto ash trees were planted at the county courthouse to commemorate the death of Chester T. French, who had been an avid horticulturist throughout most of his life.[1389] As public fervor for ecology and the environmental movement grew stronger over the following years, such events grew more numerous. Still more significant to most of the residents was what was going on in their homes and yards. Green lawns spread over once-barren mesa land; plant nurseries became big businesses as more and more citizens sought to enliven their yards with trees; housewives, students, even businessmen decorated their places with potted plants. That they were right to embrace nature was becoming an article of faith. Describing a new housing development he had just designed, Antoine Predock, one of the most influential young architects, declared in 1968:

> The concept of La Luz involves a basic attitude toward the land: An urban environment and large open natural areas should exist together, especially in New Mexico. Existing natural patterns should be recognized and reinforced, rather than eliminated. The delicate balance of plant and wild life need not be destroyed by development.[1390]

This "delicate balance," people were coming to feel, also included man. Through seeking out nonhuman forms of life, enjoying them and bringing them into their lives, the residents were enhancing their experience of the grand ebb and flow of what was going on around them. No longer so intent on controlling their worlds, they were participating enthusiastically in the largest of all living systems.

NOTES

Chapter 2

1. The statistics presented here are all necessarily approximate. In 1940 the Albuquerque population was 35,449; in 1950, 96,815. Since the biggest spurt of growth came after the conclusion of World War II, 50,000 seems a reasonable estimate. The population of Bernalillo County was 69,391 in 1940 and 145,673 in 1950, hence the estimate of 90,000. In the county as a whole in 1950, there were 43,729 Spanish-surnamed residents (30.0 percent of the total), 2,338 Indians (1.6 percent) and 1605 Blacks (1.1 percent). Although the classification "Spanish-surnamed" does not correspond precisely to an ethnic group as such, the number for that classification is close to the number who considered themselves Spanish-American. No census figures are available on the different ethnic groups in the area in 1940. But since the population growth of the decade of the 1950s consisted mainly of Anglos coming in, it is reasonable to assume that the trend began earlier and that the 1945 percentages for Spanish-Americans and Indians were larger than the 1950 percentages. U.S., Department of Commerce, Bureau of the Census, *Census of Population:1940*, vol. 2, *Characteristics of the Population*, pt. 4, Minnesota-New Mexico, p. 1019; idem, *County Data Book, 1947* (A Statistical Abstract Supplement), p. 264; idem, *Census of Population: 1950*, vol. 2, *Characteristics of the Population*, pt. 31, New Mexico, pp. 31-34, 31-58; ibid., vol. 4, *Special Reports*, pt. 3, chap. C, Persons of Spanish Surname, p. 30-53. For discussion of later proportions of ethnic groups in the area, see pp. 381-401. The figure for the area bounded by the city limits was likewise extrapolated. According to David Wing of the Albuquerque Community Development Office, the size of the city in 1946 was 11.61 square miles. Telephone conversation with David Wing, May 1, 1979. Very little annexation took place during the war years.
2. "Clyde Tingley, Ex-Governor of N.M., Dies," *Albuquerque Journal*, December 25, 1960, pp. A1, A16. Hereafter *Albuquerque Journal* is cited as *AJ*.
3. William A. Keleher, *Memoirs: 1892-1969, A New Mexico Item* (Santa Fe, N.M.: The Rydal Press, 1969), pp. 120-21. (New Edition, Santa Fe, N.M.: Sunstone Press, 2008), pp. 120-21.
4. "Tingley Remarks Added Color to N.M. Politics," *AJ*, December 25, 1960, p. A1.
5. Keleher, pp. 142-43.
6. "Clyde Tingley, Ex-Governor of N.M., Dies," *AJ*, December 25, 1960, pp. A1, A16.
7. "Husky Chinese Elms Offered Free for Digging, Tingley Says," *AJ*, March 12, 1945, p. 2.
8. "Evidence Goes to U.S. Attorney," *AJ*, January 5, 1945, p. 11.
9. "Tingley Calls Cities, Counties to Revive Municipal League," *AJ*, January 10, 1945, p. 5.
10. "Municipal League Seeks 'Home Rule' Liquor Measure," *AJ*, January 28, 1945, p. 1.
11. "Tingley to Quit Hospital Board," *AJ*, January 30, 1945, p. 2.
12. "White Replaces Tingley on Board," *AJ*, February 6, 1945, pp. 1, 2.
13. "County Board Backs Sanchez," *AJ*, February 6, 1945, p. 3.
14. "Municipal League Can't Use Public Funds Is Ruling," *AJ*, March 14, 1945, p. 1.
15. "Tingley Says Dempsey 'Steals' Policemen," *AJ*, October 25, 1945, p. 1.
16. "Dempsey Denies Tingley Charge," *AJ*, November 6, 1945, p. 1.

17. "Veteran Politician Is School Board Candidate," *AJ*, February 3, 1963, p. A12.

18. "Agrees with Tingley's Liquor License Stand," *AJ*, January 14, 1945, p. 5.

19. "Civil Service Bill for Albuquerque Passed by House," *AJ*, March 21, 1945, p. 1.

20. "'Make It for All' Is Tingley's Idea," *AJ*, March 22, 1945, p. 1.

21. "Snowball Throwers Warned by Tingley," *AJ*, July 4, 1945, p. 1.

22. "City Declares War on Culprits Killing Chinese Elms at Beach," *AJ*, July 27, 1945, p. 6.

23. Wayne S. Scott, "A Fighter, Senator Dennis Chavez Battled to Top Post," *AJ*, November 19, 1962, p. A2.

24. Ibid.

25. Gil Hinshaw, "Albert G. Simms Dislikes Attention Linked to Success," *AJ*, August 18, 1963, p. C1; "Albert G. Simms, One of Top N.M. Developers, Dies," *AJ*, December 30, 1964, p. A1.

26. "Pay Tribute to Mrs. Simms," *Albuquerque Tribune*, January 3, 1945, p. 3.

27. "John Simms Stricken by Fatal Heart Attack," *AJ*, February 12, 1954, p. 1.

28. "Writer-Historian Will Keleher Is Dead at 86 After Illness," *AJ*, December 19, 1972, pp. A1, A2.

29. "Keleher, Simms on Dinner Program," *AJ*, April 10, 1945, p. 3.

30. Clinton P. Anderson with Milton Viorst, *Outsider in the Senate, Senator Clinton Anderson's Memoirs* (New York: The World Publishing Company, 1970).

31. "Heart Attack Fatal to Clyde E. Oden, Prominent Citizen," *AJ*, May 12, l948, pp. 1, 2.

32. Bob Beier, "Veteran Chief Westerfeld Is Man Who Hates Fires," *AJ*, January 23, 1955, p. 31.

33. "Realtor Notes Change Since Board's Birth," *AJ*, May 23, 1971, p. E6.

34. "Santa Fe President Says Traffic to Hit Record During War on Japs," *AJ*, March 27, 1945, p. 2.

35. Abercrombie Holmes, "Fred Luthy's Victory over Calamity Symbol of Albuquerque Spirit," *AJ*, June 22, 1958, pp. 1, 11; "Fred Luthy Dies of Heart Attack," *AJ*, January 12, 1963, pp. A1, A5.

36. "Senior Partner of French-Fitzgerald Mortuary in Midst of Life at 77," *AJ*, February 1, 1959, p. 21; "Civic Leader C.T. French Dies at Home," *AJ*, September 28, 1966, pp. A1, A10.

37. Arthur N. Loveridge, *A Man Who Knew How to Live Among His Fellow Men, A Graphic Life Story of Chester T. French* (Boulder, Colo.: Old Trails Publishers, 1965), p. 91.

38. "Faith in Albuquerque Part of Cobbler's Success Story," *AJ*, August 12, 1951, p. 19.

39. "John Milne Dies of Heart Attack in California," *AJ*, September 6, 1956, p. 1.

40. William M, Hales, Jr., "Technological In-Migration and Curricular Change: Educational Politics in Albuquerque, 1945-1965" (Ph. D. dissertation, University of New Mexico, 1970), pp. 131-34.

41. "Harvard Man Will Head New Mexico University," *AJ*, June 8, 1995, p. 1.

42. "University Head and Family Here," *AJ*, August 9, 1945, p. 9.

43. "University Enrollment Is 1009, Includes Veterans of This War," *AJ*, March 7, 1945, p. 5.

44. "University Will Grow, Build New U.S. Culture, Says Dr. Wernette," *AJ*, August 30, 1945, p. 4.

45. "Mrs. Fergusson, Pioneer Resident, Dies Here at 85," *AJ*, September 4, 1950, pp. 1, 2.

46. "Erna Fergusson, Noted Writer, Dies," *AJ*, July 31, 1964, pp. Al, A6.

47. "Author Says U.S. Can Match Others in Illiteracy, Other Social Problems," *AJ*, May 18, 1945, p. 2.

48. "Mr., Mrs. O'Connor to Retire from Little Theatre," *AJ*, March 5, 1961, p. B3; "Mrs. O'Connor, Little Theatre Founder, Dies," *AJ*, November 17, 1965, pp. A1, A10.

49. "Legion to Aid Children Here," *Albuquerque Tribune*, March 6, 1945, p. 1.

50. "Theaters Join 'Dimes' Drive," *Albuquerque Tribune*, January 25, l945, p. 1.

51. "Barelas Council Offers 13 New Center Services; Shows Profit," *Albuquerque Tribune*, January 18, 1945, p. 2.

52. "St. Anthony's Orphanage Mingles Boys of Many Religious Faiths," *AJ*, September 22, 1946, p. 5; "St. Anthony's Orphanage History a Chronicle of Faith in Boyhood," *AJ*, August 22, 1949, p. 7.

53. "Lulacs Aim at Higher Standards for People," *Albuquerque Tribune*, February 21, 1945, p. 7.

54. "University Schedules Full Week," *Albuquerque Tribune*, January 13, 1945, p. 3.

55. "Alianza's Annual Ball November 27," *AJ*, November 7, 1946, p. 9.

56. "'Man Against Pain,' Anesthesia's History, Latest Book by Dr. H. Raper," *AJ*, September 20, 1945, p. 3.
57. "Few Residents Here Made '45 Resolutions; Pray for Peace," *Albuquerque Tribune*, January 2, 1945, p. 2.
58. Terry McShane, "The Case of the Miner's Daughter," *AJ*, October 28, 1945.
59. "State Mourns Carrie Tingley," *AJ*, November 8, 1961, p. A17.
60. For further discussion of the movies of 1945 and later, see pp. 286, 292-93, 348-49, 352-53, 361.
61. "News of Rescue Thrills Families of New Mexico Men Taken on Bataan," *AJ*, February 2, l945, p. 1.
62. "Crowd Hails Three Bataan Heroes on Arrival Home from Jap Prison," *AJ*, March 24, 1945, p. 1.
63. "Trees to Be Planted for Bataan Survivors in Memorial Service," *AJ*, March 25, 1945, p. 11.
64. "Line of March for Bataan Vets' Parade Announced," *AJ*, December 5, 1945, p.1.
65. "Quiet Emotion Shows Memory of Living for Bataan Dead," *AJ*, December 10, 1945, p. 1.
66. "Pyle's Adopted City and State Grieve at Death," *AJ*, April 19, 1945, p. 1.
67. "'G.I. Joe' Director, Frances Langford Among Hollywood Group at Premiere," *AJ*, July 13, 1945, p. 1.
68. "New Mexico Boys Tell of Battle Experiences, Leave for Fort Bliss," *AJ*, June 19, 1945, p. 1.
69. "Albuquerque Celebrates Noisily; Stores, Public Offices Close Today," *AJ*, August 15, 1945, pp. 1, 2.
70. "Congratulations—Lobos," *AJ*, January 3, 1946, p. 6.
71. "Boy Hero Chooses to Live with Neighbor," *AJ*, February 6, l946, pp. 1, 3.
72. For further discussion of crime in Albuquerque over the years, see pp. 122, 258, 277, 293-94, 309, 311, 317.
73. "More About Commission," *Albuquerque Tribune*, January 1, 1945, p. 9.
74. "Gang Fights, Beatings Still Common Here," *AJ*, September 18, 1945, pp. 1, 2.
75. "Coeds 'Kidnapped,' One Student Hurt in UNM Campus Feud Saturday," *AJ*, March 17, 1946, p. 1.
76. "UNM Suspends Three Students for Estufa Fire," *AJ*, April 11, 1947, pp. 1, 9.

Chapter 3

77. U.S., Department of Commerce, Bureau of the Census, *County Data Book, 1947* (A Statistical Abstract Supplement), p. 260; idem, *Census of Population: 1950*, vol. 2, *Characteristics of the Population*, pt. 31, New Mexico, p. 31-34; idem, *Census of Population and Housing 1960, Census Tracts*, Final Report PHC(1)-4, Albuquerque, N. Mex. SMSA, p. 13; idem, *Census of Population and Housing: 1970, Census Tracts*, Final Report, PHC(1)-5, Albuquerque, N. Mex., SMSA, p. P-9.
78. The population of New Mexico grew from 531,818 in 1900 to 1,016,000 in 1970. Idem, *County and City Data Book, 1947* (A Statistical Abstract Supplement), p. 260; idem, *County and City Data Book, 1972* (A Statistical Abstract Supplement), p. 318.
79. Ibid.
80. Ibid.
81. Idem, *Census of Population: 1950*, vol. 2, *Characteristics of the Population*, pt. 31, New Mexico, p. 31-36; idem, *Census of Population and Housing: 1960, Census Tracts*, Final Report PHC(1)-4, Albuquerque, N. Mex. SMSA, p. 31; idem, *Census of Population and Housing: 1970, Census Tracts*, Final Report PHC(1)-5, Albuquerque, N. Mex. SMSA, p. P-17.
82. U.S., Department of Commerce, *County Business Patterns: First Quarter, 1948*, pt. 2, State Reports, no. 29, New Mexico, p. 8; U.S., Department of Commerce, Bureau of the Census, *County Business Patterns:1972*, New Mexico, CBF-72-33, p. 22. The average size of firm was calculated by dividing the total number of employees by the total number of units reporting.

83. The average sizes of the business firms were calculated from data in *County Business Patterns* of 1948 and 1972 on all counties in the United States with 20,000 to 25,000 workers and with 90,000 to 100,000 workers. The data for two counties seemed highly atypical and were not used—one in Tennessee which in 1948 had 21,866 workers and firms averaging 56.79 each, and one in West Virginia which in 1972 had 21,939 workers and firms averaging 40.70 each.

84. Robert J. Levin and Amy Levin, "Sexual Pleasure: The Surprising Preferences of 100,000 Women," *Redbook*, September 1975, pp. 52, 53.

85. Alfred C, Kinsey, et al., *Sexual Behavior in the Human Female* (Philadelphia and London: W.B. Saunders Company, 1953), p. 361.

86. Levin and Levin, p. 55.

87. Robert J. Levin, "The Redbook Report on Premarital and Extramarital Sex: The End of the Double Standard," *Redbook*, October 1975, p. 38.

88. Levin, p. 42.

89. U.S., Department of Commerce, Bureau of the Census, *Census of Population and Housing: 1960, Census Tracts*, Final Report PHC(1)-4, Albuquerque, N. Mex. SMSA, p. 13.

90. Between 1950 and 1960 the number of Indians residing in Bernalillo County rose from 2338 to 3378, the Blacks from 1605 to 4672, and the Spanish-surnamed from 43,729 to 68,101; the remainder rose from 98,001 to 186,048. Idem, *Census of Population: 1950*, vol. 2, *Characteristics of the Population*, pt. 31, New Mexico, pp. 31-34, 31-58; ibid., vol. 4, *Special Reports*, pt. 3, chap. C, Persons of Spanish Surname, p. 3C-53; idem, *Census of Population and Housing: 1960, Census Tracts*, Final Report PHC(1)-4, Albuquerque, N. Mex. SMSA, p. 13; idem, *Census of Population: 1960*, vol. 1, *Characteristics of the Population*, pt. 33, New Mexico, pp. 33-49; idem, *Census of Population: 1960, Subject Reports, Persons of Spanish Surname*, Final Report PC(2)-1B, p. 164.

91. "Military Housing Problem," *AJ*, February 8, 1945, p. 6; "Yes, You Can Get Hotel Room Here if You Wait 'Till After the War," *AJ*, July 19, 1945, p. 9; "City's Crowded Catholic Cemeteries Seek More Space by Using Driveways," *AJ*, February 17, 1946, p. 1.

92. "Veterans Housing," *AJ*, November 27, 1946, p. 6.

93. "Sandia Corp. Unique Among City Industries," *AJ*, July 7, 1957, p. 10; "Area's Atomic Community Very Complex," *AJ*, May 20, 1969, p. 4.

94. "Construction at Sandia Base Tops $22 Million for 1949," *AJ*, January 1, 1950, p. 1; "Labor, Sandia Differ on Effects of Strikes," *AJ*, July 3, 1957, p. 2.

95. "Sandia Corp. Unique Among City Industries," *AJ*, July 7, 1957, p. 10.

96. "Area's Atomic Community Very Complex," *AJ*, May 20, 1969, p. A4.

97. "Sandia, Kirtland Bases Use 30 Per Cent of Work Force," *AJ*, August 10, 1957, p. 3.

98. "Sandia Corp. Unique Among City Industries," *AJ*, July 7, 1957, p. 10.

99. "Morelli Offers 10-Point Program," *AJ*, March 10, 1946, p. 5.

100. "Tingley's GA Ticket Ready, He Announces," *AJ*, March 17, 1946, p. 1.

101. "Better Gov't Ticket Wins," *AJ*, April 3, 1946, p. 1.

102. "New City Commission Rescinds Water Rate," *AJ*, April 10, 1946, p. 1.

103. "Garbage Inspector Fired as City Hall 'Clean Up' Begins," *AJ*, April 18, 1946, p. 1.

104. "North End Park Elms Go Down; Tingley Believes Cause Neglect," *AJ*, June 1, 1946, p. 3.

105. "Our Traffic Problems," *AJ*, July 11, 1946, p. 6.

106. "Albuquerque's City Government Cost to Be 43 Pct. More," *AJ*, August 1, 1946, p. 1; "City's Amazing Growth in Last Five Years Nets 250 Per Cent Boost in Government Cost," *AJ*, July 5, 1951, p. 1.

107. "Albuquerque Has Made Biggest Gains in Last Decade," *AJ*, December 20, 1959, p. A7.

108. Ibid.; "City Area Has Expanded to Five Times Size of 1940," *AJ*, April 10, 1960, p. E1.

109. "City Commissioners Move to Corral All Vast Suburban Areas," *AJ*, December 31, 1946, p. 1.

110. "Rates for Water Doubled Outside of City Limits," *AJ*, February 19, 1947, p.1.

111. "Legislature Passes Annexation Bill Despite Montoya's El Paso 'Junket,'" *AJ*, March 15, 1947, p. 1.

112. "Morelli Denounces Two-Man City Rule in Commission Battle," *AJ*, June 25, 1947, p. 1.
113. "Buck Retires from Post in Surprise Maneuver," *AJ*, August 13, 1947, p. 1.
114. "Storm Sewer Politics Costly, Tingley Says," *AJ*, August 1, 1947, p. 1.
115. "Clyde Tingley Announces He'll Seek Re-Election," *AJ*, September 11, 1947, p. 1.
116. "Tingley and Everly Elected," *AJ*, October 8, 1947, p. 1.
117. "Rankin Acting City Manager as Wells and Others Resign," *AJ*, October 11, 1947, p. 1.
118. "Rankin Appoints Rogers, Matteucci City Attorneys," *AJ*, November 11, 1947, p. 1.
119. "Charles E. Wells New Water Chief at $6000 Yearly," *AJ*, December 4, 1947, p. 1.
120. "Catchings Named City Manager by Vote of 4 to 1," *AJ*, December 20, 1947, p. 1.
121. "Tingley, Morelli Play 'Cheap Political Trick', Says Everly as Catchings Spurns City Post," *AJ*, December 27, 1947, p. 1.
122. "Sorry Performance," *AJ*, December 31, 1947, p. 6.
123. "Tingley Out, Everly Chairman," *AJ*, January 28, 1948, p. 1.
124. "Rosenberg Quits as City Manager, Blames Hostility," *AJ*, February 6, 1948, p. 1.
125. "Commission Hires Wells as Manager in Stormy Session," *AJ*, February 7, 1948, pp. 1, 2.
126. "Wells Gets Full Title of Manager," *AJ*, September 1, 1948, p. 1.
127. "City Garbage Deal Complete," *AJ*, February 26, 1947, p. 1.
128. "City Buys Garbage Firm to Avert Crisis," *AJ*, May 30, 1948, p. 1.
129. "Wells Sees 90,000 City Population as North Area Annexed," *AJ*, August 14, 1948, p. 1.
130. "City Annexes Part of Old Albuquerque," *AJ*, July 21, 1948, p. 1.
131. "Wells Sees 90,000 City Population as North Area Annexed," *AJ*, August 14, 1948, p. 1.
132. City Commission Approves $2,910,000 Bond Issue," *AJ*, September 8, 1948, p. 1.
133. "Morelli Blocks $2,910,000 Water, Sewer Issue," *AJ*, September 11, 1948, p. 1.
134. "City Deadlock on Bonds Ends in Secret Deal," *AJ*, January 28, 1949, p. 1.
135. "Old Town Dispute Given to Board for Arbitration," *AJ*, January 5, 1949, p. 1; "City Commission Annexes Old Town Despite Court Case," *AJ*, January 19, 1949, p. 1; "Old Town Put Back Outside," *AJ*, January 30,1949, p. 1; "Old Town Votes More Than 2 to 1 Against Coming into Albuquerque," *AJ*, April 13, 1949, p. 1.
136. "Annexation Victory," *AJ*, June 30, 1949, p. 16.
137. "Old Town Annexed to Increase City's Population by 4000," *AJ*, July 1, 1949, p. 1.
138. "City Annexes Part of Old Albuquerque," *AJ*, July 21, 1948, p. 1; "City Annexes Tract, Ups Population 2000 Following Hot Debate," *AJ*, September 7, 1949, p. 1.
139. "Record Annexation of Mesa Land Increases Area of City by 50 Pct.," *AJ*, November 23, 1949, p. 1; "City Annexes 3300 Acres Surrounding Bel-Air," *AJ*, January 25, 1950, p. 1; "City Area Has Expanded to Five Times Size of 1940," *AJ*, April 10, 1960, p. E1.
140. "City Commission Votes to Give Airport to U.S.," *AJ*, November 16, 1949, p. 1.
141. "30 Candidates Set New Commission Race Record," *AJ*, March 22, 1950, p. 1.
142. "New Commissioners Are Lawyer, Realtor, Cleaner," *AJ*, April 5, 1950, p. 1.
143. "Wilson, Gilbert, Batsel Win," *AJ*, April 5, 1950, p. 1.
144. "Tingley, O'Bannon Win," *AJ*, October 3, 1951, p. 1.
145. "McCallister, Graham Announce Candidacy for City Commission," *AJ*, August 14, 1951, p. 1.
146. "Tingley, O'Bannon Win," *AJ*, October 3, 1951, p. 1.
147. "Tingley Takes Chair of City Commission in Harmony Session," *AJ*, October 10, 1951, p. 1.
148. "City's Amazing Growth in Last Five Years Nets 250 Per Cent Boost in Government Cost," *AJ*, July 5, 1951, p. 1.
149. "Wells Suspends Four City Officials, Charging Politics in Working Hours," *AJ*, October 16, 1951, p. 1.
150. "Tingley Reveals Garbage Dept. $307,377 in Red," *AJ*, November 4, 1951, p. 1; "Garbage Financing Illegal, Attorney Informs Tingley," *AJ*, November 16, 1951, p. 1.
151. "City Economy Drive to Pay Garbage Debt Is Planned by Wells," *AJ*, November 17, 1951, p. 1.

152. "R.C. Schoor to Manage City Garbage Program," *AJ*, December 8, 1951, p. 1.

153. "'City Is Broke,' Declares Tingley; Wells Calls Situation 'Not So Bad,'" *AJ*, November 15, 1951, p. 1; "The City's Financial Mess," *AJ*, November 18, 1951, p. 6.

154. "City Manager Charles Wells Asks Retirement," *AJ*, January 1, 1952, p. 1.

155. "Engel Is Hired as City Manager; Commission Fixes Pay at $8000," *AJ*, January 5, 1952, p. 1.

156. "Flood Reveals Engineer Errors, Tingley Charges," *AJ*, June 5, 1952, p. 2; "Tingley Blasts Engineer on Storm Sewer Plan," *AJ*, August 27, 1952, p. 2.

157. "Tingley Bid to Run Garbage Dept. Grinds to a Halt," *AJ*, March 11, p. 1.

158. "Engel to Investigate Zoo After Commission Hears Report of Emu's Death," *AJ*, December 2, 1953, p. 2.

159. For a full and interesting account of this episode in Albuquerque politics by one of the leading participants, see Joel V. Barrett, "Citizen Participation in the Formation of Albuquerque's Bus Franchise, 1948-1953" (Master's thesis, University of New Mexico, 1954).

160. "Bus Co. Pays City $1000 a Year," *AJ*, December 13, 1945, p. 1.

161. "Local Men Buy City Bus Lines," *AJ*, August 15, 1945, p. 9.

162. "Bus Company Asks New Franchise," *AJ*, January 7, 1948, p. 1; "UNM Student Group Blasts Terms of Proposed New Bus Franchise," *AJ*, April 21, 1943, p. 1; "City Rams Through 25-Year Bus Franchise," *AJ*, May 25, 1949, p. 1; "Campaign for Election on City Bus Franchise Gains Power Rapidly," *AJ*, May 26, 1949, p. 1; "City Bus Franchise Defeated," *AJ*, December 21, 1949, p. 1.

163. "Campaign for Election on City Bus Franchise Gains Power Rapidly," *AJ*, May 26, 1949, p. 1.

164. "City Bus Franchise Petitions Are Filed," *AJ*, June 15, 1949, p. 1.

165. "City Bus Franchise Defeated," *AJ*, December 21, 1949, p. 1.

166. "Commission Rules Duke City Buses Off Streets," *AJ*, January 11, 1950, p. 1; "Policy of 'Favoritism,'" *AJ*, January 20, 1950, p. 6; "Commission Gives Duke City Bus Co. 10 Stops in City," *AJ*, February 1, 1950, p. 1.

167. "Fare Only Bar to Bus Franchise," *AJ*, March 4, 1952, p. 2.

168. "Bus Strike to End Today," *AJ*, March 27, 1951, p. 1.

169. "Fare Only Bar to Bus Franchise," *AJ*, March 4, 1952, p. 2.

170. "Commission Adopts Bus Franchise, Modifies Basis for Fare Changes," *AJ*, March 19, 1952, p. 1.

171. "Fare Only Bar to Bus Franchise," *AJ*, March 4, 1952, p. 2.

172. "Bus Fares Hike to 15 and 7 Cents Gets City Approval," *AJ*, June 5, 1952, p. 1.

173. "New Organization Formed to Fight Bus Fare Increase," *AJ*, July 1, 1952, p. 1.

174. "Petitions for Bus Fare Vote Filed," *AJ*, July 24, 1952, p. 1.

175. "Fair Fares Group Blasts Tingley as Bus Firm Ally," *AJ*, August 3, 1952, p. 1.

176. "Two-Thirds of Names Ruled Off Bus Petitions," *AJ*, August 13, 1952, p. 1.

177. "City Asks Court to Rule on Bus Fare Petitions," *AJ*, August 16, 1952, p. 1; "Bus Fares Go Up Today as City Rejects Petition," *AJ*, September 28, 1952, p. 1.

178. For a fuller treatment of Albuquerque's practice and legislation in regard to racial matters at this time, see A. Rosenfeld, "New Mexico's Fading Color Line," *Commentary* 20 (September 1955): 203-11.

179. "UNM Is One in 37. It Omits All 'Discriminatory' Queries," *AJ*, March 6, 1951, p. 5.

180. "City Passes Measure Barring Discrimination; Referendum Predicted," *AJ*, February 13, 1952, p. 1.

181. "Referendum Vote Petitions Fall Short," *AJ*, March 14, 1952, p. 1.

182. "Union Would Serve as Bargaining Agent for City Employes," *AJ*, February 15, 1952, p. 1.

183. "Tingley Out, Everly Chairman," *AJ*, January 28, 1948, p. 1.

184. "Paul Shaver Named Chief of Police," *AJ*, November 16, 1948, pp. 1, 6.

185. "Union Would Serve as Bargaining Agent for City Employes," *AJ*, February 15, 1952, p. 1.

186. "AFL Gets Commission Approval as City Employes' Bargaining Agent," *AJ*, February 27, 1952, p. 1.
187. "That Auditorium Jinx," *AJ*, July 20, 1950, p. 6; "City May Build Auditorium, NPA Officials Decree," *AJ*, November 10, 1950, p. 1; "Auditorium Deal with U. Ruled Out," *AJ*, January 20, 1952, p. 1.
188. "City Will Ask Bids on Parking Meters," *AJ*, November 29, 1950, p. 1.
189. "Auditorium Is War Casualty," *AJ*, February 7, 1951, p. 1; "Auditorium Maneuvering," *AJ*, February 22, 1951, p. 6; "Court Dismisses Suit to Block City Auditorium," *AJ*, March 7, 1951, p. 1; "Auditorium Deal with U. Ruled Out," *AJ*, January 20, 1952, p. 1.
190. "Mention of Auditorium Greeted with Laughter," *AJ*, October 29, 1953, p. 1.
191. "New Auditorium Site Approved by City Voters," *AJ*, November 11, 1953, p. 1.
192. "Tingley Still Has Unsigned Contract," *AJ*, December 10, 1953, p. 1.
193. "City Commission Cancels Auditorium Contract," *AJ*, January 27, 1951, p. 1.
194. "10-Year Master Plan for City Voted," *AJ*, November 5, 1947, p. 1.
195. "City Commission Adopts Master Water-Sewer Plan," *AJ*, September 26, 1952, p. 1; "1954 Water Bans Are Likely Unless Commission Acts," *AJ*, July 25, 1953, p. 1.
196. "City to Name Special Board for Water Woes," *AJ*, July 15, 1953, p. 1.
197. "Tingley, O'Bannon Block $3 Million Bond Issue," *AJ*, July 30, 1953, p. 1.
198. "Quits Water Board, Hits at Tingley," *AJ*, July 30, 1953, p. 1.
199. "City to Issue $2,400,000 in Water, Sewer Bonds," *AJ*, August 1, 1953, p. 1.
200. "Problems of Growth," *AJ*, March 6, 1947, p. 6.
201. "City Suddenly Bans Parking on Fourth Street," *AJ*, July 12, 1946, p. 1.
202. "Traffic Survey Hit by Tingley," *AJ*, November 7, 1996, p. 2.
203. "Traffic Report Asks Engineer, More Parking," *AJ*, May 22, 1950, pp. 1, 4; "Arterial Street Net Is One Big Reform Urged by Engineers," *AJ*, May 23, 1950, pp. 1, 11.
204. "City Votes Traffic Commission into Existence, Starts Model Traffic Measure Toward OK," *AJ*, June 7, 1950, p. 1.
205. "City Lays Groundwork for Traffic Regulation," *AJ*, December 24, 1950, p. 14.
206. "City Commission to Reopen Talks on Bus Franchise," *AJ*, September 6, 1950, p. 13.
207. "City Commission Approves Model Traffic Ordinance," *AJ*, September 13, 1950, p. 1.
208. "City Lays Groundwork for Traffic Regulation," *AJ*, December 24, 1950, p. 14; "Dabney Resigns Post with City," *AJ*, November 14, 1952, p. 3.
209. "City to Remove Stop Signs, Change Lights to Flash Red," *AJ*, December 29, 1950, p. 1.
210. "City Purchases 1700 Meters at Total Cost of $106,250," *AJ*, January 7, 1951, p. 1.
211. "One-Way Street System Is OK'd; Starts in Month," *AJ*, January 24, 1951, p. 1.
212. "Commission Initiates First Paving District Program in 20 Years," *AJ*, April 26, 1950, p. 1.
213. "Avalanche of Objections Blocks East Central Resurfacing Program," *AJ*, March 7, 1951, p. 1; "City Drops Paving on East Central; Starts New Move," *AJ*, March 14, 1951, p. 1; "Property Owners Would Cut East Central Outlay in Half," *AJ*, March 31, 1951, p. 1.
214. "Paving Program Surfaces 78 Miles of City Streets," *AJ*, January 23, 1952, p. 1.
215. "Commission Approves 16 New Street Names," *AJ*, February 9, 1951, p. 1.
216. "Tingley Takes Blast at Dabney as Park Cut Wins Approval," *AJ*, January 23, 1952, pp. 1, 7.
217. "Dabney Protests Tingley 'Interfering,'" *AJ*, March 8, 1952, p. 1.
218. "Vast Residential Street Lighting Program Approved by Commission," *AJ*, July 16, 1952, p. 1; "Traffic Chief Dabney Bows Out of City Post," *AJ*, December 7, 1952, p. 33.
219. "Dabney Resigns in Long Battle with Tingley," *AJ*, November 14, 1952, pp. 1, 3.
220. "Francis Burton, UNM Grad, New Traffic Engineer," *AJ*, May 30, 1953, p. 1.
221. "Naming of Board to Handle Parking Is Authorized," *AJ*, June 17, 1953, p. 1.
222. "Citizens to Form Traffic Commission," *AJ*, January 13, 1954, p. 13.

223. "Dorothy Cline Announces Candidacy for Council," *AJ*, January 20, 1954, p. 2.

224. "Citizens' Group Outlines 'Cures' for City Ills," *AJ*, February 12, 1954, p. 2.

225. Jack Gill, "Many Sandia Employes on Citizens Committee," *AJ*, February 16, 1958, p. 30.

226. "Citizens' Group Selects Sanchez, Bice and Halama," *AJ*, February 10, 1954, p. 7.

227. "Citizens' Group Not Criticizing Engel, Employes," *AJ*, February 13, 1954, p. 5.

228. "Citizens' Group Outlines 'Cures' for City Ills," *AJ*, February 12, 1954, p. 2.

229. "City Commission Has Made Good Start, Bice Says," *AJ*, March 11, 1958, p. 1.

230. "Tingley, Cline Targets of Political Meeting," *AJ*, February 18, 1954, p. 2.

231. "Tingley, Sanchez Offered TV Time for Debate," *AJ*, March 5, 1954, p. 13.

232. "Tingley Will Support, Campaign for Bingham, Latham, Hogan in City Commission Election," *AJ*, March 14, 1954, p. 1.

233. "Clyde Tingley Ready to Quit Chairman Post," *AJ*, March 29, 1954, p. 1.

234. "Tingley Brands as 'Lie' Statement by City Manager," *AJ*, April 3, 1954, p. 1.

235. "Tingley Gives His Views in Talk on TV Program," *AJ*, April 3, 1954, p. 2.

236. "Bice, Halama, Sanchez Win," *AJ*, April 7, 1954, p. 1.

237. "New Commission Members Assume Control of City," *AJ*, April 14, 1954, pp. 1, 2.

238. "Tingley Misses 41 of 65 Meetings of City Commission," *AJ*, June 2, 1955, p. 1.

239. "Pair Is Endorsed for Commission," *AJ*, September 11, 1955, p. 4; "Atkinson and Lanier Win Commission Seats," *AJ*, October 5, 1955, p. 1.

240. "Voters Put Citizens Ticket Back in Office," *AJ*, April 9, 1958, p. 1.

241. "Sanchez Flays Tingley, O'Bannon for Absences," *AJ*, November 10, 1954, p. 1.

242. "City Commission Worries over Correct Use of Words," *AJ*, September 19, 1955, p. 30.

243. "Firemen Face Disciplinary Action for 'Horseplay,'" *AJ*, August 12, 1954, p. 2.

244. "Mr. Betts' Fishing Trip," *AJ*, May 26, 1955, p. 6.

245. "City Commission Bans Acceptance of Gifts, Favors," *AJ*, May 27, 1955, p. 1.

246. "City Employes Ordered to Quit Political Posts," *AJ*, May 18, 1956, p. 2.

247. "Commission Puts Laborers Under the Merit System," *AJ*, August 4, 1954, p. 1.

248. "City Personnel Records to Be Standardized," *AJ*, December 19, 1957, p. 2.

249. "City Commission Has Made Good Start, Bice Says," *AJ*, March 11, 1958, p. 1.

250. "Albuquerque Sales Tax Becomes Effective Today; Revenue Headache Begins," *AJ*, May 1, 1955, p. 1.

251. "One Unit Tax System Step Virtually Completed Here," *AJ*, March 1, 1957, p. 4.

252. "Citizens' Committee Raps Tax Commission Again," *AJ*, March 3, 1956, p. 10.

253. "One Unit Tax System Step Virtually Completed Here," *AJ*, March 1, 1957, p. 4.

254. "Albuquerque Property Tax Hiked," *AJ*, August 18, 1959, p. A1.

255. "Should Be Commended," *AJ*, November 27, 1955, p. 6; "Some of Changes in Albuquerque Are Behind Scene," *AJ*, February 2, 1958, p. 10.

256. "Vast Building Program Marks City's Growth," *AJ*, February 2, 1958, p. 10.

257. "Some of Changes in Albuquerque Are Behind Scene," *AJ*, February 2, 1958, p. 10.

258. "City Board Eases Out Humane Ass'n as Shelter Advisor," *AJ*, May 8, 1957, p. 1; "Rouse Removed as Shelter Head; Dismissal Asked," *AJ*, May 11, 1957, p. 1; "Rouse Fired as Shelter Manager," *AJ*, May 18, 1957, p. 1.

259. "Commission OKs Bond Ordinance on First Reading," *AJ*, August 27, 1959, p. C6.

260. "City Commission Has Made Good Start, Bice Says," *AJ*, March 11, 1958, p. 1.

261. "Sponsors Defend Sanchez' Views on Union Plea," *AJ*, January 11, 1955, p. 2.

262. "Commission Puts Laborers Under the Merit System," *AJ*, August 4, 1954, p. 1.

263. "Anti-Union Activities Are Charged," *AJ*, December 25, 1954, p. 2; "Tingley Favors City Employes' Union Contract," *AJ*, January 4, 1955, p. 2; "Central Labor Union Hits City Commission Stand," *AJ*, January 10, 1955, p. 2; "Sponsors Defend Sanchez' Views on Union Plea," *AJ*, January 11, 1955, p. 2.

264. "Engel Outlines Program for City to Keep Pace with New Tax Revenue," *AJ*, June 16, 1955, p. 1.

265. "Night Bus Service Sharply Curtailed in East Albuquerque," *AJ*, May 15, 1954, p. 1.

266. "City Board Orders Manager to Make Bus Survey," *AJ*, May 19, 1954, p.1.

267. "Sanchez Doubts Cuts Necessary," *AJ*, May 29, 1955, p. 2.

268. "Bus Company to Reinstate Four of Seven Discontinued Lines," *AJ*, May 31, 1954, p. 1.

269. "Bus Drivers Accept Guaranteed Hourly Wage," *AJ*, July 12, 1955, p. 1.

270. "City Approves Zone Rate Plan and School Token Hike for Buses," *AJ*, July 20, 1955, p. 1; "City Bus Fare Increase Ordinance Is Passed," *AJ*, July 27, p. 1.

271. "Auditorium Study Here Is Approved by Commissioners," *AJ*, May 5, 1954, p. 1.

272. "Civic Center Being Planned by Commission," *AJ*, August 26, 1954, p. 1.

273. "City Commission Majority Picks Site for Auditorium North of St. Joseph Hospital," *AJ*, January 5, 1955, p. 1.

274. "New City Auditorium, Five Stations Included in 1956 Improvements," *AJ*, December 24, 1956, p. 4.

275. "City's Auditorium Is Officially Opened," *AJ*, April 27, 1957, p. 1.

276. "Vast Building Program Marks City's Growth," *AJ*, February 2, 1958, p. 10.

277. A.J. Brumbaugh, ed., *American Universities and Colleges*, 5th ed. (Washington, D.C.: American Council on Education, 1948), p. 619.

278. "Popejoy Named UNM President," *AJ*, January 30, 1948, p. 1.

279. "Wernette Says His Drive to Raise UNM Standards Was Met with Hostility," *AJ*, May 21, 1947, p. 1.

280. "Popejoy to Succeed Wernette as UNM President in June," *AJ*, January 30, 1948, p. 1.

281. "City School System Marks Tenth Year of Consolidation," *AJ*, December 27, 1959, p. A7.

282. "Spain to Head School System," *AJ*, May 25, 1955, p. 1; "Dr. Spain to Become Superintendent of Schools Today; No Changes Planned," *AJ*, July 1, 1956, p. 37.

283. William M. Hales, Jr., "Technological In-Migration and Curricular Change: Educational Politics in Albuquerque, 1945-1965" (Ph.D. dissertation, University of New Mexico, 1970), pp. 135-39.

284. Donald Ducoff, "The Springer Transfer Company: A Study of Business Growth and Top Management Leadership" (Master's thesis, University of New Mexico, 1963), pp. 6-43.

285. "'Uncle Doc' Lovelace Is Dead Here at 85," *AJ*, December 5, 1968, pp. A1, A16.

286. "Lovelace Has Faced Huge Odds in the Past," *AJ*, December 15, 1965, pp. A1, A2.

287. "'Uncle Doc' Lovelace Dies," *AJ*, December 5, 1968, p. A16.

288. "U.S. Appoints Lovelace Top Defense Dept. Doctor," *AJ*, May 9, 1951, p. 1.

289. "Dr. Lovelace Given High AF Award," *AJ*, October 20, 1955, p. 1.

290. "UNM Graduates Hear of New Business Code," *AJ*, June 5, 1953, pp. 1, 5.

291. "House Building Increasing Here," *AJ*, March 7, 1997, p. 13.

292. "New 450-Home Princess Jeanne Project Planned," *AJ*, July 13, 1958, p. 2.

293. "Home Builders, Lenders Hail FHA Boost," *AJ*, December 2, 1956, p. 24; "FHA Increases Interest Rates to 5 3/4 Per Cent," *AJ*, September 24, 1959, p. A1.

294. "Dale Bellamah Heads $7 Million-a-Year Business," *AJ*, May 11, 1957, Talking House Section, p. 4; "War Altered Bellamah's Plan to Become Lawyer," *AJ*, April 20, 1958, p. 35; "Bellamah's Philosophy: Dream," *AJ*, January 31, 1971, p. A7; "Albuquerque Magnate Dale J. Bellamah Dies," *AJ*, April 21, 1972, pp. A1, A5.

295. "Builder Buys 640 Acres on Mesa," *AJ*, April 27, 1953, p. 2; "Snow's Reputation as Builder Cited," *AJ*, July 23, 1968, p. A2.

296. "F & S Construction Co. Now Builds a House Every Hour, Every Day," *AJ*, September 9, 1951, p. 24; "Builder Hoffman Kills Wife, Turns Gun on Himself," *AJ*, October 14, 1959, p. A15.

297. "Hoffmantown Shopping Center Located in Huge Suburban Area," *AJ*, January 6, 1952, p. 10.

298. "Builder Buys 640 Acres on East Mesa for New Homes," *AJ*, April 27, 1953, pp. 1, 2.

299. "$10 Million Home-Building Project Is Underway in Northeast Heights," *AJ*, November 14, 1953, p. 1.

300. "1600-Home Addition Announced," *AJ*, June 19, 1954, p. 1.

301. "Many Downtown Business Moves, New Theater to Enliven Central," *AJ*, December 4, 1946, p. 1.

302. "New Penney Store Opens Its Doors Today," *AJ*, August 4, 1949, J.C. Penney Section, p. 1.

303. "Nob Hill Business Center Once Scoffed At, Now Vast Success," *AJ*, March 2, 1952, p. 26.

304. "Construction Starts on 10-Store Shopping Center Designed to Serve Self-Contained Community," *AJ*, February 11, 1949, Second Section, p. 1.

305. "Hoffmantown Shopping Center Located in Huge Suburban Area," *AJ*, January 1, 1952, p. 10; "Hoffmantown Shopping Center to Be Expanded at Cost of $750,000," *AJ*, January 24, 1956, p. 1.

306. "1600-Home Addition Announced," *AJ*, June 19, 1954, p. 1.

307. "Erna Fergusson Proposes Long-Term Planning for Cities of New Mexico," *AJ*, September 8, 1948, p. 12.

308. "Commission Votes Planning Board, New Fire Station," *AJ*, December 8, 1948, p. 1.

309. "Everly Appoints Planning Aides," *AJ*, December 15, 1948, p. 1; "Vollmer to Recommend Alarid to Advisory Board," *AJ*, July 1, 1956, p. 12.

310. "S.Y. Jackson Heads City Plan Advisers," *AJ*, December 22, 1948, p. 1.

311. "City Requires Gift of 5 Acres Before It Approves Plat," *AJ*, February 16, 1949, p. 1.

312. "Planning Group Issues 'Guide' for Subdivisions," *AJ*, April 21, 1950, p. 18.

313. "Commission Gives City Planning Board First Say in Platting," *AJ*, June 21, 1950, p. 1.

314. "Planning Engineer Cites Loss to City by Early Neglect," *AJ*, November 4, 1951, p. 2.

315. "Planners Disapprove Utility Cost Measure," *AJ*, February 29, 1952, p. 1.

316. "City to Require Builders to Pay for Utility Lines," *AJ*, February 18, 1953, p. 1.

317. "City Will Require Developers to Pay to Extend Mains," *AJ*, May 27, 1953, p. 1.

318. "Builders Now Must Pay for Paving of Side Streets," *AJ*, April 22, 1955, p. 43.

319. "Land Use Survey Basis for Zoning," *AJ*, September 23, 1950, p. 14.

320. "City Zoning Defined as Property Protection Move at Public Meeting," *AJ*, May 22, 1953, p. 4.

321. "Commission Votes to Keep Old Town Free of Trucks," *AJ*, May 6, 1953, p. 1.

322. "City Approves Big Bellamah Shopping Area," *AJ*, January 11, 1956, p. 1.

323. "Home Builder Here Plans $10 Million Area Development," *AJ*, May 7, 1955, p. 1.

324. "Dale Bellamah Announces Plan for $6 Million Shopping Center," *AJ*, December 12, 1955, p. 1.

325. "$5 Million Shopping Center Is Planned for Northeast Area," *AJ*, January 6, 1956, p. 1.

326. "City Approves Big Bellamah Shopping Area," *AJ*, January 11, 1956, p. 1.

327. "Option Granted for $7-Million Shopping Center," *AJ*, March 12, 1957, p. 1.

328. "Planning Board Loses Bellamah," *AJ*, June 20, 1957, p. 2.

329. "Complaints Are Voiced Shopping Unit Would Be Unfair Competition," *AJ*, August 13, 1957, p. 2.

330. "Planning Board OKs Winrock Center, 4-2," *AJ*, September 10, 1957, p. 1.

331. "Winrock Shopping Center Zone Change Gets Full Approval," *AJ*, October 23, 1957, p. 1.

332. "Court Upholds City Zone Change in Suit to Block Winrock," *AJ*, June 13, 1958, p. 1.

333. "New $6 Million Home Project Is Planned Here," *AJ*, July 30, 1954, p. 1.

334. "Snow Buys Anderson's Farm for Housing," *AJ*, July 15, 1955, p. 1; "Big Housing Project Set for Valley," *AJ*, August 15, 1958, p. 1.

335. "Exclusive Housing Planned," *AJ*, February 13, 1958, p. 1.

336. "Plans for Two Home Projects Announced Here," *AJ*, July 6, 1958, p. 8.

337. "Bellamah Is Sixth Largest Building Firm in World in '58, Records Show," *AJ*, February 5, 1959, p. 2.

338. "New Bellamah Model Homes Open Sunday," *AJ*, February 6, 1959, p. 1.

339. "New Northwest Development Is Scheduled," *AJ*, September 9, 1959, p. 1.

340. "100 Acres in Heights Purchased for Housing Facility for Elderly," *AJ*, June 4, 1958, p. 1.

341. "Construction Firm Starts $1 Million, 47-Acre Mobile Home Park Project," *AJ*, August 26, 1959, p. 1.

342. "Business Area Problems Noted in Study Report," *AJ*, November 2, 1958, p. 28.

343. "12-Story Office Building to Replace Old Simms Structure at 4th, Gold," *AJ*, June 19, 1952, p. 1.

344. "Million Dollar Telephone Building Will Be Built at Silver, Seventh," *AJ*, June 2, 1955, p. 1.

345. "Bank of New Mexico Announces Plan for 14-Story Office Building," *AJ*, August 30, 1957, p. 1.

346. Medical Center Ready for Occupancy," *AJ*, October 8, 1950, p. 1.

347. "Lovelace Clinic Dedication Will Mark Start of 'Medical City,'" *AJ*, November 2, 1950, p. 13.

348. "700 at Dedication of Bataan Hospital," *AJ*, April 21, 1952, p. 1.

349. "Albuquerque Area Industrial Parks and Districts," leaflet published by Albuquerque Industrial Development Service, Inc., 1976.

350. U.S., Department of Commerce, Bureau of the Census, *Census of Population: 1950*, vol. 2, *Characteristics of the Population*, pt. 31, New Mexico, p. 31-37; idem, *Census of Population and Housing: 1960, Census Tracts*, Final Report PHC (1)-4, Albuquerque, N. Mex. SMSA, p. 13. The figures for the median family income of the bottom tenth percentile were interpolated from the income categories listed. The figures were corrected for inflation by means of a "Consumer Price Index for Urban Wage Earners and Clerical Workers" produced by the U.S., Department of Labor, Bureau of Labor Statistics.

351. U.S., Department of Commerce, Bureau of the Census, *Census of Business: 1948*, vol. 3, *Retail Trade—Area Statistics*, p. 30.06; idem, *Census of Business: 1958*, vol. 2, *Retail Trade—Area Statistics*, pt. 2, Missouri-Wyoming and Alaska, Hawaii, Guam, and Virgin Islands, p. 31-12.

352. Idem, *Census of Housing: 1940*, vol. 2, *General Characteristics*, pt. 4, Nebraska-Pennsylvania, p. 240; idem, *Census of Housing: 1950*, vol. 1, *General Characteristics*, pt. 4, Michigan-New York, p. 31-14; idem, *Census of Housing: 1960*, vol. 2, *Metropolitan Housing*, pt. 2, Abilene-Corpus Christi Standard Metropolitan Statistical Areas, pp. 14-3, 14-4.

353. "Home-Building," *AJ*, May 1, 1948, p. 8.

354. "It's Cheaper to Buy Than Rent, Say Real Estate Experts," *AJ*, March 17, 1957, p. 36.

355. U.S., Department of Commerce, Bureau of the Census, *Census of Housing: 1940*, vol. 2, *General Characteristics*, pt. 4, Nebraska-Pennsylvania, p. 247; idem, *Census of Housing: 1960*, vol. 2, *Metropolitan Housing*, pt. 2, Abilene-Corpus Christi Standard Metropolitan Statistical Areas, pp. 14-3, 14-4.

356. Ibid.

357. Idem, *Census of Housing: 1940*, vol. 2, *General Characteristics*, pt. 4, Nebraska-Pennsylvania, p. 240; idem, *Census of Housing: 1960*, vol. 2, *Metropolitan Housing*, pt. 2, Abilene-Corpus Christi Standard Metropolitan Statistical Areas, pp. 14-3, 14-4.

358. Idem, *County Data Book, 1947* (A Statistical Abstract Supplement), p. 266; idem, *County and City Data Book, 1962* (A Statistical Abstract Supplement), p. 256.

359. Idem, *Census of Housing: 1940*, vol. 2, *General Characteristics*, pt. 4, Nebraska-Pennsylvania, p. 254; idem, *Census of Housing: 1960*, vol. 2, *Metropolitan Housing*, pt. 2, Abilene-Corpus Christi Standard Metropolitan Statistical Areas, pp. 14-3, 14-4.

360. "New Temple Combines Comfort with Reverence," *AJ*, April 15, 1951, p. 10.

361. "New $75,000 Christ Methodist Church to Be Dedicated," *AJ*, March 30, 1957, p. 5.

362. "Freedom Train Viewed by 7265 as Hundreds Are Turned Away," *AJ*, February 17, 1948, p. 1.

363. "City to 'Request' Non-Communist Oath of Workers," *AJ*, August 9, 1950, p. 1.

364. "Freedom Crusade Leaders Chosen," *AJ*, September 5, 1950, p. 1.

365. "Milne Tells School Staff to 'Teach Americanism,'" *AJ*, August 30, 1952, p. 11.

366. "Students at Ernie Pyle to Study Americanism," *AJ*, February 12, 1953, p. 13.

367. "Rapid Growth of City Catholic Schools Outlined," *AJ*, December 27, 1959, p. A14.

368. "Impressive Ceremonies Initiate New College of St. Joseph," *AJ*, June 13, 1950, p. 1.

369. "College of St. Joseph-on-the-Rio Grande Buildings Are Dedicated; Hundreds Attend," *AJ*, October 16, 1952, p. 9.

370. "Throngs Hear Evangelist Billy Graham Speak Nightly at Specially Built Tabernacle," *AJ*, November 16, 1952, p. 1.

371. "Dr. Wyatt Lambastes Kinsey's Sex Report," *AJ*, August 31, 1953, p. 11.

372. "Beauty Contest Off; No Reason Given," *AJ*, July 1, 1952, p. 1.

373. "Can't Be Sidestepped," *AJ*, February 9, 1950, p. 6.

374. "Indecent Movies, Comics Target of Campaign Here," *AJ*, May 24, 1955, p. 15.

375. "Theater Here Cancels Film Showing After Protest by Legion of Decency," *AJ*, June 4, 1955, p. 1.

376. "Vandalism Increases in Bernalillo County; Schools Primary Targets," *AJ*, October 30, 1961, p. C1.

377. "Marijuana Traffic Gaining in City Area, Officials Warn," *AJ*, July 25, 1951, p. 10.

378. John Leahigh, "Use of Drugs by GI Tied to Vietnam War," *AJ*, February 21, 1971, p. A2.

379. "Police Slayer Hunted Here," *AJ*, December 2, 1954, p. 1; "Slaying of Police Officer Stirs Criticism of Lack of Funds for Additional Men," *AJ*, December 2, 1954, p. 4; Bob Beier, "Friends of Gunmen Tell of Fatal Flight and How They Tried to Aid Police," *AJ*, December 9, 1954, p. 1.

380. "City Commission Approves Civilian Defense Program," *AJ*, August 16, 1950, p. 1.

381. "Women's Clubs to Raise Civil Defense Fund for Air Raid Warning Equipment," *AJ*, January 26, 1951, p. 9.

382. "Popularity of Bomb Shelters Begins to Grow in Nation—and Albuquerque," *AJ*, January 23, 1951, p. 3.

383. "Mysterious Green Fireballs of 1951 Probably Were Meteors, Dr. LaPaz Says," *AJ*, January 2, 1952, p. 4.

384. "Tired of Being Afraid," *AJ*, May 5, 1952, p. 6.

385. "'Toy Dance' at University to Brighten Yule for Tots," *AJ*, December 3, 1953, p. 17.

386. "Kirtland Airmen 'Adopt' St. Anthony's Youngsters," *AJ*, June 16, 1951, p. 1.

387. "Sigma Chi Pledges Initiate 'Help Week' to Replace 'Hell Week' for Initiation," *AJ*, February 10, 1952, p. 4.

388. "Fledgling Legal Aid Here Helps 183; Officials Now Sure It Fills a Need," *AJ*, January 6, 1951, p. 5.

389. "For a United Fund," *AJ*, June 29, 1954, p. 6.

390. "2500 Albuquerque Mothers March Here Tonight for United Fund," *AJ*, November 10, 1955, p. 1.

391. "Accident Investigation Squad Inaugurated by City Police," *AJ*, December 19, 1952, p. 8.

392. "City Starts Efforts to Reduce Employes High Mishap Rates," *AJ*, February 2, 1952, p. 1.

393. "Teenage Traffic School Stresses Good Attitudes," *AJ*, December 12, 1954, p. 42.

394. "Police and Pretty Girls Will Patrol City to Promote Safe Driving Day," *AJ*, December 15, 1954, p. 1.

395. "Driver Clinic Inaugurated in View of City Accidents," *AJ*, September 21, 1956, p. 14.

396. "Safety Council Organized for Greater Albuquerque," *AJ*, September 24, 1958, p. 26.

397. "KOB Television Starts Regular Programs Monday," *AJ*, November 28, 1948, p. 1.

398. "KOAT-TV Begins Television Tonight; Third Station Starts Programs Sunday," *AJ*, October 2, 1953, p. 2.

399. "UNM, City School Venture into TV Made Big News," *AJ*, January 5, 1959, p. 9.

400. Robert A. Barnes, "Addiction to High Fidelity Is Filling New Mexico Homes with Melody," *AJ*, April 17, 1955, p. 25.

401. "County School Bonds Approved—Only 3 Votes Against in Entire County," *AJ*, April 24, 1946, p. 1.

402. In 1953 City Commission Chairman Clyde Tingley and U.S. Senator Dennis Chavez supported Dr. Max Sanchez, who was campaigning to unseat S.Y. Jackson, the chairman of the school board, but the voters reelected the incumbent overwhelmingly. "Chavez Silent on Why He Dips into School Race," *AJ*, January 31, 1953, p. 1; "Incumbents Take City School Board Election," *AJ*, February 4, 1953, p. 1. Another attempt to defeat incumbent members of the board was made in 1957 by three employees of the defense-related industries, who wanted more emphasis on science teaching. They too were turned back at the polls. "School Board Candidates Would Boost Sciences," *AJ*, January 18, 1957, p. 56; "Incumbents Retain Board Positions by Large Margins," *AJ*, February 6, 1957, p. 1.

403. U.S., Department of Commerce, Bureau of the Census, *County Data Book, 1947* (A Statistical Abstract Supplement), p. 264; idem, *Census of Population: 1950*, vol. 2, *Characteristics of the Population*, pt. 31, New Mexico, p. 31-34; idem, *Census of Population and Housing:1960, Census Tracts*, Final Report PHC(1)-4, Albuquerque, N. Mex. SMSA, p. 13.

404. New Mexico, Superintendent of Public Instruction, *Eighteenth Biennial Report*, pp. 96, 122; "University Enrollment Is 1009, Includes Veterans of This War," *AJ*, March 7, 1945, p. 5.

405. New Mexico, Superintendent of Public Instruction, *Annual Statistical Report on New Mexico Schools, for the Period July 1, 1959 to June 30, 1960*, p. 8; U.S., Department of Health, Education and Welfare, Bureau of Educational Research and Development, Educational Statistics Branch, *Total Enrollment in Institutions of Higher Learning, First Term, 1959-60 Basic Data*, p. 38.

406. "Albuquerque High Official Answers Why Students Should Attend School," *AJ*, August 24, 1955, p. 13.

407. "Scientific Thinking Fits Any Subject, PTA Told," *AJ*, February 22, 1958, p. 2.

408. "O'Beirne Stresses Need of Science Students," *AJ*, January 27, 1956, p. 10.

409. "Program Reflecting Need for Technical, Scientific Skills Urged by Spain," *AJ*, January 26, 1957, p. 2.

410. "Educators Would End Athletic Scholarships," *AJ*, April 7, 1957, p. 1.

411. "Educated Man Taking Over, U. Grads Hear," *AJ*, June 6, 1957, p. 1.

412. "Heavy Majority for UMT, Draft in Vote at UNM," *AJ*, March 25, 1948, p. 1.

413. John Robert Powers, "Secrets of Charm," *AJ*, November 20, 1950, p. 2.

414. "Hints on Hair-Do and Charm Spark Pan-Hellenic Luncheon," *AJ*, January 20, 1953, p. 8.

415. "Bob Feller Selects Henry Whately, 12, as 'Outstanding Youth of Albuquerque,'" *AJ*, May 14, 1950, p. 1.

416. "Wayne Will Pick Queen of Fiesta; Crowning Friday," *AJ*, April 27, 1952, p. 2.

417. "U. Panty-Raiders Score 'Lightly'; Balked by Police," *AJ*, May 23, 1952, p. 1.

418. "It's Disgusting," *AJ*, May 24, 1952, p. 4.

419. "Popejoy Terms Panty Raid at U 'Disgraceful Outbreak,'" *AJ*, May 29, 1952, p. 1.

420. Joy Gallagher, "Don't Worry if Teen-Ager Is 'Nervous'; That Means He's 'Crazy,' She's 'Frozen,'" *AJ*, October 22, 1953, p. 13.

421. "Police Will Open Juvenile Division Here This Month," *AJ*, December 6, 1955, p. 2.

422. "Rock 'n' Roll Beat Keeps Teenagers Jumpin' Here," *AJ*, August 4, 1956, p. 9.

423. "Elvis Presley 'Influence' Hit by U.S. Judge," *AJ*, December 20, 1956, p. 2.

424. "2000 Expected at First Duke City Hop Sunday," *AJ*, August 23, 1957, p. 38.

425. "City Males Are 'Ordered' Not to Shave Until July," *AJ*, April 13, 1956, p. 39.

426. "'Come Clean' Edict Issued for Women," *AJ*, May 1, 1956, p. 2.

427. "City Founders Didn't Wear Beards, Study of Record of Period Shows," *AJ*, May 26, 1956, p. 17.

428. "Pony Express Ride Will Start 250th Anniversary Today," *AJ*, July 3, 1956, p. 1.

429. "Parade to Reflect Spirit of '76, Tradition of 1706," *AJ*, July 3, 1956, p. 15.

430. "History of Albuquerque to Be Dramatized in Enchantorama Stage Show Wednesday," *AJ*, July 2, 1956, p. 11.

431. "Distinguished Guests, Frontier Show Top Today's Features," *AJ*, July 7, 1956, p. 1.

432. "Duke and Duchess Get Giant Welcome from 3800 Persons," *AJ*, July 8, 1956, p. 1.

433. "Role of Religion in History Here Takes Spotlight," *AJ*, July 8, 1956, p. 1.

434. "Cardinal Applauds 250th Celebration as Strong 'Front Against Communism,'" *AJ*, July 9, 1956, p. 1.

435. "Role of Religion in History Here Takes Spotlight," *AJ*, July 8, 1956, p. 1.

436. "Russia's Success with Moon Is Danger to Free World, Says Dr. Lincoln LaPaz," *AJ*, October 10, 1957, p. 1.

437. "Teachers Face More Courses in Science Study," *AJ*, December 21, 1957, p. 1.

438. "HS Graduation Requirements Hiked," *AJ*, April 9, 1958, p. 1.

439. "Education Board Puts A-B-C Grade System into Effect Next Fall," *AJ*, June 11, 1958, p. 1.

440. "University Faculty, Staff Offered Pay Boosts Next Fall," *AJ*, April 24, 1958, p. 1.

441. "Science Fair Scholarships Are Increased," *AJ*, February 11, 1958, p. 1.

442. "Youthful Rocketeers Organize Club at AHS, Fire First Test Shot on Mesa," *AJ*, November 10, 1957, p. 11.

443. "100 Top Science, Math Students Taken on Tour of Sandia Corp. Facilities," *AJ*, February 12, 1958, p. 15.

444. "Chamber of Commerce, Other Business Groups Announce Affiliation," *AJ*, August 19, 1953, p. 18.

445. "Heights Assn. Ends Affiliation with Chamber," *AJ*, February 8, 1958, p. 1.

446. "Heights Body Backs Shift of City, County Offices," *AJ*, September 17, 1959, p. A1.

447. "11 Girls Flee Welfare Home," *AJ*, October 9, 1958, p. 1.

448. "Harms Resigns as Fair Manager," *AJ*, November 27, 1958, p. 9.

449. "Tingley's Name in Red Neon Will Cost Fair $1905," *AJ*, December 13, 1958, p. 1.

450. "Gov. Burroughs Renames Banes as Member of State Fair Board," *AJ*, March 10, 1959, p. 1.

451. "Teenage Dance Sponsors Hoped for by Baker," *AJ*, March 3, 1959, p. 5.

452. "Commissioners Name Brunacini County Manager," *AJ*, December 17, 1958, p. 1.

453. "County Board Democrats Split on Manager," *AJ*, May 27, 1959, p. 1.

454. "Dorothy Cline Retains County Commission Post," *AJ*, May 30, 1959, p. 1.

455. "Miss Cline Is Asked to Quit as Chairman," *AJ*, June 26, 1959, p. A1.

456. "Miss Cline Votes Against Budget, But It Passes," *AJ*, July 1, 1959, p. C8.

457. "Miss New Mexico to Participate in Contest Despite Church Penalty," *AJ*, July 4, 1959, p. A1.

458. "More Clergymen Enter POAU-Catholic Hassle," *AJ*, July 7, 1959, p. A2.

459. "Miss New Mexico Gets Mail on Controversy," *AJ*, July 7, 1959, p. B12.

460. "Sue Ingersoll Feels She Learned Much in Contest Dispute," *AJ*, July 22, 1959, pp. A1, A2.

461. "Man-Made Floods Here Helping Prove Old Indian Anecdote," *AJ*, August 10, 1955, pp. 1, 15.

462. "10-Year Progress in Flood, Reclamation Projects Listed," *AJ*, March 6, 1959, p. 2.

463. "Arroyo Flood Control Up to City, Parley Decides," *AJ*, August 8, 1951, p. 1.

464. "City Commission Backs Flood Control District Plan to Cut Danger," *AJ*, August 22, 1951, p. 1.

465. "City Group Asks for Special Flood Control District," *AJ*, January 12, 1952, p. 1.

466. Wayne S. Scott, "Here's How $9.5 Million in Local Costs Would Be Spent on Twin Ditch Project," *AJ*, August 11, 1963, pp. A1, A6.

467. Wayne S. Scott, "Big Ditch Designed to Trap Rain of State's Record Fall," *AJ*, August 7, 1963, p. A1.

468. Wayne S. Scott, "Southern 'Big Ditch' to Haul Less Water," *AJ*, August 8, 1963, p. A1.

469. Wayne S. Scott, "Sandia Flood District Formed Nine Years Ago, But No Dirt Turned Yet," *AJ*, June 25, 1961, p. E7.

470. "Flood District, Knocked Out by Court, to Close Office Sept. 1," *AJ*, August 9, 1958, p. 1.

471. "Flood District Protest Meeting Draws Thousands in Heights," *AJ*, October 19, 1957, p. 1.

472. "Conservancy Protests Increase; N.M. State Fair Joins Objectors," *AJ*, October 20, 1957, p. 1.

473. "Year's Worst Flood Brings Big Damage to Streets in City," *AJ*, October 21, 1957, p. 1.

474. "Voters Put Citizens Ticket Back in Office," *AJ*, April 9, 1958, p. 1.

475. "Flood District, Knocked Out by Court, to Close Office Sept. 1," *AJ*, August 9, 1958, p. 1.

476. "POPA's Slate Sweeps Positions in Sandia Dist.," *AJ*, October 7, 1959, p. 1.

477. "O'Toole, Atkinson to City Commission," *AJ*, October 7, 1959, p. 1.

478. "City-County Bldg., Consolidation Plan Defeated by Voters," *AJ*, October 7, 1959, p. 1.

Chapter 4

479. "Commissioners Hit Campaigning of City Judge," *AJ*, March 3, 1960, p. A2.

480. "City Commission Session Marked by Verbal Bout," *AJ*, May 25,1960, p. A2.

481. Marianne Johnson, "City Commission Voting Reflects Election Jolt," *AJ*, March 27, 1960, p. A4.

482. Marianne Johnson, "City Commission Charge Bid Rigging," *AJ*, June 15, 1960, p. A1.

483. Marianne Johnson, "City Commission Marred by Open Warfare," *AJ*, July 20, 1960, p. A1; "City Manager Gets Vote of Confidence," *AJ*, August 25, 1960, p. A1.

484. Judith Brimberg, "Detailed Report on Paint Buying Is Asked by City," *AJ*, December 13, 1961, p. A1.

485. Edna Steinman, "Ex-City Employe Acquitted of Embezzling," *AJ*, May 15, 1962, p. A1.

486. Judith Brimberg, "Detailed Report on Paint Buying Is Asked by City," *AJ*, December 13, 1961, p. A1.

487. Paul Wieck, "City Finance Director Kious Resigns," *AJ*, December 18, 1961, p. A1.

488. Paul Wieck, "State to Investigate City Financial Affairs," *AJ*, December 21, 1961, pp. A1, A8.

489. "Directive Seeks to Clarify City Hall Command Chain," *AJ*, January 17, 1962, p. A2.

490. Paul Wieck, "City Traffic Head Resigns," *AJ*, January 30, 1962, p. A1.

491. "Beck Gets Post as City's Traffic Engineer Chief," *AJ*, February 15, 1962, p. A1.

492. Marianne Johnson, "'Brain' Goes Berserk Here; Fuse Blows, Traffic Snarled," *AJ*, October 11, 1960, p. A1.

493. Marianne Johnson, "Citizens Group Plans to Shelve Reform Plank," *AJ*, November 13, 1960, pp. A1, A7.

494. "Clyde Tingley, Ex-Governor of N.M., Dies," *AJ*, December 25, 1960, p. A1.

495. "Tingleys Send Toys to Hospital," *AJ*, December 22, 1960, p. D1.

496. "Know Your Candidates," *AJ*, March 28, 1962, p. D1.

497. Paul Wieck, "Politics Among Workers Fails to Surprise Many," *AJ*, August 19, 1962, p. A4.

498. Paul Wieck, "ACC Sweeps City Commission Election," *AJ*, April 4, 1962, p. A1.

499. Paul Wieck, "Stand on Urban Renewal Represents Policy Shift," *AJ*, May 29, 1962, p. A4.

500. Dick McAlpin, "Schifani, Who Loves Good Fight, Expects Just That Before City Vote Is Tallied," AJ, September 26, 1963, p. B9; Dick McAlpin, "Trigg's Background Includes Many Years as an Administrator," *AJ*, September 30, 1963, p. B11.

501. Dick McAlpin, "Schifani, Trigg Win City Commission Seats," *AJ*, October 9, 1963, p. A1.

502. "Schifani, Elected as Non-Partisan, Backs Montoya," *AJ*, December 11, 1963, p. A1.

503. Wayne S. Scott, "Schifani Remarks Trigger Demand for Recall Vote," *AJ*, December 12, 1963, p. A1; "Schifani Issues Apology," *AJ*, December 17, 1963, p. A1.

504. Dick McAlpin, "Newest Members Add Zing to Commission," *AJ*, September 6, 1964, p. A4.

505. Dick McAlpin, "Commission 'Intrusion' Shakes Up City Staffers," *AJ*, November 8, 1964, p. A4.

506. "City Commission Ignores Petitions on Gasoline Tax," *AJ*, January 20, 1965, pp. A1, A2.

507. Dick McAlpin, "Court Orders City to Prepare for Gasoline Tax Referendum," *AJ*, January 30, 1965, p. A1.

508. Sam Blythe, "Voters Defeat Gasoline Tax Increase," *AJ*, November 17, 1965, pp. A1, A2.

509. "ACC Proposes Three Candidates for Commission," *AJ*, February 23, 1966, pp. A1, A2.
510. Ted Hulbert, "Domenici Would Assign Priority to Top Problems," *AJ*, March 24, 1966, p. A10.
511. "'Little Hoover' Probe Is Proposed by Gurule," *AJ*, March 26, 1966, p. C6.
512. "Candidate Kinney Feels Street Budget Adequate," *AJ*, March 24, 1966, p. C7.
513. "Successful Record Cited As Citizens Committee Issues Election Platform," *AJ*, March 4, 1966, p. F6.
514. "'People's' Ticket Adopts Platform for Board Race," *AJ*, March 9, 1966, p. D1.
515. "Schifani, Trigg to Support Rival 'People's' Ticket," *AJ*, March 11, 1966, p. A1.
516. "People's Ticket Is Given Backing of Labor Unions," *AJ*, April 2, 1966, p. A6.
517. Sam Blythe, "ACC Grip on City Hall Soundly Shattered," *AJ*, April 6, 1966, p. A1; "Vote Tide Starts in East San Jose," *AJ*, April 6, 1966, p. A1.
518. "Six Members Resign from Posts on City Planning Commission," *AJ*, May 3, 1966, p. A1; "City Commission Names 5 Members to Planning Board," *AJ*, May 25, 1966, p. A1.
519. "Plan Director Resigns," *AJ*, June 30, 1966, p. A1.
520. "F.R. Bowdich Named to Head Personnel Dept.," *AJ*, May 10, 1966, p. A2.
521. "Lack of City 'PR' Is Noted," *AJ*, January 7, 1968, p. A6.
522. Sam Blythe, "Commissioners Oust City Manager Engel," *AJ*, April 28, 1966, p. A1.
523. "Former Employes Give Engel Gift—Ape Art," *AJ*, May 18, 1966, p. C12.
524. "Triigg, Schifani Favor Mayor System for City," *AJ*, August 13, 1965, p. A1.
525. Dick McAlpin, "Veteran City Employes 'Scared of' Commission," *AJ*, May 28, 1967, p. A4.
526. "More Difficult Year Faced by Commission," *AJ*, December 18, 1966, p. A4.
527. "Urban Renewal Expert Is Hired; Salary $16,500," *AJ*, June 22, 1967, p. A1.
528. "Newcomers Are Welcomed, Results Are Expected," *AJ*, July 23, 1967, p. A4; Sam Blythe, "City's New Plan Chief Making Impression," *AJ*, August 6, 1967, p. A4.
529. Sam Blythe, "Changes Cropping Up in Board Procedures," *AJ*, April 24, 1966, p. A4.
530. "Trigg's Plan for Group on Industry Is Stymied," *AJ*, October 7, 1966, p. A2.
531. "Mistakes of Past Could Profit City," *AJ*, April 20, 1967, pp. A1, A9.
532. Sam Blythe, "U.S. Helped Mold City Vote," *AJ*, November 19, 1967, p. A4.
533. Bob Beier, "ACC Hopefuls for Retention of Manager, More Home Rule," *AJ*, September 26, 1967, p. A2; Sam Blythe, "Payne, Barnhart Elected to Commission," *AJ*, October 4, 1967, p. A1.
534. "City Commission to Create Three Assistance Panels," *AJ*, October 18, 1967, p. A11.
535. Sam Blythe, "U.S. Helped Mold City Vote," *AJ*, November 19, 1967, p. A4.
536. "$25 Million for Renewal," *AJ*, June 28, 1968, p. A1.
537. "Health Chief Quits; City Hires PR Man," *AJ*, July 27, 1968, p. B6.
538. "Gripe Sessions Idea Good," *AJ*, August 4, 1968, p. A4.
539. Bob Brown, "Commissioner Keeps Cool Under Fire," *AJ*, September 24, 1968, p. A4.
540. Martha Buddecke, "Charges of Valley Neglect Stir Pete Domenici's Ire," *AJ*, June 27, 1969, pp. A1, A2.
541. Mike Padget, "Citizens Plan City Future," *AJ*, April 20, 1969, p. A4.
542. Sam Blythe, "Observatory Deserves Look," *AJ*, January 5, 1969, p. A6.
543. "ACTION Involves Many," *AJ*, July 13, 1969, p. A6; "ACTION Workers Collect 500-Plus Tons of Refuse," *AJ*, July 27, 1969, p. A2.
544. Joline Daffer, "Urban Systems Plan Gets City Approval," *AJ*, February 24, 1970, pp. A1, A5; Joline Daffer, "City Chalks Up a 'First,'" *AJ*, March 1, 1970, p. A4.
545. "Gurule Leaves Post on City Commission," *AJ*, December 9, 1967, p. A1.
546. "School Official to Get Commission Post," *AJ*, December 18, 1967, p. A1.
547. "Baker, Gurule Convicted of Defrauding Railway," *AJ*, April 16, 1969, p. A1.
548. "R.H. Wilson to Become City Manager," *AJ*, July 3, 1968, p. A1.
549. "Domenici, Barnhart Trade City Posts," *AJ*, March 4, 1970, p. A1.

550. Ken Wilkinson, "Air Force Had Big Role in Airport Development," *AJ*, November 12, 1965, p. E10.

551. Marianne Johnson, "Present Site Urged for New Air Facility," *AJ*, June 16, 1960, pp. A1, A2; "Airport Controversy," *AJ*, June 21, 1960, p. A6; "Commissioners Approve Kirtland. as Airport Site," *AJ*, July 13, 1960, p. A1.

552. "Airport Solution Near," *AJ*, April 2, 1961, p. A4.

553. "In City's Lap," *AJ*, July 13, 1961, p. A4; "Sharrer Back with Deed to Airport," *AJ*, December 16, 1962, p. A1; Ken Wilkinson, "Air Force Had Big Role in Airport Development," *AJ*, November 12, 1965, p. E10.

554. Bill Hesch, "Profits Squeeze Has Parallel in Service Loss," *AJ*, June 24, 1962, p. C8.

555. "The City's Bus Lease," *AJ*, March 1, 1964, p. A4.

556. "City Plans Bus Company Study; Firm to Quit," *AJ*, November 20, 1963, p. A1.

557. "The City's Bus Lease," *AJ*, March 1, 1964, p. A4.

558. "City Commission Votes to Buy Bus Firm," *AJ*, December 16, 1964, p. A1.

559. "New City Hall Problem," *AJ*, July 18, 1965, p. A4.

560. Sam Blythe, "City Commission OKs Bargaining with 3 Unions," *AJ*, September 15, 1965, p. A2.

561. "Bus Union, City Reach Agreement," *AJ*, January 14, 1966, p. A1.

562. Sam Blythe, "Changes Cropping Up in Board Procedures," *AJ*, April 24, 1966, p. A4.

563. "New Civic Center Plan," *AJ*, June 9, 1960, A6.

564. "Commission Votes Go-Ahead on City Hall," *AJ*, August 31, 1960, p.A1.

565. "City, County Fail to Reach Accord on Joint Building," *AJ*, October 19, 1961, p. A2.

566. Judith Brimberg, "Growth Committee Formed, Will Seek New City Hall Here," *AJ*, January 28, 1962, p. A1; "City Commission OKs Growth Unit Bond Issue Plan," *AJ*, February 28, 1962, p. Al.

567. "$100,000 Pledged for City Hall Site," *AJ*, June 6, 1962, p. A1.

568. "City Accepts Hall Site Near Courthouse," *AJ*, June 27, 1962, p. A1.

569. "Lovelace Urges Single Building for City, County," *AJ*, July 10, 1962, p. A1.

570. "Joint Building for City, County Favored by C of C," *AJ*, July 17, 1962, p. A1.

571. "County Officials Reject Proposal on Joint Building," *AJ*, August 4, 1962, p. A1.

572. "Courthouse Bond Issue Narrowly Wins," *AJ*, May 15, 1963, p. A1.

573. "POPA Launches Drive to Change Sandia Dist. Law," *AJ*, April 6, 1960, p. A2.

574. "Property Owners Split Develops; 6 Directors Quit," *AJ*, December 31, 1959, p. A1.

575. "William Jones Resigns as POPA President," *AJ*, January 5, 1960, p. A2.

576. "Citizens Committee Protests Flood Tax," *AJ*, June 20, 1960, p. A1; Wayne S. Scott, "Sandia Flood District Formed Nine Years Ago, But No Dirt Turned Yet," *AJ*, June 25, 1961, p. E7.

577. "POPA Directors Debate Levy for Flood District," *AJ*, June 25, 1960, p. A2.

578. Wayne S. Scott, "Sandia Flood District Formed Nine Years Ago, But No Dirt Turned Yet," *AJ*, June 25, 1961, p. E7.

579. Wayne S. Scott, "Flood Control Views of Conservancy Board Modified in 4 Years," *AJ*, July 5, 1961, p. A1.

580. "POPA Board Group Renounces Conservancy Ties," *AJ*, July 30, 1961, p. A1.

581. "City, County Agree on Maintenance of Proposed Flood Control Ditches," *AJ*, April 29, 1960, p. A2.

582. Wayne S. Scott, "Sandia Flood District Formed Nine Years Ago, But No Dirt Turned Yet," *AJ*, June 25, 1961, p. E7.

583. Wayne S. Scott, "Court Rules End to SCD Stormy Life," *AJ*, January 6, 1962, p. A1.

584. "Victims of Flood Here Are Declared Eligible for Loans by SBA," *AJ*, August 16, 1961, p. A1.

585. Wayne S. Scott, "Court Rules End to SCD Stormy Life," *AJ*, January 6, 1962, p. A1.

586. "SCD Finally Quits," *AJ*, January 20, 1962, p. A4.

587. "Vote Scheduled for Flood Control Bond, Directors," *AJ*, June 21, 1963, p. A1.

588. Wayne S. Scott, "Metropolitan Flood Control Authority Unable to Place Liens on Property," *AJ*, August 17, 1963, pp. A1, A11.

589. Wayne S. Scott, "Voters Approve Twin Ditch Flood Project," *AJ*, August 28, 1963, p. A1.

590. Paul Wieck, "Urban Renewal Pitfalls Have Been Avoided Here," *AJ*, August 20, 1961, p. A4.

591. Marianne Johnson, "City's Housing Code Is Still 'Voluntary,'"*AJ*, December 16, 1960, p. B12.

592. Paul Wieck, "Urban Renewal Pitfalls Have Been Avoided Here," *AJ*, August 20, 1961, p. A4.

593. "Program Makes Progress in 1960," *AJ*, December 11, 1960, p. A7.

594. Paul Wieck, "Urban Renewal Pitfalls Have Been Avoided Here," *AJ*, August 20, 1961, p. A4.

595. Marianne Johnson, "Federal Agency OKs City Improvement Plan," *AJ*, December 2, 1960, p. A1.

596. Ibid.

597. "South Broadway s 'Face' Beginning to Shine," *AJ*, June 11, 1962, p. A1.

598. Marianne Johnson, "City Reaches Crossroads in Urban Renewal Field," *AJ*, June 11, 1961, p. A6; "Ordinance OK'd to Create Urban Renewal Board," *AJ*, June 28, 1961, p. A2.

599. "South Broadway's 'Face' Beginning to Shine," *AJ*, June 11, 1962, p. A1.

600. Paul Wieck, "Businessmen 'Given Ball' on Downtown," *AJ*, December 13, 1961, p. A1.

601. Paul Wieck, "Once a 'Loner' O'Toole Now Votes with the Team," *AJ*, September 23, 1962, p. A4.

602. Paul Wieck, "Stand on Urban Renewal Represents Policy Shift," *AJ*, July 29, 1962, p. A4.

603. "City to Start Rehabilitation Program Today," *AJ*, August 7, 1962, p. A1.

604. "Downtown Program Is Attracting Support," *AJ*, February 17, 1963, p. A4.

605. "Extensive Rehabilitation Progress Is Chalked Up," *AJ*, December 23, 1963, p. D2.

606. "City Picks Committee 'To Sell' Downtown," *AJ*, January 15, 1964, p. A1.

607. Ibid.

608. Dick McAlpin, "AMDEC's Strength Lies in Power of Persuasion," *AJ*, February 9, 1964, p. A4.

609. Dick McAlpin, "Development Group to Have Final Word," *AJ*, June 14, 1964, p. A4.

610. Martin Paskind, "Downtown Property Owners Vote to Launch Renewal Plan," *AJ*, December 17, 1964, p. A1.

611. Dick McAlpin, "'Individualism' Stalls Progress of Downtown," *AJ*, November 17, 1963, p. A4.

612. Dick McAlpin, "Aversion to Debt Is Declared Drag on Downtown," *AJ*, February 13, 1964, pp. A1, A7.

613. Martin Paskind, "Downtown Property Owners Vote to Launch Renewal Plan," *AJ*, December 17, 1964, pp. A1, A2.

614. Bob Brown, "20-Year 'Core' Plan Is Endorsed," *AJ*, January 22, 1966, p. A1.

615. Sam Blythe, "Progress Is Sure to Be Slow on Traffic Plan for Core Area," *AJ*, May 22, 1966, p. A4.

616. Bob Brown, "Program Makes Progress in 1960," *AJ*, December 11, 1960, p. A7.

617. Ted Hulbert, "Domenici Would Assign Priority to Top Problems," *AJ*, March 24, 1966, p. A10.

618. "Voters Turn Down 3 of 9 Bond Proposals," *AJ*, April 6, 1966, p. A1.

619. Sam Blythe, "Interested Citizens Want Core Redevelopment to Get Moving," *AJ*, July 31, 1966, p. A4.

620. Sam Blythe, "Downtown Architects Worried, Off the Cuff," *AJ*, September 5, 1965, p. A4.

621. Sam Blythe, "Progress Is Sure to Be Slow on Traffic Plan for Core Area," *AJ*, May 22, 1966, p. A4.

622. Sam Blythe, "Commissioners Assume Urban Renewal Role," *AJ*, August 9, 1966, p. A1.

623. "City Commission Names 5-Member Urban Committee," *AJ*, January 24, 1967, pp. A1, A5.

624. Frankie McCarty, "APS Explains Interest in City Urban Program," *AJ*, July 7, 1967, p. A2; Frankie McCarty, "Renewal Planners Lead Discussion on City Project," *AJ*, January 30, 1968, p. A6.

625. "City OKs 'Y' Plan Overpass," *AJ*, September 30, 1967, p. A1.

626. Sam Blythe, "$27 Million Urban Renewal Plan Unveiled," *AJ*, November 10, 1967, pp. A1, A8.

627. "Albuquerque to Get Model Cities Grant," *AJ*, November 17, 1967, p. A1.

628. Sam Blythe, "Friction Developing over Metro Planning Concept," *AJ*, May 7, 1967, p. A4; Martha Buddecke, "Who Plans the Planning," *AJ*, June 16, 1968, p. A4.

629. "Core Against East Heights Center Plan," *AJ*, January 5, 1967, p. A1; "Keep It Downtown," *AJ*, January 5, 1967, p. A4

630. W. Wilson Cliff, "Convention Center Site Is Downtown," *AJ*, April 17, 1968, p. A1.

631. Sam Blythe, "$25 Million for Renewal," *AJ*, June 28, 1968, pp. A1, A4.

632. John McMillion, "Urban Renewal Board Conflict Poses Threat," *AJ*, October 19, 1968, p. A4; Martha Buddecke, "Urban Renewal Sentiment Varies," *AJ*, February 2, 1969, pp. A1, A8.

633. Martha Buddecke, "Neighborhood 'Repair' Plan Supported by City Officials," *AJ*, December 6, 1968, p. A2.

634. Sam Blythe, "Crowd Asks Renewal Say of City Hall," *AJ*, February 4, 1969, p. A1.

635. "Model Cities Citizen Board OKs Neighborhood Development Plan," *AJ*, February 16, 1969, p. G5.

636. "Urban Renewal OKs Model Cities Area NDP Plan," *AJ*, March 13, 1969, p. A1.

637. Martha Buddecke, "Board Gets Needed Member," *AJ*, April 6, 1969, p. A6.

638. Martha Buddecke, "Albuquerque Finds Success Formula in Energy, Community Spirit, Unity," *AJ*, January 4, 1970, p. E4.

639. Martha Buddecke, "$19.5 Million Tijeras Urban Project OK'd," *AJ*, February 20, 1970, p. A1.

640. Joline Daffer, "City at Milestone in Core Renewal Project," *AJ*, April 5, 1970, p. A1.

641. Martha Buddecke, "Physical Improvement Program in Jeopardy," *AJ*, September 7, 1969, p. A1; Joline Daffer, "City at Milestone in Core Renewal Project," *AJ*, April 5, 1970, p. A1.

642. Mike Padget, "Barelas Families Get Better Housing," *AJ*, May 6, 1971, p. A8.

643. Wilson Cliff, "Downtown Street Plan Draws Considerable Ire," *AJ*, October 7, 1967, p. A10; Sam Blythe, "City Does Flip-Flop in OK of Core Mall," *AJ*, October 24, 1967, p. A1; "City's First Core Mall Now History," *AJ*, December 27, 1967, p. A1.

644. Martha Buddecke, "New Group to Spark Downtown Renewal," *AJ*, November 7, 1969, p. A1.

645. Mike Padget, "City's Plan for Downtown Receives Unanimous Approval," *AJ*, December 17, 1970, p. A2.

646. U.S., Department of Commerce, Bureau of the Census, *Census of Population and Housing: 1960, Census Tracts*, Final Report PHC(1)-4, Albuquerque, N. Mex. SMSA, p. 13; idem, *Census of Population and Housing, 1970, Census Tracts*, Final Report PHC(1)-5, Albuquerque, N. Mex. SMSA, p. P-9.

647. Leaflet published by the Albuquerque Industrial Development Service, 1977.

648. U.S., Department of Commerce, Bureau of the Census, *Census of Population and Housing: 1970. Census Tracts*, Final Report PHC(1)-5, Albuquerque, N. Mex. SMSA, p. P-25. The correction for inflation was calculated by means of "Consumer Price Index for Urban Wage Earners and Clerical Workers," produced by the U.S. Department of Labor, Bureau of Labor Statistics.

649. "New C of C Industrial Recruiting Brochure Cites City's Strong Points," *AJ*, April 29, 1960, p. B9.

650. "Hinkle Urges C of C to Act on Industrial Development," *AJ*, May 20, 1960, p. B4.

651. "City Industrial Assn. Outside of Chamber OK'd by Two Groups," *AJ*, August 27, 1960, p. A1.

652. "Off the Ground," *AJ*, September 29, 1960, p. A4.

653. "North Valley Businessmen OK C of C Merger," *AJ*, June 29, 1962, p. D2.

654. "Industrial Development Group Names President," *AJ*, June 21, 1963, p. A2.

655. W. Wilson Cliff, "Effort, Perseverance Rewarded in Landing of New City Industry," *AJ*, August 30, 1966, p. A2.

656. "City Industrial Fund Tops $1 Million Goal with Ease," *AJ*, February 17, 1967, p. A1.

657. "An Industrial Lift," *AJ*, March 24, 1967, p. A4; "ACF Ends City Plant Operations," *AJ*, December 1, 1967, p. A1; "State's Dynamic Growth in '60s Was Typified by Albuquerque," *AJ*, January 4, 1970, p. E10.

658. "TVI Will Offer Study in Trades," *AJ*, August 15, 1965, p. D3.

659. "T-VI Role in Industry is Valuable," *AJ*, September 17, 1968, p. A4.

660. "State's Dynamic Growth in '60s was Typified by Albuquerque," *AJ*, January 4, 1970, p. E10.
661. Ibid.
662. Ibid.
663. "Intense Job Effort to Open Monday," *AJ*, June 30, 1968, p. A4.
664. "Friden Signs Job Contract to Train 150 Unemployed," *AJ*, August 19, 1969, p. A2.
665. Rees Lloyd, "'Skills Co-op' Is Helping Dropouts Get New Start in Life," *AJ*, April 3, 1969, p. D1; Bob Brown, "Small Groups Deserve Credit for Projects," *AJ*, March 10, 1970, p. A4.
666. Ben Castillo, "Minority Businesses Given a Lift," *AJ*, January 17, 1972, p. A1.
667. Judith Brimberg, "Other City Areas Having Troubles," *AJ*, March 18, 1962, p. A16.
668. "Eastern Combine Buys Park Plaza Building," *AJ*, February 3, 1970, p. A1.
669. W. Wilson Cliff, "Locally Conceived Industries Benefit Merging Nationally," *AJ*, April 11, 1967, p. C4.
670. W. Wilson Cliff, "Springer Corp. Plans $500,000 Building," *AJ*, September 11, 1969, p. A1.
671. W. Wilson Cliff, "Springer Acquires Berger-Briggs Realty," *AJ*, March 26, 1970, p. A1.
672. "Atrisco Board Votes to Sell Huge Tract," *AJ*, April 5, 1959, p. 1.
673. "25,000 Visit New Hoffman Homes," *AJ*, June 8, 1959, p. A1.
674. "Hoffman Opening Today," *AJ*, June 7, 1959, p. D7.
675. "Incorporation Being Planned by Hoffman," *AJ*, June 9, 1959, p. A1.
676. "Fraudulent Atrisco Grant Deeds Cloud Tangled Heirship, Title Situation," *AJ*, July 5, 1969, p. A1.
677. "Hoffman Clears Title, to Start Building Soon," *AJ*, September 2, 1959, p. A2.
678. "Builder Hoffman Slays Wife, Then Himself," *AJ*, October 14, 1959, pp. A1, A5.
679. "Snow to Take Over Hoffman City Project," *AJ*, November 30, 1959, p. A1.
680. "Snow's Reputation as Builder Cited," *AJ*, July 23, 1968, p. A2.
681. Martin Paskind, "Albuquerque Realtors Agree Now Top Time to Purchase Home," *AJ*, May 17, 1963, p. A2.
682. "Snow's Reputation as Builder Cited," *AJ*, July 23, 1968, p. A2.
683. "Bellamah's Philosophy: Dream," *AJ*, January 31, 1971, p. A7.
684. "Sears Plans Multi-Million Dollar Shopping Center in NE Heights," *AJ*, January 26, 1962, p. A1.
685. Martin Paskind, "'High-Rise' Apartment to Start Here," *AJ*, August 16, 1963, p. Al.
686. W. Wilson Cliff, "Four Seasons Motor Inn Ready," *AJ*, November 28, 1971, p. A9.
687. W. Wilson Cliff, "Albuquerque Magnate Dale J. Bellamah Dies," *AJ*, April 21, 1972, pp. A1, A5.
688. "Bellamah Corp. Announces $60-Million, 450-Acre Plan," *AJ*, July 21, 1972, p. A1.
689. "Twin-Tower Luxury Office Unit Planned," *AJ*, August 25, 1972, p. A1.
690. "Building to Start on $50 Million Complex," *AJ*, May 30, 1968, p. C4.
691. "New Community Slated to Build on West Mesa," *AJ*, April 8, 1960, p. A1.
692. "Developer Buys Big Tract," *AJ*, September 7, 1961, pp. A1, A6.
693. "Albuquerque Area Industrial Parks and Districts," leaflet published by Albuquerque Industrial Development Service, Inc., 1976.
694. Judith Brimberg, "Curtiss-Wright Building New Facility," *AJ*, February 11, 1961, p. A1.
695. "Albuquerque Area Industrial Parks and Districts," leaflet published by Albuquerque Industrial Development Service, Inc., 1976.
696. "Apartments Open at Paradise Hills," *AJ*, July 2, 1972, p. G2.
697. Dick McAlpin, "State's Tough New Subdivision Bill Draws Different Reactions from Big Land Firms," *AJ*, March 12, 1963, p. A1.
698. Art Bouffard, "Views Given on County Zoning Ordinance," *AJ*, November 28, 1971, p. A10.
699. "Applications Available for Apartments in Low-Cost, Non-Profit Development," *AJ*, November 1, 1964, p. C5; Martin Paskind, "Realtor, Builder Fight on Rentals to Reach Capital," *AJ*, April 6, 1965, pp. A1, A2; "FHA Lists Apartment Rent Level," *AJ*, May 26, 1966, p. A10; W. Wilson Cliff, "U.S. to Soon Help Some Pay Rent," *AJ*, March 12, 1967, p. E5.

700. "Ordinance Approved to Permit Housing Project in Old Town Area," *AJ*, July 28, 1970, p. A2; "Ground Broken for 140-Unit Apartment Complex in NE," *AJ*, December 20, 1971, p. A2.

701. Dick McAlpin, "City Stands Firm on Housing Program," *AJ*, May 16, 1967, p. A1; Sam Blythe, "City Housing Program Moves 65 Families into Better Quarters," *AJ*, March 20, 1968, p. A12.

702. "Low-Rent Housing Dream Is Disappearance of Ghetto," *AJ*, June 6, 1968, p. C6.

703. Ted Hulbert, "Seven Living in Small House Typical Program in S. Barelas," *AJ*, September 13, 1965, pp. A1, A9.

704. Mike Padget, "Renewal Program Grew Here in 1970," *AJ*, January 31, 1971, p. E1.

705. Mike Padget, "Kirtland Addition Residents Finally Get Repair Money," *AJ*, August 10, 1969, p. A4.

706. "Subsidy Program Assists Young Home Buyers," *AJ*, December 25, 1968, p. C11.

707. Martha Buddecke, "Home Builders to Seek Turnkey Housing Role," *AJ*, March 5, 1970, p. A1; Art Bouffard, "Additional Turnkey Units Authorized by HUD for City," *AJ*, November 19, 1971, pp. A1, A6; Suzanne Burks, "First Turnkey Projects Finished and Occupied, 'Acid Test' Begins," *AJ*, October 15, 1972, p. E1.

708. U.S., Department of Commerce, Bureau of the Census, *Census of Housing: 1960*, vol. 2, *Metropolitan Housing*, pt. 2, Abilene-Corpus Christi Standard Metropolitan Statistical Areas, pp. 14-3, 14-4; idem, *Census of Population and Housing: 1970, Census Tracts*, Final Report PHC(1)-5, Albuquerque, N. Mex. SMSA, pp. H-1, H-9.

709. Martin Paskind, "Albuquerque Realtors Agree Now Top Time to Purchase Home," *AJ*, May 17, 1963, p. A2.

710. U.S., Department of Commerce, Bureau of the Census, *Census of Housing: 1960*, vol. 2, *Metropolitan Housing*, pt. 2, Abilene-Corpus Christi Standard Metropolitan Statistical Areas, pp. 14-3, 14-4; idem, *Census of Population and Housing: 1970, Census Tracts*, Final Report PHC(1)-5, Albuquerque, N. Mex. SMSA, p. H-9.

711. Idem, *Census of Housing: 1960*, vol. 2, *Metropolitan Housing*, pt. 2, Abilene-Corpus Christi Standard Metropolitan Statistical Areas, pp. 14-3, 14-4; ibid., vol. 1, *States and Small Areas*, pt. 6, New Jersey-Ohio, p. 33-15; idem, *Census of Housing: 1970*, vol. 1, *Housing Characteristics for States, Cities, and Counties*, pt. 33, New Mexico, p. 33-65.

712. "City of Albuquerque Building Permits," leaflet published by Albuquerque Industrial Development Service, Inc., 1974; Monthly Report, Department of Public Works, City of Albuquerque, 1957-1962.

713. Dick McAlpin, "Apartments Construction Booms Here," *AJ*, March 17, 1963, pp. A1, A6; "Different Factors Involved in Trend Toward Apartment Living," *AJ*, March 18, 1963, pp. A1, A8.

714. Multiple Listing Report, Albuquerque Board of Realtors, July 1976.

715. Telephone conversation with the Albuquerque office of the Federal Housing Authority, Mortgage Credit Section, October 2, 1979.

716. Dick McAlpin, "Different Factors Involved in Trend Toward Apartment Living," *AJ*, March 18, 1963, pp. A1, A8.

717. "Sears to Close Downtown Store on West Central," *AJ*, April 5, 1967, p. A1; "Action Imperative," *AJ*, April 5, 1967, p. A4; "Fedway Leaving Downtown Albuquerque," *AJ*, June 4, 1971, p. A1.

718. U.S., Department of Commerce, Bureau of the Census, *Census of Retail Trade: 1972, Retail Trade: Major Retail Centers*, New Mexico, RC 72-C-32, p. 32-12.

719. "City Typified State's Gains," *AJ*, January 14, 1970, p. E4.

720. Paul Wieck, "Downtown Area Will Continue as Government Center," *AJ*, November 25, 1962, pp. A1, A8.

721. "Picturesque Downtown Progress," *AJ*, July 1, 1966, p. A1.

722. "Big Building for Albuquerque," *AJ*, December 2, 1971, p. A4.

723. Bob Brown, "Face of City Is Changing Rapidly," *AJ*, September 24,1972, p. A4.
724. The percentages of office buildings and businesses for 1972 were calculated by counting the number of addresses in the central business district as defined by the U.S. Bureau of the Census and then dividing by the number of each kind in the metropolitan area. The source was the yellow pages of the 1972 Greater Albuquerque telephone book. The percentages of physicians, dentists and lawyers were calculated from the numbers of names rather than addresses, for the proportion of practicing professionals in the area seemed more significant than the proportion of their offices located there. The figures for 1945, which were taken from chapter two, were arrived at through a similar procedure.
725. U.S., Department of Commerce, Bureau of the Census, *Census of Retail Trade: 1972, Retail Trade: Major Retail Centers*, New Mexico, RC 72-C-32, pp. 32-6, 32-7.
726. "Del Webb, Bank Official to Open New Mexico's Tallest Bldg. Today," *AJ*, February 14, 1963, p. A1.
727. "Albuquerque Area Industrial Parks and Districts," leaflet published by Albuquerque Industrial Development Service, Inc., 1976.
728. *Decades of Destiny*, booklet published by P.F. McCanna, Inc., Albuquerque, 1973, p. 18.
729. Ibid., p. 17.
730. Dick McAlpin, "Apartment Construction Booms Here," *AJ*, March 17, 1963, pp. A1, A6.
731. Wilson Cliff, "Giant Apartment Complex Is Planned in NE Heights," *AJ*, November 19, 1967, p. A1; *Decades of Destiny*, booklet published by P.F. McCanna, Inc., Albuquerque, 1973, p. 18.
732. Martin Paskind, "Albuquerque Realtors Agree Now Top Time to Purchase Home," *AJ*, May 17, 1963, p. A2.
733. Report conducted by the Automotive Safety Foundation, 1950, p. 25.
734. "1972 Traffic Flow for the Greater Albuquerque Area," a map prepared by the Middle Rio Grande Council of Governments and the City of Albuquerque, 1973.
735. Judith Brimberg, "UNM Students Split over Racial Picketing," *AJ*, March 6, 1960, p. A1.
736. Ted Hulbert, "City Resident Is Still Deeply Moved by Fact Whites Joined Capital March," *AJ*, September 29, 1963, p. B4.
737. "Lack of Housing Forces Negroes Here to Live in Shacks, Report Says," *AJ*, April 13, 1960, p. A1.
738. Wayne Welch, "Negroes in Albuquerque Excluded from New Housing, Report Declares," *AJ*, September 10, 1961, p. B8.
739. Paul Wieck, "Housewife Overcomes Discrimination, Helps 50 Negro Families Find Housing," *AJ*, November 4, 1962, p. A14.
740. Frankie McCarty, "Landlords Turn Down Negro at U.," *AJ*, October 14, 1962, p. A1.
741. "Ordinance Asked to Bar Housing Discrimination," *AJ*, October 17, 1962, pp. A1, B2.
742. "U. Campus Group Asks Rent Units Be Unsegregated," *AJ*, October 17, 1962, p. A1.
743. "U. Action Due to Ban Racial Discrimination," *AJ*, December 5, 1962, p. A1.
744. "African Student Denied Housing Returning to U.," *AJ*, October 25, 1962, p. A2.
745. "'Fair Housing' Groups Start Tolerance Drive," *AJ*, November 20, 1962, p. A2.
746. "President Signs Ban on Housing Discrimination," *AJ*, November 21, 1962, p. A1.
747. "Discrimination Fault of People, Builders Claim," *AJ*, October 18, 1962, pp. A1, A10.
748. "City Ordinance Against Discrimination Is Passed," *AJ*, June 19, 1963, pp. A1, A2.
749. Dick McAlpin, "Fair Housing Board Ready for Action Soon," *AJ*, November 10, 1963, p. A4.
750. "Fair Housing Ordinance Called 'Unenforceable,'" *AJ*, November 16, 1964, p. A2.
751. Hal Simmons, "U. Student Court Action Stirs Up Campus Discord," *AJ*, May 4, 1961, p. A4.
752. "UNM Party Accuses Council of Racial Discrimination," *AJ*, November 21, 1963, p. A14.
753. "Motion to Ban Discriminatory Clauses Gets Varied Reaction," *AJ*, March 5, 1964, p. B7.
754. "University Regents Adopt Policy Aimed at Discriminatory Clauses," *AJ*, March 17, 1964, p. A1.
755. "U. Bid Is Given Negro Fraternity," *AJ*, April 24, 1964, p. C1.
756. "1350 Sign UNM Petitions," *AJ*, February 21, 1961, p. A2.

757. "Probe at UNM Opposed by Senate Finance Group," *AJ*, February 24, 1961, pp. A1, A14.
758. Wayne Welch, "Resolutions Hitting 'Test' Oath Backed," *AJ*, March 14, 1962, p. A1.
759. Wayne Welch, "U. Regents Oppose Reeve, Favor Both Oaths, Loan Plan," *AJ*, March 13, 1962, p. A1.
760. "NMCLU Wants Public Discussion of Oath Issue," *AJ*, March 17, 1962, p. A1.
761. "Popejoy Fires Back at Critics," *AJ*, May 12, 1962, p. A1.
762. Roy Carbine, "Student Newspaper 'Lobo' Draws Fire of UNM Regents," *AJ*, November 12, 1961, p. C5; Roy Carbine, "Two UNM Student Groups Hit Regents' Study of the 'Lobo,'" *AJ*, November 18, 1961, p. A2.
763. "Popejoy Quashes Lobo-Journalism Professor Feud," *AJ*, October 19, 1962, pp. A1, A6.
764. "University Council Praises Popejoy," *AJ*, September 18, 1964, p. A2.
765. "Democratic Group Endorses Slate of Eight Candidates," *AJ*, March 12, 1959, p. 8.
766. "Grass Roots Democrats List Platform," *AJ*, March 4, 1960, p. B11; Wayne S. Scott, "Grass Roots Group Power Questioned," *AJ*, August 17, 1962, p. A6.
767. Ibid.
768. Sam Blythe, "City Air Pollution Ordinance Enforcement Phase to Start," *AJ*, December 12, 1965, p. A1, A6.
769. "Leaf-Burning Law Effective Wednesday," *AJ*, October 1, 1963, p. D5.
770. Sam Blythe, "City Air Pollution Ordinance Enforcement Phase to Start," *AJ*, December 12, 1965, p. A6.
771. Sam Blythe, "Air Pollution Plan Slowed by Lack of Funds," *AJ*, December 13, 1965, p. B5.
772. William Montgomery, "ACC Board Votes Against Paper Mill," *AJ*, September 6, 1969, p. A1.
773. "Paper Mill for State Ruled Out," *AJ*, September 12, 1969, p. A1.
774. "The Mess in Viet Nam," *AJ*, August 24, 1964, p. A4.
775. Ben Moffett, "Dad Says Hero Died in No-Purpose Battle," *AJ*, March 3, 1968, p. A1.
776. "Protest Staged over Fallout Shelter Training," *AJ*, February 20, 1964, p. A9.
777. Paul Wieck, "Belief Racial Discrimination Wrong Motivated Allen Cooper," *AJ*, July 29, 1963, p. A10; "City Women Organize 'Rights' Workers Aid," *AJ*, July 9, 1965, p. A14.
778. "Allen Cooper Terms 'Leftist' Tag Inaccurate," *AJ*, February 27, 1965, p. A14.
779. "City Man Notifies IRS of Refusal to Pay Tax," *AJ*, April 16, 1966, p. A2.
780. Dick McAlpin, "Burton of 'The UNM Juggler': 'Yessir, We're Communists,'" *AJ*, November 1, 1967, p. A2.
781. Art Bouffard, "March on Induction Center Keys Month's Moratorium," *AJ*, November 15, 1969, p. A12.
782. "Area Boost Given War on Poverty," *AJ*, October 1, 1964, p. A14.
783. "Questioning of Official About Poverty War Reveals Some Confusion," *AJ*, February 20, 1965, p. D7.
784. Art Bouffard, "EOB Communications Criticized," *AJ*, April 20, 1970, p. A1.
785. Paul Wieck, "Anderson Calls Poverty Corps in N.M 'Mess,'" *AJ*, May 3, 1965, p. A1.
786. "Gailard Appointed County EOB Head," *AJ*, June 2, 1965, pp. A1, A2.
787. Ed Hulbert, "Youthful Leaders Represent Trend," *AJ*, September 12, 1965, pp. A1, A8; "Association Leaders Are Avoiding Politics," *AJ*, September 15, 1965, p. A15.
788. Marcia Goldstein, "Higher Values Needed to Eliminate Poverty," *AJ*, August 16, 1966, p. A12.
789. Rees Lloyd, "Community Is Key in Poverty Planning," *AJ*, November 15, 1968, p. A2.
790. "Low-Rent Housing Dream Is Disappearance of Ghetto," *AJ*, June 6, 1968, p. C6.
791. Marcia Goldstein, "EOB Officials Busy Answering Queries from Parks Dept.," *AJ*, August 20, 1966, p. C5.
792. Ted Hulbert, "Seven Living in Small House Typical Program in S. Barelas," *AJ*, September 13, 1965, pp. A1, A9.

793. Marcia Goldstein, "EOB Officials Busy Answering Queries from Parks Dept.," *AJ*, August 20, 1966, p. C5.

794. Larry Calloway, "Cost of Job Corps $5500 a Year for Each Girl," *AJ*, January 6, 1967, p. B12.

795. Fred Bonavita, "Project Head-Start in Albuquerque Described as Justified by Enthusiasm," *AJ*, June 20, 1965, p. C2.

796. "New Mexico's Approved Poverty War Programs," *AJ*, August 10, 1966, p. C15.

797. Frankie McCarty, "'Upward Bound' Means Excitement for Motivated Youths," *AJ*, July 31, 1966, p. C1.

798. "Intensive Training Given in New Careers Program," *AJ*, November 1, 1968, p. E10.

799. Marcia Goldstein, "Community Centers Are Nothing Novel—North Barelas Has Had One for Years," *AJ*, August 19, 1966, p. E2.

800. Ted Hulbert, "Progress Slow in Most Areas," *AJ*, September 14, 1965, p. A15; "Association Leaders Are Avoiding Politics," *AJ*, September 15, 1965, p. A15; "Democrat Group Pledges to Help South Barelas," *AJ*, October 10, 1965, p. A2.

801. Ted Hulbert, "Four New Centers Are Planned," *AJ*, June 5, 1966, p. D2; Marcia Goldstein, "EOB Officials Busy Answering Queries from Parks Dept.," *AJ*, August 20, 1966, p. C5.

802. Marcia Goldstein, "Welfare Centers Bring Services, Aid to Poverty Stricken Areas," *AJ*, August 15, 1966, p. B13.

803. Marcia Goldstein, "Progress in South Barelas Slow; But Poverty War May Speed It Up," *AJ*, August 14, 1966, p. E1.

804. "'Pop Art' Film Sponsored by Rights Group Here Is Confiscated by Police," *AJ*, April 2, 1965, p. A2; "U. Students Start Talkathon to Protest Events in Selma," *AJ*, March 11, 1965, p. A2; Lynne Frindell, "UNM Volunteers Combat School Dropouts with Tutoring," *AJ*, December 11, 1966, p. F5.

805. U.S., Department of Health, Education and Welfare, Bureau of Educational Research and Development, Educational Statistics Branch, *Total Enrollment in Institutions of Higher Education, First Term, 1959-60 Basic Data*, p. 38; U.S., Department of Health, Education and Welfare, National Center for Education Statistics, *Total Enrollment in Higher Education, 1972*, p. 208.

806. The dollar figures were calculated by dividing the total current fund expenditures of the university by the size of the student body. The sources for the expenditures are *University of New Mexico Financial Report for the Year Ended June 30, 1960*, p. 7; *University of New Mexico Financial Report for the Year Ended June 30, 1972*, p. 61. Adjustments for inflation were made using the Consumer Price Index published by the U.S. , Department of Labor, Bureau of Labor Statistics.

807. New Mexico, Superintendent of Public Instruction, *Annual Statistical Report on New Mexico Schools, for the Period July 1, 1959 to June 30, 1960*, pp. 8, 63; idem, *Annual Statistical Report of the Superintendent of Public Instruction, for the Period July 1, 1971 to June 30, 1972*, p. 17; New Mexico, Department of Finance and Administration, *Statistics: Public School Finance Division, 1972*, p. B25. The calculations were made in the same manner as before.

808. Johnny D. Gonzales, "Sports Boom Hits City in 1960s," *AJ*, January 4, 1970, p. F2.

809. Ibid; "Triple-A for Albuquerque," *AJ*, September 3, 1971, p. A4.

810. "Proprietors of Coffee House Find Patrons Noisy—Interesting," *AJ*, July 10, 1959, p. B5.

811. Bennie Moffett, "True 'Beats' Spurn Weekend Counterparts as 'Art Snobs,'" *AJ*, January 16, 1961, p. A8.

812. Bennie Moffett, "City's 'Beat' Bunch Stresses 'We Don't Want' Attitude," *AJ*, January 15, 1961, p. A1.

813. Roy Carbine, "Editor of Student Newspaper Has Become Center of Controversy," *AJ*, November 24, 1961, p. F11.

814. Frankie McCarty, "Campus Unrest Brings Opinions," *AJ*, May 30, 1965, p. A5.

815. Frankie McCarty, "U. Regents Adopt Policy on 'Rights,'" *AJ*, October 10, 1965, p. A1.

816. Frankie McCarty, "Unit of Group Scored by FBI Formed Here," *AJ*, October 8, 1964, p. A1.

817. "Popejoy Says U. Would Reject Club's Affiliation," *AJ*, October 10, 1964, p. A1.

818. Frankie McCarty, "U. Panel Discusses Du Bois Club Action Before Professors," *AJ*, January 12, 1965, p. A2.

819. "Du Bois Leader, Student at UNM, Admits He's Red," *AJ*, November 18, 1965, p. A1.

820. "Liberties of All Students Upheld by U. President," *AJ*, November 19, 1965, p. A1.

821. "Something of a 'Tout Sheet' Greets Students at University Registration," *AJ*, September 15, 1966, p. B4; "Student Group Hits 'Conspiracy' of Residents," *AJ*, January 8, 1968, p. A2.

822. "Dispute over Carmichael's Date at UNM Rages On," *AJ*, January 12, 1968, p. A2; Bob Beier, "Appearance at University Cancelled by Carmichael," *AJ*, January 19, 1968, pp. A1, A4.

823. Frankie McCarty, "Heady Aims to Set Tone of University," *AJ*, July 21, 1968, p. A1.

824. "Heady Requests Study of UNM Publication," *AJ*, August 25, 1968, p. A19.

825. "U. Suspends Three in Demonstration," *AJ*, October 24, 1968, p. A2; Frankie McCarty, "Suspended UNM Student Appeals," *AJ*, October 29, 1968, p. A2.

826. Frankie McCarty, "Suspension of 3 at U. Affirmed," *AJ*, November 22, 1968, p. A1.

827. Frankie McCarty, "UNM Faculty Asks Clemency in Student Suspension Appeal," *AJ*, December 6, 1968, p. E19.

828. "U. Students Reinstated," *AJ*, December 27, 1968, p. A1.

829. "'Free University' Sign-Up Starts at UNM Today," *AJ*, April 15, 1966, p. A2.

830. "Parental Burden Is Cited in New U. Housing Policy," *AJ*, January 31, 1965, pp. A1, A10; "U. Faculty Votes to End Control of Student Life," *AJ*, June 4, 1970, p. A2.

831. "UNM to Open Four Dorms to Coeducational Housing," *AJ*, April 4, 1971, p. D1.

832. "Students on More Committees," *AJ*, May 16, 1968, p. A12.

833. As early as 1967, nearly half the students were getting some form of financial aid. "Students Get Financial Aid," *AJ*, October 1, 1967, p. B9.

834. "Draft Protest Group Sparks Melee at AHS," *AJ*, May 24, 1967, p. A1.

835. "Youth Council Hopes to Be Link Between City's Teenagers and Adults," *AJ*, January 23, 1959, p. 43; Cathy Ingenhutt, "Youth Council Has Many Projects," *AJ*, February 6, 1966, p. F5.

836. "Juvenile Gangs Clash in Battle," *AJ*, April 26, 1964, p. A2; "Civic Auditorium Youth Dances Are Canceled," *AJ*, April 29, 1964, p. A1.

837. Pete Chronis, "Youths Not Content with Dance Statute," *AJ*, November 9, 1965, p. A1; "City Commission Votes Ordinance on Youth Dances," *AJ*, December 1, 1965, p. A1.

838. Wayne Welch, "A 'Panel of Experts' Gives Parents Tips on Handling Teenage Problems," *AJ*, April 23, 1961, pp. A1, A13.

839. "'Mad Mad World' Youths Complain of Rules Aplenty," *AJ*, August 14, 1965, p. C4.

840. For example, "Suspended Teenager Pleads Longhair Case," *AJ*, January 12, 1967, p. D7; "Boy Keeps Hair, Is Suspended," *AJ*, February 4, 1969, p. B4.

841. Leroy Bearman, "Several Lobo Players Denied Entrance to Award Banquet," *AJ*, December 11, 1968, p. F1; "Facial Hair Ban Scored," *AJ*, December 13, 1968, p. G3.

842. Frankie McCarty, "Teacher, Pupil Walkout Affects One City School," *AJ*, March 18, 1967, p. A2.

843. Pat Lamb, "Young Protest Marchers Want Dance, Not Picnic," *AJ*, February 18, 1967, p. A6.

844. Frankie McCarty, "Schools Are Learning to Heed Students' Ire," *AJ*, March 16, 1969, p. A9; Frankie McCarty, "Students Seek Recognition as Human Beings," *AJ*, March 17, 1969, pp. A1, A11.

845. Frankie McCarty, "Students Ask for Explanations," *AJ*, March 18, 1969, pp. A1, A15.

846. Frankie McCarty, "Schools Are Learning to Heed Students' Ire," *AJ*, March 16, 1969, p. A9.

847. Frankie McCarty, "Students Air Their Views on Dress, Appearance Code," *AJ*, April 18, 1969, p. C6.

848. Glenn Garvin, "Few Dress Code Restrictions for City High Schools," *AJ*, November 9, 1970, p. A6.

849. Frankie McCarty, "Student Rights, Responsibilities Being Written into Board Policy," *AJ*, October 10, 1971, p. A1.

850. "School Rights, Responsibilities Text Presented," *AJ*, May 11, 1972, p. F12.

851. Frankie McCarty, "Statement Adopted on Student Rights," *AJ*, May 23, 1972, p. A14.

852. Ted Hulbert, "Job Agency Aids Idle Youths Find Niche in Society," *AJ*, February 14, 1965, p. A1; "Dial-a-Teen Ideas Used as Models," *AJ*, October 24, 1971, p. G7.

853. Merith Cosden, "Youth Services Center Hitting Some Problems," *AJ*, February 8, 1971, p. A10.

854. "18-Year Vote Age Ratified into Law," *AJ*, July 1, 1971, p. A1.

855. Between 1960 and 1970, the number of Indians residing in Bernalillo County rose from 3,378 to 5,822, the number of Blacks from 4,672 to 6,740, and the number of Spanish-surnamed from 68,101 to 123,814; the remainder declined from 186,048 to 179,398. U.S., Department of Commerce, Bureau of the Census, *Census of Population and Housing: 1960, Census Tracts*, Final Report PHC(1)-4, Albuquerque, N. Mex. SMSA, p. 13; idem, *Census of Population: 1960*, vol. 1, *Characteristics of the Population*, pt. 33, New Mexico, p. 33-49; idem, *Census of Population and Housing: 1970, Census Tracts*, Final Report PHC(1)-5, Albuquerque, N. Mex. SMSA, pp. P-9, P-33, P-35; idem, *Census of Population: 1970, Subject Reports*, Final Report PC(2)-1F, American Indians, p. 138.

856. Idem, *Census of Population and Housing: 1960, Census Tracts*, Final Report PHC(1)-4, Albuquerque, N. Mex. SMSA, pp. 13, 38; idem, *Census of Population and Housing: 1970, Census Tracts*, Final Report PHC(1)-5, Albuquerque, N. Mex. SMSA, pp. P-25, P-41.

857. Idem, *Census of Population and Housing: 1960, Census Tracts*, Final Report PHC(1)-4, Albuquerque, N. Mex. SMSA, pp. 13, 38; idem, *Census of Population and Housing: 1970, Census Tracts*, Final Report PHC(1)-5, Albuquerque, N. Mex. SMSA, pp. P-9, P-35.

858. "Reies Tijerina Tells of His Early Life, Dreams," *AJ*, June 29, 1967, p. A16.

859. Jerry Lipman, "Spanish Grant Claimants Start 62-Mile March," *AJ*, July 3, 1966, pp. A1, A6; Paul Albright, "Tijerina Mapping New Plan to Push for Alianza Claims," *AJ*, July 26, 1967, p. B15.

860. "Tijerina Meet Brings $700 in Legal Fees," *AJ*, July 30, 1967, p. A2.

861. Jerry Lipman, "Spanish Grant Claimants Start 62-Mile March," *AJ*, July 3, 1966, pp. A1, A6.

862. Marcia Goldstein, "Land Grant Alliance Tells Plan of Action," *AJ*, September 5, 1966, p. A2.

863. Bill Feather, "Raid Recalled as Anniversary Nears," *AJ*, June 2, 1968, p. C12.

864. Howard Graves, "State, Federal Units Mobilized in Rio Arriba," *AJ*, June 4, 1967, pp. A1, A2.

865. Dick McAlpin, "Gunmen Raid Courthouse," *AJ*, June 6, 1967, pp. A1, A5; Bill Feather, "Raid Recalled as Anniversary Nears," *AJ*, June 2, 1968, p. C12.

866. "Tijerina Meet Brings $700 in Legal Fees," *AJ*, July 30, 1967, p. A2.

867. Bob Beier, "New Clash Spices Alliance Convention," *AJ*, October 22, 1967, pp. A1, A8.

868. "Student Group Hits 'Conspiracy' of Residents," *AJ*, January 8, 1968, p. A2.

869. "Reies Tijerina Gets 2-Year Jail Sentence," *AJ*, December 16, 1967, p. A1.

870. "Tijerina the Wrong Choice," *AJ*, April 26, 1968, p. A6.

871. Ibid.; Frankie McCarty, "1000 March Here in Poor People Drive," *AJ*, May 19, 1968, pp. A1, A2.

872. "Reies Tijerina Enters N.M. Governor Race," *AJ*, July 28, 1968, p. E10.

873. "Supreme Court Rules Tijerina, Two Others Off Nov. 5 Ballot," *AJ*, October 26, 1968, p. A1.

874. Joline Daffer, "Tijerina Found Not Guilty," *AJ*, December 14, 1968, pp. A1, A6.

875. "Tijerina Conviction Sustained," *AJ*, February 16, 1969, p. A1.

876. Kathy Mason, "Tijerina Convicted in Burning," *AJ*, September 28, 1969, p. A1.

877. Layne Vickers, "Tijerina Found Guilty on Two Counts," *AJ*, November 27, 1969, pp. A1, A6.

878. "Dissident Group Fails in Effort to Unseat Leadership of Alianza," *AJ*, May 31, 1970, p. A1.

879. "County Democrats Blast OEO, Corps," *AJ*, August 18, 1967, pp. A1, A2.

880. Frankie McCarty, "Educational Shortchange at Duranes?" *AJ*, July 2, 1967, pp. A1, A11; Frankie McCarty, "Communications Lack Cited as Big Problem at Duranes," *AJ*, July 3, 1967, pp. A1, A5; Frankie McCarty, "Struggle for Power Continues Within Los Duranes Assn.," *AJ*, August 4, 1967, p. A8; Bob Brown, "Brown Beret One of Ballejos 'Hats,'" *AJ*, August 25, 1968, p. A4.

881. "'Striking' Students to Be Suspended," *AJ*, April 23, 1968, p. C3; Bob Brown, "Brown Beret One of Ballejos 'Hats,'" *AJ*, August 25, 1968, p. A4.

882. "Shooting Protested by 'Brown Berets,'" *AJ*, August 17, 1968, p. A11; Martha Buddecke, "Brown Berets Seek Protection," *AJ*, August 22, 1968, p. A16; Bob Brown, "Brown Beret One of Ballejos 'Hats,'" *AJ*, August 25, 1968, p. A4.

883. "Proof to Be in Pudding," *AJ*, August 25, 1968, p. A4; Don Brumbelow, "Experience One Key Criteria: for Officers Picked for New Community Relations Unit," *AJ*, September 15, 1968, p. F6.

884. "EEOC Delegates Quit Conference in Protest," *AJ*, March 29, 1966, p. A1.

885. "Civil Service Unit Plans Drive to Aid Spanish-Americans," *AJ*, August 10, 1966, p. A2.

886. John McMillion, "LULAC Aims Touch Many Economic Ills," *AJ*, February 19, 1968, p. A4.

887. "Fifteen Students from Seven Tribes Form Kiva Club at University of New Mexico," *AJ*, December 12, 1952, p. 35; "Indian Bills Assailed by UNM Kiva Club," *AJ*, March 5, 1953, p. 10.

888. Bill Hesch, "Navajo Student 'Bordertown' Program in 4th Year Here," *AJ*, August 17, 1962, p. D10.

889. "Work on Indian Village to Show Tribal Cultures Started at Fairgrounds," *AJ*, July 11, 1964, p. A1.

890. Jim Newton, "Dances Keep Alive Indian Traditions," *AJ*, March 8, 1967, p. B6.

891. "Law Scholarships Offered Indians," *AJ*, March 17, 1968, p. F11.

892. Susan Craig, "CHR, Indian Involvement Hailed by Albuquerque Region Director," *AJ*, October 25, 1970, p. E9.

893. Bob Brown, "Spanish List at University Is Increasing," *AJ*, July 15, 1969, p. A4.

894. Frankie McCarty, "Forum Told Minorities Not Understood at UNM," *AJ*, February 18, 1969, pp. A1, A16.

895. "Should Have Limited Protest," *AJ*, March 1, 1969, p. A4.

896. "UNM Student Senate Votes to Cut Athletic Relations with BYU," *AJ*, March 21, 1969, p. F1.

897. Frankie McCarty, "University Faculty Refers Complaint," *AJ*, May 14, 1969, p. A2.

898. Rees Lloyd, "H.E.W. Finds Inequities at U. Plant," *AJ*, July 4, 1969, pp. A1, A2.

899. Frankie McCarty, "Heady Details UNM Action on Charges," *AJ*, July 11, 1969, pp. A1, A2.

900. "Discrimination at University 'Unintentional,'" *AJ*, September 22, 1969, pp. A1, A5.

901. "U. Committee Report Scored as 'Whitewash,'" *AJ*, September 23, 1969, p. A1.

902. Patrick Lamb, "Institution Heads in State Listening to Minority Units," *AJ*, March 9, 1969, p. F9.

903. "UNM Chicano Studies Program Introduced in Workshop Course," *AJ*, February 6, 1970, p. A1.

904. Tomas O. Martinez, "Black Cultural Exhibit Planned," *AJ*, August 28, 1970, p. A1; "New Spanish Village Opens Doors at Fair Wednesday," *AJ*, September 10, 1972, p. 16 of State Fair Section.

905. U.S., Department of Commerce, Bureau of the Census, *Census of Population: 1970, General Social and Economic Characteristics*, Final Report PC(1)-C33, New Mexico, pp. 33-154, 33-158, 33-164.

906. U.S., Department of Commerce, Bureau of the Census, *Census of Population: 1970, General Social and Economic Characteristics*, Final Report PC(1)-C33, New Mexico, p. 33-154.

907. U.S., Department of Commerce, Bureau of the Census, *County Data Book, 1947* (A Statistical Abstract Supplement), p. 265; idem, *Census of Population: 1950*, vol. 2, *Characteristics of the Population*, pt. 31, New Mexico, p. 31-36; idem, *Census of Population and Housing; 1960, Census Tracts*, Final Report PHC(1)-4, Albuquerque, N. Mex. SMSA, p. 31.

908. Idem, *Census of Population; 1950*, vol. 2, *Characteristics of the Population*, pt. 31, New Mexico, p. 31-36; idem, *Census of Population and Housing: 1960, Census Tracts*, Final Report PHC(1)-4, Albuquerque, N. Mex. SMSA, p. 31.

909. Idem, *Census of Population and Housing: 1970, Census Tracts*, Final Report PHC(1)-5, Albuquerque, N. Mex. SMSA, p. P-17.

910. Idem, *Census of Population: 1970, General Social and Economic Characteristics*, Final Report PC(1)-C33, New Mexico, p 33-152.

911. Melissa Howard, "Liberated During Explosive '60s, Women Demand Equality," *AJ*, January 4, 1970, p. B1.

912. Joline Daffer, "More Women Involved in Crime," *AJ*, April 10, 1969, p. B2; Susan Landon, "Women's Serious Crime Rate Up," *AJ*, December 11, 1972, pp. A1, A2.

913. U.S., Department of Commerce, Bureau of the Census, *Census of Population: 1950*, vol. 2, *Characteristics of the Population*, pt. 31, New Mexico, p. 31-36; idem, *Census of Population: 1970, General Social and Economic Characteristics*, Final Report PC(1)-C33, New Mexico, p. 33-152.

914. Idem, *Census of Population: 1950*, vol. 2, *Characteristics of the Population*, pt. 31, New Mexico, p. 31-36; idem, *Census of Population: 1970, General Social and Economic Characteristics*, Final Report PC(1)-C33, New Mexico, p. 33-153.

915. "Separate Listing for Men, Women in Help Wanted Ads Ruled Out," *AJ*, September 23, 1965, p. C9.

916. Melissa Howard, "Liberated During Explosive '60s, Women Demand Equality," *AJ*, January 4, 1970, p. B1.

917. "First Class for Policewomen Will Start Here in 10 Days," *AJ*, July 8, 1966, p. A8.

918. Grace Marie Arnett, "Figures Rise Following Adoption of Liberalized Law," *AJ*, August 16, 1970, p. B1.

919. Melissa Howard, "Liberated During Explosive '60s, Women Demand Equality," *AJ*, January 4, 1970, p. B1.

920. Frankie McCarty, "Slack-Wearing School Girls Debate Rages," *AJ*, November 27, 1969, p. G1.

921. Frankie McCarty, "West Mesa Suspends Girl for Wearing Bell-Bottoms," *AJ*, December 3, 1969, pp. A1, A6.

922. Glenn Garvin, "Few Dress Code Restrictions for City High Schools," *AJ*, November 9, 1970, p. A6.

923. Marie Attmore, "Angels of Mercy Sport Pantsuits," *AJ*, July 26, 1970, p. B1.

924. Melissa Howard, "Women's Group Seeking 'Equality,'" *AJ*, October 9, 1969, p. B1.

925. Melissa Howard, "Groups Seeking to Banish Female Myths," *AJ*, October 26, 1969, p. B1.

926. "Women's Protest Spoils Mother's Day for George," *AJ*, May 12, 1969, p. A1.

927. Grace Marie Arnett, "Women's Liberationists Demonstrate, Fight Men," *AJ*, August 27, 1970, pp. A1, A2.

928. Melissa Howard, "Liberated During Explosive '60s, Women Demand Equality," *AJ*, January 4, 1970, p. B1.

929. Grace M. Prather, "Female Enrollment at UNM Law School Triples in 5 Years," *AJ*, May 14, 1972, p. B1.

930. "UNM 'Second Sex' Course Explores Women's Roles," *AJ*, March 8, 1970, p. B6.

931. "U. Women's Studies OK'd by Faculty," *AJ*, February 16, 1972, p. A1.

932. Grace M. Prather, "Female Enrollment at UNM Law School Triples in 5 Years," *AJ*, May 14, 1972, p. B1.

933. "New Day Care Center Readied for Children of UNM Students," *AJ*, September 2, 1970, p. A6.

934. "Marriage Counselor Feels Family Life Is Changing, But Not 'Falling Apart,'" *AJ*, January 11, 1963, p. D4; Grace Marie Arnett, "Agency Provides Professional Counseling," *AJ*, September 2, 1970, p. B1.

935. "Garfield School Boys Put on Aprons as Girls Take Over Hammers, Saws," *AJ*, February 11, 1967, p. A6.

936. Grace Marie Prather, "'Survival of the Fittest' Is Maxim of Young Bachelors," *AJ*, February 21, 1971, p. B1.

937. Robert Meek, "Girls' Lib Hits Jr. High," *AJ*, March 29, 1971, p. B1; Ben Moffett, "Tennis Goes Coed at MHS," *AJ*, February 23, 1972, p. C1.

938. "New Coed Physical Education Courses Offer Wide Variety," *AJ*, December 10, 1972, p. B1.

939. Grace M. Prather, "Girls Invading Another Male Stronghold—Pumping Gas," *AJ*, July 25, 1971, p. B1.

940. Grace M. Prather, "Men Break Sex Sound Barrier," *AJ*, July 10, 1971, p. B1.

941. "APS Appoints Woman High School Principal," *AJ*, August 10, 1971, p. B1.

942. Grace M. Prather, "Husband Is Greatest Supporter," *AJ*, August 6, 1971, p. B1.

943. Marcia Goldstein, "Higher Values Needed to Eliminate Poverty," *AJ*, August 16, 1966, p. A12.

944. Marcia Goldstein, "Welfare Centers Bring Services, Aid to Poverty Stricken Areas," *AJ*, August 15, 1966, p. B13.

945. Wayne S. Scott, "Clubs for Women on Welfare Prove of Great Benefit," *AJ*, October 24, 1965, p. G1.

946. Frankie McCarty, "City Bar Assn., Legal Aid Society OK Compromise," *AJ*, August 25, 1966, p. A2.

947. "Welfare Recipients Circulate Handbills; Fight Lower Checks," *AJ*, October 29, 1967, p. A2.

948. Frankie McCarty, "Poor Demand Voice in Decisions," *AJ*, January 27, 1968, p. A2.

949. Rees Lloyd, "Cuts in Welfare Protested," *AJ*, January 10, 1969, p. A1.

950. Rees Lloyd, "300 Protesters Jam City Welfare 'Gripe In,'" *AJ*, January 15, 1969, p. B6.

951. Rees Lloyd, "County Poor Hit 'Welfare System,'" *AJ*, February 1, 1969, pp. A1, A6; Rees Lloyd, "Panel Is Told Fundamental Change Needed in Welfare," *AJ*, February 2, 1969, p. A2.

952. Wayne S. Scott, "HSS Board OKs Welfare Slashes," *AJ*, November 1, 1969, p. A1.

953. Martha Buddecke, "Model Cities' Approach Broad," *AJ*, December 8, 1968, pp. A1, A9; Ben Castillo, "Model Cities Area Projects, Funds Grow," *AJ*, November 29, 1970, p. D10.

954. "Moving People Out of Homes Becoming Problem for City," *AJ*, April 17, 1963, p. D1; Bob Brown, "Cordova, His Program Not Orthodox," *AJ*, May 24, 1970, p. A4.

955. Martha Buddecke, "Model Cities' Approach Broad," *AJ*, December 8, 1968, p. A1.

956. Sam Blythe, "Citizen Role Lagging in Model Cities Work," *AJ*, March 19, 1968, p. A6.

957. Martha Buddecke, "Model Cities Problems Hunted," *AJ*, December 10, 1968, pp. A1, A10.

958. Martha Buddecke, "Model Cities Executives Keep Citizens Involved," *AJ*, December 9, 1968, p. A1; Bob Brown, "Cordova, His Program Not Orthodox," *AJ*, May 24, 1970, p. A4.

959. Sam Blythe, "Model Cities Officials Need to Know People," *AJ*, January 8, 1968, pp. A1, A8; Martha Buddecke, "City Hunts Problems," AJ, December 10, 1968, p. A10; Martha Buddecke, "Model Cities 'Bridges' Teach Residents How to Speak to City," *AJ*, December 11, 1968, pp. A1, A3; Ben Castillo, "Model Cities Area Projects, Funds Grow," *AJ*, November 29, 1970, p. D10.

960. Martha Buddecke, "Model Cities' Approach Broad," *AJ*, December 8, 1968, p. A9.

961. Ben Castillo, "Model Cities Area Projects, Funds Grow," *AJ*, November 29, 1970, p. D10.

962. In the first action year, for example, the Citizens Board, the Joint Policy Board and the City Commission approved a Model Cities Budget of $33.6 million, including city funds, federal matching funds and all participating programs. "City Commission OKs $33.6 Million Model Area Plan," *AJ*, March 4, 1969, p. A1. Most of this money was approved by the bureaucracies involved and spent.

963. Joline Daffer, "Alcoholism Center Will Open April 1," *AJ*, March 27, 1970, p. A6; "Model Cities OKs Projects with $2.9 Million Tab for 1971," *AJ*, July 27, 1970, p. A2; Ben Castillo, "Model Cities Area Projects, Funds Grow," *AJ*, November 29, 1970, p. D10.

964. Ben Castillo, "Model Cities Area Projects, Funds Grow," *AJ*, November 29, 1970, *AJ*, p. D10; Mike Padget, "Quebrar Getting Model Cities Funds," *AJ*, February 2, 1971, p. A16.

965. "City Officials Score One," *AJ*, November 23, 1969, p. A4; Joline Daffer, "City Commission Approves Model Cities Cultural Unit," *AJ*, March 10, 1970, p. B8; Marie Attmore, "Model Cities Libraries Work for 'Convivial Spirit,'" *AJ*, April 11, 1971, p. C1.

966. "Model Cities Unit OKs 28 Projects for $2.9 Million," *AJ*, July 27, 1970, pp. A1, A2; Ben Castillo, "Model Cities Area Projects, Funds Grow," *AJ*, November 29, 1970, p. D10.

967. Dick McAlpin, "EOB Member Resigns, Blasts 'Ultra-Liberals,'" *AJ*, April 22, 1967, p. A1; "A Difficult Decision," *AJ*, April 23, 1967, p. A4.

968. Bob Brown, "Politics Seen as Factor in OEO Hassle," *AJ*, August 28, 1967, p. A4; Bob Brown, "Sees Davis as Able to Communicate," *AJ*, August 30, 1967, p. A4.

969. Ibid.; "Davis Calls on Gailard to Resign," *AJ*, August 21, 1967, p. A1; "EOB Funds Hinge on Greater Voice for Neighborhoods," *AJ*, August 24, 1967, pp. A1, A5.

970. Dick McAlpin, "EOB Director Gailard Fired by 19-8 Vote," *AJ*, March 1, 1968, p. A1.

971. Ibid.; Bob Brown, "Brown Beret One of Ballejos 'Hats,'" *AJ*, August 25, 1968, p. A4.

972. "Dr. Hamilton Quits as Board Member in EOB Protest," *AJ*, March 5, 1968, p. A2.

973. Bob Brown, "Cordova, His Program Not Orthodox," *AJ*, May 24, 1970, p. A4.

974. Art Bouffard, "VISTA Is Active in Neighborhoods," *AJ*, April 23, 1970, pp. A1, A4.

975. Martha Buddecke, "Most Stable Area in the City? It's Model Neighborhood," *AJ*, March 6, 1969, p. C12.

976. Art Bouffard, "Year Crucial for Poverty War," *AJ*, April 24, 1970, p. A6; Ben Castillo, "E. San Jose Youth Center Shows Pride of Community," *AJ*, January 3, 1971, p. A1.

977. Martha Buddecke, "Physical Improvement Program in Jeopardy," *AJ*, September 7, 1969, p. A1.

978. "S. Barelas Area Voted Industrial," *AJ*, December 20, 1968, p. A1.

979. Martha Buddecke, "Self-Interest Rears Head in Poor Area," *AJ*, December 24, 1968, p. A4.

980. Martha Buddecke, "Martineztown to Stay as Is," *AJ*, January 10, 1969, p. A1.

981. "Martineztown Votes Down Election 2-1," *AJ*, January 17, 1969, p. A1.

982. "Model Cities Citizen Board OKs Neighborhood Development Plan," *AJ*, February 16, 1969, p. G5.

983. Martha Buddecke, "Martineztown to Ask NDP Funds Be Set Aside for Area," *AJ*, March 7, 1969, p. D1.

984. "Urban Renewal OKs Model Cities Area NDP Plan," *AJ*, March 13, 1969, p. A1.

985. "Area Vote Turns Down Zone Change," *AJ*, March 23, 1969, p. A1.

986. Martha Buddecke, "Resident Participation Is Key," *AJ*, March 25, 1969, p. A2.

987. Tomas O. Martinez, "Martineztown Residents Win Round with U.R.," *AJ*, February 3, 1971, p. D1; Mike Padget, "Renewal Unit Halts School Land Taking," *AJ*, February 19, 1971, p. A1; Mike Padget, "Urban Renewal Unit OKs Relocation Plan," *AJ*, April 23, 1971, p. A1; "Licho Martinez Picked Citizen Board Head," *AJ*, April 29, 1971, p. A14.

988. Mike Padget, "Martineztown Action Finally Taking Form," *AJ*, December 3, 1972, p. A4.

989. Chuck Anthony, "MC Board's Chief Ousted," *AJ*, July 13, 1972, pp. A1, A7; Chuck Anthony, "Books Not Closed on Ouster of Martinez," *AJ*, July 23, 1972, p. G6.

990. Chuck Anthony, "Model Cities Board Ousts Two Officers," *AJ*, July 26, 1972, p. A1.

991. "Green Quits Board Post," *AJ*, July 28, 1972, p. A2.

992. "Joe Green Wins Place on Model Cities Board," *AJ*, August 1, 1972, p. A8.

993. Chuck Anthony, "Rudy Baca New Head of Model Cities Board," *AJ*, August 30, 1972, pp. A1, A2.

994. Mike Padget, "Martineztown Action Finally Taking Form," *AJ*, December 3, 1972, pp. A1, A4.

995. Martha Buddecke, "Model Cities Citizens Board Shows Mettle," *AJ*, July 7, 1969, p. A4.

996. Art Bouffard, "County EOB Gets 2-Year Extension," *AJ*, April 19, 1970, p. A6.

997. Rees Lloyd, "Community Is Key in Poverty Planning," *AJ*, November 15, 1968, p. A2.

998. Art Bouffard, "EOB Plans '71 Goals Despite Local Protests," *AJ*, September 18, 1970, p. B11.

999. "3500 Attend 1st Mass in English Language," *AJ*, October 13, 1964, p. A2.

1000. Frankie McCarty, "Catholic Schools Placing New Emphasis on Catechism," *AJ*, April 2, 1970, p. B6.

1001. Catherine Luther, "Two Guitar Masses Prove to Be Smash," *AJ*, February 11, 1967, p. A5.

1002. Dick McAlpin, "Protest Erupts over Rev. Boyd's Controversial Speech at UNM," *AJ*, October 14, 1967, p. A5.

1003. Jim Newton, "God Alive, UA Performers Say in Exciting Happening," *AJ*, May 5, 1967, p. F11.

1004. "'Day of Concern' Is Declared Today," *AJ*, March 12, 1965, p. A1.

1005. "St. Mary's High to Close Doors; Deficit Blamed," *AJ*, March 7, 1967, p. A2; Frankie McCarty, "28 Catholic Schools Closed," *AJ*, March 29, 1971, pp. A1, A6.

1006. Fritz Thompson, "Young Life Members Run Their Own Show," *AJ*, February 16, 1971, p. A1.

1007. Ernie Heltaley, "Mandatory Procedure Is Set Up by DA," *AJ*, June 27, 1966, p. A2.

1008. "Problems on Juveniles," *AJ*, May 17, 1967, p. A4.

1009. Joline Daffer, "Youth's New Right to Jury Trial, Court Merger Will Face Changes," *AJ*, October 20, 1967, p. A14.

1010. "Judge Robins Stresses Concern for the Little Man, Those Addicted to Drink," *AJ*, October 10, 1963, p. B8.

1011. "Harry Robins Decries Democrats in Jobs," *AJ*, December 14, 1953, p. 9.

1012. "Judge Robins Stresses Concern for the Little Man, Those Addicted to Drink," *AJ*, October 10, 1963, p. B8.

1013. "Robins Gives Views on Sentencing Addicts," *AJ*, October 10, 1969, p. B4.

1014. Mike Padget, "Drug-Use Driving Case Is Dismissed," *AJ*, November 21, 1969, p. A1.

1015. "Judge, Officer Debate in Court," *AJ*, April 30, 1970, p. D1.

1016. "Two Policemen Protest Treatment Allegedly Given Them by Judge," *AJ*, December 4, 1970, p. A2.

1017. Art Bouffard, "Robins Chastises City, Police for 'Diversionary Tactics,'" *AJ*, December 10, 1970, p. A1.

1018. Frankie McCarty, "Robins Backed by Organizations," *AJ*, December 10, 1970, p. A2.

1019. "Minorities Press Demands to City," *AJ*, December 15, 1970, pp. A1, A2.

1020. "City Enforcement of Three Laws Stopped Pending Review," *AJ*, December 18, 1970, pp. A1, A5.

1021. "AG's Court Dispute Ruling Backs Robins," *AJ*, December 18, 1970, pp. A1, A6.

1022. "Legal Aid Expansion Wins Committee OK," *AJ*, July 6, 1966, p. A1; Frankie McCarty, "City Bar Assn., Legal Aid Society OK Compromise," *AJ*, August 25, 1966, p. A2.

1023. Dick McAlpin, "Free Legal Aid Is Hottest Front in Poverty War," *AJ*, May 7, 1967, pp. A1, A8.

1024. Fritz Thompson, "UCF OKs Bar Assn. Poor Plan," *AJ*, July 3, 1970, pp. A1, A2; Eric McCrossen, "Legal Aid Conflict Draws New Answers," *AJ*, July 27, 1970, p. A4; Gary Stone, "Lawyers Volunteer to Aid Poor," *AJ*, August 8, 1970, pp. A1, A2.

1025. Dick McAlpin, "Free Legal Add Is Hottest Front in Poverty War," *AJ*, May 7, 1967, pp. A1, A8.

1026. Reuben Valdez, "Suspects Go Free When Old Criminal Cases Clog Courts," *AJ*, January 28, 1968, p. C10.

1027. Joline Daffer, "New City, State Court Procedures Installed," *AJ*, January 4, 1970, p. E11.

1028. "Court Expands Legal Rights of Poor," *AJ*, June 23, 1970, p. A4.

1029. Susan Craig, "Area Drug Prosecution Cases Increase," *AJ*, January 3, 1972, p. A1.

1030. Martha Buddecke, "Five New County Magistrates to Replace 51 Justice Courts," *AJ*, July 21, 1968, pp. A1, A8; Martha Buddecke, "Jurisdiction, Procedure of New Courts Explained," *AJ*, July 23, 1968, pp. A1, A11.

1031. "Courts Took Trial Deadlines in Stride During 1971," *AJ*, January 2, 1972, p. D9.

1032. Chuck Anthony, "Citations Will Replace Some Arrests," *AJ*, October 13, 1971, p. A8.

1033. Sam Blythe, "'Brutality Board' Unusual," *AJ*, October 15, 1967, p. A4.

1034. Chuck Anthony, "Police Dept. Settling Down Following Year of Upheaval," *AJ*, January 10, 1971, p. E1.

1035. Dave Parker, "Byrd Tells Black Coalition Beating Charge Under Probe," *AJ*, July 1, 1972, p. A1.

1036. Dave Parker, "City Patrolman Is Arrested on Black Coalition's Charge," *AJ*, July 5, 1972, p. A1.

1037. Mike Padget, "Personnel Board Expanded to 7 by Commission; Member Chosen," *AJ*, August 1, 1972, p. A2.

1038. Chuck Anthony, "Young City Blacks Protest Handling of Arrest by Police," *AJ*, November 9, 1972, p. A1.

1039. Chuck Anthony, "Police Disciplinary Action Not Warranted, Chief Says," *AJ*, November 23, 1972, p. A1; "Report Criticizes Police Procedure in Arrest," *AJ*, November 24, 1972, p. A8.

1040. "Grand Jury Indicts Two Deputy Sheriffs," *AJ*, December 31, 1971, p. A1; "Jury Reports County Jail Conditions Improved 75 Pct.," *AJ*, December 31, 1971, p. A7.

1041. Art Bouffard, "Reforms Ordered at Jail," *AJ*, July 18, 1972, pp. A1, A2; Art Bouffard, "County Commission Takes Control of Jail," *AJ*, August 18, 1972, p. A1.

1042. See, for example, "Unusual Sentence Imposed by Judge," *AJ*, July 3, 1963, p. A2; Edna Steinman, "Appeal Successfully Challenges City Judge Advisement Policy," *AJ*, July 10, 1964, p. A2; "New Punishment Trend," *AJ*, May 2, 1965, p. A4.

1043. "Supreme Court Rules Death Penalty Illegal," *AJ*, June 30, 1972, p. A1.

1044. "Experimenting Answers Questions, Pupils Learn," *AJ*, April 12, 1957, p. 15; "Biology Instructor Here State 'Teacher of the Year,'" *AJ*, June 10, 1963, p. A2.

1045. Frankie McCarty, "School System Advances Cited," *AJ*, January 25, 1965, p. A12.

1046. "'Do-It-Yourself' Math Teaching Is Tried Here," *AJ*, March 17, 1961, p. F12.

1047. "Students Learn Tricks of Politicking in Humanities Class Civil War Project," *AJ*, February 23, 1970, p. A6.

1048. "'Instant Reward' Learning Scores," *AJ*, January 2, 1968, p. C7.

1049. Frankie McCarty, "Behavior Concept Aids Reading," *AJ*, October 22, 1972, p. D1.

1050. Frankie McCarty, "Youngsters Learn at Chosen Rate in Free School," *AJ*, May 18, 1969, pp. A1, A7.

1051. Frankie McCarty, "School System Advances Cited," *AJ*, January 25, 1965, p. A12.

1052. Frankie McCarty, "Youngsters Learn at Chosen Rate in Free School," *AJ*, May 18, 1969, pp. A1, A7.

1053. "High School Offers Unusual Courses," *AJ*, June 4, 1972, p. C5.

1054. "TVI Will Offer Study in Trades," *AJ*, August 15, 1965, p. D3.

1055. "T-VI Widens Career Spectrum," *AJ*, August 13, 1972, pp. E1, E4.

1056. Frankie McCarty, "Four Acts Expand Concept of What Education Includes," *AJ*, April 26, 1965, pp. A1, A7.

1057. Frankie McCarty, "Low Income Area. Schools Funded Well, Says Report," *AJ*, March 14, 1971, pp. A1, A7.

1058. "Volunteers Manning School," *AJ*, October 25, 1970, p. E6; Frankie McCarty, "Drop-Outs, Kick-Outs Back in School," *AJ*, April 11, 1971, p. F7; Janelle Glasscock, "Freedom High-Hope for a Dropout," *AJ*, December 19, 1971, p. G6; Frankie McCarty, "School on Wheels to Graduate 27," *AJ*, May 21, 1972, p. A2; "Freedom High Triples Size as Program Proves Success," *AJ*, November 6, 1972, p. A8.

1059. "Mixed Emotions Expressed on Rio Grande's Modular System," *AJ*, March 22, 1971, p. A8; "El Dorado Students Laud Unique Schedule," *AJ*, December 13, 1970, p. C4.

1060. "Program Jobs Outnumber People," *AJ*, November 5, 1972, p. D1.

1061. Frankie McCarty, "Schools Needed to Try Non-Graded Classes; Catholic Success Told," *AJ*, June 26, 1966, p. D2.

1062. "Frankie McCarty, "School Board Problems Cited at Meeting Here," *AJ*, April 7, 1963, p. G3.

1063. Frankie McCarty, "School Administrators in Trouble," *AJ*, September 27, 1964, p. E7.

1064. Frankie McCarty, "Principal in Middle in School Problems," *AJ*, March 20, 1969, pp. A1, A5.

1065. "Dr. Charles R. Spain, Head of City Schools, Dies of Heart Attack," *AJ*, May 9, 1965, pp. A1, A8.

1066. Frankie McCarty, "Chisholm Named Superintendent of City Schools," *AJ*, August 31, 1965, pp. A1, A13.

1067. "ACTA Adopts 10-Item Program on Education," *AJ*, April 30, 1966, p. A13.

1068. Frankie McCarty, "City's Teachers on Strike," *AJ*, February 22, 1968, p. A1; Frankie McCarty, "Teachers Succeed in Closing City Schools," *AJ*, February 23, 1968, p. A1.

1069. Frankie McCarty, "City Teachers to Return to Class Thursday," *AJ*, February 28, 1968, p. A1.

1070. "Chisholm Quits Top APS Post," *AJ*, March 23, 1969, p. A1.

1071. Bob Beier, "Top School Position Goes to UNM Man," *AJ*, June 10, 1969, pp. A1, A11.

1072. Tom Wiley, "Decentralization Will Be Major Goal of APS," *AJ*, August 17, 1969, p. E1.

1073. "Retiring APS Leader Notes Financial Need," *AJ*, June 22, 1971, p. A2.

1074. "Books, Magazines Seized as Indecent Literature from 3 City Newsstands," *AJ*, February 22, 1961, p. B18.

1075. Judith Brimberg, "Judge Finds Book, Magazine Obscene, Fines 3 Dealers," *AJ*, June 2, 1961, p. A1.

1076. "New Ordinance Against Obscene Literature OK'ed," *AJ*, March 7, 1962, p. A1.

1077. Ibid.

1078. "Calendar Ruled Not Obscene," *AJ*, March 21, 1963, p. A2.

1079. Layne Vickers, "City Man 'Guilty' in Pornography Case," *AJ*, March 15, 1968, p. D1.

1080. "District Judge Dismisses Pornography Sale Case," *AJ*, November 7, 1969, p. D1.

1081. "Southwest Valley Residents Boo Annexation Plan," *AJ*, April 7, 1960, p. A1.

1082. "Valley Club to Head Battle on Annexation," *AJ*, April 19, 1960, p. A2.

1083. Marianne Johnson, "City Moves Toward Annexation as South Valley Plans New Town," *AJ*, April 20, 1960, p. A1.

1084. "Truce Is Declared in City, South Valley Annexation and Incorporation Rumpus," *AJ*, April 21, 1960, p. A2.

1085. "Snow Vista Annexation Passes over Protests," *AJ*, September 28, 1960, p. A2.

1086. "Incorporation of South Valley Soundly Beaten," *AJ*, September 20, 1961, p. A1.

1087. Dick McAlpin, "S. Valley Residents Thrown Sunday Punch," *AJ*, September 22, 1963, p. A4.

1088. Edna Steinman, "Annexation Plan Illegal," *AJ*, July 17, 1964, p. A21.

1089. Dick McAlpin, "S. Valley Residents Thrown Sunday Punch," *AJ*, September 22, 1963, p. A4.

1090. Ibid.

1091. "City Commission Annexes Tract in South Valley," *AJ*, January 29, 1964, p. A1.

1092. Dick McAlpin, "City Commissioners Approve Annexation," *AJ*, June 24, 1964, p. A1; Edna Steinman, "City Proposal of Annexation Is Ruled Illegal," *AJ*, July 17, 1964, pp. A1, A21.

1093. "City Commission OKs Annexation of 8200 Acres," *AJ*, September 23, 1964, p. A2.

1094. Troy Kemper, "City Loses Fight to Annex Mesa, N. Valley Areas," *AJ*, October 8, 1964, pp. A1, A6.

1095. "Cornelius Slate Captures Seats on Annex Unit," *AJ*, January 6, 1965, p. A1.

1096. "City Hopes Plea Will Void Board's Annexation Vote," *AJ*, February 14, 1965, p. A1.

1097. Martin Paskind, "Annexations Now Made Without Furious Uproar," *AJ*, May 23, 1965, p. A4.

1098. Ibid.

1099. "Annexation Issue Knocks," *AJ*, June 19, 1966, p. A4.

1100. "A Constructive Approach," *AJ*, November 15, 1967, p. A4.

1101. One of the best studies of shifting patterns of collective violence and their significance is Charles Tilly, "Collective Violence in European Perspective," in *Violence in America: Historical and Comparative Perspectives*, edited by Hugh Davis Graham and Ted Robert Gurr (New York: Bantam Books, 1969), pp. 1-45.

1102. U.S., Department of Justice, Federal Bureau of Investigation, *Uniform Crime Reports: Crime in the United States*, 1945-1969.

1103. "Shots Fired, One Injured in Park, Suspects Nabbed," *AJ*, September 3, 1963, p. A2.

1104. "Roosevelt Park Terrorism Cited to City Officials," *AJ*, August 18, 1965, p. A1.

1105. Layne Vickers, "Demonstrator Guilty of Assault," *AJ*, May 20, 1969, p. B4.

1106. *Word Alchemy* (New York: Grove Press, Inc., 1967), pp. 34-5. Reprinted by permission of Grove Press, Inc. Copyright 1960, 1966, 1967 by Lenore Kandel.

1107. "Four-Letter-Word Poem Draws Attack of Solons," *AJ*, March 22, 1969, p. A12.

1108. Frankie McCarty, "'Pornographic' Ode Distributed Anew to UNM Classes," *AJ*, March 25, 1969, p. A1.

1109. Ibid., pp. A1, A5.

1110. Frankie McCarty, "Prof Suspended in U. Poem Incident," *AJ*, March 27, 1969, p. A2.

1111. Ibid., pp. A1, A2.

1112. Frankie McCarty, "Faculty Unit Protests; More U. Suspensions," *AJ*, March 23, 1969, pp. A1, A8.

1113. William Montgomery, "Poetry Rally Lures Big Audience," *AJ*, March 29, 1969, pp. A1, A6.

1114. William Montgomery, "Regents Back Ferrel Heady at University," *AJ*, March 30, 1969, pp. A1, A4.

1115. William Montgomery, "Heady Meets with Student Delegation," *AJ*, April 2, 1969, pp. A1, A2.

1116. "Pornography Count Dismissed Against Store," *AJ*, August 2, 1969, p. B4.

1117. William Montgomery, "Regents Back Ferrel Heady at University," *AJ*, March 30, 1969, p. A1.

1118. "Highlights of Advisory Unit's Report," *AJ*, April 10, 1969, pp. A1, A2.

1119. Frankie McCarty, "Heady Lays Down Reinstatement Terms," *AJ*, April 10, 1969, pp. A1, A10.

1120. Bill Montgomery, "Six Arrested After UNM Night Rally," *AJ*, April 11, 1969, pp. A1, A2.

1121. "Heady Reinstates U. Teaching Assistants," *AJ*, April 13, 1969, p. A1.

1122. Frankie McCarty, "U. Community Views Aired," *AJ*, April 16, 1969, p. C1.

1123. "U. Magazine's Distribution Halted as 'Naughty' Words Are Criticized," *AJ*, August 18, 1969, p. A1; Sherman Smith, "Mid-America and the University," *AJ*, September 7, 1969, pp. B14, B15.

1124. Ibid., p. B14.

1125. "Pornography Count Dismissed Against Store," *AJ*, August 2, 1969, p. B4.

1126. Layne Vickers, "Man Charged in Slaying of Officer," *AJ*, March 27, 1969, p. A1.

1127. Joline Daffer, "Mistrial Is Declared in Garcia Murder Case," *AJ*, September 6, 1969, p. A1.

1128. "Volunteers Building Poor People's Park," *AJ*, October 5, 1969, p. F6.

1129. Frankie McCarty, "He's in Center of Dispute; His Name Is Pete Garcia," *AJ*, January 14, 1970, pp. A1, A4.

1130. "City Youth Fatally Shot After Argument in Park," *AJ*, June 23, 1969, p. A1.

1131. Layne Vickers, "Head of Legal Aid Society Calls DA 'Political Hack,'" *AJ*, October 11, 1969, pp. A1, A6.

1132. Mike Padget, "Fitzpatrick Retained as Counsel of LAS," *AJ*, November 12, 1969, p. A1.

1133. Ed Mahr, "Trash Barrage on Court Delays BYU-Lobo Game," *AJ*, March 1, 1970, p. A2.

1134. William Montgomery, "Thurmond's Talk Blocked by Hecklers," *AJ*, March 5, 1970, pp. A1, A2.

1135. Frankie McCarty, "Two UNM Students Cited for Disrupting Thurmond," *AJ*, March 6, 1970, p. A1.

1136. "Thirty Speakers Discuss 'How to Save University,'" *AJ*, March 6, 1970, p. A2.

1137. Art Bouffard, "Crude Bomb Found in ROTC Building," *AJ*, March 10, 1970, p. A1.

1138. "Two U. Students Booked in Debris Throwing Case," *AJ*, March 11, 1970, p. A1.

1139. "Many Denounce Taxes for War," *AJ*, April 16, 1970, p. F14.

1140. Mike Padget, "Rites on 'Earth Day' Join Many Together," *AJ*, April 23, 1970, pp. A1, A2.

1141. Frankie McCarty, "Punch to Jaw Decks One UNM Defendant," *AJ*, April 23, 1970, pp. A1, A9.

1142. Frankie McCarty, "Lavender to Appeal Decision on Students," *AJ*, April 29, 1970, p. A1.

1143. Mike Padget, "Reaction Is Mixed to Poetess' Visit," *AJ*, April 30, 1970, p. A8.

1144. Frankie McCarty, "University Unit Blasts Candidates," *AJ*, May 1, 1970, pp. A1, A8.

1145. "GIs Attack in Cambodia," *AJ*, May 1, 1970, p. A1.

1146. Frankie McCarty, "'Love Lust,' 26 Other Works Are Read to Packed House," *AJ*, May 2, 1970, pp. A1, A2.

1147. "Four Killed, 11 Injured at Kent State," *AJ*, May 5, 1970, p. A1.

1148. "Jane Fonda Blasts U.S. Asian Policy," *AJ*, May 5, 1970, p. A1.

1149. Frankie McCarty, "UNM Incident: Events Are Reconstructed," *AJ*, June 21, 1970, p. C4.

1150. Frankie McCarty, "Heady Stiffens Student Penalty," *AJ*, May 6, 1970, p. A1.

1151. Frankie McCarty, "UNM Incident: Events Are Reconstructed," *AJ*, June 21, 1970, pp. C4, C5.

1152. Mike Padget, "City Strikers Halt Maintenance Work," *AJ*, July 8, 1970, p. A1; Ben Castillo, "Striking City Employees Scuffle with Police at Yard Entrance," *AJ*, July 8, 1970, p. A1; "City Workers Vote to End 7-Day Strike," *AJ*, July 14, 1970, p. A1.

1153. Chuck Anthony, "Police Dept. Settling Down Following Year of Upheaval," *AJ*, January 10, 1971, p. E1; "Police, City Officials Reach Pay Accord," *AJ*, July 3, 1970, p. A1.

1154. "Metropolitan Crime Rate Second in U.S.," *AJ*, August 13, 1970, p. A1.

1155. "Report on Police Is Too Soft," *AJ*, September 27, 1970, p. A4.

1156. Chuck Anthony, "Police Dept. Settling Down Following; Year of Upheaval," *AJ*, January 10, 1971, p. E1.

1157. Art Bouffard, "UNM Students Convicted in Tiff During Nixon Visit," *AJ*, January 22, 1971, p. A8.

1158. "Sam the Queen Receives No Coronation Rite at UNM," *AJ*, October 18, 1970, p. A2.

1159. Frankie McCarty, "Focus on New Breed," *AJ*, December 20, 1970, p. C12.

1160. Tomas O. Martinez, "Black Berets Pledged to Help La Raza," *AJ*, December 20, 1970, p. B12.

1161. "Kinney Leaves Room as Minorities Lash Officials on Several Issues," *AJ*, December 16, 1970, pp. A1, A6.

1162. Tomas O. Martinez, "Black Berets Protest Police," *AJ*, March 28, 1971, p. A2.

1163. "Beret Is Found Guilty of Charges of Interfering with Police Officer," *AJ*, March 10, 1971, p. A7.

1164. "Dallas Man to Be Police Chief Here," *AJ*, March 7, 1971, p. A1.

1165. Ben Castillo, "Minority Representatives Voice Opposition to Byrd," *AJ*, March 18, 1971, p. A1.

1166. "Byrd Takes Police Chief Oath of Office," *AJ*, April 2, 1971, p. A1.

1167. "Byrd, LULAC to Work Together," *AJ*, April 8, 1971, p. A1.

1168. Ben Castillo, "Refuse Workers Given 5-Day Week," *AJ*, April 18, 1971, p. A1.

1169. Records of the Albuquerque Public Schools.

1170. Records of the Albuquerque Police Department.

1171. Records of the Employment Security Commission of New Mexico.

1172. "17 Persons Are Arrested at Yale Park," *AJ*, June 11, 1971, p. A2.

1173. Frankie McCarty, "Violence in June: The Analysis of a Riot," *AJ*, July 18, 1971, pp. E1-E3.

1174. Frankie McCarty, "Riots: A Time of Violence, Confusion," *AJ*, July 19, 1971, pp. A1, A6, A7.

1175. "Six City Policemen Suspended 10 Days," *AJ*, June 26, 1971, p. A1.

1176. Eric McCrossen, "Commission's Membership Questionable," *AJ*, June 28, 1971, p. A4.

1177. "Eight Black Berets Arrested at Capital," *AJ*, June 25, 1971, pp. A1, A2.

1178. "Riot Unit Disbanded; King Urges Jury Probe," *AJ*, July 1, 1971, p. A1.

1179. "Reyes Resigns Post, Urges Charter OK," *AJ*, June 29, 1971, p. A1.

1180. Ben Castillo, "Voters Turn Down Mayor-Districting Plan," *AJ*, June 30, 1971, pp. A1, A2.

1181. Mike Padget, "Mass Police Resignation Threatened Here," *AJ*, July 1, 1971, pp. A1, A2.

1182. Chuck Anthony, "Police Accept 11th Hour Salary Compromise," *AJ*, July 2, 1971, p. A1; "Blue-Collar Workers OK City Offers," *AJ*, July 8, 1971, p. A1; Mike Padget, "City Firemen Accept Wage, Fringe Offer," *AJ*, July 10, 1971, p. A1.

1183. Chuck Anthony, "Clues Are Few in Park Slaying," *AJ*, July 18, 1971, p. A1.

1184. Catherine Luther, "Park Kids, City Work on Pad," *AJ*, July 21, 1971, p. A5.

1185. Ben Castillo, "Commission Relents on Transients Park," *AJ*, July 23, 1971, p. A1.

1186. Mike Padget, "City Police Close Yale Park," *AJ*, August 20, 1971, p. A1.

1187. "Commission Approves Two Readings for Parks Curfew," *AJ*, September 28, 1971, p. A1.

1188. Ruth Epstein, "His House—A Place to 'Rap' About Christ," *AJ*, April 13, 1970, p. A8.

1189. Nancy Barnett, "Suicide Prevention Center Fights Alienation, Loneliness," *AJ*, January 11, 1970, p. C3.

1190. "Laudable Student Project," *AJ*, November 6, 1970, p. A4.

1191. Catherine Luther, "Ex-Users Form Group to Aid Addicts," *AJ*, February 11, 1971, pp. A1, A2.

1192. Cathy Luther, "SAADA Alive, Flourishing," *AJ*, March 28, 1971, p. C5.

1193. Mike Padget, "Urban Sprawl Oozes Toward Sandia Slopes," *AJ*, April 21, 1971, pp. A1, A5.

1194. Fritz Thompson, "Opponents of Sandia Road Plan Tree 'Plant-In' May 15," *AJ*, May 5, 1971, p. A1; "Mini-Plant-In Marks Crest Road Protest," *AJ*, May 16, 1971, p. A1.

1195. Fritz Thompson, "Sandia Mt. Road Stirs Turmoil," *AJ*, May 16, 1971, pp. A1, A2.

1196. Mike Padget, "Open Spaces Concept Born of Confrontation," *AJ*, May 30, 1971, p. A2.

1197. Art Bouffard, "'Save Volcanoes' Committee Intensifies Area Campaign," *AJ*, August 2, 1971, p. A1.

1198. Tomas O. Martinez, "Admirers Mob Tijerina on His Return to New Mexico," *AJ*, July 27, 1971, pp. A1, A10.

1199. Tomas O. Martinez, "VISTA Supervisors Claim 'Politics' Is Behind Firings," *AJ*, September 15, 1971, p. A1.

1200. "Baca, Poole, Koch Win Commission Seats," *AJ*, October 6, 1971, pp. A1, A2.

1201. "All Eight Bond Issues Approved by Voters," *AJ*, October 6, 1971, p. A1.

1202. "Citizens Ignore 'Gripe Sessions,'" *AJ*, November 21, 1971, p. A1.

1203. "Robins Defends Riot Case Handling After Jury Report," *AJ*, July 3, 1971, p. A6.

1204. Susan Craig, "Jury Rules for Guard in Bayoneting Suit," *AJ*, September 22, 1971, p. A1.

1205. Barbara Lawless, "All Cleared of Charges in U. Case," *AJ*, October 13, 1971, p. A1.

1206. Betty Keller, "City 'Storefront' Offers Aid," *AJ*, July 4, 1971, p. A1.

1207. "Police Plan Program at 80 City Schools," *AJ*, October 13, 1971, p. C6.

1208. Fritz Thompson, "Officers to Study Cultural Relations," *AJ*, February 1, 1971, p. A2.

1209. "1000 Residents Adopt Anti-Burglary Marks," *AJ*, February 13, 1972, p. A1.

1210. Chuck Anthony, "Hijackers Held in Cuba," *AJ*, November 28, 1971, p. A1.

1211. "Hijack Suspects Said 'Doing Fine,'" *AJ*, January 22, 1971, p. A1.

1212. "Garcia Conviction Reversed," *AJ*, July 31, 1971, p. A12.

1213. Barbara Lawless, "Garcia Found Guilty in Shooting of Deputy," *AJ*, December 18, 1971, p. A1.

1214. Chuck Anthony, "Pete Garcia Charged with Shooting Three," *AJ*, January 7, 1972, p. A2.

1215. Chuck Anthony, "Police Slay Two Men at Dynamite Shed," *AJ*, January 30, 1972, pp. A1, A7.

1216. Chuck Anthony, "Candlelight Vigil Set for Berets," *AJ*, February 2, 1972, p. A1.

1217. "750 Attend Memorial for Slain Beret Member," *AJ*, February 2, 1972, p. A10.

1218. Mike Padget, "Commission Seeks Probe," *AJ*, February 8, 1972, p. A1.

1219. Mike Padget, "Tijerina Makes Race Unity Plea," *AJ*, September 9, 1971, pp. A1, A5; Dave Parker, "State, City, County Officials Guests at Tijerina Dinner," *AJ*, February 11, 1972, p. A1.

1220. Barbara Lawless, "'Justifiable Homicide' Ruled in Beret Deaths," *AJ*, March 8, 1972, p. A1.

1221. Bob Brown, "Brotherhood in Our Lives," *AJ*, April 12, 1972, p. A4.

1222. Fritz Thompson, "APS Reports Disruptions Few," *AJ*, June 6, 1972, p. A1.

1223. Chuck Anthony and Dave Parker, "War Protest Blocks I-25," *AJ*, May 10, 1972, pp. A1, A8.

1224. "U. Students Condemn Nixon's Actions," *AJ*, May 10, 1972, p. E6.

1225. Art Bouffard and Dave Parker, "Tear Gas Hurled at Protesters," *AJ*, May 11, 1972, pp. A1, A10.

1226. Art Bouffard, "City Offers to Help Students Plan 'Sanctioned' Antiwar March Today," *AJ*, May 12, 1972, p. A2.

1227. Dave Parker, "Protesters Practice 'Peace Now,'" *AJ*, May 13, 1972, pp. A1, A4.

1228. Art Bouffard, "Nearly 300 Hear Speakers at War Forum at City Park," *AJ*, May 14, 1972, p. A1.

1229. Art Bouffard, "Robins Puts Demonstrator Cases Under Year's Review," *AJ*, May 18, 1972, pp. A1, A2.

1230. Art Bouffard, "Robins Fines Policeman $10 on Contempt of Court Count," *AJ*, September 14, 1972, p. A1.

1231. Art Bouffard, "Petitions for Robins' Recall Are Filed with City Clerk," *AJ*, November 22, 1972, p. A1.

1232. Ed Mahr, "Domenici, Lujan, Runnels Winners," *AJ*, November 8, 1972, p. A8.

1233. Carol Cohea, "JCS Rocks 9000 Here at Opera Performance," *AJ*, February 26, 1972, p. A2.

1234. "Nostalgia '72 48th Annual University of New Mexico Homecoming," *AJ*, October 31, 1972, p. H1.

Chapter 5

1235. The source of the 1972 figures is a leaflet published by the Albuquerque Industrial Development Service, based on information supplied by the Bureau of Business and Economic Research at the University of New Mexico, their data having been furnished by the U.S. Department of Commerce, Bureau of the Census.

1236. The source of the figure for 1972 is U.S., Department of Commerce, *Social and Economic Statistics Administration, Boundary and Annexation Survey, 1970-1973* (Washington, D.C., 1975), p. 47.

1237. U.S., Department of Commerce, Bureau of the Census, *Census of Population: 1950*, vol. 2, *Characteristics of the Population*, pt. 31, New Mexico, p. 31-36; idem, *Census of Population and Housing: 1970, Census Tracts*, Final Report PHC(1)-5, Albuquerque, N. Mex. SMSA, p. P-17.

1238. Idem, *City Finances: 1945* (Cities Having Populations over 25,000), vol. 3, *Statistical Compendium*, p. 40; City of Albuquerque Budget Estimate, Comparative Consolidated Expenditures, Fiscal Year 1973.

1239. Computed on the basis of the Consumer Price Index for Urban Wage Earners and Clerical Workers, U.S. City Average, periodically published by the U.S., Department of Labor, Bureau of Labor Statistics, Washington, D.C.

1240. U.S., Department of Health, Education and Welfare, Office of Economic Opportunity, *Federal Outlays in New Mexico: 1972*, p. 33.

1241. "New Mexico Cultural Groups Are Granted Federal Funds," *AJ*, September 11, 1966, p. C1.

1242. "City Parks Dept. Offers Variety," *AJ*, April 23, 1972, p. F4.

1243. Ibid.

1244. Sam Blythe, "Long Struggle Comes to End as City OKs Sign Ordinance," *AJ*, December 4, 1968, p. A1.

1245. Art Bouffard, "County Commission Adopts Noise Limiting Ordinance," *AJ*, December 21, 1971, p. A3.

1246. Rees Lloyd, "State 'Get Tough' Meat Inspection Is Due," *AJ*, May 16, 1969, p. A4.

1247. The aid received from other governments for fiscal year 1945 was $36,000, $31,000 of which came from the State of New Mexico. U.S., Department of Commerce, Bureau of the Census, *City Finances: 1972* (Cities Having Populations over 25,000) , vol. 3, *Statistical Compendium*, p. 22.

1248. The aid received from other governments for fiscal year 1972 was $9,658,471, $9,397,938 of which came from the federal government. City of Albuquerque Budget Estimate, Comparative Consolidated Revenues, Fiscal Year 1973.

1249. William Montgomery, "Health Agency's Job Outgrows Budget," *AJ*, February 1, 1970, p. A6.

1250. "Dial-a-Ride, 766-7546," *AJ*, December 31, 1972, p. A2.

1251. "Permanent Jobs Found for 900," *AJ*, August 15, 1972, p. B2.

1252. William Montgomery, "Health Agency's Job Outgrows Budget," *AJ*, February 1, 1970, p. A6.

1253. Art Bouffard, "Quebrar to Disband, 'Reluctantly,' May 31," *AJ*, March 18, 1972, p. A1; "County Receives Methadone Grant," *AJ*, July 19, 1972, p. C1.

1254. "S. Valley, City Water Pact OK'd," *AJ*, August 2, 1972, p. A1; Mike Padget, "1972 Saw Changes at City Hall," *AJ*, December 25, 1972, pp. A1, A6.

1255. In 1969, for example, the New Mexico Democratic Convention voted to change the composition of the State Central Committee to allow the counties to be represented proportionally according to their populations. Bob Beier, "Democrats Unite in Revising Rules," *AJ*, June 15, 1969, pp. A1, A8.

1256. W. Wilson Cliff, "No Such Thing as Instant Highway," *AJ*, March 26, 1972, p. G2.

1257. Ben Castillo, "Ray Baca Hopes He Can Expand Role in 'Service of the People,'" *AJ*, October 7, 1971, p. A2.

1258. Mike Padget, "Commission Still Uncertain on Wilson," *AJ*, January 23, 1972, p. A4.

1259. "Our Choice: Poole, Baca, Koch," *AJ*, October 3, 1971, p. A6.

1260. Grace Marie Prather, "Nancy Koch Terms Victory the Result of a Total Effort," *AJ*, October 7, 1971, p. A10.

1261. "Baca, Poole, Koch Win Commission Seats," *AJ*, October 6, 1971, pp. A1, A2.

1262. Mike Padget, "Wilson to Leave Top Post at City Hall," *AJ*, March 2, 1972, p. A1.

1263. "City Names Head Planner," *AJ*, February 19, 1971, pp. A1, A5; "Planning Director Is Named New Acting City Manager," *AJ*, March 3, 1972, p. A1.

1264. Bob Brown, "Smith Is Man of Vision," *AJ*, March 22, 1972, p. A4; "Smith Gets Top Post with City," *AJ*, July 6, 1972, p. A1.

1265. These figures were arrived at by counting the numbers of business establishments of each type listed in the classified sections of the 1945 and 1972 telephone directories.

1266. U.S., Department of Commerce, Bureau of the Census, *Census of Population: 1950*, vol. 2, *Characteristics of the Population*, pt. 31, New Mexico, p. 31-36; idem, *Census of Population: 1970, General Social and Economic Characteristics*, Final Report PC(1)-C33, New Mexico, p. 33-153.

1267. Idem, *Census of Population: 1950*, vol. 2, *Characteristics of the Population*, pt. 31, New Mexico, p. 31-36; idem, *Census of Population: 1970, General Social and Economic Characteristics*, Final Report PC(1)-C33, New Mexico, p. 33-152.

1268. Bernard Velasquez, "Flea Market: Fun Bargains," *AJ*, October 31, 1971, p. A1.

1269. U.S., Department of Health, Education and Welfare, Office of Economic Opportunity, *Federal Outlays in New Mexico: 1972*, p. 31.

1270. From 1964 to 1972, the number of people in Bernalillo County receiving public assistance rose from 11,253 (4.0 percent of the population) to 19,207 (5.7 percent). The figures for the number of persons on public assistance come from the U.S., Department of Commerce, Bureau of the Census, *County and City Data Book, 1967* (A Statistical Abstract Supplement), p. 243; idem, *County and City Data Book, 1972* (A Statistical Abstract Supplement), p. 322. The percentage for 1964 was calculated using a population figure, 283,629, derived from interpolation of census figures of 1960 and 1970. The percentage for 1972 was calculated using the population figure 339,500, presented in a leaflet published by the Albuquerque Industrial Development Service, based on information supplied by the Bureau of Business and Economic Research at the University of New Mexico, their data having been furnished by the U.S., Department of Commerce, Bureau of the Census.

1271. "FHA Will Launch Free Counseling," *AJ*, April 13, 1968, p. A11; Mike Padget and Art Bouffard, "Housing Plentiful—for Well-to-Do," *AJ*, November 14, 1971, p. A7; Mike Padget and Art Bouffard, "Rehabilitation Programs Lagging Behind Needs in City," *AJ*, November 15, 1971, pp. A1, A5.

1272. Martha Buddecke, "City, EOB to Staff San Jose Center," *AJ*, September 13, 1969, p. A1; Martha Buddecke, "City's Flood Victims," *AJ*, November 9, 1969, p. A4.

1273. "Ex-Convicts Form DESEO to Assist Selves, Families," *AJ*, February 13, 1972, p. F8.

1274. "Dial-a-Ride, 766-7546," *AJ*, December 31, 1972, p. A2.

1275. Frankie McCarty, "U. Becoming 'Urban Grant' Institution, Heady Declares," *AJ*, March 7, 1969, p. D1; "Campbell Views Institute as Extension of University," *AJ*, August 2, 1969, p. C7; "ISRAD Is Committed to Training Program," AJ, October 6, 1971, p. B9; Wayne S. Scott, "ISRAD Operations Are Criticized on Several Sides at LFC Hearing," *AJ*, September 28, 1972, pp. A1, A8.

1276. Frankie McCarty, "UNM Clinical Law Program 'Bridges Gap,'" *AJ*, January 3, 1971, p. G5.

1277. Grace Marie Arnett, "Agency Provides Professional Counseling," *AJ*, September 2, 1970, p. B1.

1278. Pat Kailer, "Parents Without Partners Share Good Times and Bad," *AJ*, October 29, 1972, pp. B1, B5.

1279. U.S., Department of Commerce, Bureau of the Census, *Census of Population: 1950*, vol. 2, *Characteristics of the Population*, pt. 31, New Mexico, p. 31-120; idem, *Census of Population: 1970, Detailed Characteristics*, Final Report PC(1)-D33, New Mexico, p. 33-481.

1280. Pat Kailer, "Consumer Credit Counseling a Life Line to Debtors," *AJ*, November 12, 1972, pp. B1, B3.

1281. "AIDS Doing Excellent Job," *AJ*, October 2, 1972, p. A4.

1282. Martha Buddecke, "Large, Small Organizations Seek Funds," *AJ*, March 23, 1969, p. A18; Catherine Luther, "Fund Raising Has Grown Since They Put 'All Beggs in One Asket,'" *AJ*, October 12, 1969, p. A3; Carol Cohea, "Innovations Are Announced at UCF Orientation Meeting," *AJ*, July 28, 1971, p. C8.

1283. Catherine Luther, "Volunteer Band Centralizes," *AJ*, October 15, 1972, p. A2.

1284. U.S., Department of Commerce, Bureau of the Census, *County Business Patterns; First Quarter, 1948*, pt. 2, State Reports, no. 29, New Mexico, p. 9; idem, *County Business Patterns: 1972*, New Mexico CBP-72-33, p. 24. The employment statistics given in these reports do not cover self-employment, agricultural employment, family employment, casual employment, domestic service, government employment, railroad employment, or employment by certain types of nonprofit organizations.

1285. U.S., Department of Commerce, Bureau of the Census, *City Finances: 1945* (Cities Having Populations over 25,000), vol. 3, Statistical Compendium, p. 51; City of Albuquerque Budget Estimate, Comparative Consolidated Expenditures, Fiscal Year 1973.

1286. "University of New Mexico Report on Examination of Accounts for the Fiscal Year Ended June 30, 1945," pp. 4, 33; "University of New Mexico Financial Report for the Year Ended June 30, 1972," pp. 30, 61.

1287. New Mexico, Superintendent of Public Instruction, *Annual Statistical Report of the Superintendent of Public Instruction, for the Period July 1, 1970, to June 30, 1971*, p. 17.

1288. U.S., Department of Commerce, Bureau of the Census, *Census of Population: 1950*, vol. 2, *Characteristics of the Population*, pt. 31, New Mexico, p. 31-120; idem, *Census of Population: 1970, General Social and Economic Characteristics*, Final Report PC(1)-C33, New Mexico, p. 33-153.

1289. Frankie McCarty, "New Medicaid Provision to Cover All State's Poor," *AJ*, April 12, 1967, p. A1.

1290. William Montgomery, "Health Agency's Job Outgrows Budget," *AJ*, February 1, 1970, p. A6; William Montgomery, "Planned Parenthood Plays Role in Drive on Poverty," *AJ*, February 5, 1970, p. B4.

1291. William Montgomery, "Public Health Service Office Guards Residents' Health," *AJ*, February 3, 1970, p. A9.
1292. "S. Valley Clinic Opens Today," *AJ*, April 17, 1972, p. A1.
1293. John Ira Petty, "Progress Is Marked by City's Hospitals," *AJ*, January 3, 1971, p. E2; Pat Kailer, "Maternity-Infant Project Holds Neighborhood Clinics," *AJ*, October 1, 1972, p. B1.
1294. "Therapists Practice Profession at Veterans Hospital," *AJ*, September 10, 1972, p. B1.
1295. Art Bouffard, "Alcoholism Plans Readied," *AJ*, May 30, 1971, p. A6; Art Bouffard, "Vet Poses Problem as Future Alcoholic," *AJ*, June 1, 1971, pp. A1, A5.
1296. Layne Vickers, "Center Means Life to Some," *AJ*, January 25, 1970, p. A1.
1297. "New Directions Center Provides a Friend, Help," *AJ*, March 5, 1972, p. D6.
1298. Chuck Anthony, "City Policemen OK Changes in Uniform," *AJ*, June 10, 1971, p. A1.
1299. "Student Advisers Named to UNM Board of Regents," *AJ*, March 29, 1972, p. B10.
1300. U.S., Department of Commerce, Bureau of the Census, *Census of Population: 1950*, vol. 2, *Characteristics of the Population*, pt. 31, New Mexico, p. 31-120; idem, *Census of Population: 1970, General Social and Economic Characteristics*, Final Report PC(1)-C33, New Mexico, p. 33-153.
1301. Idem, *County Business Patterns: First Quarter, 1948*, pt. 2, State Reports, no. 29, New Mexico, p. 9; idem, *County Business Patterns: 1972*, New Mexico CBP-72-33, p. 25. The employment data given in these reports do not include self-employment, agricultural employment, family employment, casual employment, domestic service, government employment, railroad employment, or employment by certain types of nonprofit organizations.
1302. John Ira Petty, "Military Life Style Changing at Sandia," *AJ*, February 11, 1971, p. F1.
1303. Grace M. Prather, "Sororities Are Hiring Managers to Replace Housemothers," *AJ*, April 30, 1972, p. B1.
1304. "Albuquerqueans Join in Din Welcoming '72," *AJ*, January 1, 1972, p. A2.
1305. Frankie McCarty, "Demand Exceeds Bilingual School Growth," *AJ*, July 23, 1972, p. A1.
1306. Tomas O. Martinez, "Chicano Author Exemplifies New Breed," *AJ*, October 15, 1972, p. C5.
1307. "Senior Citizens Plan Hobby Show," *AJ*, November 26, 1972, p. F1.
1308. "Clinic Takes Guesswork from Gardening," *AJ*, July 11, 1972, p. B5.
1309. U.S., Department of Commerce, Bureau of the Census, *City Finances: 1945* (Cities Having Populations over 25,000), vol. 3, *Statistical Compendium*, p. 51; City of Albuquerque Budget Estimate, Comparative Consolidated Expenditures, Fiscal Year 1973.
1310. Johnny D. Gonzales, "Sports Boom Hit City in 1960s," *AJ*, January 4, 1970, p. F2; "Triple-A for Albuquerque," *AJ*, September 3, 1971, p. A4.
1311. Johnny D. Gonzales, "Sports Boom Hit City in 1960s," *AJ*, January 4, 1970, p. F2.
1312. Ibid.
1313. Martha Buddecke, "Performing Arts Need Finance Aid," *AJ*, January 17, 1972, p. A2.
1314. Martha Buddecke, "'Change or Die' Is Challenge Facing U.S. Performing Arts," *AJ*, January 18, 1972, p. A2.
1315. Carol Cohea and Art Bouffard, "3000 Go on Musical Safari," *AJ*, May 29, 1972, p. A1.
1316. Scott Beaven, "15,000 Fans Hear Stones at U. Arena," *AJ*, June 16, 1972, p. A1.
1317. "U.S. Champion to Compete Here in Balloon Race," *AJ*, April 7, 1972, p. D1.
1318. Bob Brown, "Brotherhood in Our Lives," *AJ*, April 12, 1972, p. A4.

Chapter 6

1319. In *Colliers*, November 10, 1945, p. 7.
1320. In *Colliers*, November 3, 1945, p. 96.

1321. In *Colliers*, November 10, 1945, p. 33.

1322. In *Albuquerque Tribune*, January 22, 1945, p. 3.

1323. William P. Wyatt, "Special Services Planned," *AJ*, September 9, 1950, p. 18.

1324. In *AJ*, October 16, 1951, p. 19.

1325. In *AJ*, May 16, 1952, p. 15.

1326. In *AJ*, September 19, 1952, p. 16.

1327. In *AJ*, September 26, 1952, p. 16.

1328. In *Reader's Digest*, May 1972, p. 42.

1329. In *Reader's Digest*, May 1972, p. 7.

1330. In *Reader's Digest*, May 1972, p. 64.

1331. In *AJ*, July 7, 1971, p. C8.

1332. In *AJ*, July 21, 1971, p. C9.

1333. In *AJ*, February 2, 1948, p. 10.

1334. "Film Stars Appear Here Tomorrow at World Premiere of 'Albuquerque,'" *AJ*, February 1, 1948, p. 1.

1335. "St. Mary's Pupil Writes Best Slogan for City," *AJ*, November 18, 1951, p. 2.

1336. "Janet Latsha, Asthma Sufferer, Regains Health in Albuquerque," *AJ*, April 23, 1950, pp. 1, 14.

1337. "In Pace with El Paso," *AJ*, July 19, 1948, p. 4.

1338. "Will We Be Outdone?" *AJ*, July 19, 1953, p. 4.

1339. "Miracle City," *AJ*, September 7, 1958, p. 6.

1340. "In 200,000 Class," *AJ*, November 9, 1960, p. A6.

1341. Edmund. Engel, "Doubling of Population, Physical Growth of City Brought Many Problems," *AJ*, January 30, 1962, p. B2.

1342. "Frightening Picture," *AJ*, January 26, 1968, p. A6.

1343. Fritz Thompson, "City Groping with Population Boom Woes," *AJ*, February 27, 1972, pp. A1, A14.

1344. "Let's Help Santa Fe Opera," *AJ*, October 20, 1969, p. A4.

1345. Bill Withers, "Lean on Me," Interior Music Corp. (B.M.I.), on record album *The Best of Bill Withers*, Sussex Records, Inc., 1975.

1346. Richard Bach, *Jonathan Livingston Seagull* (New York: The Macmillan Company, 1970).

1347. Kathleen Winsor, *Forever Amber* (New York: The Macmillan Company, 1944).

1348. Mack Gordon and Henry Warren, "The More I See You," A.S.C.A.P., sheet music, n.d.

1349. In *AJ*, January 28, 1947, p. 8.

1350. In *AJ*, April 18, 1947, p. 16.

1351. In *AJ*, August 2, 1947, p. 10.

1352. In *AJ*, August 2, 1947, p. 10.

1353. In *AJ*, May 17, 1972, p. C11.

1354. "Missing Bride-to-Be Safe in Dallas," *AJ*, January 7, 1947, p. 1.

1355. "Man Admits Slaying Soldier's Wife Here 'Because I Loved Her,'" *AJ*, March 5, 1950, pp. 1, 2.

1356. In *Albuquerque Tribune*, January 24, 1945, p. 4.

1357. Franklin D. Roosevelt, "A Just and Honorable Peace," in *Vital Speeches of the Day*, March 1, 1945, p. 290.

1358. Buddy Kaye and Ted Mossman, "Till the End of Time," Saintly-Joy Inc., sheet music, 1945.

1359. Flo Wilks, "Victor Emert Using Found Items to Decorate U of A Campus Chapel," *AJ*, December 13, 1970, p. C2.

1360. "Policeman's Art to Enhance Building," *AJ*, March 10, 1971, p. B6.

1361. Ewan MacColl, "The First Time Ever I Saw Your Face," Stormking (B.M.I.), on record album *First Take* by Roberta Flack, Atlantic Recording Company, 1969.

1362. Dicky Betts, "Blue Sky," No Exit Music Co., Inc. (B.M.I.), on record album *Eat a Peach* by the Allman Brothers Band, Warner Brothers, Inc., 1972.

1363. "ZIP Code Starts Operation Today," *AJ*, July 1, 1963, p. A1.

1364. Frankie McCarty, "Electronic 'Brain' Now Fully Controls City Water Supply," *AJ*, March 19, 1958, p. 1

1365. "City Puts New Traffic Signal Controls into Use Today," *AJ*, April 17, 1959, p. 35.

1366. Mike Padget, "Computer Data on Accidents Helps Spot Trouble Locations," *AJ*, November 2, 1969, p. E9.

1367. Art Bouffard, "County to Buy New Computer System," *AJ*, October 13, 1971, p. A16.

1368. "Computer Bulges with Data from 2 Million Documents," *AJ*, December 31, 1972, p. A14.

1369. Ted Hulbert, "Jargon Used by Teenagers Is Ever-Changing," *AJ*, December 8, 1963, p. E1.

1370. U.S., Department of Commerce, Bureau of the Census, *Census of Population: 1950*, vol. 2, *Characteristics of the Population*, pt. 31, New Mexico, pp. 31-119, 31-120; idem, *Census of Population: 1970, Detailed Characteristics*, Final Report PC(1)-D33, New Mexico, p. 33-480.

1371. Don McLean, "American Pie," Mayday Music Inc. and Yahweh Tunes Inc., sheet music, 1972.

1372. Flo Wilks, "Fair Visitors, Exhibitors Stage Gala Fashion Show," *AJ*, July 27, 1962, p. B1.

1373. "State Arts and Crafts Fair Tabbed as Total Success," *AJ*, August 2, 1969, p. A1.

1374. Charles Lumpkin, "Utah Symphony a Hit as Hall Is Christened," *AJ*, October 2, 1966, p. A1.

1375. "Museum for City Is Opened," *AJ*, September 8, 1967, p. A1.

1376. "Fine Arts College Has Rapid Growth," *AJ*, September 2, 1966, p. E10; "Art Student Enrollment Rises 95%," *AJ*, February 6, 1972, p. C3.

1377. "UNM Gets Lithography Study Center," *AJ*, April 29, 1970, p. A1.

1378. Frankie McCarty, "Joint Art Center Programs to Be Expanded," *AJ*, August 27, 1972, p. E6.

1379. "Highland High Students Making Films," *AJ*, July 25, 1971, p. A1.

1380. "UNM Arts, Crafts Courses to Be Offered During Fall," *AJ*, July 23, 1972, p. C4.

1381. Valerie Gonzales, "Culture-Oriented Dancing Done at Model Cities," *AJ*, July 31, 1972, p. A10.

1382. "Dr. Alexander Masley Notes Changes in Art," *AJ*, May 18, 1969, p. C2.

1383. W. Wilson Cliff, "Two Dillard Stores Closing Doors to Prepare for Winrock Opening," *AJ*, October 27, 1972, p. D1.

1384. "Model Neighborhood Gets Playground—and Theater," *AJ*, September 30, 1971, p. C1.

1385. "Pierce, Crowley Homes Awarded Top Prizes in Landscaping Contest," *AJ*, July 17, 1965, p. A2.

1386. Marie Stephenson, "City Beautification Interest, Activities Said on Increase," *AJ*, September 12, 1965, p. E1.

1387. "Arbor Week Activities Stressing Care, Value of Trees to City," *AJ*, March 12, 1967, p. E1.

1388. "Aspencade Tour Called Success; Planned Yearly," *AJ*, October 3, 1966, p. A12.

1389. "Tree Planting to Honor Memory of C.T. French," *AJ*, October 16, 1966, p. F2.

1390. "La Luz, 'Young' Development West of Rio to Add to City Size," *AJ*, March 10, 1968, p. C16.

Bibliography

Albuquerque Journal, 1945–1972.

Albuquerque Tribune, 1945.

Anderson, Clinton P., with Milton Viorst. *Outsider in the Senate, Senator Clinton Anderson's Memoirs*. New York: The World Publishing Company, 1970.

Bach, Richard, *Jonathan Livingston Seagull*. New York: The Macmillan Company, 1970.

Barrett, Joel V. "Citizen Participation in the Formation of Albuquerque's Bus Franchise, 1948–1953." Master's thesis, University of New Mexico, 1954.

Brumbaugh, A.J., ed. *American Universities and Colleges*, 5th ed. Washington, D.C.: American Council on Education, 1998.

Ducoff, Donald. "The Springer Transfer Company: A Study of Business Growth and Top Management Leadership." Master's thesis, University of New Mexico, 1963.

Graham, Hugh Davis, and Gurr, Ted Robert. *Violence in America: Historical and Comparative Perspectives*. New York: Bantam Books, 1969.

Hales, William M., Jr. "Technological In-Migration and Curricular Change: Educational Politics in Albuquerque, 1945–1965." Ph.D. dissertation, University of New Mexico. 1970.

Kandel, Lenore. *Word Alchemy*. New York: Grove Press, Inc., 1967.

Keleher, William A. *Memoirs: 1892–1969, A New Mexico Item*. Santa Fe, N.M.: The Rydal Press, 1969.

Kenner, Hugh. *Bucky: A Guided Tour of Buckminster Fuller*. New York: William Morrow & Company, Inc., 1973.

Kinsey, Alfred C.; Pomeroy, Wardell B.; Martin, Clyde E.; and Gebhard, Paul H. *Sexual Behavior in the Human Female*. Philadelphia and London: W.B. Saunders Company, 1953.

Levin, Robert J. "The Redbook Report on Premarital and Extramarital Sex: The End of the Double Standard." *Redbook*, October 1975, pp. 38-42, 190-192.

Levin, Robert J., and Levin, Amy. "Sexual Pleasure: The Surprising Preferences of 100,000 Women." *Redbook*, September 1975, pp. 52-58.

Loveridge, Arthur N. *A Man Who Knew How to Live Among His Fellow Men, A Graphic Life Story of Chester F. French*. Boulder, Colo.: Old Trails Publishers, 1965.

New Mexico. Department of Finance and Administration. *Statistics: Public School Finance Division, 1972.*

New Mexico. Superintendent of Public Instruction. *Eighteenth Biennial Report.*

New Mexico. Superintendent of Public Instruction. *Annual Statistical Report on New Mexico Schools, for the Period July 1, 1959 to June 30, 1960.*

New Mexico. Superintendent of Public Instruction. *Annual Statistical Report of the Superintendent of Public Instruction, for the Period July 1, 1971 to June 30, 1972.*

Northrop, F.S.C. *The Meeting of East and West*. New York: Collier Books, 1966.

Roosevelt, Franklin D. "A Just and Honorable Peace." *Vital Speeches of the Day*, March 1, 1945, p. 290.

Rosenfeld, A. "New Mexico's Fading Color Line." *Commentary* 20 (September 1955): 203-11.

Shapiro, Karl, ed. *Prose Keys to Modern Poetry*. New York: Harper & Row, 1962.

U.S. Department of Commerce. *County Business Patterns: First Quarter, 1948*. Pt. 2, State Reports, no. 29, New Mexico.

U.S. Department of Commerce. Bureau of the Census. *Census of Housing: 1940*. Vol. 2, *General Characteristics*, pt. 4, Nebraska-Pennsylvania.

    Census of Population: 1940. Vol. 2, *Characteristics of the Population*, pt. 4, Minnesota-New Mexico.

    City Finances: 1945 (Cities Having Populations over 25,000). Vol. 3, *Statistical Compendium*.

    Census of Business: 1948. Vol. 3, *Retail Trade-Area Statistics*.

    Census of Housing: 1950. Vol. 1, *General Characteristics*, pt. 4, Michigan-New York.

    Census of Population: 1950. Vol. 2, *Characteristics of the Population*, pt. 31, New Mexico.

    Census of Population: 1950. Vol. 4, *Special Reports*, pt. 3, Chap. C, Persons of Spanish Surname.

    Census of Business: 1958. Vol. 2, *Retail Trade-Area Statistics*, pt. 2, Missouri-Wyoming and Alaska, Hawaii, Guam, and Virgin Islands.

    Census of Housing: 1960. Vol. 1, *States and Small Areas*, pt. 6, New Jersey-Ohio.

    Census of Housing: 1960. Vol. 2, *Metropolitan Housing*, pt. 2, Abilene-Corpus Christi Standard Metropolitan Statistical Areas.

Census of Population: 1960. Subject Reports, Persons of Spanish Surname, Final Report PC(2)-1B.

Census of Population and Housing: 1960. Census Tracts, Final Report PHC(1)-4. Albuquerque, N. Mex. SMSA.

County and City Data Book, 1962 (A Statistical Abstract Supplement).

County and City Data Book, 1967 (A Statistical Abstract Supplement).

Census of Housing: 1970. Vol. 1, *Housing Characteristics for States, Cities, and Counties*, pt. 33, New Mexico.

Census of Population: 1970. General Social and Economic Characteristics, Final Report PC(1)-C33, New Mexico.

Census of Population and Housing: 1970. Census Tracts, Final Report PHC(1)-5, Albuquerque, N. Mex. SMSA.

County and City Data Book, 1972 (A Statistical Abstract Supplement).

County Business Patterns: 1972. New Mexico, CBP-72-33.

Census of Retail Trade: 1972. Retail Trade: Major Retail Centers, New Mexico, RC 72-C-32.

U.S. Department of Commerce. Social and Economic Statistics Administration. *Boundary and Annexation Survey, 1970–1973.*

U.S. Department of Health, Education and Welfare. Bureau of Educational Research and Development. Educational Statistics Branch. *Total Enrollment in Institutions of Higher Learning, First Term, 1959–60 Basic Data.*

U.S. Department of Health, Education and Welfare. National Center for Education Statistics. *Total Enrollment in Higher Education, 1972.*

U.S. Department of Health, Education and Welfare. Office of Economic Opportunity. *Federal Outlay in New Mexico: 1972.*

U.S. Department of Justice. Federal Bureau of Investigation, Uniform Crime Reports: Crime in the United States, 1945–1969.

Whitrow, G.J., ed. *Einstein: The Man and His Achievement.* New York Dover Publications, Inc. , 1967.

Winsor, Kathleen. *Forever Amber*, New York: The Macmillan Company, 1944.

INDEX

Ortega Hall, 159
Ortiz, Rudy, 165, 247
Orzen, William, 157, 304, 306

P

Pacely, Homer, 304
panty raid, 129
Paradise Hills, 199-200, 208
Parents Without Partners, 337
Paris Shoe Store, 41-42
Park Plaza, 194, 208
Parsons and Whittemore, 218
Parsons, Howard W., 202
Parsons, W. Howard, 213
Payne, Word, 170
People's Committee for Better Government
  (PCBG), 168-70, 319
perfection, 354-56
Phillips, Howard, 170
Pickett, Roy, 299
Plaza Del Sol, 206
Poetry Series Committee, 305
Pollack, Kenneth, 298-300
Poole, Robert, 319, 331
Poorbaugh, Fred, 178
Popejoy Hall, 344, 365
Popejoy, Tom, 101-2, 130, 155, 172, 215-16,
  229-30, 303, 305-6
pornography, 21, 286-87, 300, 301
Potenziani, A.F., 177, 191
Pravitz, Don, 114
Predock, Antoine, 369
Princess Jeanne Park, 106-7, 109-10, 199
Property Owners Protective Association
  (POPA), 144, 177, 178
Protestant churches, 135, 270
Public Health Service, 339-40
Pyle, Ernie, 49, 51, 120, 122

Q

Quebrar, 260, 302, 329

R

Ramirez, Reuben, 170, 189
Rankin, Herbert W., 72
Raper, Howard R., 48
rectangular, 57, 357
Red Cross, 44, 46, 48, 125
Redd, C.K., 183

Regina School of Nursing, 46, 116
Reidy, Robert, 287
Reineke, Mrs. Robert, 262
Reinicke, William, 355
religion, 21, 118, 120-21, 213-14, 252, 269-
  71, 285, 340, 356
Reyes, G.P., 172, 315, 319
Rich, Edna, 341
Rio Arriba courthouse, 242
Rio Grande Estates, 200
Rio Grande Park, 32, 295
Rio Rancho, 200, 208
Roach Ranch West, 315
Robb, John, 100
Robertson, G.B., 165, 169-70, 173, 276
Robins, Harry, 54-55, 272-74, 287, 302, 311,
  319, 324
Rockafellow, W.R., 162
Rogers, Waldo, 72, 132
Roosevelt Park, 11, 143, 158, 253, 295, 302,
  312-13, 315-16
Roosevelt, Eleanor, 49
Rosenberg, Lyle, 73
Rosenbloom, Robert, 320
Roswell law, 74, 75
Runnels, Harold, 298
Russell, Larry, 230

S

Saavedra, Louis, 172, 319, 331
Salazar, Ernest, 48
Salazar, Eulogio, 242-43
Salazar, John, 228
Salazar, Victor, 196-97, 200
San Felipe de Neri Church, 146
San Jose, 76, 171, 221, 223-24, 258-59, 264,
  267
San Martin, Mauro, 267
San Pedro Village, 208
San-Bar Construction Company, 114
Sanchez, Al (Hurricane), 133
Sanchez, Gilbert, 302
Sanchez, Manuel, 30, 33, 165, 264
Sanchez, Maurice, 92-95, 99, 124, 133, 135,
  161-62, 165
Sandia Conservancy District, 141-45, 177-79
Sandia Corporation, 10, 67-68, 92, 102, 106,
  128, 137, 164, 168, 179, 250, 331, 359

CPSIA information can be obtained
at www.ICGtesting.com
Printed in the USA
FSOW01n1836061214
3697FS